D1554570

The Search for Modern Tragedy

The Search for Modern Tragedy

Aesthetic Fascism in Italy and France

MARY ANN FRESE WITT

CORNELL UNIVERSITY PRESS

Ithaca and London

First published 2001 by Cornell University Press

Printed in the United States of America

Permission granted by Duke University Press to reprint portions of "Fascist Discourse and Pirandellian Theater," which appeared in somewhat different form in *South Atlantic Quarterly*, 1992.

Permission granted by Alpha Academic to reprint portions of "Fascist Ideology and Theatre under the Occupation: The Case of Anouilh," which appeared in somewhat different form in *The Journal of European Studies*, 1993.

Portions of chapter two appear with the permission of the IAPL Series in Philosophy, Literature, and Culture (series editor Hugh J. Silverman), which holds initial rights to this material; it will be published in significantly different form under the title "Aesthetic Fascism and Modern Tragedy: D'Annunzio's *Fedra*," in *Cultures in Contention: Differences, Affiliations, Liminalities*, edited by John Burt Foster, Jr., and Wayne J. Froman.

Library of Congress Cataloging-in-Publication Data

Witt, Mary Ann Frese.
   The search for modern tragedy : aesthetic fascism in Italy and France / Mary Ann Frese Witt.
      p. cm.
   Includes bibliographical references and index.
   ISBN 0-8014-3837-3 (cloth : alk. paper)
   1. Italian drama—20th century—History and criticism. 2. Italian drama (Tragedy)—History and criticism. 3. Fascism—Italy. 4. Politics and literature—Italy—History—20th century. 5. Fascism in literature. 6. French drama—20th century—History and criticism. 7. French drama (Tragedy)—History and criticism. 8. Politics and literature—France—History—20th Century. 9. Fascism—France. I. Title.
   PQ4145 .W58 2001
   842'.0512090912—dc21

                                                                    2001003142

Cornell University Press strives to use environmentally responsible suppliers and materials to the fullest extent possible in the publishing of its books. Such materials include vegetable-based, low-VOC inks and acid-free papers that are recycled, totally chlorine-free, or partly composed of nonwood fibers.

Cloth printing   10 9 8 7 6 5 4 3 2 1

For Ron

Contents

Preface

For Americans of my generation who were children during World War II, the notion of fascism seemed simply evil in some primordial way, and thus, as Susan Sontag reminded us, fascinating. As a literary scholar, I am interested in fascism less for its politics than for the peculiar aesthetic and "spiritual" appeal that it exercised. Research in cultural studies, art history, and literature, especially since the 1970s, has refined not only our understanding of fascist aesthetics, but also the understanding of the nature of the fascist presence in art and literature and of the involvement of those writers, artists, and intellectuals who came to the movement primarily through aesthetics. It is this latter phenomenon that I have termed "aesthetic fascism."

The idea for this book began when I was spending a sabbatical year in Rome and in Paris, working on Pirandello and the French theater in the light of dramatic theories of space. Pirandello's well-known membership in the fascist party and association with Mussolini aroused my curiosity to the extent that it impeded my progress in the area of theoretical dramaturgy; I felt that I simply had to deal with it in some way. Gaspare Giudice's 1963 biography—the first major study to treat the problem openly and seriously—was invaluable in providing documentation for the nature of the association, but I felt that I could not accept Giudice's contention (and that of most Italian critics since) that Pirandello's literary work had nothing whatsoever to do with his political affiliation. Could a writer so neatly divide his politics from his art? Pirandello's idiosyncratic statements on fascism seemed more literary than political. Was the playwright and director merely an opportunist, eager to woo Mussolini's support for his theater?

While Pirandello was hardly above lobbying for what he needed, the depth of his commitment to the theater seemed to preclude such a simplistic splitting. The key, perhaps, lay in the theatrical nature of fascism itself.

While I continued to work in the area of dramatic theory, my research on Pirandello led me down a different path. I read for several years in the ideology of Italian fascism, convinced by Pier Giorgio Zunino's work that the only way to get a sense of the movement's shifting, unsystematic, and activist nature was to read the periodicals of the *ventennio*. I began to focus on the association between fascism and theater, finding that the theatricality of fascism's presentation of itself and the importance of theater to the movement had been theorized by fascist ideologues. What surprised me was the fascists' support for the revival of ancient tragedy along with their belief in modern tragedy as the genre befitting the "new era." Yet, although they praised Pirandello's innovations in the genre and pointed out correlations between his "philosophy" and fascism, no contemporary dramatist seemed to meet the criteria to become the tragedian of fascism. I decided to concentrate on this unexplored field of the fascist search for modern tragedy.

The ideal modern tragedy, according to the fascist ideologues, would not be a piece of base propaganda but rather a great work of art capturing the public through poetry. While awaiting the ultimate work, models could be found in revivals of the modern tragedies of "the Bard," Gabriele D'Annunzio, sometimes promoted as "the soul of fascism." If D'Annunzio's intellectual and artistic roots were in turn-of-the-century aestheticism, so, perhaps, were some of fascism's. At this point, Walter Benjamin's seminal theory on the link between fascism and *l'art pour l'art* along with Zeev Sternhell's much debated argument that the origins of fascism lay in early twentieth-century Franco-Italian cultural movements, were crucial. The mutual influences between the French and Italian intellectual and cultural currents that eventually entered fascist ideology suggested that the link between fascism in France and Italy, at least in the domain of culture, might be stronger than links between either of the two and Nazi Germany, or other national fascist movements. The conflation between aesthetic and political discourse at the turn of the century, as well as the attraction to fascism through aesthetics on the part of artists and writers, suggested to me the term "aesthetic fascists" to designate those whose commitment to fascism seemed more aesthetic than political. Seminal to the aesthetic fascists in both Italy and France was their reading of the works of Nietzsche, in particular *The Birth of Tragedy*. The origins of tragedy in ancient Mediterranean Dionysian sacrificial rapture justified its promotion as the literary and theatrical form most apt to fuse antiquity with the present, violence with beauty, and the individual with the totalitarian corporate body.

French fascism, lacking a sustaining regime and thus often more divorced from politics than its Italian counterpart, has received much attention in recent years. Closest to my interests is David Carroll's *Literary Fascism*, whose title also suggests a conviction that "fascism" can extend beyond politics. While recent scholars of French fascism have tended to stress the native roots of the movement and its independence from German Nazism, relatively little has been made of the Italian connection. My reading in the best-known fascist intellectuals—Pierre Drieu La Rochelle and Robert Brasillach—suggested that, in the 1930s at least, Italian fascism, along with the earlier Franco-Italian cultural movement, exercised considerable influence over the French variety. Certain French fascist literati, more explicitly than the Italians, approached fascism through aesthetics. Like the Italians they showed, under the influence of Nietzsche, a strong interest in the revival of ancient and the creation of modern tragedy. The French claimed their own classical tragedians as well, Corneille and Racine, as precursors of the movement. Antisemitism, of little importance in early Italian fascism, was a strong current in the French aesthetic as well as political variety. Under the German Occupation, writers for the collaborationist press continued to call for a modern tragedy worthy of French fascism or of the National Revolution. Although the dramatic works of Jean Anouilh and Henry de Montherlant came closest, the ultimate fascist tragedy was never created. The search for modern tragedy ended, I believe, with the trial and execution of Robert Brasillach, cast by Anouilh in the role of Antigone.

The reader will decide whether the claims outlined schematically here are adequately substantiated in this book. If not, the fault is of course entirely my own. The work, however, is not entirely my own, for I have been greatly helped by a number of people. The late Edouard Morot-Sir read and encouraged my work on Anouilh. Alexander De Grand, who kindly read several drafts of various portions of the manuscript, suggested bibliography and set me straight on several aspects of fascism. Russell Berman and Paul Schue read and made important remarks on the introduction. Faculty members and Fellows at the University of Utah, at the Tanner Humanities Center seminars and elsewhere, asked helpful questions and made suggestions for my work. Members of the French Studies Seminar at the National Humanities Center, in particular Alice Kaplan and Steven Vincent, raised important questions on portions of the manuscript, forcing me to rethink several concepts. Robert Dombroski read and commented on the chapters on D'Annunzio and Pirandello; Carol Harrison did so for chapter 4. John Burt Foster helped me with the section on Thierry Maulnier. Exchanges of ideas with Joe Golsan at conferences over the years have been most useful. Wladimir Krysinski, Joan Stewart, Alice Kaplan, Daniela Bini, and Susan Suleiman have generously read proposals on the book and given support for grants. I received invaluable research assistance from Claudia Bolgia in Rome and Eric Witt in Paris. Debora Godfrey was extremely helpful to me in preparing versions of the manuscript. Special thanks go to Andrew Sparling for his painstaking editing and his preparation of the index.

I thank the staff at the libraries where I did much of the research for this book: those at the Biblioteca Burcardo in Rome and the Bibliothèque de l'Arsenal in Paris have been particularly helpful. The Newberry Library in Chicago kindly provided me with a space to work during a sabbatical leave in 1991 when I also made use of the resources of the University of Chicago Regensburg Library. I have also worked in the D'Annunzio Vittoriale library in Garda, the Biblioteca nazionale in both Rome and Florence, the Bibliothèque nationale in Paris, and the University of Utah, Duke University, and North Carolina State University libraries. The American Academy in Rome, where I began and am now finishing the writing of the book, has often provided excellent working conditions.

Financial support for this project has come from a Fulbright research grant and leaves, a summer stipend, and travel grants from the College of Humanities and Social Sciences at North Carolina State University. An Eccles Fellowship from the Tanner Humanities Center at the University of Utah in 1996–97 enabled my progress by providing an ideal situation for writing and research as well as interaction with stimulating colleagues.

The staff at the Cornell University Press have of course contributed in bringing this book to light. Special thanks go to my editor, Bernhard Kendler, for his intelligent and professional readings, suggestions, and encouragement. Trudie Calvert and Candace Akins showed patience and painstaking exactitude in the copyediting process.

My children, Eric, Martha, and Daria Witt, have been unfailing in their support and encouragement of my work. My most exacting critic, as well as my prime source of intellectual and emotional support, is my husband, Ronald Witt. This book would not have been the same without him.

All translations in the book are mine unless otherwise indicated.

MARY ANN FRESE WITT

Introduction

The question of fascism's relationship to European high culture is still under debate. Although numerous studies have moved us away from the postwar contention that fascism was an anomaly or a "parenthesis" in European history, there seems at the present time to be no general agreement on the intellectual sources of the movement or on its influence on the writers and artists who were in various degrees and forms attracted to it. Zeev Sternhell's thesis that fascism was already a "culture" at the turn of the century before it became political has met with criticism from historians for whom economic and social conditions take precedence over intellectual currents and ideology in the consideration of fascism;[1] David Carroll's term "literary fascism," applied to cultural trends in France, has come under similar fire. Yet it is undeniable that many of the writers who either joined fascist

---

[1] Sternhell has been criticized for erroneously attributing the origins of fascism to France and for adopting the term "fascism" to describe pre-World War I intellectual currents *avant la lettre* as well as for overemphasizing the intellectual and ideological aspects of the movement. The historian of French fascism Robert Soucy has been one of his most outspoken critics. See his *French Fascism: The Second Wave, 1933–1939* (New Haven, Conn.: Yale University Press, 1995), 1–25. For surveys of the Sternhell controversy among historians, see Antonio Costa Pinto, "Fascist Ideology Revisited: Zeev Sternhell and His Critics," *European History Quarterly* 16, no. 4 (1986):465–83; and Robert Wohl, "French Fascism, Both Right and Left: Reflections on the Sternhell Controversy," *Journal of Modern History* 63, no. 1 (March 1991):91–98. Whatever its value to political, social, and economic history, Sternhell's study of fascist ideology is useful to the student of artistic and literary aspects of fascism. His use of the term "fascist" to describe ideological currents operating before Mussolini's *Fasci* of Revolutionary Action of 1914–15, not to mention his organization of the *Fasci italiani di combattimento* in 1919 and the March on Rome in 1922, seems to me far preferable to such awkward terms as "prefascist" or "protofascist."

parties or sympathized with fascism came to the movement through litera-ture or aesthetics. Our modern view of them as politically naive or deluded does not mean that their commitment was less real. Neither should a pri-marily aesthetic approach to fascism be dismissed as frivolous or harmless.

This book does not address the controversies involving the origins of fas-cism or the relation of the ideological to the political. I do contend, how-ever, that the term "aesthetic fascism" can be useful in describing certain currents in literature and the arts from the early twentieth century into the 1940s. On one level, this phenomenon can be seen as part of the early modernist belief that innovation in art could lead to revolutionary change in politics, or rather, that art and politics were two sides of the same coin. On another, it is a product of the aesthetic nature of certain political ex-periences such as the merging of self with a crowd representing national identity—the totalizing work of art representing the totalitarian state made famous by Walter Benjamin. It is of course Benjamin's gloss on Filippo Marinetti's elegy to the beauty of war— "the logical result of fascism is the introduction of aesthetics into political life"[2]—that is still the starting point for any discussion of fascism and aesthetics.

The phenomenon of writers and intellectuals drawn to fascism through aesthetics, while small in size, was international in scope. Examples in-clude Mircea Eliade in Romania, Rafael García Serrano in Spain, Wyndham Lewis in England, Ezra Pound, transplanted to Italy from the United States, Martin Heidegger in Germany, and the young Paul de Man in Belgium.[3] An aspiring writer who pursued another career, Joseph Goebbels, pub-lished a novel, *Michael,* in 1927, extolling the concept of the statesman as artist. Although this notion, along with the related one of the national state as a work of art, can be found in fascism regardless of national origin, some important distinctions among nationalities as among individuals exist.

---

[2] Walter Benjamin, "The Work of Art in the Age of Mechanical Reproduction," in *Illumi-nations,* trans. Harry Zohn (New York: Schocken, 1969), 242.

[3] Alastair Hamilton's *The Appeal of Fascism, 1919–1945: A Study of Intellectuals and Fascism* (New York: Macmillan, 1971) is still a good source on intellectuals and fascism. On Serrano, see Janet Pérez, "Fascist Models and Literary Subversion," in *Fascism, Aesthetics, and Culture,* ed. Richard J. Golsan (Hanover, N.H.: University Press of New England, 1992), 128–42.

The cases of Heidegger and de Man have of course occasioned a great deal of writing and discussion since Victor Farias's *Heidegger et le nazisme,* trans. Myriam Benarroch and Jean-Baptiste Grasset (Paris: Verdier), published in 1987, and the contemporary discovery of the articles Paul de Man wrote for the pro-fascist Belgian journal *Le Soir* during World War II. In-teresting for our purposes here is the work of Philippe Lacoue-Labarthe, who argues that for Heidegger (as for others), Hitler's project was a "National Aestheticism" whose political model is the *Gesamtkunstwerk* (*Heidegger, Art and Politics: The Fiction of the Political,* trans. Chris Turner [London: Basil Blackwell, 1990], 61–76). Reed Way Dasenbrock ("Paul de Man: The Mod-ernist as Fascist," in Golsan, *Fascism, Aesthetics, and Culture,* 229–41), makes a convincing case for the influence of aesthetics, as well as of Italian fascism on de Man's early interest in fas-cism. De Man seems to have believed that the climate of Mussolini's Italy was conducive to the creation of beautiful and original poetry.

Sternhell's argument that fascism as an intellectual movement originated in the work of French and Italian thinkers at the turn of the twentieth century makes a convincing case for distinguishing a Franco-Italian fascist ideology from its German counterpart.[4] (This is not to say that Italian and French fascisms did not also diverge in important ways.) Most important for our purposes here will be the "Latin" emphasis on the poetic word, above the sentiment of race, as the binding force between leader and crowd. The emphasis did not of course exclude the existence of antisemitism and racism, particularly in French fascism. Although it was clearly the profound upheaval of World War I that made fascism as a political movement possible, I will argue that it is justifiable to speak of an "aesthetic fascism," albeit *avant la lettre*, in France and Italy at the turn of the century. Two important early representatives, Maurice Barrès and Gabriele D'Annunzio, call upon the power of the word and the classical heritage from Greece and Rome, along with indigenous traditions, in evocations of national sentiment that intertwine the aesthetic and the political.[5] It is in part the desire to recuperate the classical heritage within the national literary tradition, along with the profound influence of Friedrich Nietzsche's *Birth of Tragedy*, that will make the creation of a modern tragedy seem so important. The French, who did not experience the fascist state, were perhaps able to maintain an aesthetic approach to fascism longer than the Italians. As late as 1943, the poet and fascist Jean Turlais could say that fascism was "above all an aesthetic."[6] Throughout the 1930s, French intellectuals drawn to fascism were on the whole more interested in its Italian than its German face; this changed after 1943, when Il Duce was no longer important on the European scene. Even under the German Occupation, however, French aesthetic fascists continued to seek to define a *French* fascism. Modern tragedy—in the classical "Latin" and French tradition—emerged in their vision as the literary form best suited to embody the ideals of fascism.

"Aesthetic fascism," in my use of the term, is not the same as "fascist aesthetics." Although in the brief chapter that follows this introduction, I find it useful to outline the relations between official fascist culture in Italy in the

[4] Sternhell's arguments appear in Zeev Sternhell, *La Droite révolutionnaire: Les Origines françaises du fascisme* (Paris: Editions du Seuil, 1978); Zeev Sternhell, *Neither Right nor Left: Fascist Ideology in France*, trans. David Maisel (Princeton, N.J.: Princeton University Press, 1996); and Zeev Sternhell, with Mario Sznajder and Maia Asheri, *The Birth of Fascist Ideology: From Cultural Rebellion to Political Revolution*, trans. David Maisel (Princeton, N.J.: Princeton University Press, 1994).

[5] David Carroll cites a representative passage from *Les Déracinés* on the funeral of Victor Hugo: "Above all, words, words, words! That's his title, his force, to be master of French words: their totality forms the entire treasure and the entire soul of the race" (*French Literary Fascism: Nationalism, Anti-Semitism, and the Ideology of Culture* [Princeton, N.J.: Princeton University Press, 1994], 39).

[6] Jean Turlais, "Introduction à l'histoire de la littérature fasciste," *Les Cahiers français* 5 (May 1943): 25.

1920s and 1930s and the production of modern tragedy, I am primarily interested in the aesthetic approach to fascism on the part of certain exemplary writers in Italy and France as it relates to their theories of modern tragedy and their attempts to create it. Yet the productions of these writers, especially since we are concerned with theater, must also be viewed in the context of their reception, and this inevitably involves fascist aesthetics. In the case of D'Annunzio, especially, I am aware that my term will be highly controversial. D'Annunzio was never a political fascist, and even his role as precursor is now contested by some. Yet D'Annunzio was a leader in the early twentieth-century cultural climate sketched out above. Also important to my treatment of D'Annunzio is that his modern tragedies, written much earlier, were produced and received to much acclaim during the fascist *ventennio* with official sponsorship and in the context of fascist aesthetics. The last example in the book will probably be as controversial as the first. Jean Anouilh (unlike D'Annunzio) claimed to have no interest in politics but to be simply a man of the theater. Yet, as I hope to show, the texts of his modern tragedies, in particular *Antigone*, in the context of both the cultural influences on them and their reception, place them within the parameters of aesthetic fascism.

Neither aesthetic fascism nor fascist aesthetics can be understood without an attempt to define fascist ideology—an attempt that has seemed doomed to failure. The movement was so protean that it incorporated the most divergent political and economic as well as cultural tendencies. Indeed, one inherent characteristic of fascism seems to be its tendency to fuse and bind apparent opposites (one need only think of the origin of the word and the image of the *fasces*). Thus we find at various times and places juxtapositions of conservative nationalism with revolutionary ardor, agrarian nostalgia with futurist modernism, anticapitalist and antibourgeois rhetoric with the courting of the bourgeoisie, traditional Christianity with militant atheism or paganism, humanist reason with irrationalist nihilism, avant-garde and "pure art" with propagandistic art, myths of the nation as nurturing mother with myths of the cruel and conquering hero, or simply right with left. These polarities do not even take into account the differences among the "fascisms" in the first half of the twentieth century in Italy, Spain, France, Germany, Belgium, England, Hungary, Romania, and elsewhere, not to mention their derivatives and revivals today.

This heterogeneity of fascism does not mean, however, that it is impossible to ascertain certain ideological constants of the movement. Drawing on others who have attempted to summarize the core elements of fascist ideology,[7] as well as on my readings in the journalism of the period, I will attempt my own list here.

[7] Roger Griffin offers "palingenetic ultranationalism" as an all-purpose definition of fascism. By this he intends to imply an emphasis on the decadence and degeneration of the present coupled with an organic nationalist myth of the past and a future-oriented myth of

1. A rejection of the values of the Enlightenment, the bourgeoisie, and all forms of rationalism, notably Marxism and parliamentary democracy.
2. The notion that "true" individuality can be achieved only through fusion with the people or the corporate body.
3. Faith in the authority of the man who emerges as a natural leader and who leads his followers by establishing a mystical bond with them.
4. Religious syncretism, often combined with a cult of the leader and the state and with an institutionalization of ritual. Fascism often presents itself as "spiritual" as opposed to "political."
5. Moral and philosophical relativism. While fascist ideologues may accept Nietzsche's contention that "nothing is true," they grant power to the dictator to construct his own "truths" or "myths" and impose them on the people.
6. Philosophical antirationalism, sometimes sustained by reference to Nietzsche and Henri Bergson.
7. The promotion of action in opposition to intellectual ideals or discussion. An understanding of life as Darwinian struggle and of violence and will as necessary and beautiful. Mussolini's trilogy of verbs in the imperative mode in his slogan "Believe, Obey, Fight," contrasted with the abstract nouns "Liberty, Equality, Fraternity," exemplifies the opposition well.
8. A rejection of certain aspects of modernity, including capitalism, combined with nostalgia for agrarian existence and utopian visions of corporate, class-fusing societies. (This ideological tenet did not, of course, prevent the fascists from courting bourgeois capitalists.)
9. An embracing of technology, speed, and modern warfare.

---

regeneration and rebirth. See his "Fascism" in *International Fascism: Theories, Causes and the New Consensus*, ed. Griffin (New York: Oxford University Press, 1998), 35–39, and "Staging the Nation's Rebirth: The Politics and Aesthetics of Performance in the Context of Fascist Studies," in *Fascism and Theatre*, ed. Günter Berghaus (Providence: Berghahn Books, 1996), 11–29. Emilio Gentile discusses the use of these myths, particularly the latter, in *The Sacralization of Politics in Fascist Italy*, trans. Keith Botsford (Cambridge: Harvard University Press, 1996). Umberto Eco, in "Ur-Fascism," *New York Review of Books* 42 (June 22, 1995): 12–15, postulates ten "archetypal foundations" of fascist ideology. Other efforts to synthesize the ideology of fascism, either generally or nationally, include Walter Laqueur, "The Essence of Fascism" and "Fascist Doctrine," in *Fascism: Past, Present, and Future* (New York: Oxford University Press, 1996), 13–27; George Mosse, "Toward a General Theory of Fascism," in *Masses and Man*, ed. Mosse (New York: Howard Fertig, 1980); Stanley Payne, *Fascism: Comparison and Definition* (Madison: University of Wisconsin Press, 1980); Robert Soucy, "The Nature of Fascism in France," in *Fascism: An Anthology*, ed. Nathanael Greene (New York: Thomas Y. Crowell, 1980), 275–300; Pier Giorgio Zunino, *L'ideologia del fascismo: Miti, credenze e valori nella stabilizzazione del regime* (Bologna: Il Mulino, 1985).

10. A dismissal of the "easy life" (Mussolini's "Il Fascista è contra la vita comoda"[8]) or "decadence" (often equated with city life) and a value placed on physical fitness, devotion, and self-sacrifice.
11. A romantic exaltation of death, especially as heroic sacrifice.
12. A cult of virile power and the subjection of women, along with the extolling of woman as mother/madonna.
13. A cult of one's own race or ethnic group as superior, sometimes combined with justification of imperialism. Antisemitism, however, is not a central tenet of fascism in its early stages.

I would be the last to claim that this list is either exhaustive or true in all cases. Since fascist ideology is so shifting, as Pier Giorgio Zunino argues, the best way to get a sense of it is to read the journals of the period, which he has done extensively.[9] I have done my own reading of journals, particularly in regard to the theater, in both Italy and France. The corporate state, as one journalist reminds us, is "never made, but is continually in the process of making";[10] the same may be said of its ideology.

Attempts at generic definitions of fascist ideology tend to reinforce its *cultural* importance. Fascists themselves liked to present their "spiritual" movement as somehow beyond or above mere "politics." Both Benito Mussolini and Adolf Hitler envisioned themselves as "artists," using the disparaging term "politicians" for their democratic or socialist enemies. Mussolini confided to Emil Ludwig that "everything depends on dominating the mass like an artist" and that his ambition was to make a dramatic masterpiece of his own life.[11] Hitler cultivated the image of himself as an equivalent to Wagner. Fascism's extensive use of the theatrical and the spectacular is well known, and its effect was not lost on fascist-leaning writers involved in theater. Both Luigi Pirandello and Robert Brasillach praised Mussolini as a great poet of the theater, and Brasillach defined fascism as government by poetry.[12]

A high confluence of aesthetic and political discourse, mingling the two so that they are at times indistinguishable, occurred at the turn of the century in both France and Italy. A complex formed of the art-for-art move-

---

[8] Benito Mussolini, "Fascismo," in *L'enciclopedia italiana* (Florence: Treves, 1932), 14, 847.

[9] Zunino, *L'Ideologia del fascismo*.

[10] Luigi Chiarini, "Individuo e stato," *Il giornale d'Italia*, March 9, 1934, 3. Since the state draws its power from the inner spirit of individuals by representing their "universal moment," it is "mai completamente fatto, ma un continuo farsi."

[11] Emil Ludwig, *Colloqui con Mussolini* (Milan: Mondadori, 1932), 125, 219.

[12] Pirandello in *Quadrivio*, November 3, 1935, 71. Brasillach, in a review of René Benjamin's *Mussolini et son peuple*, agrees with Benjamin that il Duce is "a great dramatic poet" and adds: "The directors [*Les animateurs*] of peoples is an idea dear to me, government by poetry" (in Robert Brasillach, *Oeuvres complètes* [Paris: Club de l'honnête homme, 1966] 12: 33, hereafter cited as *OC*).

ment, irrationalist thinking in the wake of Nietzsche and Bergson, along with reactionary, imperialist, and syndicalist-revolutionary thinking, foreshadowed the intertwining of the aesthetic in later fascist rhetoric and spectacle. Yet the relationship between fascism and fin-de-siècle aestheticism has not received a great deal of attention. Benjamin's provocative suggestion that the fascist aesthetization of politics is "the consummation of *l'art pour l'art*"[13] is less frequently quoted and less unpacked than his remark on the introduction of aesthetics into political life. Simonetta Falasca-Zamponi, however, has made a convincing argument for the relationship between *l'art pour l'art* aesthetics and Mussolini's politics of spectacle. In her view, the prevalence of form over ideological norms, as noted by Benjamin, characterizes Mussolini's aestheticized politics.[14] In Russell Berman's reading of Benjamin, the fascist state is the heir of l'art pour l'art in a formal rather than an ideological sense in that both are constructed so as to refuse intersubjective communication. Thus Benjamin's concept of "aura" could encompass the mystifying authority of the political figure as well as the perfection of artistic form. Berman also offers the following schematic definition of fascist modernism in literary aesthetics: "In place of bourgeois teleology, fascist modernism operates with iteration, a perpetual repetition of the same, suggesting the eternal return of a cyclical history. In place of identity construction [here he seems to mean the Bildungsroman], it offers the spectacle, unnuanced and unquestioned."[15] In this schema, fascism would seem to privilege the "spectacular" genre of theater over the temporal one of the novel. Although Berman's frame of reference is primarily to German fascist modernism, the definition is broad enough to be useful for the French and Italian varieties as well.

Berman goes on to criticize Benjamin's theory for being at once too narrow (aestheticism hardly characterizes all the aspects of fascism, even Italian fascism) and too broad (contemporary politics of spectacle fit into the definition as well). These criticisms, while true, point out the fact that more work remains to be done on the specific relationship between fin-de-siècle aestheticism and the aesthetic component of early fascism, as well as on later aesthetic approaches to fascism. In terms of early twentieth-century aesthetic-political relations, futurism has received the lion's share of attention.

---

[13] Benjamin, *Illuminations*, 241.

[14] Simonetta Falasca-Zamponi, *Fascist Spectacle: The Aesthetics of Power in Mussolini's Italy* (Berkeley: University of California Press, 1997). See, for example, her discussion of Mussolini's idea of substituting "artistic vision" for political democracy. "Mussolini's aspiration to transform Italy and create it anew was yet another variation on the theme of the God-like artist-creator" (12).

[15] Russell Berman, "Written Right across Their Faces," in *Modern Culture and Critical Theory: Art, Politics, and the Legacy of the Frankfurt School* (Madison: University of Wisconsin Press, 1989), 105–6.

Walter Adamson's *Avant-Garde Florence: From Modernism to Fascism* fills a gap by demonstrating how Italian avant-garde and aestheticist movements other than futurism were instrumental in the formation of the culture of fascism, a culture which for him as for Sternhell occurred before the movement became politicized or the term invented. Many of the "cultural" fascists, however, were reluctant to make the leap into politics. Adamson stresses the French connection with the symbolists and decadents in the formation of this culture, as well as the influence of Bergson and Nietzsche. The modernist project of the search for cultural renewal, rejection of bourgeois norms for a recuperation of the primal, a transvaluation of values and a Sorelian heroic regeneration, along with the ideal of "pure beauty" first found a voice in the journal *Il Marzocco* begun in 1896 by Gabriele D'Annunzio and Mario Morasso.[16] Under the editorship of Enrico Corradini (1897–1900) the journal's aesthetic ideals fused with those of nationalism and imperialism. Adamson traces the continuity of this culture through several other journals but primarily through the figures of Giovanni Papini and Giuseppe Prezzolini. Important for an understanding of cultural fascism are the essays written by Mussolini from 1905 to 1908 on such figures as Baudelaire, Verlaine, Wilde, D'Annunzio, and Nietzsche (140). An emphasis in Mussolini's writing at this time is on "spiritual elevation" (142), a term that he continued to use in his later political writings and that found sympathetic receivers in Papini and Prezzolini, who were searching for a "secular religion." In 1913, Prezzolini, who was familiar with Giovanni Gentile's idealist thought, formulated the notion of "a spiritual revolution that would culminate in a new politics of lyricism and pageantry, in a 'world as theater'" (189), an ideal he believed would be in part realized with Italy's entrance into the war.[17] In 1923, Prezzolini, although growing disillusioned with the political movement, recognized that fascism, as a secular-religious movement complete with pageantry and theatrics, was heir to his earlier avant-garde modernism (248).

The conflation of the literary, the religious, the theatrical, and the political does indeed seem to be a constant in the intellectual discourse of early twentieth-century France and Italy. It can be seen in the work of the syndicalist Georges Sorel, a prime influence on Mussolini. Although Sorel began as a Marxist, he repudiated the materialism, rationalism, and utopianism of Marxism and was able to accept an "organic" concept of nationalism, both regionalized and extended to Italy, the sister "Latin" nation. Sorel's notion that violence is the motivating force of history, his cult of en-

[16] Walter Adamson, *Avant-Garde Florence: From Modernism to Fascism* (Cambridge: Harvard University Press, 1993), 8–13.

[17] Other conflations of politics and theater occur in Enrico Ruta, "Il mito e il fatto," *La Voce*, May 13, 28, 1914, and in articles on Claudel in *La Voce*, April 11, June 13, 1912, October 10, 17, 24, 1912, quoted in Adamson, *Avant-Garde Florence*, nn. 119–20, p. 292.

ergy and heroism as sources of morality and virtue, and his call for an irrational system of "myths"—in particular the myth of the general strike—to replace Marxist materialist utopias as sources of revolutionary inspiration were all important legacies to fascism. Violence, in Sorelian thought, was not a means to an end but a thing of beauty in itself: thus Sorel can esteem heroic war as praised by poets over base war waged by politicians.[18] On the other end of the political-aesthetic spectrum was Charles Maurras, founder of the Action française, for whom beauty in politics represented classical-traditional order rather than revolutionary violence. What these two poles had in common was a revulsion against the Enlightenment and nineteenth-century "bourgeois" values already decried by Nietzsche: universalism, individualism, progress, natural rights, equality, parliamentary democracy, and the like. The followers of Maurras and Sorel were thus able to make common cause for a while, and it is with their brief rapprochement that Sternhell marks the beginning of the fusion of right and left from which fascist ideology would grow. It was, however, in Italy, according to Sternhell, that the "nationalist-syndicalist" synthesis solidified, first around the Libyan war of 1911 and then around the interventionist movement in World War I.[19] It was at this time too that the discourse of imperialism entered into what can by then be called a nascent fascism.

Some of the aesthetic-political language that Sorel bequeathed to fascism is specifically theatrical in nature. Like D'Annunzio, and partly under the influence of the popular *Psychology of Crowds* by Gustave Le Bon, he understood well the nature of the dynamic between leader and crowd, a phenomenon of theatrical aesthetics that would culminate in Mussolini's "dominating the mass like an artist" and, in a different form, in Hitler's mass rallies. Sorel's concept of *myth*, which he describes as "expressions of a determination to act" and "a body of images" to be understood "by intuition alone,"[20] fuses political activism, Bergsonian philosophy,[21] religion, and notions from literature and visual arts. In praising the beauty of violence, Sorel also glorifies the Homeric hero, "the indomitable hero confident in his strength and putting himself above rules," whose values "are approximately the same as the Cornelian values."[22] These values are not necessarily extinct but may live on in art, which may inspire action. Sorel here seems to anticipate the cult of Corneille and of a neo-Cornelian tragedy of will and

---

[18] Georges Sorel, *Réflexions sur la violence* (Paris: Rivière, 1946), 246–49, quoted in Sternhell, *Birth of Fascist Ideology*, 67.

[19] Sternhell, *Birth of Fascist Ideology*, 32.

[20] Georges Sorel, *Reflections on Violence*, trans. T. E. Hulme (London: Collier Books, 1969), 50, 122.

[21] For the influence of Bergson on Sorel, see Sternhell, *La Droite révolutionnaire*, 393–94 and Mark Antliff, *Inventing Bergson: Cultural Politics and the Parisian Avant-Garde* (Princeton, N.J.: Princeton University Press, 1993), 4–7, 156–59.

[22] Sorel, *Reflections on Violence*, 232.

sacrifice that would be dear to the later French fascists' fusion of aesthetics and politics. His notion of myth also had a profound effect on Mussolini.

It was in the wake of the diffusion of Nietzsche's *Birth of Tragedy* at the end of the nineteenth century that the fusion of aesthetic discourse specifically on tragedy with that of political ideology took shape. Two books from the formative fascist culture of early twentieth-century Italy and France are exemplary: *L'Imperialismo artistico* by Mario Morasso (1903) and *Les Méfaits des intellectuels* by Sorel's disciple Edouard Berth (1914). The latter, written at the time when the syndicalists, disillusioned with the materialist socialist left, were exploring rapprochement with Maurras's Action française, shows that the more youthful Berth may have gone farther than Sorel in embracing the new synthesis.[23] But an equally important influence on *Les Méfaits* is evident as well. An enthusiastic reader of *The Birth of Tragedy*, Berth was eager to fuse Nietzschean aesthetics with the discourse of political theory. The following passage is exemplary:

> From the fraternal alliance of Dionysus and Apollo emerged the immortal Greek tragedy. . . . Similarly, L'Action française—which with Maurras, is a new incarnation of the Apollonian spirit—through its collaboration with syndicalism—which, with Sorel, represents the Dionysian spirit—will be able to give birth to a new grand siècle, one of those historical achievements which afterward for a long time leave the world dazzled and fascinated. [24]

Berth further explains that syndicalist violence "calls for order, as the sublime calls for the beautiful; Apollo must complete the work of Dionysus."[25]

Drawing on Sorel and Nietzsche, Berth equates beauty with violence and with Dionysus and opposition to the Dionysian spirit with decadence. Stating that Nietzsche calls Socrates "the first decadent," Berth gives his explanation of the term that, originating with Barrès, will become a favorite in fascist language. Decadence is "a dissolution of the social idea, a retreat of each individual into his shell, which he hypocritically calls his liberty" (211–12). "Decadence," which is antitragic, stems from rationalism as well as individualism: thus Descartes, who had "no tragic sense of life" (293), is decadent; Pascal, whose thought confronts beyond rationality the paradoxes of Christianity such as the *felix culpa*, is nondecadent and tragic. (Berth cites feminists and emancipated women as modern examples of decadence.) In contrast to decadent individualism, Dionysian mass fervor brings each soul into contact with the universal soul, creating a true free-

[23] See Sternhell, *Birth of Fascist Ideology*, 82ff.
[24] Edouard Berth, *Les Méfaits des intellectuels*, 2d ed. (Paris: Rivière, 1926), 355, quoted in Sternhell, *Birth of Fascist Ideology*, 89.
[25] Berth, *Les Méfaits*, 1st ed. (Paris: Rivière,) [1914], 329.

dom of the will superior to rationalistic-individualistic illusory freedom. Thus Berth ardently believes that the "myth" of the Sorelian general strike will bring about a new incarnation of Dionysus (215) as it enables the people to become conscious of its spiritual unity, thus abolishing decadence. While there is undoubtedly more of Sorel than of Maurras in his book, Berth does not neglect to return to his modern Apollonian. Mythical delirium demands clarity of organization, and *grandeur tragique* will be achieved only through their fusion.[26] Aesthetics, politics, and social analyses are so intertwined in Berth's discourse that it is sometimes hard to know of which area he is speaking. Thus the mythical and the heroic are necessary elements of the general strike, and the renaissance of tragedy Berth calls for (here, 288, he seems to mean actual stage tragedy) will serve as a remedy against social as well as artistic decadence.

In Berth's fusion of Sorel and Maurras with Nietzsche, modern tragedy appears to be the ideal form with which to express the intuited notion of myth, Sorel's replacement for the Marxist utopia. For Sorel, it is not the reality but the myth of the general strike that will effect the cohesiveness of the proletariat. Tragedy, for Berth, will represent the culmination of this mythic hope; the synthesis of Dionysian movement and Apollonian form. Berth's view in a sense resembles the theory of the contemporary Marxist critic Franco Moretti. For Moretti, modern tragedy as a genre aspires to what he calls "the moment of truth"[27] or a resolution resulting from a turning point out of ordinary time that reveals as false the temporal dimension of everyday life, as represented in the genre of the novel. Tragedy thus encodes and anticipates revolutionary politics. The "tragic" mode of political thinking is, in Moretti's view, best illustrated by Sorel's myth of the general strike. For Sorel, peace and stability represent a compromise masking the social truths that the strike will reveal through violent conflict.

One point on which all historians of fascism agree is the crucial role of World War I in the development of the movement. Both mobilization itself and the political, economic, and spiritual vacuum left in the wake of the Great War, along with the fear of "bolshevism," made possible the spread of a political vision that promised strong leadership and a new order in every domain. For Italian interventionists, going to battle seemed to afford the opportunity for a realization of a heroic sense of life absent during the years of liberal, parliamentary government and "mediocrity." After the war, Italian fascism incorporated myths of violence, sacrifice, and regeneration from memories of experience in combat. Emilio Gentile goes

---

[26] Berth here follows Nietzsche, who defines the "tragic myth" as "a symbolization of Dionysian wisdom through Apollinian artifices" (Friedrich Nietzsche, *The Birth of Tragedy and The Case of Wagner,* trans. Walter Kaufmann [New York: Random House, Vintage Books], 1967, 131).

[27] Franco Moretti, "The Moment of Truth: The Geography of Modern Tragedy," in *Contemporary Marxist Literary Criticism,* ed. Francis Mulkern (London: Longman, 1992), 114–24.

so far as to suggest that the myth of "resurrection," created from the sacrifice of martyred soldiers for the renewal of the *patria*, became "the founding myth of the Fascist symbolic universe."[28] Pirandello, in search of myths, makes use of this one in one of his modern tragedies. In France, Pierre Drieu La Rochelle's writings exemplify nostalgia for the heroic, violent, and "tragic" universe of the battlefield. Violent struggle, heroic death, and renovating sacrifice to a spiritualized nation realized the longing for a tragic solution to decadent modernity inspired by reading Nietzsche.

Drieu's nostalgia for what might be called the ecstasy of war went hand in hand with his critique of postwar society, which seemed to him to relapse into decadence. Along with other French fascists, however, Drieu found hope for the renewal and renovation of France in the riots in Paris on February 6, 1934, the event they saw as an incarnation of Sorel's notion of the myth of the general strike. These demonstrations against the Stavisky affair, they believed for a short time, would initiate the revolution that would bring about the demise of parliamentary government and the advent of fascism in France. The title character of Drieu's novel *Gilles* perceives the moment thus: "Looking to his right and his left, he saw himself surrounded by Fear and Courage—the divine couple who preside over war had returned. . . . On a beauteous theater of stone and sky, a people and a police separated like two halves of a chorus."[29] Robert Brasillach refers to the same event as "that tragic night" and "that exalting night" of which the German papers wrote, "The dawn of fascism is rising over France."[30] In Drieu's text, it is as if an epic, Homeric moment of war presided over by divine beings reforms itself into a tragic performance, complete with a choral agon in a beautiful outdoor theater. For both Drieu and Brasillach, the violence of the streets is literally sublimated—rendered sublime—and aestheticized as tragic form. The night of tragic struggle will give birth to the dawn of the moment of truth, the coming of fascism. Franco Moretti's sense that Sorel's myth of the general strike represents a "tragic" mode of political thinking seems to receive an almost literal illustration in the description in *Gilles*.

If, as Moretti suggests, Sorelian "tragic" thinking is in some way a culmination of the actual modern tragedies of Hebbel, Hauptmann, Ibsen, and Strindberg, important distinctions must nonetheless be made between these and the new thinking about modern tragedy that arose at the turn of the century in the wake of Nietzsche and aestheticism. Whereas nineteenth century bourgeois tragedy tends to substitute specific social condi-

---

[28] Gentile, *Sacralization of Politics in Fascist Italy*, 39.

[29] Pierre Drieu La Rochelle, *Gilles* (Paris: Gallimard, 1939), 595–96, trans. and cited by Alice Yaeger Kaplan, *Reproductions of Banality: Fascism, Literature, and French Intellectual Life* (Minneapolis: University of Minnesota Press, 1986), 69.

[30] Robert Brasillach, *Notre avant-guerre* (Paris: Plon, 1968), 135–36, trans. and quoted in Kaplan, *Reproductions of Banality*, 69–70.

tions for ancient tragic fate, thereby suggesting that if conditions changed, tragedy might be avoided, the condemnation of modernity in the discourse on and production of tragedy both in the formative and in the postwar culture of fascism is absolute. A case in point is Mario Morasso's *Imperialismo artistico* (1903).

Morasso's treatise, whose very title conflates the political and aesthetic, puts forth a theory of modern tragedy for the nascent new age. The original coeditor (with D'Annunzio) and a prime contributor to *Il Marzocco*, Morasso was closely involved in the movement fusing l'art pour l'art with nationalism. Attempting to create a theory of aesthetics and civilization, he comes up with the following schema. There are three types of civilization: the "barbarous" (inferior), the dominating and military (superior), and the mercantile, bourgeois (intermediate). The art of superior civilizations (for example, classical Greece) is realist in the classical sense, expressive of the "sublime and profound," tending toward harmony and perfection. The art of intermediate civilizations such as materialistic bourgeois democracy is characterized by superficial realism and banal propaganda, typified by Emile Zola. Intermediate civilizations may be either "decadent," tending from superior to inferior, or "ascendant," tending from inferior to superior. In the first case, the art they produce is "romantic"—nostalgic toward the past—and in the second it is symbolic, fantastic, and visionary, disdainful of the present and yearning toward a future of dominance, which at the present time takes the form of imperialism and colonialism.[31]

Morasso sees a great age of imperialistic expansion dawning. As the Western powers prepare to conquer inferior peoples, democracy will be transformed into nationalism. The art of the new imperialism will shed both symbolism and the modern, democratic, everyday (inferior) realism epitomized by Zola to return to a "grandiose realism" celebrating nature, the hero, the race, and the nation (27). It is *tragedy* that will be the primary art form of the superior civilization to come (35).

In the section of the book (pp. 169–185) devoted to the discussion of "modern tragedy," Morasso makes no mention of German bourgeois tragedy but judges existing modern tragedy, characterized by the work of Ibsen and Maeterlinck, to be "symbolic"—thus moving away from realism but yearning for a new tragic form, having not yet found a modern equivalent for tragic fate (177). Classical tragedy represented the "terrible and magnificent duel between the hero, incarnating with supreme excellence all of human virtue and energy . . . and fate, including all the unknown forces, mysteries of earth and heavens" (170) made possible by an aristocratic society (Morasso, like the fascist theorists who followed him, skirts the fact that tragedy was

[31] "And the greatest dream is that of dominion" (Mario Morasso, *L'imperialismo artistico* [Turin: Fratelli Bocca, 1903], 22).

produced under Athenian democracy). Modern tragedy will have to create its own form of the classical agon by drawing on the energies of mass society, inventing a hero with the will to combat fate in the form of imperial domination, a hero who incarnates the "brute force" of the masses and who is capable of cutting through the "imbecilities" and false egalitarianism of parliamentary democracy.[32]

The most promising author for the resurrection of the new tragedy is for Morasso his colleague D'Annunzio, who had by then written only one play in the new genre, *La Città morta* (*The Dead City*). Unlike most modern tragedies, *La Città morta* is not "symbolic" but rather embodies the "pure classic scheme" (180) of the agon between hero and fate. Yet Morasso has reservations: the hero does not have truly heroic stature; the concept of "fate" is still too verbal and too psychological. These failings, however, are not the fault of D'Annunzio but rather of Italian society, which, run by opportunistic parliamentary imbeciles, has not yet produced the strong leader who could inspire tragic grandeur (185). Morasso, however, is optimistic that the new, heroic, and imperialistic society is in the process of being formed and that D'Annunzio, along with others to come, will be its tragic poet. Denunciation of liberal, parliamentary democracy and of "L'Italietta" of Giolitti was of course commonplace among the nationalists of early twentieth century Italy. Nor was Morasso alone in making such accusations. Angelo Olivetti, reader of Nietzsche and an architect of the fusion of Sorelian syndicalism and nationalism in Italy, used similar terms when he accused Italian bourgeois society of lacking a sense of the tragic and of heroism.[33] (Olivetti went on to become one of several enthusiastic Jewish fascists in the Italy of the 1920s, but he died before the imposition of racial laws in 1938.) In the years before World War I, Enrico Corradini, one of the key figures to bridge late nineteenth-century aestheticism with early twentieth-century nationalism, and later fascism, wrote several not very successful modern tragedies, including *Charlotte Corday*. Although D'Annunzio was in many respects his rival, Corradini like Morasso recognized in the national bard a tragedian worthy of the new age, calling *La Nave* (*The Ship*) the first heroic tragedy of Italy, in that it united imperialism with modern consciousness.[34]

[32] See the discussion by Roberto Tessari in "Crudités archéologiques e spezie saporose: La 'tragedia moderna' di D'Annunzio, tra altri modelli di restauro del Tragico," *Gabriele D'Annunzio: Grandezza e deliria nell'industria dello spettacolo* (Turin: Centro regionale universitario per il teatro del Piemonte, 1989).

[33] Angelo Olivetti, "Sindacalismo e nazionalismo," in *Pro e contro la guerra di Tripoli: Discussioni nel campo rivoluzionnario* (Naples: Società Editrice Partenopea, 1912), 15–17, quoted in Sternhell, *Birth of Fascist Ideology*, 167.

[34] See Paul Colombani, "Enrico Corradini: Un Dannunzien en politique?" in *D'Annunzio e il suo tempo*, ed. Francesco Perfetti (Genoa: SAGEP, 1992), 1: 329–68.

Even though Sternhell's contention that fascism developed as a culture before the actual political movement may be open to debate, it seems clear that the confluence of what I call aesthetic fascism and a new theory and practice of modern tragedy began in French and Italian discourse at the turn of the century. The key figure here is indeed D'Annunzio: not because he was necessarily the unequivocal "John the Baptist of fascism" or because he was politically a fascist, which he was not, but because, specifically in his rediscovery of Greek tragedy and his theories of modern tragedy under the influence of Nietzsche, he was the first to bring together aestheticism and nascent twentieth-century antidemocratic nationalist and imperialist ideology. There is general agreement that D'Annunzio's political/theatrical *style* heavily influenced Mussolini's. In conceptualizing aesthetic fascism, such a style must be taken seriously. D'Annunzio was, of course, promoted by the fascists as the "soul" of fascism and the poet of the regime, a concept he did not discourage. Finally, D'Annunzio's modern tragedies were revived under the fascist regime in outdoor settings and praised as drama befitting fascism. If D'Annunzio's tragedies both prefigured, and in later productions seemed to exemplify, a totalitarian binding of poet and public, those of the "apolitical" but longtime party member Pirandello were constructed on the bases of irrationalism and philosophical relativism. On opposite ends of the spectrum in most of their life and literary styles, the two major dramatists of early twentieth-century Italy were nonetheless nourished by the same turn-of-the-century cultural fusions.

The search for a literary modern tragedy "worthy" first of nationalism and imperialism and later specifically of fascism appears throughout Italian journalism, theory, and criticism from the beginning of the century through the 1930s. It is taken up, in a different guise, by fascist intellectuals in the France of the 1930s, who felt that a shared "Latinity" and classical heritage allied them in aesthetic matters more closely to Italy than to Nazi Germany.[35] The influence of Nietzsche is primary in both contexts. If D'Annunzio introduced the Dionysian and the superman as hero to Italy, Thierry Maulnier emphasized a "Mediterranean" and "classical" Nietzsche for France. Robert Brasillach, in his book on Corneille, finds an "eternal fascism" in the heroic tragedian of *le grand siècle*. Calling for the creation of a new modern tragedy based on the neoclassical, Brasillach attempts one himself with his *Bérénice*.

[35] The Germans at times made attempts to reclaim the achievements of classical Greece as *their* heritage. In general, however, they seem to have viewed admiration of the Greco-Roman tradition as a product of the Enlightenment, too "universal" to express the aesthetics specific to the "Germanic soul." Alfred Rosenberg, in a chapter titled "Racial Aesthetics" in his *Myth of the Twentieth Century*, attempts to argue that the classical Greek emphases on beauty, universalism, and "static" art are inferior to the organic, dynamic, and ethical creations of the "nordic racial soul" (*The Myth of the Twentieth Century: An Evaluation of the Spiritual-Intellectual Confrontations of Our Age*, trans. Vivian Bird [Torrance, Calif.: Noontide Press, 1982], 169–96).

Drieu La Rochelle also wrote essays and criticism on modern tragedy and fascism and produced two heroic modern tragedies. The key words in French fascist discourse on tragedy—*grandeur* and *pureté*—are, in the manner of the language of Sorel and Berth, equivocally both literary and political. *Pureté* can apply at once to aesthetic form, to heroic virility, and to matters of race. Vichy France, while presenting an obviously different political situation from that of fascist Italy, demonstrates certain parallels in theatrical matters. The French authorities, although exercising a censorship controlled by the Nazis, encouraged theatrical activities from the revival of Greek tragedies in the original to outdoor sports dramas, from promoting French classical drama at the Comédie française to staging the latest Anouilh, Montherlant, or even Sartre. As in Italy, there was much talk of reviving for the modern age the ancient "theater of the people." In Paris, the brief, intense years of the Occupation offer a veritable laboratory situation for theatrical reception studies, given the importance of theatergoing and the politicized public with a highly charged "horizon of expectations." Contrary to popular perceptions there were no plays produced during the Occupation that spoke directly to the call for resistance, although individual lines or even words were sometimes received as such. Since the figure of Joan of Arc was used for propaganda by both Vichy and the Resistance, plays on the French national heroine tended to be received favorably at both ends of the political spectrum. In Paris as in Rome, critics and other intellectuals—writing for Vichy- or Nazi-sponsored journals—theorized on the aesthetics of a modern tragedy informed by fascism, found them in certain plays of their contemporaries, but continued to speak of the advent of the ideal representative of the genre in the future. Brasillach, by then an important theater critic, in line with Italian critics such as Silvio D'Amico, argued that the true source of theater was not spectacle but rather the poetic word, and called for a revival of *literary* theater.

Both D'Annunzio, who lived and wrote in France for extended periods, and Pirandello, whose *Six Characters in Search of an Author*, in particular, helped to revolutionize French theater, were well known and influential in France. In two of the major French playwrights who produced modern tragedies in the Paris of the Occupation—Anouilh and Henry de Montherlant—one can perhaps speak of a Pirandellian and a D'Annunzian mode, or of aesthetics of relativity on the one hand and of totality on the other. While Anouilh's links to fascism were tenuous—he published articles in collaborationist papers, worked with fascist sympathizers in producing his plays, and admired Brasillach—Montherlant's were more complex and more troubling. The plays of both, however, were well received and discussed in the fascist press, and plays such as *Antigone* and *La Reine morte* (*The Dead Queen*), I will argue, in certain ways exemplify the modern tragedy informed by aesthetic fascism.

The question now poses itself: what differentiates such a tragedy from other modern tragedies? I attempted above to make a rough distinction between nineteenth-century bourgeois tragedy and a developing nationalist-fascist ideology of tragedy in the wake of Nietzsche. (This does not, of course, preclude other, "leftist" receptions of Nietzsche.) The definition of bourgeois tragedy can be extended to later twentieth-century examples. In playwrights such as Eugene O'Neill, Arthur Miller, Jean Giraudoux, and Jean-Paul Sartre, we find what I would call a domesticizing of tragic fate, or an application of social, psychological, and philosophical problems of the present to the tragic genre. Willy Loman, like Hedda Gabler, is "done in" by his environment: social strictures replace the ancient religious sense of fate. Even though, as in all tragedy, no solution to the catastrophe can be postulated, the spectator is nonetheless left with the suggestion that if only society could change, a particular tragic problem might disappear. In the case of Sartre, an existentialist assertion of freedom and renunciation of bad faith could have changed the tragic configuration of *No Exit*. Even Frantz von Gerlach in *The Condemned of Altona*, although a victim of historical forces, retains the possibility of existentialist choice. This domesticizing of tragedy is one of the reasons why George Steiner concluded in 1960 that tragedy in modernity was "dead." While Steiner's thesis is still open to debate, it is true that both nineteenth- and twentieth-century bourgeois tragedy becomes, as it were, cross-pollinated with narrative realism. The tragedy informed by aesthetic fascism, on the contrary, seeks to transcend temporal narrative, linear plot, and "democratic" dialogue to search for a more organic or spatial form that gives primacy to the poetic word of the author. It tends to reject the "decadent" present for a refuge in childhood, death, myth, atemporality, or totality[36]—what Pirandello's modern character "Henry IV," who has imprisoned himself forever in the eleventh century, calls "the great pleasure of history." No social or political solution can be postulated in such tragedy—"politics" belongs to the realm of the socialists and democrats, not to the "spiritual." These dramatists seek a new form of ancient tragic fate and heroic sacrifice as well as new poetic languages.

Self-consciousness, endemic to a genre resurrected and recreated for modernity, is a major characteristic of modern tragedy in general. In the tragedies to be studied here, it manifests itself in particular ways: D'Annunzio is the first to attempt to apply Nietzsche's theories in *The Birth of Tragedy* to the actual creation of tragedy for a dawning heroic age; the plays of Pirandello, Drieu La Rochelle, Brasillach, Montherlant, and Anouilh all make meta-tragic statements implicitly or explicitly contrasting tragedy with decadence. The language and tragic configurations of Pirandello and Anouilh

---

[36] Jean-Pierre Faye, in *Langages totalitaires* (Paris: Herman, 1972), 80, calls this phenomenon fascism's "grosses Zurück" ("great regression").

display an ironic and pessimistic commentary on modernity, along with a peculiar fatalism; those of D'Annunzio and Montherlant strive to recreate heroic sacrifice for a possible purer future. The condemnation of "plutocratic" corrupt bourgeois society, "mediocrity," and "the easy life," along with a certain cult of youth and "purity," is implicit in all.

Whereas Pirandello and Anouilh reflect ideological fascism's moral and philosophical relativism, D'Annunzio and Montherlant reflect its spirit of totalitarianism, or the word and deed that rush to fill in the nihilistic void. D'Annunzio, in particular, configures fascism's binding and fusing operations: in his theoretical writings as in his plays, the relationship between political leader and crowd is aesthetically conflated with that between tragic poet and audience. Drieu and Brasillach deal more explicitly with the fascist concept of the Other and its racial implications. Brasillach's Bérénice incarnates the Jew, the Female, and the Colonized, all of which are destined to be subjugated by the Roman (or the Latin), the Male, and the Colonizer, embodied in the Emperor Titus. Drieu's Charlotte Corday represents the spirit of French nationalism in opposition to the supposedly foreign and Jewish Marat. Charlotte, like Anouilh's Antigone and like the figure of Joan of Arc in other fascist-leaning plays, figures a masculinized virgin who rises above the category of "Woman" to serve as a sacrificial and purifying victim. The female may also be valorized, as in some of Pirandello's plays, as the sacrificing mother. Generally, however, Woman represents a corrupting threat to the male will to power and virile virtues. Montherlant's Ines de Castro is exemplary, as is the subtitle to *The Dead Queen: How to Kill Women*.

The attempt to circumscribe the parameters of a modern tragedy informed by aesthetic fascism must be not only text-based but also reception-based, as the politically charged environments of Italy in the *ventennio* and France in the 1930s and especially under the Occupation brought new dimensions to texts in some instances written in quite different circumstances. I have therefore devoted some time not only to the consideration of reviews of the plays in question but also to journalistic commentary of the period on modern tragedy. Discussion of tragedy in relation to aesthetic fascism also appears in more extended forms as in Thierry Maulnier's books on Nietzsche and Racine and Robert Brasillach's book on Corneille. These theoretical discussions are also central to my book. One of the reasons that this book is called the *search* for modern tragedy is that in the minds of fascist critics an ideal or perfect fascist modern tragedy never emerged, although the works of the writers under discussion all approximated it. I should state clearly that I do not intend to imply that these plays or their authors can be somehow reduced or dismissed by the label "fascist" or that this approach marks the entire or even the primary scope of their importance. Underlying my research, however, is the conviction that the exploration of links between the ideology and aesthetics of fascism and high modern culture continues to be crucial.

CHAPTER ONE

Theatricality and Tragedy in Fascist Italy

Although the focus of this book is on literary drama informed by aesthetic fascism rather than the practice of fascist aesthetics in theatrical production, some notion of the latter is essential to an understanding of fascist ideology in regard to theater. Theater under fascism in turn can hardly be disassociated from the carefully orchestrated staging of public spectacles throughout Italy such as sporting events, commemorative ceremonies, rituals, parades, holidays, and even Catholic masses, all designed to build the consensus necessary to fuse the individual with the fascist collectivity, the crowd with the leader.[1] Indeed, the mere thought of Benito Mussolini's Italy suggests a kind of everyday theatricality, with mass gatherings in the piazza, the stadium, and the amphitheater, parades, costumes, the loudspeaker, the chant—all the trappings of mass performance. Fascist architecture and urban planning created spaces suited to the development of a mass aesthetic. A structure such as the vast "Foro Mussolini" (renamed the "Foro italico"), devoted to sports and physical culture, exemplifies the fusion of *romanità* or reverence for Italian tradition with modernist and functional architecture of the 1930s. Mussolini's orations to the crowds in Piazza Venezia, with their totalitarian organization of space and time

---

[1] For an analysis of various fascist rituals, along with an overview of theater under the regime, see Paolo Puppa, "Pubblico e popolo nel teatro fascista," *Rivista italiana di drammaturgia* 5 (December 18, 1980), 65–83. Puppa concludes that the best drama produced by the regime was in its rituals rather than in its theatrical productions. Studies of fascist mass spectacles and rituals in conjunction with the political goals of fascism include Simonetta Falasca-Zamponi, *Fascist Spectacle: The Aesthetics of Power in Mussolini's Italy* (Berkeley: University of California Press, 1997), and Mabel Berezin, *The Making of the Fascist Self: The Political Culture of Interwar Italy* (Ithaca: Cornell University Press, 1997).

and their manipulation of an orchestrated "dialogue" between the words of the leader and the responses of the crowd was, as many contemporaries noted, a dramatic performance. The March on Rome itself was more of a spectacle than a genuine historical event; its annual commemoration served to inscribe the spectacle with myth.[2] Appropriating many aspects of D'Annunzio's use of ceremony and commemoration during his brief, highly theatrical occupation of Fiume, Mussolini sought to inculcate his "spiritual" values through the development of an aesthetic style. The major events commemorated and exalted in fascist ritual were the founding of Rome, World War I (and the sacrifice of the heroic dead for the nation), and the March on Rome. Through all of them, of course, ran the emotional bonding of Il Duce with the masses and the fabrication of consensus.

Fascism sometimes presented itself as a new "religion" more than a political party. Mussolini, pointing out that his forum for addressing the people was the piazza and not the chambers of parliament, said in a 1926 speech, "Fascism is not only a party, it is a regime, it is not only a regime, but a faith, it is not only a faith, but a religion that is conquering the laboring masses of the Italian people."[3] In his 1927 "Manifesto of Fascist Intellectuals," Giovanni Gentile attempted a more sustained definition of fascism as religion, emphasizing fascism's "spiritual" nature and that, unlike merely "political" systems, adherence to it engages the whole person.[4] The identification of fascism with religion is certainly valid in the etymological sense, in that the nature of both is to bind and to fuse. Such a definition is misrepresentative, however, in the sense that fascism had nothing that can be considered a theology. Emilio Gentile is more accurate in his characterization of fascism as a "sacralization of politics,"[5] although he perhaps forces the attempt to create a kind of theology with Mussolini or the state as God. Investing politics with a sacred nature required both the creation of myths and the dramatic ceremonies, liturgies, and rites designed to solidify the masses, to bind them into a *fasces* or a community of believers. Yet it did not really offer a system of belief. Unlike Nazism, fascism did not draw on a pagan pantheon as an alternative to Christianity. What it could and did draw on was both classical antiquity and a *romanità* that also included aspects of Roman Catholicism. Thus Mussolini's "religious" cer-

---

[2] Berezin, *Making of the Fascist Self*, 77–86.

[3] "Discorso di Pesaro," in *Opera omnia di Benito Mussolini*, ed. Edoardo Susmel and Duilio Susmel (Florence: La Fenice, 1956), 2: 197, trans. and cited in Berezin, *Making of the Fascist Self*, 50.

[4] Giovanni Gentile, "Manifesto degli intelletuali fascisti," reprinted in Emilio R. Papa, *Fascismo e cultura* (Venice: Marsilio, 1975), 186–94.

[5] Emilio Gentile, *Il culto del Littorio: La Sacralizzazione della politica nell'Italia fascista* (Rome: Laterza, 1993), translated as *The Sacralization of Politics in Fascist Italy*, trans. Keith Botsford (Cambridge: Harvard University Press, 1996).

emonies could recall Greek and Roman outdoor theater and Catholic ritual, recuperating them for modernity.

With such dramatization in public life, what theatrical production could compete with the stagings of Il Duce? One possible answer is "none," that the best drama of the fascist era was in the piazza. Yet the regime gave much support and encouragement to actual theatrical production. It encouraged popular participation in theater with traveling "Thespian carts" designed to mount productions in rural areas, "Theatrical Saturdays" offering low-price tickets to workers, and amateur theater groups in the "Dopolavoro" recreation organizations. The Corporation of Spectacle, the first and, according to Gaetano Salvemini, the *only* successful fascist corporation, was founded in 1931.[6] In an attempt to improve acting and directing techniques, the government founded an Academy of Dramatic Art, headed by Silvio D'Amico, in 1935 and appointed an inspector general for the theater in the same year. Mussolini himself showed a great deal of interest in theater. In a major speech on April, 28, 1933 at the Argentina Theater in Rome, Il Duce announced: "It is necessary to prepare a mass theater [*il teatro di masse*] that will be able to contain 15 or 20 thousand people. . . . Theater, which, in my opinion, is more educationally effective than cinema, must be designed for the people. . . . [The theatrical work] must agitate great collective passions, be inspired by a sense of deep humanity, put on stage what really counts in the life of the spirit."[7] While Mussolini seems to have felt that mass media such as the cinema and radio were more effective for purely propagandistic purposes, he counted on the theater to give aesthetic expression to fascism's "spiritual" revolution. His call was not only for a change in theatrical architecture to incorporate the masses but also for a poet capable of forging them into a collectivity—in the manner of his own totalizing speeches, it would seem.

One of the most original endeavors to create a fascist mass spectacle, the epic production of the story of a tank called *18 BL* staged outside of Florence in 1934, proved to be a colossal failure.[8] Much more successful were the fascist-sponsored productions of Italian opera in grandiose outdoor Roman settings such as the Baths of Caracalla in Rome and the Roman Arena in Verona. Already in August of 1913, on the occasion of the centennial of Giuseppe Verdi's birth, the performance of Verdi's *Aida* in the Verona Arena served to fuse the audience into a group commemorating *italianità*, the uniting of Italians into a nation. Verdi's music in the outdoor Roman setting certainly must have stirred collective Dionysian emotions,

---

[6] Gaetano Salvemini, *Under the Axe of Fascism* (London: Victor Gollancz, 1936), 129.

[7] Quoted in Pietro Cavallo, *Immaginario e rappresentazione: Il teatro fascista di propaganda* (Rome: Bonacci, 1990), 16.

[8] Jeffrey Schnapp analyzes this event and its effect in *Staging Fascism: 18 BL and the Theater of Masses for Masses* (Stanford: Stanford University Press, 1996).

but so did the particular tragic force of *Aida* with its representation of individuals heroically sacrificed to the power of the state and, perhaps, its subtext of Italian imperialist ambitions in Africa.[9] Clearly Verdian musical tragedy could be incorporated into the fascist regime's theatrical ideals of consensus, collectivism, and national sentiment. In addition to "mass" productions of romantic opera in Verona and Rome, the regime to some extent encouraged the composition of new operas by composers such as Pietro Mascagni and Gian Francesco Malipiero.[10] Puccini's *Turandot* (1926), which music critics view as the last Italian opera in the great tradition, was staged in a lavish production at the Verona Arena in 1928 and in 1938. For Jeremy Tambling, *Turandot* (as to some extent *Madame Butterfly*) stages aspects of fascist discourse with its use of the chorus to represent the masses as obedient subjects of imperial power, the taming of woman by the male representing the nation-state, and its cult of violence. Unlike Verdi's heroes, Puccini's Calaf is a "new" activist, daring and improvising in the manner of Mussolini. The tragic sacrifice of Liù, accompanied by haunting but funereal music, could stir the collective will to Dionysian fusion and violent death.[11]

In the fury to create outdoor theater for the fascist education of the masses, interest in ancient tragedy also played a role. It can be seen in theatrical organization, productions, scripts, ideological pronouncements, and even in some of the classical scholarship of the period. An example of the latter is Rodolfo de Mattei's study titled "La Politica nel teatro romano." In imitating Greek drama, de Mattei argues, the ancient Romans chose subjects such as war, patriotism, discipline, and the sacrifice of the hero for the *patria*—subjects that fit their own cultural and political outlook.[12] Tragedy, according to the author, can flourish only in a "fiery" (*infuocato*) religious and political climate—not in a squabbling democracy or in decadence.[13] The implications for the present, though not explicitly stated, seem clear enough. Speaking to an international conference on theater in London, the inspector for the theater Nicola de Pirro, echoing Nietzsche, praises Greek tragedy for its union of the "primeval forces of nature" with an "ideal equilibrium." Outlining what seems to be the ac-

[9] See Giovanni Morelli, "L'Opera," in *I luoghi della memoria: Simboli e miti dell'Italia unita*, ed. Mario Isnenghi (Rome: Laterza, 1996), 45–65, and Jeremy Tambling, *Opera and the Culture of Fascism* (Oxford: Clarendon Press, 1996), 73–93. The latter deals primarily with the discourse of imperialism in *Otello* but often refers to *Aida*.

[10] See Erik Levi, "Towards an Aesthetic of Fascist Opera," in *Fascism and Theatre: Comparative Studies on the Aesthetics and Politics of Performance in Europe, 1925–1945*, ed. Günter Berghaus (Providence: Berghahn Books, 1996), 270–74.

[11] Tambling, *Opera and the Culture of Fascism*, 144–58.

[12] Rodolfo de Mattei, "La Politica nel teatro romano," Part I, *Rivista italiana del drama* 1 (January–May 1937): 194.

[13] Ibid., 210.

cepted fascist schema for the history of drama, de Pirro contends that with the abandonment of open-air productions and the development of small indoor theaters in the Renaissance, the people lost its "totalitarian predominance," and the drama, disconnected from "collective passions," degenerated from "mythical epos" to mere story. (Theatrical greats such as Shakespeare and Lope de Vega remain exceptions.) Further decadence occurred as the bourgeois-controlled realist and naturalist theater limited itself to an external imitation of bourgeois life, completely divorcing the theater from "the primitive soul of the people." Under fascism, with the reinstatement of ancient and outdoor theater, as well as popular festivals, the relationship between theater and people is being recovered. The only modern plays de Pirro mentions, however, are D'Annunzio's *La Figlia di Iorio* and *La Città morta*, both recently revived in outdoor productions. De Pirro sounds a theme often reiterated by fascist intellectuals writing on theater. The ideal theater under fascism is *not* one of political propaganda or rhetoric but a mystical transformation of consensus ideology through art: "a consecration in which feelings and ideals held in common by all meet and are elevated by poetic truth." The revival of ancient tragedy, combined with the modern revolt against realist drama, will, it seems, recreate the popular communicative function of theater lost under bourgeois decadence.[14]

De Pirro's ideas were to some extent put into practice. The Istituto del Dramma Antico, founded in 1929, promoted the study and production of ancient drama, particularly Greek tragedy. The dialogue of the hero and the chorus resounding in the open-air ruins where the tragedies were often performed could no doubt be seen as a theatrical replication of the grander-scaled ecstatic dialogue between the hero and the crowd taking place in the piazza. Mussolini, according to de Pirro, was particularly moved by *Antigone* and *The Seven against Thebes*.[15] Tragedies such as Sophocles' *Ajax* fit the contemporary glorification of the military hero. In certain cases alterations were made to emphasize a message. For example, in a 1930 production of *Iphegenia at Aulis*, the ending speech of the messenger was cut so that the tragedy would close with the "sublime" sacrifice of the virgin for her country.[16] The theatrical use of outdoor spaces such as the Greek and Roman ruins at Paestum, Fiesole, and Syracuse, as well as in Rome itself, served not only to reinforce the link the regime wished to promote between classical glory and fascist present but also to inspire an emotional and "religious" binding of the masses analogous to the exaltation produced in the political festivals. Theatrical productions in classical ruins were not

[14] Nicola de Pirro, *Il teatro per il popolo* (Rome: Novissima, 1938), 57–68. The text is reprinted in French and English translations as well as in Italian. I quote from the English translation.
[15] Ibid., 67.
[16] Puppa, "Pubblico e popolo," 81.

of course limited to performances of classical drama and of opera. Some of the most spectacular and most successful were, as I will discuss in the next chapter, those of D'Annunzio's tragedies.

The bourgeois theater produced within four walls did not, however, die under fascism. Escapist, so-called white telephone plays were one of the most popular forms of entertainment.[17] Also produced in traditional theaters were fascist propaganda plays, written not only by theater professionals but also by amateurs encouraged by the theatrical organizations of the regime. Many of these scripts—some recently discovered—tend to be thematically oriented either to the "trenches" or the "march": that is, like fascist rituals and commemorative events, they extol the origins of fascism in World War I, or portray the growth and success of the movement as symbolized by the march. Others are concerned with the experience of a religious "conversion" to fascism on the part of a former skeptic and of the sacrifice made possible by fascist "faith." Called in fascist parlance "sublime dramas," these are exemplified by Roberto Farinacci's *Redenzione,* the story of a former communist who finally succeeds in being admitted to the fascist party as he dies a hero's death, or the winner of the 1938 Premio San Remo, *I figli* by Renata Mughini, that portrays an antifascist mother who is "converted" when her son volunteers for the African campaign and she kneels before a portrait of Il Duce. Others portray fascism as a "rebirth" from the ruins of a decadent civilization. These propaganda scripts tended on the whole to follow conventional nineteenth-century formats.[18] Some of them did attempt to create a "myth" of Mussolini, exalted as "more than Caesar, more than Napoleon . . . , having "in his blood all the power of immortal Rome [and] . . . the best qualities of the race,"[19] and shown in dialogue with a popular chorus. The mythical Mussolini was also on occasion identified with Moses and with Christ.[20]

The most serious attempts to write a heroic modern tragedy, historical and therefore not *specifically* propagandistic, are the three plays written by

[17] See Enzo Maurri, *Rose scarlatte e telefoni bianchi: Appunti sulla commedia italiana dall'Impero al 25 luglio 1943* (Rome: Abete, 1981).

[18] The historian Pietro Cavallo discovered in the state archives in Rome a considerable number of scripts submitted to the censure authorities during the fascist period. He has categorized them and analyzed them from the point of view of their statements on fascist propaganda in his *Immaginario e rappresentazione: Il teatro fascista di propaganda* (Rome: Bonacci, 1990). His findings are also summarized in his article "Theatre Politics of the Mussolini Regime and Their Influence on Fascist Drama," trans. Erminia Passannanti and Gunter Berghaus, in Berghaus, ed., *Fascism and Theatre: Comparative Studies of the Aesthetics and Politics of Performance in Europe, 1925–1945* (Providence: Berghahn Books, 1996), 113–32. See also the earlier essay by Paolo Puppa, "Motivi pirandelliani e condizionamenti di regime nel teatro italiano degli anni '30," in *Pirandello e la drammaturgia tra le due guerre,* ed. Enzo Scrivano (Agrigento: Centro Nazionale di Studi Pirandelliani, 1985), 211–43.

[19] Emmanuele Iacano, "28 ottobre," cited in Cavallo, *Immaginario,* 74.

[20] Cavallo, "Theatre Politics," 123.

Giovacchino Forzano in collaboration, he claims, with Mussolini.[21] They are *Campo di Maggio*, 1930 (made into a film in 1934), on Napoleon; *Villafranca*, 1932, on Victor Emmanuel II and Cavour; and *Cesare*, 1938, produced on the eve of the war in 1940, on Julius Caesar. Written in a prosaic language, they follow a conventional three-act dramatic schema. *Campo di Maggio* portrays in the first act Napoleon's return from Elba, in the second his return from the defeat at Waterloo, and in the third the eve of his exile to St. Helena. Much emphasis is placed on Napoleon's conflict with the assembly, the implication being that if he had been able to dissolve it and rule with a "temporary dictatorship" (11), he might have saved the nation. The nation (*la patria*), he affirms in his soliloquies, is not "those five hundred lawyers," the deputies, but rather the workers, the soldiers, the people (59). True leadership does not take place through corrupt elected officials but emanates from the person and the "voice" of the leader. "The army and the country know only my voice" (115). The minister of the police Fouché, the man in whom "all of the bourgeoisie, the liberals, and the democrats of France place their hopes" (31), clearly represents the corruption of those elements, as the journalists of the "free press" represent its scandal-mongering. Forzano and Mussolini attempt to emphasize the tragic solitude of the figure who had "always dominated destiny" through will (167) now facing his downfall and to bring out the pathos in the human being in a final dialogue with his mother. In spite of these efforts, the figure remains wooden, the dramatic structure banal, the language adequate for a historical text but not for a tragedy. This judgment, however, was apparently not shared by most of the play's first spectators, who interrupted the performance with multiple and prolonged applause, nor by the normally judicious critic Renato Simoni, who used words of hyperbolic praise, calling Napoleon a tragic figure and comparing the play to Greek tragedy.[22] Another reviewer, however, called the play "boring" and its propaganda effect "pleonastic"—that is, it was all true, but as good fascists we already knew it.[23]

---

[21] Giovacchino Forzano, *Mussolini autore drammatico, con facsimili e autografi inediti* (Florence: G. Barbèra, 1954). This book contains the Italian texts of *Campo di Maggio, Cesare,* and *Cavour,* as well as facsimiles of letters of Mussolini and D'Annunzio. In the introduction, Forzano explains how Mussolini suggested the subjects and the plots of the three plays and even wrote part of the dialogue. Mussolini's name never appeared as author in any Italian edition or production, but Mussolini is cited as coauthor of the French, English, and German translations of the play on Napoleon, *Campo di maggio.* (His photograph, with a dedication to the translator, appears in the German translation titled *Hundert Tage.*) See Mario Verdone, "Mussolini's 'Theatre of the Masses,'" in *Fascism and Theatre*, ed. Berghaus, 139 n. 6. For a discussion of the three plays, see Giorgio Fontanelli, "Mussolini drammaturgo," *Dimensioni,* 3: 43–56.

[22] Review of December 30, 1930, in *Trent'anni di cronaca drammatica,* 3: 372–73.

[23] Alberto Cecchi, "Campo di Maggio," *Rassegna italiana,* February 1931, 153–55.

Even duller as drama is *Villafranca*, although it ends with the solitary figure of Victor Emmanuel II heroically proclaiming that "Italy will be made" by himself and the Italian people, without foreigners, but then confessing that he has endured the most painful night of his life (321). Closer to the persona that Mussolini was constructing for himself is the figure of Caesar in the play by that name. This Julius Caesar is a benevolent dictator, like Napoleon loved by the common people, peasants, slaves, and women but hated by the jealous republicans. He is furthermore a cultivated man who speaks Greek, identifies with Sophocles' *Antigone* (446), and is even the author of a tragedy (an *Oedipus*) himself (385). Personally, he is dazzling. Mark Antony claims he has received the gift of "eternal youth" ("Giovinezza eterna," 397) from the gods. Cleopatra, though recognized as "a true *king*" by Caesar (463), cries "for the power that she envies and loves" (471) and begs to be nothing but Caesar's slave so she can participate in his glory. One of the Roman women characters claims that whereas the republicans reduced women to mere females (*femmine*), under Caesar they were true women (*donne*) (350).

The contrast between republican and totalitarian law is emphasized here even more than in *Campo di Maggio*. In the opening scene, a republican schoolmaster asks a pupil, "What happens to one who rebels against the laws?" Wiser than his master, the pupil answers, "If he conquers and makes new laws, better than the old ones, he is a great man!" (340). The legalistic pettiness of the republicans (or "democrats" as they are sometimes called) contrasts with the greatness of the person of Caesar and his vision of the Roman *patria* and empire throughout the play. It is not the laws of the republic that preserve liberty, Caesar argues; rather they take away the liberty fundamental to Rome, which is the liberty to become a great empire (416).

Forzano and Mussolini did not attempt to imitate classical tragedy in the form of this play, since it takes place in an array of settings and times. To show Caesar's relations with the barbarians, they introduce at various points an Arab, a black African, a British man, and a Gaul. (The latter, in contrast with the former three, shows civilized characteristics in his appreciation of Italian taste—perhaps a sign of the "Latin" bond with France.) Classical decorum is observed in that the violent act of the assassination takes place offstage, but since Caesar, unlike Napoleon, is given no onstage opportunity to express his awareness of the fate that will befall him, it is difficult to see him as a tragic hero. Indeed, the authors seem to be unwilling to acknowledge either his death or his downfall. Caesar, Metellus declares in the final scene, has been welcomed in heaven among the gods. The people, wreaking vengeance on the assassins, will carry out their true leader's legacy, proclaiming the birth of the empire from the death of the republic. The crowd, described at the end of the play as "mad with tragic furor"

(512), seems to receive a transfusion of Dionysian energy from the sacrifice of their hero-god. Unlike most tragic heroes, Caesar is not permitted to suffer and to doubt but rather is transposed to another order of glory.

Although the Forzano-Mussolini tragedies met with some success, the Italian public seems to have grown tired of repetitive propaganda pieces, and among fascist intellectuals a sentiment that the theater was "in crisis" prevailed. Massimo Bontempelli, who was himself a playwright and party member and who claimed in the 1920s that his *novecentismo* movement was *the* style of fascism, pronounced in 1934 that the prose theater was just as dead as epic poetry and that the theatrical production most in conformity with the fascist ideal of mass spectacle was the sporting event since a soccer game was, for most people, more dramatic than a play.[24] For Silvio D'Amico, the major theater critic during the *ventennio*,[25] mass theater meant not huge spectacle but rather the communication of a poet with the masses. Commenting on the fiasco of *18 BL*, he argued that great dramatic theater has been and will always be the reign of the word.[26] The producer-director Anton Giulio Bragaglia, often in polemic with D'Amico, contended that great theater results from the collaboration of the writer with the *metteur en scène*, rather than from the domination of the writer. He calls for a "total revolution against base nineteenth century bourgeois theatricality," a revolution open to modernity and avant-garde experimentalism while not neglecting Italian tradition—a revolution worthy of Mussolini's. The true fascist theater will be born not just from redoing the classics but from the "faith," "spiritual values," and new aesthetic consciousness of the people.[27]

The opinions of Bontempelli, D'Amico, and Bragaglia are representative of major trends in the varied and contradictory attempts of intellectuals to formulate a fascist aesthetic of theater. Typically, they speak in the future: the true and complete fascist theatrical revolution has not yet taken place. They agree that the bourgeois, realist, and naturalist theater of the previous century belongs to the era of liberalism and socialism and must be discarded. They also concur that a theater of propaganda is to be rejected as unworthy of fascism—artists, says Bragaglia, for example, must follow their intuition just as Mussolini follows his, and "good politics" do

---

[24] Massimo Bontempelli, *L'avventura novecentista* (Florence: Vallecchi, 1974), 235.

[25] A Catholic and an extremely cultivated man as well as a prolific writer, D'Amico, according to his later memoirs and according to most Italian critics, was not a proponent of fascism. His writings from the 1920s and 1930s, as indicated in some of the quotations here, however, give every indication of consensus with the regime and of participating in the quest for a theater worthy of fascism. I have therefore included his voice with those of other fascist intellectuals interested in theater.

[26] Silvio D'Amico, "Teatro di Masse, 18 BL" in *Cronache del teatro*, 2 (Rome: Laterza, 1964), 283.

[27] Anton G. Bragaglia, *Il teatro della rivoluzione* (Rome: Edizioni Tiber, 1929).

not necessarily make good art.[28] The "revolution" in theater, as in other aspects of culture, will develop in some organic way out of the total, or totalitarian revolution led by Mussolini. It is as if the visions of theater they represent—mass spectacle, poetic rapture, and revolutionary avant-garde, combined with occasional reverence for classicism and "Italian tradition"— have as models the March on Rome, Mussolini's discourses in Piazza Venezia, and the futurist revolutionaries, all with a dash of *romanità*. Models could also be the stadium soccer game, D'Annunzio's poetic orations at Fiume and in the theater, and the futurist happenings or the premiere of *Six Characters in Search of an Author*. In theater as in the other arts, however, it is clear that an open attitude toward experimentalism, the avant-garde and trends in European modernism was much more prevalent in the 1920s than in the 1930s. The discussions of culture in *Critica fascista* in the 1920s are representative. Writing on fascist art in 1926, for example, Ardengo Soffici argued that art must be a free manifestation of the spirit, never a political instrument. Since fascism is "a total movement that blends poetry with politics," it will necessarily produce art that unites the classical and the modern, the revolutionary and the traditional.[29] Even in the more repressive atmosphere of the 1930s, however, pronouncements that fascist art was above base propaganda but was rather a free creation of the spirit continued. The logic was simply that true art, under fascism, would necessarily be in keeping with the "spiritual" tenor of the times, that is, would necessarily be fascist. As Massimo Bontempelli put it in 1936, "A work of art, if it has artistic value, implicitly has political value."[30]

Pronouncements on the "crisis" of the theater along with various proposal for remedies occur throughout the *ventennio*. Writing in 1927, Alberto Ghislanzoni laments that writers for and practitioners of the theater have not yet penetrated the "collective soul" or seized the "corporative spirit" but remain too imbued with foreign individualism and commercialism.[31] Since the theater is not yet truly fascist, Ghislanzoni recommends a "surgical operation" by the state. But he views D'Annunzio and Pirandello as precursors of the fascist theater to come: D'Annunzio in that he successfully renewed Italian theater by attacking and overcoming the bourgeois naturalism of the dominant French theater and Pirandello in that he portrayed the *smarrimento* (disorientation, rootlessness) of the postwar bourgeoisie. While he mentions Forzano as someone who is attempting to create fascist theater, he concludes that he is a good theatrical technician, but incapable of portraying "spiritual torment."[32]

---

[28] Ibid., 22, 72.
[29] Ardengo Soffici, "Arte fascista," *Critica Fascista*, October 1, 1926, 383–85.
[30] Bontempelli, *L'Avventura novecentista*, 207.
[31] Alberto Ghislanzoni, *Teatro e fascismo* (Mantua: Edizioni "Mussolinia" Paladino, 1929), 8.
[32] Ibid., 28ff.

Mussolini's often-quoted call for a "mass theater" received its most notable responses at the fourth international conference of the Alessandro Volta Foundation, held in October 1934 with the support of Mussolini and the royal academy. The conference that year was devoted to the question of the "dramatic theater"—its role in the state, with the masses, and in comparison with other spectacles throughout Europe. Presided over by Pirandello and featuring his production of D'Annunzio's *La Figlia di Iorio*, the conference participants included Marinetti, D'Amico, Jacques Copeau, William Butler Yeats, and Walter Gropius. Pirandello, in his opening speech, alluded to the ancient function of the theater in festival and religious ritual, the revival of the mass spectacle in modern Italy, and the necessity of contemplating its implications for the modern theater.[33] The theme of the "religious" function of theater, primarily in its etymological sense, is sounded throughout the conference. Yet along with the discussions on the role of mass spectacle and sport, the conference proceedings on the whole reaffirm the primacy of the theater of *words*, a literary drama that would effect the "religious," "mythical" binding of the masses through *poetry*.[34] This is perhaps because Silvio D'Amico dominated much of the discussion. Beginning with the rhetorical question, "What mass theater could be more authentic than that of the people gathered in Piazza Venezia, when Mussolini speaks from his balcony?"[35] D'Amico goes on to argue that only the power of the word, the text of the true poet—in the tradition from Aeschylus to Pirandello—has the power to communicate theatrically with the masses. The dramatic poet is a "mystic revealer." Implicit is the notion that Il Duce, too, is in his way a poet of the theater. The analogy is taken up by Pirandello in his speech closing the conference and made even more explicit in a 1935 speech in which Mussolini figures not only as "poet" and "author" of the theater but also as "hero" and the Ethiopian campaign as "a spectacle of real and great beauty."[36] (It is interesting, however, that no one mentions the dramas purportedly written by Mussolini with Forzano.) Another important theme, consonant with the general fascist line on art discussed above, is that true fascist theater (in contrast to more vulgar Nazi

---

[33] Luigi Pirandello, "Discorso al Convegno 'Volta' sul Teatro Drammatico," in *Opere di Luigi Pirandello* vol. 6, *Saggi, Poesie, Scritti varii*, ed. Manlio Lo Vecchio Musti (Milan: Mondadori, 1960), 1039–1040.

[34] An example is the following quotation from Guido Salvini, who had worked with Pirandello in the Teatro d'Arte. Criticizing the theater of political propaganda in other nations and claiming that Il Duce's spiritual revolution marked an Italian way, Salvini says, "We believe in a theater of propaganda, but not . . . strictly political. . . . The public wants to feel its passion vibrating, it wants the new spirit to be expressed on the stage, today as always, with the miracle of *poetry*" (Reale Accademia d'Italia, Fondazione Alessandro Volta, *Atti dei Convegni*, 4: 45).

[35] Ibid., 314.

[36] Speech given at Teatro Argentina on the anniversary of the March on Rome, October 29, 1935, in *Quadrivio*, November 3, 1935.

and Soviet aesthetics) is *not* a theater of propaganda. Propaganda can be made, but "not on purpose" (323). The genuine fascist poet will "feel" the climate of the times spiritually, will naturally reject the bourgeois aesthetics of realism and naturalism, and will create a work of art, itself the best propaganda.[37] Even in 1934, we seem here close to a notion that the true expression of fascism is art for art!

But where were these national dramatic writers? An article announcing the Volta conference in the Neapolitan journal *Il Mattino* recapitulates what one could call the messianic hope for the arrival of the true fascist poet of the theater. The reform of the theater, the author tells us, is necessary for the progress of art, civilization, and the "vast passion of the people" under fascism. "In the meantime," he continues, "it is good to remember that the theater of Gabriele D'Annunzio and that of Luigi Pirandello contain the most significant real and ideal values of our National Theater."[38] Still in 1937, shortly after the death of Pirandello, a writer in the fascist journal *Gerarchia* envisions the coming of a truly fascist theater in the future. Mentioning Jacques Copeau's ideas on popular theater and Léon Chancerel's experiments with bringing theater to the people (destined to become important under Vichy), the author reiterates the call for a theater "for the people" based on new "myths." Rejecting the realistic aesthetics of bourgeois theater, this coming theater will resemble ancient tragedy. Transcending "reality," it will create the "Hero who personifies in Myth and who purifies in the catharsis of tragedy our life and our society just as the Prometheuses and the Oedipuses represented the spiritual problems of ancient Greece."[39] Again in 1938, in a lecture given in Budapest on Italian theater reprinted in the fascist theater journal *Scenario*, the regime's inspector for the theater, Nicola de Pirro, still speaks of an ideal fascist theater in future terms. Such a theater, in Mussolini's words, must be directed to the "people"; it must presuppose a "faith," a binding "religiosity" and communion of spirits; and it must be "profoundly classical." De Pirro concludes with a statement of messianic hope for the advent of the Tragic Poet. "With the period of bourgeois theater closed, perhaps tomorrow this art form [the Italian theater] will be able to return to be one of the greatest expressions of civil and social life, rite and festival of a people spiritually united to hear the word of the poet."[40] But this literary soul mate of Il Duce, destined to refashion the spirit of ancient drama for the age of fascism,

---

[37] See my "Fascist Discourse and Pirandellian Theater," *South Atlantic Quarterly* 91, no. 2 (Spring 1992): 303–31, for statements of this theme in the fascist press generally.

[38] Riccardo Forster, "Prima del Convegno 'Volta' sul Teatro," *Il Mattino* (Naples), March 4, 1934.

[39] Alberto Vigevani, "Problemi del nostro teatro. Attesa del Mito," *Gerarchia*, no. 8 (August 1937): 572, cited in Cavallo, *Immaginario*, 223.

[40] Nicola de Pirro, "Verso il teatro di domani," *Scenario* 7, no. 5 (May 1938): 247–49.

clearly never arrived. As late as 1939, articles summarized in the *Rivista italiana del dramma* envision a "theater of tomorrow" capable of expressing the "heroic reality" of fascism, necessarily involving a revival of tragedy, the "sublime" form killed, through an odd metaphor of miscegenation, by the bourgeois theater: "With the coming of the bourgeoisie, tragedy descended from its sublime spheres to mate with the grotesque and give life to the drama."[41] Once again, Pirandello is credited with portraying the decadence of the bourgeoisie.[42]

"In the meantime" there were D'Annunzio and Pirandello, both of whom were regularly cited in the press as the creators of modern tragedy in Italy. If the "true fascist" theatrical poet never arrived, it seemed in part, in the minds of those concerned with fascist art, to be because no worthy successor to Italy's greatest modern dramatists could be found. Yet the two rivals, radically divergent in their approach to literature, were both formed by important strands in the culture of early fascism. D'Annunzio's pioneering efforts to create a modern tragedy belong to the turn-of-the-century reading of Nietzsche with the critique of bourgeois liberalism discussed in the Introduction. Pirandello's creation of a theater out of the sense that nothing is true and everything is to be constructed connects intimately, as we will see, with aspects of fascist discourse. In any case, our interest lies not in reductively labeling either playwright as "fascist"—a label that would be blatantly false—but rather in exploring to what extent aesthetic fascism and modern tragedy converge in the projects of each.

[41] "Giornali e Riviste" (review of the press), *Rivista italiana del dramma*, July–November 1939, 131.

[42] Ibid., 12.

CHAPTER TWO

D'Annunzio's Nietzschean Tragedy
and the Aesthetic Politics of Fusion

Claims of association between Gabriele D'Annunzio and fascism at the present time are bound to raise some strenuous objections. In the early 1980s, D'Annunzio criticism, particularly in Italy, entered a phase of reevaluation that is still ongoing. If the postwar period tended to dismiss the "national bard" as a bombastic fascist whose language, along with his politics, were a disgrace to Italy, the D'Annunzian revisionists have brought out the considerable political and personal differences between Il Commandante and Il Duce, while rethinking the original and important contributions of the writer to European—not only Italian—poetry, theater, and fiction.[1] A representative article is that of Giovanni Antonucci, titled "Political Language in the Theater of Gabriele D'Annunzio" but written to prove that there is no such thing. Beginning with a revealing anecdote from his student days in the 1940s that tells of a university assistant's refusal even to speak about D'Annunzio ("Era stato un fascista e basta") ("He was a fascist and that's enough"), Antonucci goes on to describe D'Annunzio's theater as one of poetry, not politics, of myths, not ideology.

---

[1] See, for example, Paolo Valesio, *Gabriele D'Annunzio: The Dark Flame* (New Haven, Conn.: Yale University Press, 1992); Giorgio Barberi Squarotti, *La Scrittura verso il nulla: D'Annunzio* (Turin: Genesi, 1992); and Giovanni Antonucci, "Introduzione generale" and "Introduzione a D'Annunzio drammaturgo," in Gabriele D'Annunzio, *Tutto il teatro*, ed. Giovanni Antonucci (Rome: Newton Compton, 1995), 1: vii–xxiii. An American scholar, Jared M. Becker, *Nationalism and Culture: Gabriele D'Annunzio and Italy after the Risorgimento* (New York: Peter Lang, 1994), however, argues forcefully that the poet made important contributions to fascism. As Becker notes, foreign scholars, including George Mosse and Zeev Sternhell, have tended to see more association between D'Annunzio and fascism than have Italians.

He dismisses as "absurd" the ideas of any scholar from Luigi Russo to Paolo Alatri who ever suggested that a play of D'Annunzio's contained a political message.[2] What is missing in this argument and in similar criticism is a willingness to consider that "poetry" and "politics" are not necessarily mutually exclusive categories or that there was an aesthetics along with an ideology of fascism. It is indeed time to reevaluate D'Annunzio's theater, as well as his writing in other genres, in their European and even world context, for he is still little known outside of Italy. Among other things, he was the primary figure responsible for attempting to apply Nietzsche's ideas in *The Birth of Tragedy* to the actual creation of a modern tragedy. But just because the pendulum swung too far in one direction does not mean it should do so in the other. There seems to be a tendency in Italy to move from a view of D'Annunzio as a bad writer and a fascist to D'Annunzio as a good or even great writer and (therefore?) a non- or even antifascist. In the case of Pirandello, the tendency has been rather to accept the fact of his adherence to fascism but to affirm a complete and radical split between his literary production, especially his theater, and his avowed political ideology.

Recent scholarship has indeed revealed that D'Annunzio's fascist credentials are highly ambivalent, that the differences between the legionari of Fiume and the fascists were considerable, and that relations between the poet and the duce were less than ideal.[3] D'Annunzio, for example, never joined the party and, at least until giving Benito Mussolini his wholehearted support for the Ethiopian campaign, undoubtedly regarded Il Duce as his inferior rival. Similarly, the fascists preferred to keep D'Annunzio more or less imprisoned in his "Vittoriale," where they could make use of him when convenient without having too much to do with him. Yet make use of him they did. If the movement felt the need for grounding in a "spiritual father," D'Annunzio was unquestionably the chosen one. The duo of D'Annunzio as the "soul" or the "poet" of fascism and Mussolini as its "body" or "force" became a prevalent cliché. No other writer, it would seem, so richly deserved the title of the poet of the new Italy. In the theater, it was widely recognized that he alone had been able to resurrect the spirit of ancient tragedy, to unite antiquity and modernity through a theatrical poetics that communicated with crowds in a manner

[2] Giovanni Antonucci, "Il Linguaggio politico nel teatro di Gabriele d'Annunzio," in *D'Annunzio e il suo tempo*, ed. Francesco Perfetti (Genoa: SAGEP, 1992), 2: 157–67.

[3] The renowned historian of fascism Renzo de Felice, in his *D'Annunzio politico, 1918–1938* (Bari: Laterza, 1978), has been primarily responsible for the revisionist position regarding D'Annunzio's politics. In particular, he makes the case for a D'Annunzio in Fiume close to leftist politics. See also Vito Salierno, *D'Annunzio e Mussolini: Storia di una cordiale inimicizia* (Milan: Mursia, 1989), and Francesco Perfetti, "D'Annunzio, ovvero la politica come poesia," in *D'Annunzio e il suo tempo*, ed. Perfetti, 1: 369–85.

anticipating Il Duce's. Drawing on the poet's spiritual strength could only enhance Mussolini's political effectiveness.

Nor is it at all evident that D'Annunzio did anything to discourage fascist "use" of him. Although he abhorred Mussolini's pact with Adolf Hitler because of his dislike of Germany, he made no protest against any fascist brutality. Certainly he sang Mussolini's praises at the time of the Ethiopian campaign. If he otherwise preferred to keep his distance from political fascism, it seems to have been because he saw in it an inferior, prosaic realization of his own vision. Far from being "exploited" by fascism, as some commentators have argued, D'Annunzio could in a sense have the best of both worlds, allowing the fascists to praise his poetry, his "spiritual guidance," to pay for lavish productions of his plays, to publish his *opera omnia*, while maintaining a posture of godlike independence.[4] The details of D'Annunzio's politics cannot concern us here. More cogent are the arguments made by Renzo de Felice, Paolo Alatri, and Emilio Gentile that Mussolini inherited from D'Annunzio, most notably from the Fiume period but originating earlier, a certain political style as well as a particular kind of patriotic "religion." Thus D'Annunzio anticipated the aesthetics of fascist mass politics with rituals such as the speech from the balcony, the call-and-response dialogue and the mystical fusion of leader with crowd, the Roman salute, and the ritual cry—in other words, a politics of *spectacle*. Like Mussolini after him, he fused religious metaphors with political rhetoric, defined the piazza as a "sacred space," and developed a liturgy for use in addressing crowds.[5] If we are to accept the argument that aesthetics were an integral part of fascist culture from the beginning, the question of

---

[4] The fascist press and other publications throughout the *ventennio* are full of statements of adulation of D'Annunzio in relation to fascism. Here are a few examples: *La Rivista d'Italia*, May 26, 1925, reports that Mussolini's stay at the Vittoriale was of "profound spiritual significance" for the "two brothers in the same faith." *La Tribuna*, two days later, quotes D'Annunzio as saying that in his capacity as poet, he can translate the country's spiritual state into lyrics. According to Luigi Tonelli in *La Rivista d'Italia*, September 15, 1926, D'Annunzio's greatness in the theater was to renew contact with the "brutal force" of the crowd. The Belgian priest Antonio Bruers, who wrote on D'Annunzio and was sympathetic to fascism, finds that D'Annunzio, through aesthetics, prepared Italy's antimaterialist, spiritual revolution. Bruers at times even adopts religious language, comparing D'Annunzio to a prophet who prepares the coming of the Messiah (*Gabriele D'Annunzio e il moderno spirito italico* [Rome: La Fronda, 1921]). D'Annunzio, ahead of his time, understands the need for violence, a heroic ethic, imperialism, and the surpassing of "feminine" love. Through his tragedies, he demonstrates the need for redemptive sacrifice, thus affirming the values of the community above those of the individual (*Nuovi saggi dannunziani* [Bologna: Zanichelli, 1938], 32ff.). A Belgian journal, *La Renaissance*, April 21, 1923, explains that Italy was reborn from fascism with D'Annunzio as its "soul" and Mussolini as its "body." We will see numerous other examples in the reviews of individual plays.

[5] De Felice, *D'Annunzio politico*, ix–xi; Paolo Alatri, *Gabriele D'Annunzio* (Turin: Unione tipografica-editore torinese, 1983), 45ff.; Emilio Gentile, *The Sacralization of Politics in Fascist Italy*, trans. Keith Botsford (Cambridge: Harvard University Press, 1996), 17.

style cannot be dismissed as merely superficial. A related and indeed more important element, not much discussed by the Italian historians but analyzed in some detail by Barbara Spackman, is D'Annunzio's use of language. But if Spackman sees Il Commandante's rhetoric at Fiume as anticipatory of fascist "rhetoric of virility,"[6] I want to emphasize his poetics. While in one sense nothing could be further apart than the bare, paratactic discourse of Mussolini the former journalist and the dense tropes, esoteric vocabulary, and complex syntax of the Bard, this may be the very reason why Il Duce felt the need of the "spiritual" poet, at least standing behind him as a figurehead. The dramatic poet and the dictator-orator both used language for a similar purpose: the fusing and the binding of individuals into a crowd and of the crowd with the poet/speaker. This D'Annunzio had anticipated in his early writings on aesthetics and politics, in which he intertwines the two discourses in the manner of Berth and Morasso. As D'Annunzio himself said in a 1902 interview, "Art and politics have never been disassociated in my thought."[7]

If aesthetics were never absent from D'Annunzio's politics, neither were politics—a peculiar *style* of politics—entirely absent either from his writing on aesthetics or his literary writing. As Antonio Gramsci once suggested, D'Annunzio may have succeeded politically without ever having had a political idea in his head.[8] For Renzo de Felice, it was not until World War I and the contact with common people that the poet was politicized. Yet what can be described as the inauguration of the mass politics of spectacle which the Commandante created so effectively at Fiume has its origin in the turn-of-the-century years that saw the development of D'Annunzio's interest in the theory and practice of modern tragedy along with an early political experience that can be characterized as theatrical. These should be considered not as "prophetic" of fascism, as the earlier argument went, but rather as integral to the context of the contemporary intellectual/artistic/political syntheses that constituted the matrix for the culture of fascism. With D'Annunzio, the fusion of aesthetics and political thought (or political mythology) already existent in turn-of-the-century discourse reaches a higher and more complex level.

One of D'Annunzio's important contributions to political-aesthetic thought in Italy was his reading of Nietzsche in an early essay. Although, as Guy Tosi has carefully demonstrated, much of it was plagiarized from a French article on Nietzsche, "La Bestia elettiva," published in 1892, was one of the first commentaries to appear in Italy on the German philoso-

---

[6] See Barbara Spackman, *Fascist Virilities: Rhetoric, Ideology, and Social Fantasy in Italy* (Minneapolis: University of Minnesota Press, 1996), 1–33.

[7] "Arte e politica non furono mai disgiunte nel mio pensiero." Interview in *La Tribuna*, June 20, 1902, in Paolo Alatri, ed., *Scritti politici di Gabriele D'Annunzio* (Milan: Fetrinelli, 1980), 11.

[8] Antonio Gramsci, *Passato e presente* (Turin: Einaudi, 1951), 12–13.

pher.[9] Not unlike the young Mussolini, in his 1908 essay on Nietzsche,[10] D'Annunzio applies Nietzsche's concept of slave and master morality to the contemporary political situation, concluding not only that democracy, founded on universal suffrage, is based on empty, abstract ideas but that it entails the triumph of bourgeois mediocrity, thus tyrannizing the people it is supposed to serve. Beginning his essay with the question of why more writers do not respond to democracy's call to express its ideals in literature (he seems to have the naturalists in mind), D'Annunzio implies that only a new system grounded on the Nietzschian ideals of the right of the strongest, force, power, and a morality beyond good and evil will be able to inspire poets. By the end of the essay, in another example of the conflating of the literary and the political, it is unclear whether D'Annunzio has in mind a new leader or a poet when he describes his "aristocrat" who will never "contaminate his hands" with an election ballot. In any case, this superior man is, for the time being, forced to seclude himself.

Given his wholehearted denunciation of parliamentary democracy, it might seem odd that D'Annunzio would campaign for a seat in parliament, but such contradictions never bothered Il Vate, and the use of elections to destroy the electoral system is hardly unprecedented in political history. What is of interest here is that the composition of his first modern tragedy, *La Città morta* (*The Dead City*, 1896), barely preceded his political debut as a right-wing candidate for the Chamber of Deputies in August 1897. D'Annunzio campaigned with a speech that has remained famous in Italy, "il discorso della siepe" (the "hedge speech") in which the hedge symbolized the importance of private property. His defense of beauty in this speech also earned him the title of "deputato della bellezza." Thus we find the lines: "The fortune of Italy is inseparable from the destinies of Beauty, of which she is the mother. . . . The latin spirit cannot reestablish its hegemony in the world without reestablishing the cult of One Will and holding sacred

---

[9] D'Annunzio's essay appeared in *Il Mattino di Napoli*, September 25–26, 1892. It has been translated and edited, with an introduction, by Jeffrey Schnapp in "Nietzsche's Italian Style: Gabriele D'Annunzio" in *Nietzsche in Italy* (Saratoga, Calif.: Anma Libri, 1988), 247–77. Guy Tosi, in "D'Annunzio découvre Nietzsche," *Italianistica* 2, no. 3 (1973): 418–513, lists the parallels between D'Annunzio's essay and Jean de Néthy's "Nietzsche-Zarathustra," which appeared in *La Revue blanche*, April 1892, 206–12. Schnapp argues that D'Annunzio was the first to give a concrete political interpretation to Nietzsche's theory, thus anticipating later fascist incorporations of Nietzsche.

[10] "La filosofia della forza (postille alla conferenza dell'on. Treves)" appeared in *Il Pensiero romagnolo*, no. 48, November 29, 1908. It is reprinted in *Scritti politici di Benito Mussolini*, ed. Enzo Santarelli (Milan: Feltrinelli, 1979), 99–109. Mussolini is not concerned with the role of the poet as is D'Annunzio, but he argues that Nietzsche's writings are "poetry" rather than abstract philosophical treatises. Having obviously read *The Birth of Tragedy*, he refers to the "tragic grandeur" of the Nietzschean conquering hero (101) and his "tragedy of danger" (107). Like D'Annunzio, but not specifically on universal suffrage, he decries the "morality of mediocrity" of contemporary society, proclaiming that "Nothing is true, everything is permitted!" will be the motto of the coming generation.

the sentiment that in ancient Latium inspired the terminal Festivals."[11] D'Annunzio's rhetoric here postulates a recuperation of individuality in collectivity and festival along with an identification of nationalism with aestheticism, all bound with the reestablishment of Latin hegemony. He goes on in the speech to deplore the discontinuation of the war in Africa, also identifying war and imperialism with the cult of Beauty.[12]

Once elected, D'Annunzio did very little in parliament. His most famous action, on March 21, 1900, was a theatrical gesture symbolic of the politics of fusion he advocated: his flamboyant walk from the benches of the extreme right to those of the extreme left. He explained this gesture in the following way: "After today's spectacle, I know that on one side there are many dead men screaming and on the other a few live men: as a man of intellect, I go toward life."[13] During his campaign, however, D'Annunzio had already suggested, in Nietzschean language, that the political categories of right and left held no meaning for him: "I am beyond the *right* and the *left*, as beyond good and evil . . . I am a man of life and not of formulas."[14] D'Annunzio's theatrical gesture not only signifies his disdain for parliamentary procedures but also suggests that right and left are to be fused and transcended in something beyond bourgeois politics as usual.

D'Annunzio adapted the Nietzsche of *Zarathustra* into his aesthetic/political program; he read *The Birth of Tragedy* with a view toward the creation of his own modern tragedies and toward a vision of a new kind of theater. There were other influences as well. While he admired Wagner, he was attracted by the "Mediterranean," anti-Germanic side of Nietzsche, by Romain Rolland's concept of a theater of the people, and by current French ideas on creating a "Latin" theater in opposition to Wagner through the revival of tragedy in outdoor productions in the Roman theater at Orange.[15] He was undoubtedly aware of Paul Claudel's activity in the rebirth of "religious" theater and certainly felt himself to be part of the general European movement against bourgeois realism. The most immediate stimulus to his think-

---

[11] Cited in Alatri, *Gabriele D'Annunzio*, 189.

[12] Jared Becker, in *Nationalism*, 47–49, reads this speech as the inauguration of a new politics, fusing mass socialism with the traditional right. Adopting the rallying points of "beauty" and the "stirpe," or racial-national identity, D'Annunzio uses the power of the poet to bring the working classes into a program of nationalism and imperialism. Using a left/right synthesis consonant with the culture of "prefascism," he looks toward a "spiritual" socialism, substituting aesthetic for material rewards.

[13] Quoted in Francesco Perfetti, "Dannunzio, ovvero la politica come poesia," in *D'Annunzio e il suo tempo: Un bilancio critico: Atti del convegno di studi, Genova, Rapallo, 1989* (Genoa: SAGEP, 1992), 2: 370.

[14] Letter to Luigi Lodi, July 15, 1897, cited by Alatri, *Gabriele D'Annunzio*, 193.

[15] Luisetta Elia Chomel, *D'Annunzio, un teatro al femminile* (Ravenna: Longo, 1997), 33–35, describes D'Annunzio's interest in the group "Félibres." According to her, "The first *Chorégie* in Orange had in fact been accompanied by an anti-Wagnerian declaration, in which someone expressed 'the desire to oppose Mediterranean clarity to nordic obscurity'" (35).

ing on tragedy as well as to the creation of his first modern tragedy was his trip to Greece, "the mythic motherland," with Eleonora Duse in the summer of 1895.

In August 1897, in an article entitled "The Rebirth of Tragedy," dedicated primarily to the theater at Orange, D'Annunzio defines drama as the only form through which poets can effectively communicate to a crowd "the virile and heroic dreams which suddenly transfigure life." The religious spirit of Dionysian ritual, which the modern dramatic poet must recapture, will bind individuals together with something resembling the frenzy of the ancient sacred festival. The soul of tragedy as envisioned by the poet, however, lies neither in dramatic dialogue, nor in the interchange between hero and chorus, nor in any form of dialogical relationship between actors and audience. The actors are rather reduced to beings in whom "the word of the Revealer is made incarnate on the stage" before "the multitude, mute as if in a temple." The starring, indeed the only real role in the dramatic-religious ceremony of modern tragedy will be that of the author. It is not then so much through spectacle as through a kind of verbal enchantment that individuals will be fused and bound into one entity, prepared as it were to receive and consent to a new vision of "virile and heroic dreams." Drama, in D'Annunzio's words, is both a "rite" and a "message." Since the nature of the message is not merely rational but aesthetic and transformative, it must be communicated through rite.[16] D'Annunzio's vision of the performance of tragedy, then, appears both as an *Aufhebung* of his aesthetic/political rhetoric in speeches such as "Il discorso della siepe" and as a prefiguration of his speeches at Fiume where he did for a time play the role of poet-revealer-commander before a bound and receptive crowd. Poetry and rhetoric, as we will see in D'Annunzio's tragedies, are to some extent inseparable. They will separate in the speeches of Mussolini, who seems to want to retain the "revealing," binding, and fusing properties developed by Il Vate while transforming the discourse of "beauty" into one of action.[17]

D'Annunzio explained his plans to create his own outdoor theater on the lake of Albano south of Rome—an Italian version/fusion of Orange

---

[16] The crucial passage reads as follows: "It will be the glory of poets to elevate that form to its primitive dignity, grounding it on the ancient religious spirit. Let the great metamorphosis of the Dionysian rite—the frenzy of the sacred festival transformed into the creative enthusiasm of the tragedian—be always figured as a symbol in their votive soul. Drama can only be a rite or a message. The living person in whom the word of a Revealer is incarnated on the stage, the presence of the multitude, mute as if in temples: do these not even today give to the production of a Sophoclean tragedy in the ancient theater of Orange the character of a cult, of a ceremony, of a mystery?" (La Rinascenza della tragedia," *La Tribuna*, August 3, 1897, in Valentina Valentini, *La Tragedia moderna e mediterranea: Sul teatro di Gabriele d'Annunzio* [Milan: FrancoAngeli, 1992], 80).

[17] Barbara Spackman, *Fascist Virilities*, 114–55, analyzes Mussolini's "anti-rhetorical rhetoric" and its ideological content, drawing parallels with D'Annunzio's.

and Bayreuth—in an October 1897 interview with Mario Morasso. His goal for the theater, which was never built, was to "cooperate in the rebirth of tragedy. We would like to restore to the representation of drama its ancient character of *ceremony*" and to "recall the rural and Dionysiac origin of drama."[18] In Morasso's gloss, the rebirth of tragedy in D'Annunzio's hands will enable the poet, as in ancient times, to relate dramatic ritual to political and religious ceremony. D'Annunzio, it should be understood, does not want simply to revive ancient tragedy, as in Orange, but rather to create an Italian modern tragedy, drawing on both classical drama and the "total theater" of modernity, with its synthesis of the arts, that he finds in Wagner. The understanding of modernity, in D'Annunzio's reading of Nietzsche, entails the recovery of primal Dionysian energies and a sweeping away of nineteenth-century rationalism and realism as manifested in both parliamentary democracy and bourgeois drama. In another 1897 interview, D'Annunzio defines succinctly what he wants to represent in the Albano theater: "Tragedies, in which the absolute modernity of inspiration joins with a purity of form not unworthy of the temples of Athens."[19]

D'Annunzio approached the problem of creating modern tragedy in different ways, sometimes in poetry, sometimes in prose. The most important of these forms, for our purposes, are the tragedies that make use of myth, those in some way concerned with history, and the "political" tragedies set in modernity. The two of the first type to be discussed here are *La Città morta* (*The Dead City*) and *Fedra*; the second is represented by *La Nave* (*The Ship*), and the third by *La Gloria* (*Glory*) and *Più che l'amore* (*Beyond Love*). D'Annunzio prepares himself and his readers for his approach to modern tragedy in his novel *Il Fuoco* (*The Flame*), begun in 1894 and published in 1899.

In *The Flame*, as Jared Becker has shown, D'Annunzio moves from the influence of French decadentism, with its elitist view of the artist and disdain of the mass expressed in earlier novels such as *The Virgins of the Rocks*, to a discovery of the poet as communicator with, perhaps more accurately a manipulator of, the crowd.[20] Thus the hero Stelio Effrena rejects a group of stuffy aristocrats to discover his true oratorical power over the plebian crowd, whom he hopes to "aestheticize" by bringing them the gift of eternal poetry. This project concurs with his desire to transform Venice from a city representative of backward-looking decadence to the site of a re-

[18] Mario Morasso, "Il Futuro teatro d'Albano: Colloquio con G. d'Annunzio," *L'Illustrazione italiana*, October 20, 1897.

[19] Angelo Orvieto, "Il teatro di festa: Colloquio con Gabriele D'Annunzio," *Il Marzocco*, December 12, 1897, in Valentini, *La Tragedia moderna*, 86.

[20] Becker, *Nationalism*, 20–22. Since *Le Vergini* is the only literary work of D'Annunzio's that Spackman discusses in *Fascist Virilities*, she disassociates D'Annunzio's "aristocratic" figure of the superman from later fascism. This, however, is to ignore D'Annunzio's own aesthetic-political development.

nascent nationalism, and both blend into the theory of the rebirth of tragedy that Stelio (as D'Annunzio's mouthpiece) develops throughout the novel.

Although diffused in a rich prose evoking the beauties of the city and the trajectory of a passionate but waning love affair between the thinly disguised figures of himself and Eleonora Duse, the discourse on modern tragedy in *The Flame* can be summarized by a few distinct notions, some found in the 1897 "Rebirth of Tragedy." First, although Stelio/D'Annunzio expresses his admiration for Wagner's total artwork with its "religious" bonding of performance and spectators, as well as its synthesis of theater, music, dance, festival, and myth, he reproaches Wagner for not giving enough importance to the word, which he calls the "foundation" of the work of art and which he sees as most expressive of the Latin, as opposed to the Germanic, genius. Like the symbolists, D'Annunzio finds that the word confers power on the poet: the poet does not imitate reality but recreates it and, in the theater, dominates the crowd through his revelation. Second, the poet's enchantment of the audience through the magic of the word in the theater acts as an aesthetically enhanced version of the political orator's domination of the crowd in the piazza. Stelio discovers the power of the oral, as opposed to the written word for himself when he holds forth to a crowd in Venice on the politics of beauty, replicating his author's speech titled "L'Allegoria d'autunno," delivered in Venice in September 1895 at the opening of the first *biennale* exhibit of modern art. Feeling a mysterious communication between his soul and the soul of the crowd, Stelio concludes: "The word of the poet communicated to the crowd was thus an act, like the deed of the hero."[21] Later in the novel, Stelio refines the simile relating poetic to military action to portray each as a form of conquest enabled by the energy of passion. "When the fury of glory takes hold of us, we believe that the conquest of art resembles the assault on a towered city" (290). At this point, it is the revelation of the word as act that leads him to imagine new possibilities for the theater, liberated from its suffocating urban interiors to outdoor spaces peopled by "the true crowd, the immense unanimous crowd" (96).[22]

If the dramatic poet partakes of both the political orator and the military hero, he is also a lover of women. Foscarina, the Duse figure, acquires mythic proportions as a Dionysian woman whose erotic energies serve Stelio's creative ones as her acting serves as the instrument to convey his words. Sexual desire and the sexual act acquire ritual and mythic overtones.

[21] Gabriele D'Annunzio, *Il Fuoco*, ed. Anco Marzio Mutterle (Milan: Mondadori, 1990), 95–96.

[22] D'Annunzio seems to have known and been interested in Gustave Le Bon's writing on crowd theory. He was no doubt also influenced by Romain Rolland's ideas on popular mass theater.

Early in their affair, "She wanted to die, and wanted to be taken and suddenly overcome by that masculine violence. . . . And he desired . . . [the woman] who was moved by the eternal servitude of her nature . . . the ardent actress who passed from the frenzy of the crowd to the force of the male, the Dionysian creature who with the act of life crowned the mysterious rite as in an orgy" (101). Foscarina will tell Stelio that she feels in his "virile passion" "the heroic need of moral domination" (291). The feminization of the actor completes the poet-actor-audience relationship D'Annunzio outlined in "The Rebirth of Tragedy." Receptacle and incarnation of the poet's word, rather than a competing originator, the Dionysian actress, her energies possessed and harnessed by the poet's virile force, serves as mediator between poet and crowd. Yet one Dionysian woman cannot suffice the dramatic poet-orator-hero. Stelio must have the singer as well as the actress, the virgin as well as the mature woman, in the person of the "winged victory" Donatella. The sexual "possession" of women enables the poet to capture Dionysian beauty in the Apollonian word and, through the actress, to possess the theatrical audience in metaphorical relation to the hero's possession of a city and the political orator's possession of a crowd. It is as if, by a kind of ritual rape, the male acquired powers secretly guarded by females, powers that through a process of virilization into word and deed enable him to dominate and mold the feminized crowd. We will see how similar acts of possession and sacrifice of women play themselves out in D'Annunzio's own tragedies.

Related to this theory of possession are Stelio's meditations on tragedy as "Medusan." The poet explains to his friend Daniele that great tragedy resembles the gesture of Perseus, who cuts off the head of Medusa and holds it up to the crowd (157). With the head, in Stelio's words, resembling "the entire universe," this ritual of violence enacts the "victory of man" over destiny (161). Thus the playwright-poet becomes a hero, figured as Perseus, endowed with the power to petrify his audience. But what is the significance of the Perseus-Medusa myth for the creation of modern tragedy?

D'Annunzio's interest in Medusa was not limited to *Il Fuoco*.[23] In another theoretical discussion of modern tragedy, the letter to Vincenzo Morello that serves as an introduction to *Più che l'amore* (*Beyond Love*, 1905), he imagines the creation of a tragic hero out of the act of slaying Medusa. "In order to conquer horror . . . it is necessary to invent *virtù* . . . with a splendid and speedy force that resembles a resurrection."[24] What is the horror that the hero must conquer? For Freud, there was no doubt: the myth of

---

[23] Barbara Spackman discusses the Medusan motif in *Le Vergini delle rocce* (*Fascist Virilities*, 99–106) but does not mention its development in *Il Fuoco* or in the theater.

[24] Gabriele D'Annunzio, "Dell'ultima terra lontana e della pietra bianca di Pallade," *Tutto il teatro di Gabriele D'Annunzio*, 2: 82.

Medusa's head signified horror of the forbidden sight of the mother's genitals, the revelation that women have no penis, and the consequent fear of castration on the part of the little boy. At the same time, the boy continues to believe that his mother and other powerful females have phalluses.[25] D'Annunzio, as Barbara Spackman suggests, may have been acquainted with a classical gloss on Medusa, a passage in Plato's *Symposium* in which the Gorgon's head suggests the power of rhetoric to turn the speech of other men to stony silence.[26] In the context of *Il Fuoco*, it seems clear that the significance of the Medusa encompasses both mastery over a female threat and the "petrifying" power of speech. The act of decapitating the Medusa may, as Freud says, signify the act of castration, but of what? The mother's phallus? The virility of other men? It seems to make possible the "resurrection" of the decapitator's *virtù*-virility. Both woman and the audience could, potentially, petrify and emasculate the poet-hero-orator; to defy this threat he must "possess" them, silencing their speech by himself controlling the Gorgon's head, which he turns back on them. The orator/tragic poet thus feminizes (castrates) the crowd, possessing it as he would a woman.

The Medusa for D'Annunzio also seems to bear a meaning more specifically directed toward the creation of Nietzschean tragic poetry. Possession of the Dionysian woman entails not only erotic bliss but also the almost archaeological discovery of secret powers she alone contains. The Apollonian poet is threatened by these powers but needs to recuperate them in order to create; the decapitation of the Medusa enables him to possess them and her, not the other way around. In Julia Kristeva's terms, preoedipal *jouissance* is absorbed into the paternal symbolic order. Kristeva finds historical corroboration for the psychoanalytic phenomenon in the fact that in patriarchal Western society "oriental" figures of Great Mothers and queens remained as a source of semiotic power within the symbolic order. For example, the sacred stone of Cybele was worshipped with or-

[25] Freud briefly discusses the Medusa myth in two papers, "The Infantile Genital Organization" (1923) and "Revision of the Theory of Dreams" (1932) in *The Standard Edition of the Complete Psychological Works of Sigmund Freud*, trans. and ed. James Strachey (London: Hogarth Press, 1978), 14: 144–45, and 22: 24. A posthumously published sketch is devoted to the subject: "Medusa's Head" (1940), ibid., 18: 273–74. The theory remains essentially the same, except that in the last paper Freud elaborates on decapitation as castration and on the goddess Athena, who wore the Medusa's head on her shield, as symbol of the unapproachable woman.

[26] Spackman, *Fascist Virilities*, 105. The passage in *The Symposium* reads: "I feared that Agathon in his final phrases would confront me with the eloquent Gorgias' head, and by opposing his speech to mine would turn me thus dumbfounded into stone" (Plato, *The Symposium*, trans. W. R. M. Lamb [Cambridge: Harvard University Press, Loeb Classics, 1975], 163). Speaking with characteristic irony, Socrates puns with the name of the ridiculed rhetorician Gorgias and the Gorgon.

giastic rites in which priests were required to castrate themselves.[27] We will see how D'Annunzio adds "oriental" to his female-Medusan cluster.

Interspersed with the discussion of Perseus and Medusa are Stelio's reflections on *Antigone* and his project for a modern tragedy to be titled *La vittoria dell'uomo* and that outlines the plot of D'Annunzio's first tragedy, *La Città morta*. Central to this tragedy will be "the virgin destined to die" like Antigone, killed by the "pure act" of her brother, who thus frees himself from the curse of a "monstrous Fate" (158). Thus the tragic sacrifice of the virgin carries the symbolic weight of the slaying of "Medusan" horror—in this case primal incest. The tragic hero, like the tragic poet, acquires virtue and power in part through the domination, indeed the slaughter, of woman. If D'Annunzio's first attempt at creating a modern tragedy does not exactly follow the plot outlined for *La Vittoria dell'uomo*, his theoretical concerns continue to be in evidence in the text of *La Città morta*.

The Dead City or Archaeology as Metatragedy

The intertextuality of D'Annunzio's first tragedy, performed initially in Paris with Sarah Bernhardt in 1897 as *La Ville morte* and then in Milan with Eleonora Duse in 1901, is overwhelming. Not only does D'Annunzio make use of his theories in "The Rebirth of Tragedy" and *The Flame*, he alludes to Nietzsche's *Birth of Tragedy*, Heinrich Schliemann's alleged discovery of Mycenae in 1876,[28] pieces of Greek sculpture such as the *Winged Victory*, Aeschylus's *Oresteia* (especially the *Agamemnon*), and Sophocles' *Antigone*. Passages from the latter two are read within the play. To these should be added the myth of Iphigenia, background to the tragic action of *Agamemnon*. The threads of the intertext constitute a metatext on the theory of recuperating ancient tragedy in modernity. Refashioning Nietzsche's "eternal return," D'Annunzio seeks to abolish what he calls "the error of time" by freeing his text of both historical continuity and social context, embedding his characters in a cycle of mythological events. Highly conscious of creating a modern tragedy in opposition to the canons of bourgeois and naturalist drama, he adheres to the classical five acts and three unities.

The Dead City reads at times like a symbolist drama, recalling Maeterlinck. The figure of Bianca Maria, ethereal virgin with long, flowing locks dressed in a white tunic and draped against neoclassical columns, then a ghostly

---

[27] Julia Kristeva, *La Révolution du langage poétique* (Paris: Seuil, 1974), 487.

[28] Although Schliemann at first believed that he had found the tombs of the Atrides, the ruins he excavated were actually from a few centuries earlier. D'Annunzio seems to have read of Schliemann and his discoveries in the book he used as a guide on his trip to Greece, Charles Diehl, *Excursions archéologiques en Grèce* (1890). See Maria Teresa Marabini Moevs, *Gabriele D'Annunzio e le estetiche della fine del secolo* (L'Aquila: L. U. Japadre, 1976), 325–26.

pale corpse drowned like Ophelia, seems to step out of a pre-Raphaelite painting. The unreality of the characters' world, steeped in myth and fantasy but divorced from social ties and responsibilities, the play's almost static action, the rich poetic and descriptive speeches, and the use of symbols such as the dead flowers and the dead lark to foreshadow Bianca Maria's death, along with the pervasive melancholy that accompanies the tragic foreboding, belong to the same dramatic universe as *Pelléas et Mélisande.* But D'Annunzio is closer to Claudel's *Tête d'or* in his concern with the creation of a modern tragic hero. D'Annunzio's conqueror, however, will operate not in the field of politics but in that of archaeology.

D'Annunzio in fact divides his tragic hero into two characters: the archaeologist Leonardo and the poet Alessandro (a character not included in the sketch of *La Vittoria dell'uomo*). They are united by their passion for their work and by their passion for the woman who is *both* Dionysian *and* a virgin, Leonardo's sister Bianca Maria. Leonardo is driven by his desire to discover the treasures of Mycenae and tormented by incestuous desire for his sister. He is in part a D'Annunzian Schliemann—a middle-aged German amateur archaeologist transformed into a young, passionate Italian whose excavations suggest the heroics of imperialist war on foreign shores. Bianca Maria announces his approach: "I see him! Now he is coming out of the Lion Gate . . . white with dust. . . . He has discovered the sepulchres. . . . God be praised! . . . Ah, what joy, what joy! . . . My brother! . . . Here he comes!"[29] Leonardo enters, according to the stage directions, covered with dirt, perspiration, and blood, as the room floods with sunlight. Bianca Maria then assumes the role of the mother of a war hero—those mothers whose praises D'Annunzio will later sing at Fiume: "You must rest now. . . . You have covered yourself with glory. . . . Poor hands! They are all wounded, stained with blood. . . . I will give you an ointment. . . . Come, come to your room! Let me help you. Let me be like a mother to you! You must sleep" (78). Leonardo's first words, "The gold, the gold,"[30] suggest a similarity between archaeologist and imperialist. His "glory" foreshadows that of those heroes, descendants of Ulysses, that D'Annunzio will praise in his epic poem *Maia* (1903).[31] The imperialist hero, like the heroic archaeologist, sails to a foreign land to struggle to bring treasure and wealth back to the native land, along with glory for self and country; he is welcomed back by a wife, mother, or sister who bears comfort, repose, and praise. The archaeologist, however, seeks not the domination of "exotic" or "inferior" civilizations but rather the reconquest or the reclaiming of classical antiquity. If Leonardo, as Morasso thought, represents the first

[29] D'Annunzio, *Tutto il teatro,* 1: 68.

[30] Moevs (*Gabriele D'Annunzio,* 328) shows that these were also, but in a different context, Schliemann's first words after his discovery.

[31] See Becker's analysis of this epic in *Nationalism,* 84–87.

attempt to create a tragic hero worthy of the dawning age of heroic imperialism, he is, unlike the heroes of either classical or bourgeois tragedy, a
hero without a social context. Symbolically, the archaeologist may represent the imperialist warrior, but materially he represents no nation, no society, no class.

If Leonardo is part Schliemann and part warrior, he is also part Nietzsche.
Alessandro prepares Leonardo's entrance by stating that the archaeologist's
excavations are bringing him into contact with the curse of the Atrides.
Leonardo has not only conquered the gold of Mycenae, he has also purportedly gazed upon the very corpses of Agamemnon, Clytemnestra, and
Cassandra—corpses that disintegrated immediately upon contact with the
air. Like the author of *The Birth of Tragedy*, he "uncovers" and rediscovers
for modernity the original terror of the archaic Dionysian myth below
the surface of its Apollonian form. With Leonardo's dis-covery, the "error
of time" disappears; present, history, and myth merge. Such a vision, as
Alessandro remarks, cannot pass with impunity. The archaeologist's moment of glory is his moment of *anagnorisis*—quite literally in the sense of
discovery—and in the sense of tragic turning point. To uncover the
Atrides is to share their destiny. The victorious Agamemnon returned to
a wife turned murderess; the victorious archaeologist recoils in horror at
the loving sister-mother. If quite differently from Clytemnestra, Bianca
Maria represents for Leonardo a trap in which he could be ensnared by
desire. Like Oedipus, the archaeologist-detective digs toward discovery
only to gaze upon the face of primeval horror that is also within himself.[32]

The "other half" of D'Annunzio's tragic hero, Alessandro, also bears the
sign of Nietzsche: he is the Apollonian poet. To reach the height of his creative powers, he must, of course, seek to possess the Dionysian woman. As
the archaeologist abolished the error of time by gazing into the tomb, the
poet does the same by gazing on the devoted sister as she arranges the treasures brought back by her brother, artifacts to which she seems to give new
life. He says to her: "Has the error of time not yet disappeared for you? . . .
When your hand takes the diadem that adorned the head of the prophetess, the gesture seems to evoke her ancient soul. . . . There is in you a
reawakening power of which you are yourself unconscious" (79). In ac-
cordance both with symbolist aesthetics and with his archaeological theme,
D'Annunzio's dramatic poetry works by a static uncovering and fusing of
layers rather than by a linear development. Thus overlaid on the desire of
a man to possess a woman is the desire of the poet to possess female erotic
power as well as the desire of modern man to repossess antiquity. In ful-

[32] Moevs makes the parallel between Leonardo and Oedipus, calling the former "the new Oedipus, solver of archaeological mysteries" (*Gabriele D'Annunzio*, 331). She also discusses the impact of *The Birth of Tragedy* on the play. See chap. 5, "La Città morta: L'Innesto del mito."

filling his amorous-archaeological passion, Alessandro hopes to discover the treasures in his soul and thus to produce poetry that fuses Apollo with Dionysus and the archaic with the modern.

In the last scene of the second act, Leonardo confesses to Alessandro the terrible secret (he calls it the "monster" within him) of his passion for his sister. This too is a dis-covery: he is able to unearth his secret only after he has unearthed the Atrides. It is his hope that Alessandro will "save" him. Perhaps the monstrous passion can be contained in the Apollonian word.

Alessandro's wife, Anna, classically in the third act, reveals to Leonardo the knowledge that will turn the action to its resolution in tragedy: Alessandro and Bianca Maria are in love and she, Anna, wishes to sacrifice her own happiness to allow this love to flourish. She, too, speaks in "layered" mythological terms. Bianca Maria must not, like Antigone, sacrifice her life for her brother. Instead, she must be Nike: "the Victory who will crown his [Alessandro's] life" (95). She herself is only an impediment to the flourishing of the poet-superman's creative power. With classic tragic irony, Anna's attempt to give happiness plants in Leonardo the seeds of jealousy that will bring about the catastrophe. (Indeed, Leonardo recalls Racine's, rather than Euripides', Phaedra, to the extent that he struggles against the guilt of a monstrous passion and that it is jealousy that finally incites him to violence.) In the final scene of act 3, Anna encourages Bianca Maria not to sacrifice her vitality but to yield to her love for Alessandro. Yet this message seems strangely undercut by a suggestion of eroticism between the two women. Bianca Maria clings to Anna, recalling that she kissed her on the lips; Anna caresses Bianca Maria, kissing her eyes. Thirsty in the aridity of the dead city, Anna can "hear the water run over your body, as over the statue of a fountain" (99), both suggesting her desire and inadvertently "prophesying" the young woman's death. The promise of eros liberated and joy achieved in the eventual union of Alessandro and Bianca Maria is also undercut by Bianca Maria's reading, first from the dialogue between Cassandra and the elders in *Agamemnon* and then from *Antigone*. Before dying, Antigone sees the statue of Niobe. "But forever with weeping eyes she bathes those crags, / I resemble her, for a god brings to me sleep" (101). The reading of the ancient tragedy within the modern tragedy uncovers fatality and impending death, swallowing time within eternal return as did the uncovering of the Atrides. This reading of Antigone recalls the reading in the first words of the play: "O Eros, invincible in strife. . . . You lead the erring minds of the just to ruin" (55). An instrument of tragic destiny, Eros is fated to bring doom rather than liberation and joy.

Leonardo then decides that, in order to preserve her "purity," his sister can no longer live. By the opening of the fifth act, he has (offstage) accomplished the sacrifice of his sister at the fountain of Perseus. Bianca Maria has, as it were, merged with her mythological essence, pre-Raphaelite and classical. The corpse, the stage directions tell us, lies "supine, rigid, pure. Her wet clothes cling to her body; her hair, soaked with water, winds around her face in broad bands; her arms are stretched out along her sides; her feet are joined together like those of the statues on the tombs under the arches" (111). By his "pure act," as it was called in *Il Fuoco*, Leonardo believes he has purified himself: no longer "stained," his love has become immaculate and absolute, expressed in a vocabulary more Christian than classical. "I have become pure, all pure. All the holiness of my first love has returned to my soul like a torrent of light. . . . Another benefit from her through death!" (112).

But there is more. The sacrifice, it seems, has been made not only for the purification of Leonardo's love but also for that of Alessandro, whom Leonardo now incorporates into a kind of eternal male bonding. "O my brother, O my brother in life and in death, joined to me, forever joined to me by this sacrifice I have made for you" (113). Strangely, at least within the psychological and realistic conventions that have not been entirely absent from the play, Alessandro expresses no terror, no surprise, makes no objection to Leonardo's act. In what seems to be an act of solidarity, or an acquiescence to the "purity" of their new bond, he prostrates himself next to his friend at the feet of the dead girl. In an intense and tragic moment, archaeologist and poet are one, possessing the common object of their desires in "purity," combating the fatal power of Eros through sacrifice and brotherhood.

In *Il Fuoco*, after Stelio defines tragedy through the image of Perseus decapitating Medusa and then holding up her head before a fascinated crowd, the name of Perseus suggests to him the ending of the tragedy he plans to write—the sacrifice of the virgin in the fountain of Perseus, the only living spot in a land where everything is burned and dead.[33] This leads him to define the "pure act" that will make the tragedy "modern." "The pure act signals the defeat of ancient Destiny. The new soul breaks in one gesture the iron circle in which it is bound, with a determination generated by madness, by a lucid delirium similar to ecstasy. . . . Monstrous fate is vanquished."[34] The modern tragic hero thus recuperates both Perseus's slaying of the Medusa and Agamemnon's sacrifice of Iphigenia; monstrosity is overcome by purity through an Apollonian-Dionysian moment of "lucid delirium."

This analysis describes why Stelio's tragedy was to be called *The Victory of Man*, but does it apply to *The Dead City*? To some extent, yes. Leonardo's act does seem to be generated by a "lucid delirium": he strikes against both the "monster" within himself and the curse of the Atrides. In place of the

---

[33] The fountain of Perseus and the aridity of the surrounding land were actually described by Schliemann. See Moevs, *Gabriele D'Annunzio*, 333 n. 51.

[34] D'Annunzio, *Il Fuoco*, 158.

head of Medusa, he presents to the theater audience the corpse of his beloved. The act also bonds and fuses two modern heroes, the archaeologist and the poet, one who plunders and recuperates treasure (avatar of the warrior-imperialist) and the other who creates and fascinates by means of words (avatar of the political orator). If the tragedy ended with the scene of the bonded heroes at the feet of the sacrificial corpse, it could bear Stelio's title. But it does not. After the ritual bonding, the two rise up "terrified" by the approach of Anna. Alessandro's reactions seem those of a common criminal: Where shall they hide the body? What shall they tell Anna? (113). When Anna actually appears, they are both, in the language of the stage directions, "deadly pale, stiff with terror, unable to move" (114). It is Anna, who, after touching the corpse, has the last word: "Ah . . . I see! I see!" (114), an exclamation often interpreted to mean that her lost sight has actually returned. But this medical magic would be exaggerated even in a play that contains not a few improbabilities. More likely, Anna in her personae of Cassandra and Tiresias now "sees" everything: the incest, the tragic sacrifice, the ancient and archaeological fusions.

Mario Morasso, who saw in *La Città morta* the first modern tragedy for the dawning age of heroic imperialism, nonetheless had several criticisms of the play. One can see how Morasso might have been somewhat disappointed by a tragedy that ends with the heroes terrified before the approach of a blind woman. D'Annunzio's change in title from "La Vittoria dell'uomo" is no doubt significant, for "the victory of man" over ancient destiny is certainly undercut by this ending. The victory, if there is one, seems rather to lie with the titular dead city, as well as with the figure of Anna. In Anna Meda's Jungian reading of the play, the dead city represents a kind of phallic mother, a "negative archetype of the Mother in her devouring and destructive quality," and Anna too is a maternal figure who abolishes her own "error of time" in her final "vision."[35] Leonardo, with his digging in the city, is also for Meda returning to the archetypal mother, discovering the secret of the maternal libido. Yet Meda, following the assertions in *Il Fuoco* too literally, concludes that the tragedy ends with "the victory of modern over primitive man."[36] Rather, this victory is, in the name under which D'Annunzio grouped this tragedy along with *La Gioconda* and *La Gloria*, a "mutilated victory." The archaeologist, in spite of his heroic discovery, has not succeeded in conquering the dead city; the hero, in spite of his sacrifice, has not emerged free and victorious; the Apollonian poet has not quite succeeded in containing and dominating the Dionysian energies; the male has not entirely subdued the female nor the son the mother.

[35] Anna Meda, *Bianche statue contro il nero abisso: Il teatro dei miti in D'Annunzio e Pirandello* (Ravenna: Longo, 1993), 51, 75.
[36] Ibid., 79.

Do we have then "the victory of woman"? With the performances of Bernhardt and Duse in the role of Anna, this was no doubt in a sense the case. Yet Anna, although noble and to be pitied in her own right, remains external to the central tragic action.[37] In her last appearance—white, barren, but terrifying like a phallic mother—she seems to represent the as yet not entirely dominated Medusan force contained in the titular "dead city." We are, in a sense, still in the middle of the *Oresteia*. The furies defending Clytemnestra may yet avenge Iphigenia. D'Annunzio's actual text, as opposed to the one envisaged in *The Flame*, betrays the author's doubt that modernity can produce the hero-poet capable of recuperating and vanquishing ancient destiny. Or perhaps D'Annunzio cannot relegate that task to one of his characters but can accomplish it only by himself. In this play, however, the tragic poet has not quite succeeded in displaying the slain head of Medusa to an enraptured audience.

If D'Annunzio did not write his ideal modern tragedy with *The Dead City*, he did perhaps write the first modern metatragedy. Leonardo-as-Nietzsche discovers and uncovers within antiquity and within himself powerful Dionysian forces obfuscated by neoclassical aesthetics describing a "still and noble" Greece. Tragedy is rediscovered not as victory but as an endless dialectic of striving and suffering. How can it then be represented in modern Apollonian poetry? D'Annunzio's text, heavy with intertextuality, displays the problem endemic to the writing of all modern tragedy: self-consciousness. A primarily static drama, with its themes of dis-covery and the abolishing of "the error of time," it radically alters the modern bourgeois theatrical conventions of plot, character, and verisimilitude of language and setting in the same way that D'Annunzio's theatrical political gestures defied parliamentary conventions. It announces the modern tragic hero, product of the fusion of archaeologist-imperialist and poet, though it suggests that the time for heroic "victory" is not yet ripe.

Despite its self-conscious, literary nature, D'Annunzio's first tragedy seems to have had something of the "Medusan" effect he desired. Although its early performances were in traditional theaters, where the audience's enthusiasm was primarily for Bernhardt and Duse, in 1922 *La Città morta* was revived in the outdoor Roman theater in Fiesole. The reviewer in *Il Marzocco* sees the performance as a realization of D'Annunzio's visions for the transformation of theater twenty years earlier. Thus he finds that in the summer Tuscan evening, in the ancient Roman setting, the "collective soul" of the audience remained "enchanted" for three hours in "an attitude of religious atten-

---

[37] Chomel, *D'Annunzio*, 53–64, makes an interesting case—with which I cannot agree—for Anna as the true tragic protagonist of *La Città morta*.

tion."[38] The Italian "collective soul" was of course at the time about to experience a new sort of rapturous attention in the theatro-political sphere, an apprenticeship in rapture which D'Annunzio helped to prepare.

The Dead City fits Moretti's definition of tragedy as the revelation of a "moment of truth" divorced from "novelistic" or everyday existence. Yet the dead city of the past is still too vast and multifaceted to be contained in the present; it defies and in a sense engulfs both the poet and the archaeologist. D'Annunzio's other "Greek" modern tragedy, *Fedra* (1909), will deal with its intertextuality differently by directly staging the myth.

Fedra or the Tragedy of Possession

Written in an archaic and precious language with heavy use of predecessors (Euripides, Seneca, Racine, and Swinburne) along with archaeological references, particularly to recent excavations in Crete, D'Annunzio's reworking of the classical myth in *Fedra* is in one sense an exquisite humanistic-scholastic exercise. Again drawing on both *The Birth of Tragedy* and his trip to Greece, D'Annunzio self-consciously sought to create a "primitive," Cretan Phaedra modeled on her mother, Pasiphae, a chaotic, "Dionysian" natural force. He had another interest in the myth as well. In a 1909 interview, he explained that his tragedy was also about Phaedra's father, "Minos, the first lord of the Mediterranean, the first of the Thalassocrats, the ancient founder of marine imperialism."[39] Written just after *La Nave* and shortly before the Italian invasion of Libya in 1912, D'Annunzio's tragedy was conceived in a cultural climate afire with imperialistic fervor and the desire to possess the Mediterranean, *mare nostrum*.

Fedra is dedicated to D'Annunzio's mistress of the moment, Nathalie de Gouloubeff, whom he calls, significantly, "Thalassia." Like her predecessors, "Thalassia" serves the poet-creator as a Dionysian woman, or an erotic muse. The metaphor D'Annunzio used to describe her role in a December 1908 letter, however, develops a new variation. He writes (in French) of his decision to treat the myth of Phaedra thus: "I jumped on my prey with the speed of great predatory birds. Truly, I *possessed* Phaedra in the shade of the myrtle tree pierced by her gold pin. After Euripides, after Seneca, after Racine, I dare to produce a new Phaedra. You have given me

[38] "Gaio," "*La Città morta* a Fiesole," *Il Marzocco*, September 3, 1922, reprinted in Laura Granatella, *Arrestate l'autore! D'Annunzio in scena* (*Cronache, testimonianze, illustrazioni, documenti inediti e rari del primo grande spettacolo del '900*) (Rome: Bulzoni), 1: 176–79.

[39] Interview with Renato Simoni in *Corriere della sera*, April 9, 1909, quoted in Pietro Gibellini's introduction to Gabriele D'Annunzio, *Fedra*, ed. Pietro Gibellini (Milan: Mondadori, 1989), 12.

the power to fertilize the worn-out womb."[40] The beloved-as-muse appears here as the bestower of power in the accomplishment of a kind of literary rape! The origins of the drama are thus formulated in terms of possession. What we might call the aesthetics of sexual-aesthetic-imperialistic possession will function significantly in the tragedy. *Fedra* is indeed a mythic drama in the D'Annunzian sense in that it transcends both linear time and history, transporting dramatic action to an agon of ritual and frenzy where events seem to emerge from the depths of time rather than actually to take place. The refuge in myth and poetry suggests not only a revolt against bourgeois drama in the attempt to "re-fertilize the womb of ancient tragedy" but concurrently a flight from liberal-parliamentary "Italietta" into the emerging metahistorical vision of heroic-imperialist Italy.[41]

O thanate paien—healing death—: the epigraph to all three acts suggests the motivating force of the drama. Fedra's first words, after hearing the false rumor of Theseus's death, are "O Thanatos, light is in your eyes!"[42] She seems at first to belong to the chorus of mourning women, but her diversity manifests itself almost immediately. Whereas the other women uphold the laws of Athens and of the Olympian gods, the "Titaness" or "Minoan," as she is repeatedly called, exists without and beyond the rule of both Athens and Mt. Olympus. Her being is dominated by the gods' curse as visited on her mother, rendered in a powerful image as she tells another woman, "nor do you, fraught with horror, hear bellowing within you the monster brother" (56).

The curse of Aphrodite becomes in D'Annunzio's version the source not only of Fedra's downfall but also of her "titanic" and "Dionysian" strength to revolt and defy. Fedra finds a model for herself in the tale of Evadne, the wife of Capaneus, the hero who defied the gods during the war against Thebes. For Fedra, Evadne's self-immolation on her husband's funeral pyre signifies a "titanic" triumph, a renunciation of service to the Olympian gods (72) in a fusion of revolt, erotic desire, and healing death in the "beautiful flame" of the sacrificial act. This fusion will function importantly in the tragedy.

One of D'Annunzio's inventions is the character of a beautiful Theban slave named Ipponoe, a gift from the spoils of war for Hippolytus. Fedra's decision to sacrifice the virgin to Hecate is usually seen as a manifestation of her extreme jealousy, which of course it is, but it is more complex. Struck by a vision of Aprhrodite, Fedra seizes her long hairpin (the one we heard about in Gabriele's letter to Nathalie) and, "drunk with sacrilege," pierces leaf by leaf the myrtle tree sacred to the goddess. Frenzied both with the

---

[40] Letter to Nathalie de Goloubeff, December 10, 1908, quoted in Pietro Gibellini's introduction to *Fedra*, ed. 9.

[41] This is suggested by Meda, *Bianche*, 140.

[42] D'Annunzio, *Fedra*, 50.

horror of the family curse and with pride as a Titan defying an Olympian, she is now prepared for the sacrifice. But the language with which she addresses her victim, recalling Anna's erotic discourse with Bianca Maria, resembles more the language of a lover than of a rival. "You are hidden in a thousand folds, like a flower closed with a thousand petals. . . . Open yourself. Do not tremble. I will be gentle to you. . . . You are beautiful" (87). In the language of the stage directions, the moment of sacrifice resembles a rape. "Under the cruel and devouring glare, the virgin grows stiff with terror. . . . Burning with mad desire . . . is the daughter of Pasifae" (96). The sacrificial scene is in fact a veritable whirligig of transsexuality. Ipponoe, whose name suggests Hippolytus and the horses he loves, describes herself as a young Spartan athlete. The pin with which Fedra pierces the tree of Aphrodite and kills the young girl may be seen as a manifestation of the "virile vulva"—synecdoche for the masculinized female hero identified in D'Annunzio's rhetoric by Barbara Spackman.[43]

Fedra's scene with Ipponoe is in some ways a dress rehearsal for her scene with Hippolytus. The latter repeats the movement from eroticized sweetness to the frenzy of desired possession. Departing from tradition, this Fedra violently declares the passion that consumes her, causing Hippolytus to see in her a panther preparing to leap on her prey (159). In conformity with tradition, she asks Hippolytus to stab her, begging, however, not for *his* sword but for the sword of his mother, the Amazon Antiope. She then seems to assume for herself the role of the sacrificed virgin as she attributes *her* previous role as lover/rapist to Hippolytus: "Be gentle. . . . Then pierce me with all your strength, treat me like prey"(161). We have here not only the stereotypical lustful woman begging for male violence but also a complex intertextual weaving of a mythology of rape, possession, power, and transsexuality. Fedra's desire to be loved-killed by Hippolytus fuses with her desire to be avenged on Theseus, who raped her as a young girl. It also represents solidarity with the Amazons who stormed the "masculine towers of Athens" (167). While desiring Hippolytus as lover and son she also desires the maternal phallus, the virile vulva, Antiope's sword.

From the point of view of Hippolytus and Theseus, desire of rape as the affirmation of virility is clearly fused with desire for imperial conquest. Unlike the chaste adolescent of antiquity, D'Annunzio's Hippolytus envisages his access to manhood as an identification with the father-as-rapist through a father-son expedition to abduct the young Helen of Troy—a reenactment, in this play of eternal returns, of Theseus's abduction of the young Fedra. The expedition will at the same time initiate Hippolytus into con-

---

[43] Barbara Spackman, "The Fascist Rhetoric of Virility," *Stanford Italian Review* 8, no. 1–2, *Fascism and Culture*, 81–101. The term "virile vulva" actually comes from a novel by Carlo Emilio Gadda satirizing fascism; Spackman, however, applies it to D'Annunzio, who uses such terms as "heroic womb" in his "virilization of women."

quest and power over the sea, thus fusing imperial with sexual possession. Attempting to dissuade him from this route to manhood, Fedra offers him the ships of Crete: like her father, the founder of maritime imperialism, Hippolytus can thus become a "Thalassocrat" (130). Fedra's stepson rejects her offers of power as he rejects her desire, responding that he will accompany his father on an "enterprise of men" (131). To accept Fedra would connote for him the subversion of paternal Athens and regression into the maternal labyrinth of Crete.

In the context of this web of mythical rapes, Fedra's revenge on Hippolytus and Theseus is tinged with more irony than in the classical and subsequent versions. The Hippolytus that she portrays in her accusation to his father— "drunk with desire to rape" (183)—is the very Hippolytus that Theseus would initiate into manhood in Troy. Preparing, like her model Evadne, to die next to Hippolytus's body, Fedra avenges herself on her rapist husband and becomes the possessor of the Amazon's sword. Her triumph resides also in the subversion of the laws of Athens (called the law of Cronus, the seemingly incontrovertible law of linear time). "My name is ineffable, like the name of one who subverts ancient laws to impose her own arcane law" (205), she says.[44]

What are we to make of this tangle of eros, thanatos and sacrifice; rape, imperial desire, eternal return, and subversion of time and law? It would be a facile distortion to label D'Annunzio as macho-rapist-imperialist or indeed to identify the rapist-imperialist Theseus as the hero of the play, which he clearly is not. The "Dionysian" and "Titanic" figure (the parallel between the two is found in *The Birth of Tragedy*), the force to be reckoned with here, is Fedra— "unforgettable Fedra" as she is called in the closing line of each act. The domain of the feminine—Crete, the primitive land of the "Great Mother," the labyrinth, and unconscious, unbridled lust—is indeed in D'Annunzio's view "unforgettable"; that is, we "forget" that domain at our peril if we rely solely on Apollonian-Athenian masculine linearity, law, and obedience to the gods. But the tragic figure is also in a sense Hippolytus, and one way of reading his tragedy is as society's failure to realize in the young hero an ideal, transcendent fusion of Apollo and Dionysus, modernity and myth, rational and arcane law, clarity and desire, the realms of the father and of the mother. Hippolytus's tragedy might also be read as the failure to fuse modern imperialistic venture—represented by Theseus's

---

[44] Maria Iolanda Palazzolo has discussed the function of the two worlds identified with two different systems of law in the play: the world of Theseus, marked by obedience to the gods and respect for clarity, civil law, and order, and the world of Fedra, marked by revolt against law and gods and the attempt to create a law of "supermen" ("Le due leggi: La *Fedra* di D'Annunzio," in Vanna Gentile, ed., *Transgressione tragica e norma domestica: Esemplari di tipologie femminili dalla letteratura europea* (Rome: Edizioni di Storia e Letteratura, 1983), 211–38. D'Annunzio is surely influenced by Nietzsche in his Dionysian concept of Fedra and Apollonian concept of Theseus.

raping and plundering—with mother Italy's deep-rooted claim to *mare nostrum*—represented by the first "Thalassocrats" of Minoan legendary imperialism. Hippolytus "forgets" at his peril what his stepmother offers.

There is another sense in which Fedra is "unforgettable" and in which she is "possessed." This has to do with a character whose role is crucial to the binding and fusing operations in the play: the messenger turned bard, Eurito (another D'Annunzian invention). It is he who recounts the death of Hippolytus to Theseus, serving Fedra's revenge. If the Minoan queen is unforgettable, it is because Eurito will, as they both acknowledge, give her "an eternal robe" through his poetry. He is the poet, too, of the eternal return: "What was, woman, will return" are his words to Fedra. Her sacrifice acquires power and meaning only through the poet's iteration. D'Annunzio, it would seem, has "possessed" his Fedra by inscribing himself into the figure of the bard. The poet alone has the capacity to transform primitive desire into the forms and words with which to inflame and possess the masses. Just as Nathalie's erotic energy gave Gabriele the power to "fertilize the worn-out womb," so Fedra's triumphant sacrifice to Aphrodite becomes an "eternal return" (as opposed to a linear narrative) through the bard's poetic word.

"Venus genetrix, Venus victrix sia la parola d'ordine dell'Italia fascista" ("May generating and victorious Venus be the word of order of fascist Italy"), a fascist admirer of D'Annunzio's was to write later in interpreting the Commandante's desire.[45] Part of D'Annunzio's disillusion with the actual fascist regime seems to stem from its failure to incorporate in its ideology and ritual the erotics of early fascist culture, tending instead toward a simplistic *maschilismo*.[46] Yet the D'Annunzian aesthetics of binding, fusing, and possessing in a myth of eternal return became an important legacy to fascism. The fusions here include binary poles such as male and female, classical and modern, archaic and historical, mythical and modern imperialism, Apollonian and Dionysian. The locus of power in D'Annunzio's modern tragedy lies finally neither with Theseus nor Phaedra but with the poet whose verses will render not only Phaedra but her author "unforgettable." The enchanting word of the poet, like that of the orator, as Stelio discovered in *Il Fuoco*, aesthetically binds the speaker to the crowd, whether in the theater or the piazza. D'Annunzio's aesthetics of binding and fusing seem to have been realized in productions, especially in the revivals just preceding and during the fascist period. Produced among the ruins of the Palatine in October 1922, on the eve of the March on Rome, in "the cradle

---

[45] Ferdinando Pasini, *D'Annunzio* (Rome: Augustea, 1928), 118 (Book in series "I Prefascisti").

[46] See Spackman, "Fascist Rhetoric of Virility."

of Rome and of all of Western civilization," *Fedra*, according to one reviewer, acquired a new "fascination." The production achieved a "perfect fusion between stage and audience that seemed to transform the spectacle into a rite, a celebration."[47] For another reviewer, this production proved D'Annunzio to be the glory of Italian theater and his celebration of ancient heroes a prefiguration of his celebration of Italian war heroes.[48] But even in a closed theater, the Costanzi, in a production starring Ida Rubenstein, the audience appears to have experienced a "delirium," enthusiastically calling for the (absent) poet. The same audience requested and applauded the playing of the fascist hymn "Giovinezza" between the second and third acts.[49] Poetic and political "glories of Italy" must have seemed fused together in the "religious" fascination of the tragedy.

Iorio's Daughter and the Myth of Eternal Italy

In the play that is generally considered to be D'Annunzio's most significant contribution to the theater, the poet attempts a different approach to the recuperation of myth in modern tragedy: rather than discovering or staging classical Greek mythology for modernity, he explores the pagan and Christian folklore of his native Abruzzo to dissolve the error of time in a specifically Italic form of ritualistic tragedy. A 1903 letter to his friend the artist Michetti (whose painting suggested the subject of *La Figlia di Iorio*) shows some of his intentions regarding the fusion of time and space. "I felt the living roots of my native earth and I derived from it an unspeakable joy. Everything in this tragedy is new and everything is simple; everything is peaceful and violent at the same time. Primitive man, in immutable nature, speaks the language of elementary passions. The stage direction for the time is this: 'In the land of Abruzzo, many years ago.' The substance of these figures is the eternal human substance; that of today, that of two thousand years ago."[50]

La Figlia di Iorio takes what could have been a naturalistic plot about a troubled and violent family and transposes it into a mythical mode. As in D'Annunzio's Greek-based tragedies, the setting and action of the drama

---

[47] *Fedra* was revived in a spectacular outdoor production on the Palatine, October 10–22, 1922. The review in question, however, was published on October 29, the day after the March on Rome. The original reads: "Quella perfetta fusione tra scena e platea che sembra trasformare effettivamente lo spettacolo stesso in un rito, in una 'celebrazione'." G. M. Andriulli, in *Il Secolo*, October 29, 1922, reprinted in Granatella, *Arrestate l'autore*, 2: 734.

[48] "Gaio" (A. Orvieto) in *Il Marzocco*, October 29, 1922, in Granatella, *Arrestate l'autore*, 2: 737–39.

[49] Vicenzo Tieri, "'Fedra' di Gabriele d'Annunzio interpretata da Ida Rubinstein," *Il Popolo di Roma*, April 20, 1926.

[50] In Valentini, *La Tragedie moderna*, 192.

place it in a legendary time and space where events are absorbed by ritual and the power of the poetic word becomes the prime unifying factor. Here the poet experiments with a different type of language: instead of the literary, densely intertextual verse of *Fedra*, he uses a partly dialectical but poetic speech of his own invention, making use of musicality in his variation of verse and meter. One of D'Annunzio's statements of his intentions indicates the influence of Nietzsche and possibly of Sir James Frazer on his concept of "rural" drama: "Thus we would like to recall the rural and Dionysian origin of drama, the birth of tragedy in dithyramb, the creative impulse of earthly energies at the return of spring."[51] Fertility rites and the agricultural rhythm of seasons will in fact play a major role in *La Figlia di Iorio*. With a more extensive use of a chorus than in *Fedra*, a soberly classical plot, although with onstage violence, a thematic tension between Christian ethics and pagan superstitions, and a poetic language adapted to each, D'Annunzio blends ancient Greek tragedy, Christian sacred drama, and his concept of primitive Italic ritual to create, as his reviewers will proclaim, a uniquely national tragedy.

There are essentially three dramatic "worlds" in the tragedy: first, the interior, domestic space of women, controlled by mothers and especially by the Mother Candia della Leonessa; second, the fields, the patriarchal domain of masculine work, in harvest season during the play; and third, the pastoral domain of the mountain where Candia's son Aligi, incapable of farm work, was sent by his father to be a shepherd. The mountain, where Aligi and Mila live chastely in a cave and where they encounter the holy man Cosma and the herbalist women, is the space of diversity, extracommunal life, spirituality, and untamed nature, functioning outside of the rhythms of domestic and agricultural cycles. In this sense it also defines the world inhabited by Iorio and his daughter. The sparse dramatic action of the play takes place through the invasion of one "world" into another.[52] In addition to these dramatic worlds, defined primarily in spatial terms, there exist two interpenetrating poetic worlds, discursive practices in terms of which the characters define their Christian or pagan motivations. The first act, static and ritualistic, takes place in the first dramatic world. The initiation of Vienda, the wife chosen by his mother for Aligi, into the circle of women, seems to reenact an ancient ceremony, reinforced by ritualistic language such as the refrain of the three daughters, "So let it be, mother. We kiss the earth,"[53] and the gifts of grain denoting fertility. The power of the mother, not only over her daughters and daughter-in-law but also over

---

[51] Quoted in Meda, *Bianche*, 83.

[52] For the concept of plot based on the invasion of one poetic "world" into another, see Jurij M. Lotman, "The Origin of Plot in the Light of Typology," *Poetics Today* 1, no. 2 (1979): 161–84.

[53] Gabriele D'Annunzio, *La Figlia di Iorio* (Milan: Mondadori, 1991), 43.

her son, is affirmed. Yet Aligi's allegiance is also to a different world: he reiterates several times his desire to return to the mountain, and the strange
statement to his mother that he thinks he has just slept for seven hundred
years and comes "from far away" also indicates his desire for a space outside of the communal domains of man and woman. Thus the reader/spec-
tator is prepared for his attraction to Mila, daughter of the wizard Iorio,
the other "stranger." It is her entry into the house that initiates the dramatic action. Her first speech effects a marked change in poetic rhythm.
After incantatory, endecasyllabic lines such as "Questa è la pace che vi
manda il Cielo. / E che i capegli vi si faccian bianchi / su l'istesso guan-
ciale, in gran vecchiezza!" (50). ("This is the peace that Heaven sends you.
/ May your hair turn white / on the same pillow, at a ripe old age!") Mila
cries: "Gente di Dio, salvatemi voi! / La porta! Chiudere la porta! / Met-
tete le spranghe! Son molti, / hanno tutti la falce. Son pazzi, / son pazzi
di sole e di vino" (51). ("People of God, save me! / The door! Close the
door! Bolt it! There are many of them, / they all have sickles. They are mad,
/ they are mad with sun and wine.") The staccato, interrupted rhythms announce not only her own disruptive invasion into the cyclical, eternalizing
world, but also the threat of the irruption of the men's world into the
women's.

The pagan/Christian superstitious rituals enacted to prevent the entrance of "evil" into the sanctuary of the nuptial rites (for example, spray-
ing holy water on the door hinges) (51) serve to create a sense of fatality:
evil *will* inevitably disrupt the domestic cycle. Mila's destiny is foreshadowed too as the group of harvesters coming in from the fields demand that
the women release "the rotten sheep" for them to use sexually (60). The
tainted, "rotten" wizard's daughter is also the sheep who will innocently
follow the shepherd to the mountains as well as the sacrificial lamb who
will be burned to purify the community. Mila's invasion upsets the entire
social order. The mother, Candia della Leonessa, who normally should rule
the household, falls into silence and passivity as the youngest daughter,
Ornella, takes charge to welcome the persecuted woman out of Christian
charity. The men, having left their work and households, become "bestial"
(59) in pursuit of Mila, threatening not only to interrupt the female ceremony but to rape all the women.

Candia, faced with these circumstances, is at last roused to reassume her
authority, demanding that Mila leave her house. As Louis Kibler notes,
Mila's pleas for Christian pity have no effect, but her threats of a pagan
curse, a curse that will rouse the dead ancestors, throw the women into con-
sternation.[54] Yet Christian discourse and symbols dominate the end of the

---

[54] Louis Kibler, "Myth and Meaning in D'Annunzio's *La Figlia di Iorio*," *Annali d'Italianistica* 5 (1987): 180–81.

first act. Aligi is won over to Mila by the vision of the guardian angel who stands behind her; he controls the "bestial" crowd, including his father, preventing them from harming Mila by putting up a cross; the women chant "Kyrie eleison" and "Mater purissima, ora pro nobis." Yet the Christian poetic world is inevitably penetrated (contaminated?) by the pagan one. We are never sure of the provenance of Mila's angel; the cross functions as a superstitious, rather than a religious, icon; and the women, although they use the language of the church, could be praying to the Great Mother as well as to the Virgin. By the end of the first act, then, the interpenetration of discursive and dramatic worlds has effected a disruption in the cycle of communal life without, however, really constituting a dramatic action in the temporal, progressive sense.

The mountain cave in which the second act takes place constitutes, as Lynn Gunzberg demonstrates, an attempt at "recreating domesticity in the region of nature," thus another interpenetration of worlds that will ultimately destroy the freedom that Aligi and Mila seem to be seeking outside of the community.[55] The mountain and the cave are also maternal spaces, "Madre Montagna" in the words of the "herb woman" Anna Onna,[56] the space where the woman known primarily as the daughter of her father, Jorio, "reborn" through love, prays to the Virgin Mother that she might spiritually return to her dead mother (102). Aligi, for his part, intends to override the laws of both father and mother by traveling to Rome, where he hopes that the Shepherd of shepherds (and the Father of fathers) will dissolve his unconsummated union with Vienda, allowing him to marry Mila. The most lyrical part of the tragedy occurs, in fact, as Mila and Aligi envision their pilgrimage: "O compagna, preparati al viaggio. / Lungo è il cammino, ma l'amore è forte. / Aligi, passerei sul fuoco ardente, / e che l'andare non avesse fine!" ("O my companion, prepare yourself for the journey. / The way is long, but love is strong. / Aligi, I would go through burning fire [a foreshadowing of Mila's sacrifice], if only the journey would have no end") (99). The almost operatic love duet expresses not so much the goal but the joy of motion, the dream of freedom from all the laws and restrictions of community, taboo, and belief. This project, however, seems doomed from the start by the words of the wise man Cosma, who warns Aligi that the "walls of the city are high" (94) and that he ought not to break the commandments of father and mother (99).

The dream of freedom, or the illusion of unbounded love, is brutally interrupted by the invasion into the mountain world of Aligi's father, Lazaro,

---

[55] Lynn Gunzberg, "*La Figlia di Iorio, La lupa* and the Locus of Patriarchy," *Annali d'Italianistica* 5 (1987): 227.

[56] Anna Meda notes the maternal value of mountain and cave, as they appear in this play, in Jungian psychology.

representative, as has often been observed, of patriarchy in its most primitive and brutal form. Lazaro, who has come to take Mila away from his son for his own desires, states the essence of patriarchal rule in no uncertain terms: "I am your father; and with you / I can do as I please / . . . because I am the father and you the son, do you understand? All power was given to me over you from time immemorial, above all laws" (123). Similarly, he asserts his claim to authority over Mila: "Woman, now you have seen / that I am the master. I make the law" (127). The rough language, irregular rhythm, and paratactic syntax of Lazaro's discourse contrasts sharply with the lyrics of love and longing. The dramatic climax, the *onstage* parricide (D'Annunzio abandons the Greek convention here) takes place at the moment when all three worlds have interpenetrated: the father has come from the fields to the mountain, and the female and maternal sphere is represented by the cave as well as by the presence of Aligi's sister Ornella. In killing the representative of archaic power and patriarchal law, Aligi is potentially the hero-creator of a new law and a new order. The murder weapon, the ax with which Aligi is carving an image of Mila's guardian angel, represents Aligi's spiritual, creative, artistic nature, the side that revolts against the law of the father.

The third act, however, reveals Aligi's limitations as hero. In the stage directions, all three dramatic worlds are represented scenically. Although we are in the village domain of the women, the men's threshing instruments are onstage, and the fields and the mountains can be seen (131). Candia, temporarily gone mad, suggests a desire to return to the former rhythm of life by repeating several lines from the first act (for example, Aligi's "I slept seven hundred years" [143]). It is clear that disaster has interrupted the agricultural rhythms of the community as the chorus of women chants that the grapes remain unharvested and even the earth is in mourning (146). Candia, more in mourning for her condemned son than for her dead husband, assumes the role of *mater dolorosa*. Aligi has assumed the role of penitent, consumed with guilt as he presents himself to be judged by the people. As in the first act, the abrupt entrance of the stranger Mila di Codra disrupts the communal, female-controlled ritual, changing its course. This time she clearly comes from the mountain world, sent, she says, by the "saint of the mountains" to confess (154). Mila's confession to the murder of Lazaro convinces even Aligi (provoking Mila's moving line, "Not you, Aligi!)" when she asserts that not only did she bewitch him but that the guardian angel was apostate. Aligi, in fact, demands that she not be burned because fire is beautiful ("la fiamma è bella" [164]), but that she be instead cursed by all his ancestors. He then falls asleep in the arms of his mother, regressing to the eternal, ancestral, female-dominated domain. In repeating Aligi's words ("La fiamma è bella") as she accomplishes her act of sacrifice, Mila dies not only for love but as an act of ritual purification, recompensing the community for the disruptive terror brought into being, it is true, by her. As in *Fedra*, the very existence of the foreign woman is the cause of the tragic conflict between father and son, and her sacrificial death serves to heal the communal bonds that she tore apart. At the same time, the community has failed to produce the hero who would be able to fuse the old, patriarchal law and the matriarchal ritual with the wilder, arcane, Dionysian power of the "strange" woman. Such a hero would transcend and bind all three traditional worlds, affirming his own new order. Although Aligi, unlike Hippolytus, is allowed to live, he is in a similar sense a failed tragic hero.

And yet, it is not true that by the end of the play nothing has changed. Like his more sophisticated D'Annunzian counterparts, Aligi the folk artist, under the influence of the Dionysian-Medusan woman, found the force to murder and create. With his parricide, he destroyed the arbitrary, primitive law of the old patriarchy. The chorus, representing the crowd and the community, also undergoes an important transformation. Rigorously divided into bestial men and archaic women in the first act, it appears in the third act as the voice of the people, exercising judgment for the community. Paolo Puppa argues: "The D'Annunzian Crowd grows progressively calmer, recomposes itself aesthetically until it becomes an allegory of the People, of Nationality, in which the hero, a new Anteus, finds his own authentic roots. . . . The mass . . . has become the People, reorganized in the sacred ceremonies of funeral rites and tribunal. . . . [It thus anticipates] the unanism and the interclassism of the fascist Festival!"[57]

As in *Fedra*, there is another sense in which the fusion, transcendence, and creation of a new order takes place, and that is through poetry, through the aestheticizing of Mila's tragic sacrifice. Here, however, there is no persona of the poet to render Mila "unforgettable." Still, it is again only through the "Medusan" art of the poetic word that the conflicting dramatic worlds *are* bound and fused into a ritual capturing, or so it seemed to audiences, of the primitive soul of the Italian people. Through the poetry of sacrifice, it is suggested, a new social order, founded on the spiritual and the tragic, might be born.

La Figlia di Iorio opened March 2, 1904, at the Teatro Lirico in Milan. It caused more of a sensation and aroused more enthusiasm than any of D'Annunzio's earlier plays. The Florentine reviews of the nationalist right—*Leonardo, Hermes, Il Regno,* and *Il Marzocco*—seemed to concur that D'Annunzio had succeeded not only in overcoming the all too prevalent

---

[57] Paolo Puppa, *La Parola alta: Sul teatro di Pirandello e D'Annunzio* (Rome: Laterza, 1993), 124–26. Lynn Gunzberg, on the other hand, sees the masses who taunt and finally sacrifice Mila as a symbol of "the despised parliamentary democracy, the so-called 'bestia elettiva'" (*La Figlia di Iorio,* 235). Since the chorus acts as a unanimous mass, rather than as a debating and legalistic body, Puppa's argument seems more convincing.

bourgeois (and foreign) drama but also in restoring vitality through collective consciousness, thus writing the national tragedy of Italy. Mario Maffi, writing in *Il Regno* on March 6, points out the blending of elements from Greek tragedy (Mila resembles Antigone) and Christian sacred drama. The tragedy represents the first step toward "the conquest of a national theater, to be the highest and most vast expression of our italic soul."

Writing in November 1911 in *Il Mattino*, D'Annunzio's friend Edoardo Scarfoglio muses on the contrasts between the political scene around him and the poetic tragedy which D'Annunzio had just read to him and Michetti. Whereas in the present government he sees "marionettes," endless talk, and superficial laws that have no effect on the true Italy, *La Figlia di Iorio* reveals the treasures of this true, eternal unknown nation that can never be governed by the present system. (One is reminded of Charles Péguy's contrast between *mystique* and *politique* as well as Maurice Barrès's search for *énergie nationale*.) Thus D'Annunzio's tragedy is "a more important political work than the formation of a ministry."[58]

In May 1922, *La Figlia di Iorio* was revived at the outdoor Roman theater in Fiesole with much success. The most important outdoor revival, however, was the first production to take place under the auspices of the newly founded government organization devoted solely to the staging of D'Annunzio's plays, L'Istituto nazionale per la rappresentazione dei drammi di Gabriele D'Annunzio, whose artistic director was Giovacchino Forzano (see Chapter 1). Much touted by fascist officials and litterati, the September 1927 performance, directed by Forzano, made use of almost all the outdoor spaces at D'Annunzio's estate, Il Vittoriale. The ecstasies of the reviewers in the fascist press know almost no bounds. Mario Maria Martini, writing in the Genovese journal *Caffaro* on September 13, 1927, contrasts the 1904 with the 1927 production. In the Italy of Umberto I, the Italian public was "spiritually limited" by a "nonwarlike, nearsighted, and petty society" represented on stage by tired romantic and realist plays. It was thus unprepared for the exceptional literary-theatrical phenomenon brought before it by D'Annunzio. And yet the play "won a memorable battle for the poetic theater. . . . Suddenly, the audience found itself before a lyric evocation, expression of a nation. . . . A whole mediocre mentality suddenly fell . . . the deaf and blind spirit . . . reflourished in an unexpected spring, in a renewing and persuasive religiosity. . . . The Tragedy of the People was reborn." In Mussolini's Italy of 1927, by contrast, the public was spiritually prepared so that a true mass theater could be realized with a huge, "enraptured" audience. Forzano's direction made the tragedy current and "vital." Renato Simoni, writing in *Il Corriere della Sera*, notes that in the outdoor setting, without the walls of a theater, the audience was "transformed

[58] Edoardo Scarfoglio, "Durante la crisi," in Granatella, *Arrestate l'autore*, 1: 471.

in poetry, by poetry" and that D'Annunzio's poetic voice seemed "the voice of an entire people," an expression of true "italianità." In the outdoor production, the poetic tragedy and its "religious spirit" acquired a "transforming aura" that no theater could have given it.[59] Clearly the D'Annunzio-Forzano production of *La Figlia di Iorio* seems to have at least come close to fulfilling the expectations of Mussolini's Italy for a national tragedy.

The October 1934 production, although in a closed theater (the Argentina in Rome), evoked comments recalling the rapture of the 1927 spectators, and if anything more political in their overtones. This was the play that Pirandello chose to direct for the Volta conference, with costumes and sets by Giorgio de Chirico, featuring Marta Abba and Ruggero Ruggeri. Nearly all the reviews played up the "artistic fraternity" (a phrase Pirandello had used in a letter to D'Annunzio) between the two old rivals and cited Pirandello's attempt to respect the play's atmosphere of "primitive religiosity." *Regime fascista* (October 12, 1934) describes "that spontaneous impetus which reaches from the purest voice of heroic tragedy and succeeds in creating the living atmosphere of modern tragedy." *La Cirenaica* (October 14, 1934) recalls how the play seemed an important "political act" in the badly governed Italy of 1911, while praising its actuality and its "tragic furor." *Scenario* (November 1934, p. 589) comments on Pirandello's "spiritual fidelity" to the text and the "cry of purification" accompanied by the sacrifice.

All of the reviewers give much attention to the presence of Mussolini and several cabinet members at the performance. Silvio D'Amico, writing in *La Tribuna* on October 13, 1934, speaks of "two spectacles": one taking place when Il Duce, in his box, received a clamorous standing ovation between the second and third acts, and the second, also widely applauded, Pirandello's success in remaining "spiritually faithful" to D'Annunzio's text. The coming together of the political and the poetic spectacles and of the two rival dramatists with Mussolini thus reaffirmed the sense of fulfillment of the long-desired national modern tragedy already present in the 1927 production of *La Figlia di Iorio*. Only one other production of a modern tragedy throughout the *ventennio*—that of *La Nave* in 1938—was to receive such acclaim.

These three examples of what I have called D'Annunzio's "myth" tragedies each take a different and original approach to the problem of the recuperation of ancient tragedy for modernity and to the application of Nietzschean theory to poetic creation. *La Città morta* presents a palimpsest of antiquity and modernity caught in a tragic net that abolishes "the error of time"; *Fedra* rewrites the Greek tragic myth, thickening it with

---

[59] Renato Simoni, "La Figlia di Jorio al Vittoriale," September 12, 1927, in Granatella, *Arrestate l'autore*, 1: 478.

Gabriele D'Annunzio, *La Figlia di Iorio* at the Teatro Argentina in Rome, October 10, 1934, directed by Luigi Pirandello, scenery and costumes by Giorgio De Chirico. Marta Abba as Mila di Codro, Ruggero Ruggeri as Aligi, chrous of women with baskets. From the Burcardo Library, Rome, Italy.

both modern and preclassical intertexts; *La Figlia di Iorio* retains only the schema of classical tragedy to explore through syncretic pagan-Christian ritual the depths of *italianità*. Yet they have important characteristics in common. All three reach tragic resolution through the sacrifice of a woman whose erotic power has in some way disrupted an established order. Although a woman, in all three plays, is the major and the most "unforget-table" character (Anna for the first, the title character for the others), she is not, I would argue, a tragic hero. She represents rather a "Medusan" figure possessing Dionysian energies, a diverse and almost natural creature standing to some extent outside of the human community. Even the sweet, virginal Bianca Maria contains powers, potentially either beneficial or horrible, of which she is unaware, while Anna, like Fedra, appears overcome by desire to possess the virgin.

Tragedy in these plays—consistent with D'Annunzio's theories—exists not in an act of heroic sacrifice in pursuit of an ideal (even Mila's almost sentimental gesture of love is not heroic) but rather in the ritual killing of a victim chosen to purify and exalt the community. The sacrifice becomes the staged equivalent of Stelio's metaphorical decapitation of the Medusa:

the bloody severed head is aestheticized through the poetry in which it is presented to the crowd. In each case, the creation of a modern tragic hero through the act of female sacrifice seems possible but does not quite occur. The bonding of the poet and archaeologist is undercut by the presence of Anna; Hippolytus does not rise to the new imperial challenge; Aligi, having killed the old order, does not seem capable of creating the new. One possible reading of this failure is societal: conditions in early twentieth-century Italy did not permit the portrayal of the leader who was nonetheless understood to be on his way. Another is more personal: could D'Annunzio create a character more heroic than he was himself? Spiritual communion made possible by the new tragedy, as he envisioned it, was not to be between the actor/character and the audience but between poet and crowd.

Tragedy as Historical Extravaganza on *The Ship*

La Nave (*The Ship*) is unique in D'Annunzio's theater. A huge multimedia spectacle, it comes closer to realizing the poet's ideal of a Latin total theater than any of his other dramatic works. With a cast of hundreds, including several choirs, instrumental music (by Ildebrando Pizzetti in the original production), dancing, exotic and extravagant costumes, and most notably expensive stage sets that include the principal buildings of Byzantine Venice as well as the entire titular ship, a production might give the impression that here the poet had allowed the word to cede to the Dionysian and spectacular effects of music, dance, and visual splendor. Yet a reading of the text affirms that this is far from the case. With its dense poetry, including unusual rhyming and rhythmic effects, its use of rhetoric, its chants in medieval Latin, its technical naval and archaic lexicon, *La Nave* is in fact the most linguistically rich text in all D'Annunzio's theater. This is only one of the apparent contradictions in this highly unusual play. It presents itself as a "historical" drama, but it is far richer in fantasy than in fact. It claims to be a tragedy (the final stage directions, in Latin, read, "Explicit tragoedia adriaca") without classical conventions, with "episodes" rather than acts, and it is almost as full of sex and violence as a modern movie. It is also at once a typically fin-de-siècle decadent piece, complete with sensuous perfumes, colors, sounds, and a Salomé figure; a futurist happening designed to shock the audience;[60] and a modern mass spectacle easily adapted to the 1938 fascist production. It is arguably the work in which the peculiarly D'Annunzian fusion of aesthetics and politics is most perfectly achieved.

[60] Charles Klopp, in "Form and Foam in D'Annunzio's 'La Nave,'" *Esperienze: letterarie* 14, no. 1 (1989): 36, makes the comparison between D'Annunzian "incantation" and the futurist aesthetic.

The plot has features that are both tragic and epic. The setting is a Venetian island in the year 552, and the subject is the celebration of the birth of an autonomous and imperial Venice, struggling to free itself from Byzantium in the south and the barbarians in the north, to ally itself with the destiny of ancient Rome and proceed to the conquest of the seas.[61] The ship that dominates the scene and is launched at the end of the play stands for the achievement of Venetian independence, strength, and imperial destiny but also, clearly, for D'Annunzio's contemporary hopes for an imperial Italy and its growing naval power. A prologue introduces the two rival families contending for power in Venice, the Faledros and the Graticos, each represented by a chorus as well as by principals. Accused of "fornicating" with the Greeks,[62] in effect of treachery, Orso Faledro and his sons have been blinded with a red-hot sword and the sons' tongues removed, by the Gratico faction. Two ships arrive: one brings back the Gratico brothers, Sergio and Marco, from a naval expedition, and the other bears "the siren" Basiliola, the Faledro daughter determined to carry out vengeance for the mutilation of her father and brothers. The play's final scene is foreshadowed as workers and sailors repeat that their country (*la patria*) will be constructed on the ship (160, 168). Sergio is "elected" bishop and Marco tribune by the people, but *eletto* here signifies chosen by unanimous popular acclaim and not, as in "La Bestia elettiva," voted by democratic process. Marco, who carries on an incantatory call-and-response dialogue with a reverent and enthusiastic *popolo*, pronounces for the first time a refrain that will be repeated throughout the play: "Arma la prora e salpa verso il Mondo" ("Arm the prow and set sail toward the world")—a line that seems to fulfill the last verse of the "prayer" that precedes the prologue, "Fa di tutti gli Ocèani il Mare Nostro!" ("From all the Oceans make Our Sea!"). Basiliola makes her first appearance as the treacherous temptress; pretending to submit herself to the Gratico brothers and their widowed mother the deaconess, she performs a "victory dance" for the "elected" tribune. The mother alone seems to understand the danger she poses.

By the opening of the first "episode," Basiliola and Marco have become lovers, and power lies in the hands of the woman. In a scene exuding not only eroticism and violence but also sadomasochism, "La Faledra," as she is called, kills a group of imprisoned Gratico supporters who participated in the violence against her family as they beg for the arrows she shoots as

[61] Richard Drake's *Byzantium for Rome: The Politics of Nostalgia in Umbertian Italy, 1878–1900* (Chapel Hill: University of North Carolina Press, 1980) demonstrates the symbolic value of Byzantium and Rome—the former representing decadence and effeminacy and the latter representing virile strength and conquest—in fin-de-siècle Italy.

[62] D'Annunzio, *Tutto il teatro*, 2: 162.

if they were kisses. At the end of the orgiastic massacre, a voice cries out, "Sancta Venus, vicisti." At this point the monk Traba, emissary of the deaconess, arrives on the scene to denounce the actions of "Jezebel," whom he accuses of being a pagan. Marco, under her spell, accompanies the monk, whom Basiliola further shocks by performing a striptease, baring her breasts. Repeating to Marco his own words, "Arma la prora e salpa verso il Mondo" (211), Basiliola suggests that, together, they can rule in the Orient. The extent of Marco's confusion is evident in his final words to her: "God has left me. . . . the Idol is more powerful, since you have conquered me. . . . Do you love me? Do you hate me? . . . But your kiss, whether it be of love or of hate, is worth the World" (213).

In the second episode, Basiliola, still in pursuit of vengeance, fully reveals her pagan allegiances as she is acclaimed by a group of participants at an orgiastic feast as the goddess Dione, a feast in which the bishop Sergio Gratico, also her lover, participates. The choral group of pagan feasters is opposed by another composed of zealous Christians who condemn the "contaminated" temptress. By performing another erotic dance, Basiliola succeeds in provoking a duel between the two Gratico brothers, aroused both by sexual jealousy and by rivalry for power. Basiliola tries to help Sergio by covering Marco's eyes with a cape, but Marco kills his brother and the people's rage turns against the "Greek woman," "the enemy," as they proclaim the victory of both Christ and "the prince of the sea" (246). Marco, apparently cured of his enthrallment, orders that La Faledra be tied and bound to an altar and calls for the people to be at arms and on shipboard (247).

The third and final episode begins with the appearance of the great ship named *Totus Mundus*, prepared to set sail in the Adriatic. The deaconess returns, acclaimed by the people as the prophetess Deborah, revealing the future City of light and gold (254). Marco promises to lead them in founding the promised city but recognizes that he must first purify himself of the sin of fratricide. His sea voyage to Egypt on the *Totus Mundus* (which can be translated as "all pure" as well as "the whole world") will serve both as a personal baptism and as the inauguration of Venice's imperial conquests. But Basiliola, reminding Marco that she is his worthy enemy, pleads with him for a worthy death ("la bella morte"). He decides to tie her to the prow of the ship as a living Victory figure, but she frees herself and leaps into the "expiatory fire" on the sailors' altar, declaring that she will have only the death she chooses for herself (265). As her flame-colored hair catches fire, the united choruses of all the people praise God for the expiating sacrifice and conclude the play with incantatory lines including "La patria è su la Nave! Alleluia!" . . . "O Lord, bless the Ship! God of the strong, bless the Ship! . . . Our Lord, redeem the Adriatic! Free the Adriatic to your people!" (267).

There is no question that Basiliola, D'Annunzio's most powerful dramatic "superfemmina," is the most "unforgettable" character of the play. But is she, as Luisetta Elia Chomel argues, the protagonist and the tragic heroine?[63] In a sense, she seems hardly a character in the conventional sense at all but rather a centripetal force collecting layered identities. In the course of the drama, she becomes more and more identified as "foreign" until, like Mila, she is transformed into the exemplary other, the expiatory victim whose immolation will reintegrate and purify the community. The names by which she is called are many and varied: she is an animal ("leonessa," "lonza," "belva," "serpente"); various incarnations of witch, seductress, whore, or excessively libidinous (in one speech, the monk Traba equates her with Hecate, Circe, Mirra, Pasiphae, Delilah, Jezebel, and other more esoteric figures [204–5]); and she is "la grecastra," the "Greekish" woman whose very name, containing "Basil," the Byzantine monarch, identifies her with the foreign dominating power impeding the autarkic state that Venice, synecdoche for Italy, is struggling to become.

In this play "Greece" does not carry the archaic-classical semantic connotations identifying it with true Italian tradition as in *The Dead City* and *Fedra* but rather those of an "orientalizing" opposition. And Basiliola is nothing if not "oriental," with all the connotations of the period. Her jewels, perfumes, scarves, extravagant clothing, the seductions of her exotic dancing and outrageous libido, and her "impurity" identify her with Western constructions of the feminized Orient. But this daughter of a leading family is no conventional harem slave: her familial and political loyalty as well as her strength of will ally her with figures such as Cleopatra, Zenobia, Dido, Bérénice—the entire tradition of "oriental" princesses entangled erotically and politically with an occidental ruler. She has "impurely" mingled with other races ("yellow" Huns and black Moors are mentioned), and she has reverted from Christianity to paganism. Her most important avatar is that of the goddess Dione: the frenzied chorus at the banquet, worshiping her, repeats the refrain "Omnes trahit Diona" (221). A rather obscure figure in the Greek pantheon, Dione (in English) in one version of the myth was the mother of Aphrodite by Zeus. Yet the chorus also sings that she was generated in the sea (224) as in the more prevalent story of the birth of Aphrodite. Possibly, as with Phaedra and Pasiphae, D'Annunzio has deliberately conflated mother and daughter, making his Basiliola both the embodiment of female eroticism and its mother. Certainly, as Charles Klopp shows, Basiliola belongs with "foam," not only the sea but all the bodily and earthly fluids constituting a primordial formlessness that must be dominated by the masculine "form" represented by the ship if the nation is to be saved from chaos and pursue its destiny to colonize, rather than to be

---

[63] Chomel, *D'Annunzio*, 148–61.

ruled by, the Orient.[64] In the most daring simile of the play, the chorus of Christians, identifying female fluidity with evil, declares her to be "filthy as a rag of menstrual blood" (222).

Although, as in the tradition of woman-as-whore, she is sterile, Basiola in some ways suggests the phallic mother. An Amazonian sharpshooter, she never misses the prisoners who beg for her blows. Throughout her erotic dance, she brandishes the "nude sword" that she carries at her side (223–25)—another sign of the "virile vulva" possessed by D'Annunzio's superwomen. Basiliola's humiliation of Marco (among other things, she makes him give her his royal purple mantle) suggests the possibility of castration: as Sergio says, "The sword of the female frightens him" (240). It is in fact only after he has fought his brother, brandishing a sword himself, that Marco's subservience to the woman ends. But Basiliola is also another incarnation of the Dionysian woman, not only dangerous but also necessary to the hero. The beauty of her voice (185), her songs and dances, in addition to her considerable erotic power, ally her with the cult of Dionysus. (D'Annunzio may even have chosen the name "Diona" for its phonic proximity to Dionysus.) She speaks some of the richest poetic lines, resonant with alliteration and assonance, for example: "Laggiù, di là dai lidi, il primo/groppo del nembo strappa dalle labbra/anelanti del mare un'acre bava" (194). The incantatory seductions of poetry are hers. Furthermore, this Amazon-princess-goddess-whore does demonstrate some characteristics of a tragic heroine. In a stage direction, D'Annunzio intends her attitude to be that of someone who puts herself "body to body with destiny" (223). She pursues the revenge for the outrage to her father and brothers with the stubbornness of an Antigone. Her final speeches, in which she recognizes her defeat but offers herself as sacrifice, show her to be a "worthy enemy" and a "warrior," as she calls herself, to the end. Although as antagonist she tries to destroy the hero, as Dionysian woman she also energizes him, contributing to the triumph of the finale. "Venice," in Luigi Russo's words, "was fecundated in the vagina of Basiliola."[65]

Yet this is not Basiliola's tragedy. It is not she who represents the city and the principles destined to be victorious; rather, she is their adversary as well as a primal force threatening to enact their dissolution. More than *The Dead City* and indeed more than all his subsequent tragedies, *The Ship* works out tragedy as "the victory of man," fulfilling the ideas outlined in *The Flame* on modern, as opposed to ancient, tragedy as the defeat of ancient destiny. For Basiliola, to be sure, is also Medusa and Marco Gratico a somewhat slow

---

[64] Klopp, "Form and Foam," 31–43.

[65] Luigi Russo, "Il teatro dannunziano e la politica," in *Il tramonto del letterato* (Bari: Laterza, 1960), 447 (essay from 1938).

Perseus initially captured by her gaze but able to free himself and his city at last. But can Marco be called a heroic figure? As almost all commentators have noted, there is something not quite right about him; as a character he lacks depth and interest. In a sense, however, there are no real characters in this play, only figures, and D'Annunzio has created a far more interesting figure in Basiliola. Then too, Marco, because of his long submission to Basiliola, has few lines for much of the play. What is important about Marco is his ability to speak in dialogue with the crowd in a discourse that combines rhetoric with poetry. We see this already in his first speech to "il popolo" in the prologue: "O people of the new nation, do not hear / me. . . . Hear the floods / of spring, the fullness that roars / and blocks the ports. . . . / . . . the thunder of the great / waters that grows as shadows grow. / O people whose land the rivers ravage, / hear this thunder without terror / . . . because God will send over you / days that were never seen, / not of dissolution but of empire" (182). Thus Venetians must not fear the fluidity that surrounds and threatens to engulf them but rather dominate and harness its strength to fulfill their imperial destiny. Marco goes on to promise them youth, liberty, and continuity with the traditions of Rome, emphasizing the three through rhetorical repetition and ending with the thematic refrain, "Arm the prow and set sail toward the World." To which "the people" respond: "The World! The World! Arm the great ship! Call it The Whole World! *Totus Mundus!*" (183). They then promise to follow the commands of their leader, "prince of the seas" (184).

This is no oriental despot giving orders, nor a republican following the interests of the voters, but rather a new type of leader, in harmonious dialogue with a unified *vox popoli*, interpreting its wishes, building its consensus through the power of words. Yet during most of the play, this leader is almost absent, overpowered by the Amazonian seductress. Such a dialogue does not occur again until the conflict arises between the Gratico brothers at the end of the second episode. Sergio is ready with his sword; Marco does not want to fight "the mutilated one" (Sergio has no thumb); he requests that a judgment be made. Since the people, speaking as if with one voice, call for a duel, not a judgment, Marco, in killing his brother, follows their collective wish for violence rather than debate. The collectivity in turn declares, "Victory to the Prince of the Sea!" "roaring" against "the enemy," Basiliola (246). By the end of the third episode, the true mother—Marco's mother the deaconess—has returned to replace the potential castrator. Marco, it would seem, has succeeded in decapitating his Medusa by killing "the mutilated one" and vanquishing the seductress-enemy. His virility and his command over the people regained, he is prepared both for his personal voyage of purification (to become *totus mundus*) and for his mission, with his sailors, to impose naval "form" on the "foam." Headed toward "the

Orient," the ship has become the synecdoche for an Italian civilization inherited from imperial Rome on its colonizing mission.

The true hero of this tragedy-extravaganza is neither Basiliola nor Marco
but the huge chorus, which, musically and visually in production but also
in language, has the overwhelming, dithyrambic role. Composed of groups
of workers representing various medieval "corporations" such as sailors,
shipbuilders, musicians, and stonecutters, the chorus speaks in one voice
as "il popolo" in the prologue, in dialogue, as seen above, with Marco
Gratico. In the central part of the play, however, the chorus loses its unanimity. In the first episode, it is represented only by the prisoners, reveling
in Basiola's arrows; in the second, while Marco is still under the spell of
Basiliola, it becomes antiphonal, representing the quarreling factions of
zealous Christians and pagan feasters, worshipers of Dione. Tumult among
the factions ensues (234–35). Yet the "popolo" speaks again with one voice
in persuading Marco to fight his brother and after the demise of Basiliola
becomes once again "tutto il popolo," turned against "the enemy" and in
unison with its leader. In a symbiotic relationship, the leader's power comes
from the people and the leader commands and guides the people united
in consensus.

What unites the people finally is clearly no rational ideology but a new,
ecstatic fusion of religious, political, and Nietzschean ideals. The choir now
sings of politics in liturgical form and vocabulary: "Hosannah! Hosannah!—
The future City!—The City of gold!—The City of light!—To the Orient! To
the Orient!" (254). Yet the people have not forgotten their Dionysian allegiances: at the sight of the flaming Basiliola, they chant, "Dione burns! . . .
The sacrifice is consumed!" (267). She is still Dione—the Dionysian energies are not negated but incorporated through the sacrifice. If this cry is
followed by "Praise God! Christ is victorious! (267), this is a militant Christ,
the Christ of the crusades, and a "God of the strong" (267). One could almost speak of an oxymoronic Nietzschean Christianity, a triumphant
"Mediterranean" religion stripped of piety, beyond good and evil. Is not
this ecstatically fused onstage crowd also a synecdoche for the audiences,
in theaters and piazzas, that the poet-politician wanted to reach, to enthrall
through the power of the word? If Marco Gratico, like D'Annunzio's other
male characters, does not rise to heroic stature, it is because he is in the
end only a medium: the true dialogue is once again between the tragic poet
and the crowd.

La Nave was both a huge theatrical success and a political event when it
was staged at the Argentina Theater in Rome in January 1908, though it
shocked Catholic critics. As Austrian ships menaced the Adriatic and Italy
seemed on the verge of a new age of heroic imperialism in the Mediterranean, the ecstatic call for mastery of the seas resonated with the audiences who packed the theater, while the critics spoke of the arrival of a new

national modern tragedy.[66] Because of the difficulties involved in staging and because of the objections of the church to its licentious aspects, it was not mounted again until thirty years later. Then it received the production which D'Annunzio had said he wanted: an outdoor spectacle with a chorus of five hundred and a real ship on the island of Sant'Elena in Venice itself. D'Annunzio having died just a few months previously, the occasion became among other things a hagiographical commemoration of the National Bard. The minister of popular culture, Dino Alfieri, pronounced a eulogy, informing the spectators that the production was made possible by "the will of the regime." The audience was estimated at four thousand and included royalty, dignitaries from the fascist hierarchy, and trainloads of ordinary people brought up for the occasion. As Paolo Puppa argues, the spectacle bore all the signs of the prototypical fascist festival, "la grande Festa del popolo."[67] Much of the text could indeed be made to seem prophetic of contemporary events and sensibilities. The ecstatic chorus of workers, from different "corporations" but fused into one classless mass in dialogue with their leader, must have appeared not unlike ideology and aesthetics in another Venezia, the piazza in Rome. The disciplined, consensual, inspired crowd resembles, as Puppa points out, fascism's ideal *polis*.[68] The links to Venice's foundations in the Roman Empire, along with its destiny to rule the seas and to colonize, were still in line with Mussolini's vision of Italy's history and future in 1938.

The reviewers in the fascist press on the whole waxed ecstatic over the production.[69] Given the official and commemorative nature of the event, they could hardly do otherwise, but what they have to say about both text and performance reveals much about fascist reception of D'Annunzio. Many of the reviewers recall the political and artistic significance of the 1908 performance, which not only struck another blow to the bourgeois theater and put forth a new vision of modern tragedy but also helped to arm prewar Italians with a vision of their destiny. In their view, however, the audience of Mussolini's Italy is much better prepared to understand that imperial vision than was the audience under a government "in slippers." There is general agreement that the tragedy was "prophetic": that the poet had intuited the shaping of the Italian people into a great nation, the revival of the glory of ancient Rome, and the reclaiming of the

[66] See Valentini, *La Tragedia moderna*, 278, and Puppa, *La Parola alta*, 159–61.

[67] Puppa, *La Parola alta*, 158. The entire chapter, titled "'La Nave' a Venezia" (155–72), discusses the 1938 production.

[68] Ibid., 168.

[69] The summary here is taken from press reviews in the following journals, all published September 3, 1938, unless otherwise noted: *Il Piccolo di Trieste*, *La Gazzetta di Venezia*, *La Nazione* (Florence); *Il Messaggero* (Rome); *Il Polesine Fascista* (Rovigo, preview), September 1, 1938; *Scenario* 7, no. 9 (September 1938): 474–75. The clippings can all be found in the Vittoriale archives.

Gabriele D'Annunzio, *La Nave,* directed by G. Salvini, produced in Venice, Campo Sant'Elena, September 1, 1938. View of ship and church with entire cast. From the Burcardo Library, Rome, Italy.

Gabriele D'Annunzio, *La Nave,* directed by G. Salvini, produced in Venice, Campo Sant'Elena, September 1, 1938. Adami as Basiola, R. Riccii as Marco. From the Burcardo Library, Rome, Italy.

empire that were taking place under Mussolini. The play is described as a kind of ritual, a celebration of the glorious past and future of Italy. The tragedy consists of the struggle of the virile, Roman spirit against the corruption, seductions, and chaos of the Orient. Tragedy belongs to the heroic West; magnificence and (corrupt) splendor to the East; virile form is to be imposed upon feminine chaos. D'Annunzio's poetry is also praised as an important factor in the production's success. Its musical, incantatory qualities "inflamed" the audience, "elevating" it to an understanding of the tragedy. Nor did the reviewers fail to point out the qualities that made the spectacle a festival of the people. The chorus effectively portrayed the multitude shaping itself into a "popolo" or nation, and the audience, in its enthusiastic reception, reflected this same popular unanimity.

While it is evident that the writers in the fascist press simplified interpretation of the drama for propagandistic purposes, it is also true that the text could and did lend itself well to this sort of spectacle; that on some level it was "prophetic." Whether or not D'Annunzio would have approved of this use of his "Adriatic tragedy" is another story. It is true that he ardently desired an outdoor production in Venice and had no more objection to the regime's help with it than he did to the Vittoriale production of *La Figlia di Jorio*. Yet he certainly had no desire to be reduced to the role of prophet of Mussolini's Italy. Il Vate did not want to be upstaged by anyone; especially not by Il Duce.

The revival of ancient mythology for modernity, the discovery of an Italic Dionysus in Abruzzo, and the adaptation of a historical period to an atemporal theatrical and poetic extravaganza represent divergent but related strategies by D'Annunzio to abandon the contemporary settings and language of the bourgeois theater and to create a modern poetic tragedy in the wake of Nietzsche. In other experiments with modern tragedy, however, such as *La Gioconda*, *La Gloria*, and *Più che l'amore*, he makes use of the contemporary setting and some of the conventions of bourgeois and naturalist theater and, although he never reverts to a naturalistic imitation of everyday discourse, he writes in prose. The latter two, D'Annunzio's "political tragedies," will interest us here.

Glory, Tragedy, and Politics

La Gloria, written and first produced in 1899, is in spite of the difference in genre and style in many ways a precursor of *La Nave*. Its opening was, however, a resounding fiasco: not until its revival in 1928, when it was, like the spectacle ten years later, received by the fascist public as "prophetic," did it achieve any success. Part of its fame came perhaps from the fact that

Mussolini purchased a manuscript of *La Gloria* in September 1924[70] and that he adopted as a slogan the line of the female lead: "Chi s'arresta è perduto" ("Whover stops is lost"). The 1928 production, like that of *La Figlia di Jorio* a year earlier, was sponsored by the National Institute for the Performance of Plays by Gabriele D'Annunzio.

While some commentators have seen in this "political" play a kind of *pièce à clef* on turn-of-the-century Italian politics, in particular the rivalry between the statesman Francesco Crispi and his rival Felice Cavallotti, there is little in the text to suggest reference to such a particular situation. What interests D'Annunzio here, more than the immediate politics of Italy, are questions of political theory and political vision, especially the aesthetics of politics. It is true that the play is concerned with contemporary issues in that it reflects, as usual, D'Annunzio's disdain for an Italy weakened by bourgeois parliamentary democracy and his quest for a reawakening of a heroic vision for an imperial Italy. In this case, however, the democrats do not even appear; the struggle for power is between two dictators in Rome: the elderly Cesare Bronte, a conservative, and the young Ruggero Flamma, a revolutionary. Since Flamma began as a socialist, has the rhetorical gifts to dominate crowds, and does not hesitate to use violence as a way of maintaining dictatorial control and advancing his program, it is not surprising that later viewers and readers of the play saw in him a prefiguration of their *duce.* Yet Flamma dies defeated, an outcome that could again be attributed to the notion that liberal "Italietta" was not yet prepared for the hero who would lead it to its true destiny.

In this tragedy even more than in the others, the central figure, the one who wields power and controls the dramatic action, is a woman. Elena Comnèna, called the "Byzantine princess" and the "Empress of Trebizon," is married to the old Bronte but attracted to the young Flamma's rising power. Taking matters into her own hands, in collaboration with her equally Byzantine mother, she poisons her husband and offers herself as well as her political advice to the new leader. Desperate to keep control of the crowd, and more and more in submission to la Comnèna, Flamma comes to rely on violence, becoming a ruthless tyrant. A popular revolt ensues, and a fervent young man comes to try to assassinate Flamma but, overcome by his guard, departs, leaving his knife. Flamma, who confesses that he almost welcomed the assassination, makes a gift of the weapon to his mistress, begging her to kill him. When Elena sees that he no longer has the courage to try to recapture the crowd through his oratory, she stabs him, ready to give herself to the rising young popular hero Claudio Messala.

---

[70] Alatri, *Gabriele D'Annunzio,* 525.

Rather than transmitting a clear ideological statement, as seems evident to some, the text portrays the conflict of a variety of forces, interweaving politics, psychology, erotics, and aesthetics. The old Cesare Bronte, as in *Le Vergini delle rocce*, embodies an aristocracy of a certain grandeur but no longer able to cope with the demands of the rise of mass politics. *La folla* here, the Roman crowd, is a character in its own right, listed as one of the dramatis personae, speaking with a unanimous voice and making a major impact on the drama. Although the action takes place in closed rooms as in bourgeois dramas, there is always a balcony or open window that allows the voice of the crowd to be heard and the onstage characters to report its movements. The opening of the first act is dominated by the report of the mass so huge it turns the piazza "black"; its "clamor," its "popular fervor," and its "civic fever" (174). At other times, the mass appears to be less, or more, than human, "bellowing" like a "herd" (183), emitting an "oceanic roar" (190, 220).

Ruggero Flamma, at the height of his power, has the gift of intuiting the "soul of the *patria*" (180), the nationalistic and "Latin" fervor, the "occult energies" of "a whole race that is again struggling to exist" (184) within the masses, and of giving form to these forces through his power of speech. Yet as his friend the sculptor Sigismondo Leoni observes, he has not overcome his "physical horror" of crowds and needs to be physically above them in order to dominate them (180). He is thus in a sense caught in between the D'Annunzian protagonists of *Le Vergini delle rocce* and *Il Fuoco*: he no longer disdains the masses, but he has not yet experienced the erotic pleasure of being in dialogue with them, of "possessing" them. The harmonious possession of crowd, city, and woman discovered by Stelio Effrena is not to be his. Indeed, his tragedy lies in this failure to possess. Confronted by the most formidable of D'Annunzian Dionysian superwomen, Ruggero, as the sculptor again perceives, is himself "possessed" (182). He comes to the realization that whereas he should have had the strength to "fecundate" Rome (214), all his desire has been for the "sterile" Byzantine woman. He gradually loses his possession of the crowd and by the end of the play, it is the crowd that demands of Elena, as of Salome, his severed head.

Although Ruggero Flamma may be a "failed hero," as Elena calls him, his early political-aesthetic aspirations and his pursuit of "glory," not unlike his author's, reveal an intuition of the "new" politics fermenting in early twentieth-century Italy and which the fascists believed they had realized. In addition to his understanding of the patriotic and nationalistic desires of the crowd, Flamma, in his followers' eyes, shows "virile energy, masculine will," and the ability to reconstitute the "City, the *Patria*, the latin Force" (179). Before his transformation into a tyrant at the hands of Comnèna, his discourse on the necessity of violence appears in a positive light. "No work of life can be completed without blood on a people" (183); "the right to human sacrifice is necessary [for the truth of a people] to affirm itself" (185). The people require of him the invention of "a new force and a new law" (183). Everything, particularly the necessary Latin conquest of the seas, can be achieved through the exercise of "heroic will" (184–85). He even invents a refrain, chanted by his followers, "Everyone beyond his strength!" D'Annunzio's fascist admirers saw this speech in act 1 as particularly prophetic of Mussolini.[71] Other aspects of Flamma's program, including his emphasis on *Romanità* and on the importance of Festival (201), seem equally "prophetic."

Viewed as a tragic hero, this Nietzschean-D'Annunzian superman might seem to be guilty of hubris. But the nemesis he meets, in the form of Elena Comnèna, does not warn him of boundaries but on the contrary continues to urge him to go beyond. More goddesslike than woman, la Comnèna, with rather too obvious symbolism, wears on her breast no other jewel but a small head of Medusa, shining like a shield (186, 204). This might seem to relate her to Athena, to whom Perseus gave the Medusa's head to wear on her shield, but apart from her implacable strength, this lustful and outrageous princess has little in common with the chaste goddess of wisdom. Her appearances, however, turn out to be more important than her reality. Shortly before killing Ruggero, she tells him that the "Glory" he has been seeking resembles her. To which her prey responds: "Everything that is terrible and unknown resembles *your mask*" (223, emphasis added). The princess, it seems, wears more than one mask. She appears as Athena in *her* mask as mentor to a young hero; at other times she shows the face of the beloved. Like her successor Basiliola, she incorporates the mythological identities of such figures as Circe, Jezebel, and Delilah, devourers of men. She is also, of course, Medusa herself.

Freud could have used *La Gloria* to illustrate his theory of castration anxiety induced by the sight of Medusa. Just before la Comnèna takes away the knife, Ruggero Flamma confides to his friend Daniele that he has experienced the horror of feeling himself "turned to stone little by little by the face of the Gorgon" (215). At the end of the play, having lost the virile energy evidenced in his speech in act 1, he finds himself unable to kill his lover-enemy and trembles before the very idea of addressing the crowd. It is Elena who kills him with the knife she now possesses.

Erotics, in this tragedy perhaps even more than in D'Annunzio's others, are inseparable from politics. As Ruggero grows more desperate to possess Elena and the crowd, which he is losing, he resorts to violence and crime, swearing never to end until he "satisfies" her. "I will see you trembling with pleasure [*ti vedrò gioire tutta*], from your crown to your feet, in the palpitations of my war" (210). But Elena, of course, is insatiable. It is not Ruggero's

[71] See, for example, Pasini, *D'Annunzio*, 62–63.

hubris that brings about his downfall but rather the desperation in his "going beyond" that results in his becoming, fatally, "possessed."

"Who are you?" Ruggero asks Elena, desperate to understand before he dies. As if she were a Pirandellian character, an onion composed of a series of masks (she first appears wearing a thick veil), Elena does not, cannot, answer the question. One of her most important masks, however, is her ahistorical "Byzantine" identity. As her dying husband understands, centuries of perfidy, greed, vendetta, lust, and other vices live in her "deadly race" (195–96). She is deadly to Roman men as the ways of Byzantium threaten *Romanità*, as the seditious female threatens the virile male, as chaos and tyranny threaten order and the leader, another example of the "oriental" menace. It is not that her considerable erotic power is to be disdained or shunned. Rather, it is to be *possessed*, just as Dionysian force is to be possessed by the Apollonian word, woman by man, and the East is to be colonized by the West—not the other way around. The later hero Marco Gratico will be able to possess the Venetians' fascination with the Byzantine woman through her sacrifice; Ruggero Flamma is himself sacrificed.

The tragic conflict in *La Gloria* is not between two men (Bronte and Flamma never appear onstage together) and not even between a man and a woman but rather between a man and a superhuman, transhistorical, eternal force encountered in the "mask" of a woman. In Stelio Effrena's concept of modern tragedy, man would emerge victorious over the forces of ancient destiny. But in this play, even more than in the other two D'Annunzio called "les victoires mutilées" (*La Città morta* and *La Gioconda*), victory is indeed mutilated. Perseus encounters the Medusa but is undone—in effect castrated—by her. In historical terms, an Italy dominated by bourgeois ideals and a bourgeois government is itself mutilated, not yet ready to emerge victorious in the pursuit of its historic destiny. Although *La Gloria* is certainly not without its flaws, it has been unjustly dismissed either as a vehicle of propaganda or as an uninteresting realistic piece on contemporary politics. Instead, with its agon between human and eternal forces, it offers an original solution to the problem of modern tragedy as well as to the creation of a non-naturalistic drama within some of the conventions of the bourgeois stage.

Reviewers of the 1899 production, as might be expected, protested that the play was confusing and that it was impossible to understand what the author was trying to do. A French critic called "Enrico Bérenger" in *L'Illustrazione italiana*, claimed that it was unique in modern European literature in its poetic rendering of "the agitations of contemporary society."[72]

---

[72] Quoted in Granatella, *Arrestate l'autore*, 1: 263. Granatella reprints reviews from the 1899 and 1912 productions but none from the 1928 production.

The 1928 reviewers (and, from their reports, the audiences) were far more enthusiastic. Calling it a "political tragedy," they remark that the public of contemporary Italy is far better prepared to understand such a work than that of prewar Italy. Liberating itself conceptually as well as formally from the petty bourgeois mentality of the end of the last century, the modern tragedy contains a foreshadowing of concepts that would play a role in fascism's political and social reconstruction of Italy. In his antinaturalistic tragedy, D'Annunzio writes a "national" tragedy, proclaiming the right to violence in order to attain spiritual liberty. In bourgeois Italy, *La Gloria* was a cry for imperial Italy. In 1938, a commentator wrote: "It seems a prophecy of what will occur . . . when Italians have found their *Duce.*"[73] One must assume that this loyal fascist was not referring to the demise of the hero! Some reviewers seem to consider only the first act of the play. Others, however, blame Ruggero's downfall on that very society as yet unable to understand either the formal innovations or the political message of D'Annunzio's tragedy.

Più che l'amore (Beyond Love): The Tragedy of Modernity

Whereas *La Gloria*, although set in modern Rome, emphasizes the timeless nature of the conflicts and personalities involved, D'Annunzio's other "political tragedy" is set squarely in modernity. It therefore runs the risk of having to use some realist conventions while at the same time attempting to go beyond realism. Partly because of this confusion in genre—the audience interpreted the hero's crime rather too literally for D'Annunzio's intentions—and partly because of a mediocre production, the opening of *Più che l'amore*[74] in October 1906 was even more of a resounding failure than that of *La Gloria*. Apparently scandalized by the immorality or amorality of the hero's attitude toward the crime he commits, the crowd after the performance was said to have cried out, "Carabinieri, arrestate l'autore!" ("Police, arrest the author!").[75] Public outrage and (with important exceptions) critical panning induced the author to write a long defense of the play, later published as a preface, in which he also refines his thinking on the problematic nature of modern tragedy.

In this play even more than in others, D'Annunzio has fused together

[73] Reviews in the Vittoriale archives from *Il Popolo di Brescia, Il Resto del Carlino,* and unidentified journals. The last quotation is from Goffredo Bellonci, "Il Teatro di Gabriele D'Annunzio," *Scenario* 7, no. 4 (April 1938): 162–66.

[74] Literally translated, the title means "More than love" and refers to the superior importance Corrado grants to his dream of Africa, compared to his love for Maria. "Beyond Love" seems to me a better expression of this idea.

[75] Review by Domenico Oliva in *Il giornale d'Italia,* October 30, 1906, in Granatella (who takes the anecdote for her title *Arrestate l'autore!*), 2: 625.

an eclectic bundle. While much of the plot and the setting seem to come straight out of realist drama—sometimes even out of melodrama—the dense, often poetic language, the frequent narration, the use of symbolism, and the somewhat static nature of the action situate the play outside of realist conventions. Although the tragedy on the whole follows classical canons in time, place, and action, it is divided not into acts but into two "episodes." D'Annunzio also introduces three lyric interventions: a "symphonic" prelude, an intermezzo, and an exode, stating the poetic themes and evoking related mythological deities. The tragic destiny of antiquity, although less obviously than in *The Dead City*, also hangs over the characters living in modern Rome, in the Italy of Giolitti.

At the outset, we find Corrado Brando, an architect, telling his longtime friend the hydraulic engineer Virginio Vesta, of his desire to return to his explorations in Africa. Attempting to finance the enterprise, he gambled and lost. The idea of killing the winner, a grotesque old moneylender (*usuraio*), by using a specific Somalian method, crossed his mind. Virginio senses "something strange" in his friend. Virginio extracts from his sister Maria the confession that she is in love with Corrado; he tells her that Corrado intends to leave for Africa. Two friends, an architect and a doctor, arrive with the news that the usurer Paolo Sutri was robbed and killed and his nephew Simone,[76] whom the old man forced to live in poverty, has been arrested. Virginio is shaken by the news. After the men leave, Maria tells her brother that she has already "given herself entirely" to Corrado. In the language of the stage directions, "it seems that the face of the universe has suddenly changed for him [Virginio]."[77] The first episode ends as Maria tells her brother that she is carrying Corrado's child.

In the second episode, in Corrado's lodging, Maria shows herself worthy of a hero. Having learned that he is leaving for Africa, she tells her lover: "I am free, freely given: not a chain but a gift" (129). She does not cry or beg him to stay as would a sentimental dramatic heroine, yet the pathos of the lovers' separation rises to an intensity that makes it the most successful scene in the play. Left alone with his Sardinian servant, Rudu, Corrado evokes their former exploits and adventures together in Africa while preparing for his voyage but hesitates in deciding whether to go. Virginio arrives and Corrado at last confesses (in lurid detail) the crime he committed: it was he, as Virginio suspected, who killed the old usurer. The deed done, Corrado continues, "I don't know what wild delirium cried inside me, 'The new Erinyes!'" (144). Virginio, the faithful (pure, virginal) comrade, now sees Corrado's departure as his friend's opportunity to purify himself and offers his help. But Rudu reports that three policemen have

---

[76] Oliva calls the usurer and his son Davide and Stefano Cave (ibid., 627).

[77] D'Annunzio, *Tutto il teatro*, 2: 116.

come for Corrado. Corrado, in a deflated version of Aligi's and Mila's "la flamma è bella," exclaims, "E una bella sera" (146). As he makes Virginio leave and grabs a gun, we are left to believe that the hero and his faithful servant will shoot it out with the police until death.

Some similarities with *The Dead City* are evident. The brother-sister couple is again threatened by the love of the brother's best friend for the sister. Maria, like Bianca Maria, is associated with flowers, poetry, water, and purity, with the addition of music (she is a pianist). Although incestuous desire is not suggested explicitly, the brother adores his sister and cannot envisage life without her, his "purity," his "harmony." Virginio also resembles Marco Gratico in his domination of the force of water through technology and Alessandro in that he sees engineering as a kind of "poetry," recuperating Dionysian forces in Apollonian form (93–94). Corrado, tormented, almost mad, and obsessed by his overseas conquest and glory, more closely resembles the "artistic imperialist" Leonardo. There is even an archaeological motif in the play—one of the minor characters is working on excavations in Rome. The play's literary-mythological overlay, discussed at length in the preface, is more oblique than in *The Dead City* but present nonetheless. The first words of the prelude, from D'Annunzio's own poem "Laus Vitae," make clear the author's intentions: Corrado is a *Ulisside*, a descendant of Ulysses in his restless inability to stay home, his need to transcend limits, to push on toward knowledge and conquest. By the end of the play, however, he appears as a new Orestes, followed by the new Eumenides. In the preface, D'Annunzio also compares him to Sophocles' Ajax, evokes his "Promethean" qualities, and likens him to other tragic heroes driven to crime, such as Macbeth. Other intertexts are evident: Corrado is an offspring of Dostoevsky's Raskolnikov as well as of D'Annunzio's reading of the Nietzschean superman. Virginio, defining Corrado's "lucid madness," cites one of Mussolini's favorite sayings from Nietzsche: "Nothing is true: everything is permitted" (118).

In contrast to *The Dead City* and the other "myth" tragedies, however, the text of *Beyond Love* is not overwhelmed by intertextuality. In his tragedy of modernity, D'Annunzio seems to make a self-conscious attempt to rewrite the classical agon between hero and fate in the contemporary context. He may well have also been trying to rise to Morasso's challenge to create a tragic hero worthy of the dawning age of nationalist imperialism. Morasso's words, written in 1903, seem almost designed for Corrado Brando: "As the individual no longer recognizes boundaries to his will, so nations seek beyond their boundaries the universal domain of glorious empires."[78] Brando,

---

[78] Mario Morasso, *Imperialismo artistico* (Milan: Bocca, 1903).

however, is another tragic hero ahead of his time: the national will does not yet coincide with his individual one.

Because of his desire to modernize his tragedy, D'Annunzio paradoxically falls back into certain nineteenth-century dramatic conventions. An example of a melodramatic element that has little or nothing to do with the tragedy is Virginio's narrative on his and Maria's mother—we learn that she left her husband and children for another man and had a son with him whom Maria, in a "domestic angel" role, helps to care for. The seduction motif, and Virginio's reaction to it, is of course straight from melodrama, although it is interesting to see how the "superwoman" transcends the convention. The moneylender is described in almost Balzacian terms as a grotesque figure with a hanging lip, consumed with an evil passion for money, as is the squalor of modern Trastevere, evoked in the narrative of the crime. A la Balzac, even the hero's tragic downfall is essentially based on money. Squarotti points out the "irony of bourgeois reality" in Corrado's need for money in order to carry out his individualistic, heroic expedition.[79]

In other respects, D'Annunzio has left the nineteenth-century bourgeois world to move into the technological twentieth century. Thus the tools of the engineer's trade, complete with hydraulic models, are described in some detail in the stage directions opening the first episode and Corrado's collection of guns in those at the opening of the second. These modern tools are juxtaposed with nonmodern objects, thus effecting a fusion of modernity, tradition, and exoticism that transcends the otherwise realist setting. Virginio's room contains the "sublime images" of Dante, Leonardo da Vinci, Michelangelo, and Beethoven (92) and Corrado's has trophies of elephants along with utensils and arms from African tribes. The objects become more metaphorical than metonymical as the reader or spectator comes to understand that Virginio (a twentieth-century Faust?) hopes to fuse hydraulics with poetry in his striving toward a modern version of the sublime while Corrado intends to use his modern weapons to recover "primitive" energies. Together, in an ideal world, they could create an Apollonian/Dionysian ancient/modern technological/poetic synthesis.

The tragic conflict occurs in the clash between the urge toward a new, superhuman heroism and the mediocrity of the existing bourgeois world. Some critics, no doubt including the spectators who called for the arrest of the author, have seen in the play nothing more than the story of a sordid crime with pseudo-Nietzschean overtones.[80] Yet D'Annunzio's justification of his hero deserves attention. "In Corrado Brando, it is not crime that is glorified . . . but the efficacy and the dignity of crime conceived as

---

[79] Squarotti, *La Scrittura verso il nulla*, 257.
[80] See, for example, Oliva's review in Granatella, *Arrestate l'autore*, 2: 625–31.

Promethean virtue" (524). The logic of the committing of a crime lies in the desire to rise above the mediocrity of the rule of law as well as beyond good and evil. At the end, "The duty of the tragic hero is fulfilled. The most sacred instinct of life, of life to come, of life that perpetuates itself, is translated in the last gesture with religious grandeur" (524–25). D'Annunzio here seems to have in mind Nietzsche's notion that the tragic hero, like Dionysus, is immolated for our pleasure and thus participates in the eternal return. The "new Erinyes" Corrado calls for would thus be forces that not only allow him to expiate his crime through suffering but also joyfully to perpetuate life through his child. The superwoman ready to sacrifice anything for love, we may assume, will one day be elevated to the sublime role of mother of the hero.

Now it is true that the text does not quite bear the weight of this theoretical argument. Yet it does not simply represent the story of a sordid crime: bad acting and a mediocre production apparently contributed to the first spectators' desire to "arrest the author." What D'Annunzio seems to be attempting here is to write the tragic agon of heroic desire struggling against bourgeois mediocrity in the context of the *Italietta* of his day. Just three years previously he had published a modern epic, *Maia*, that celebrated as "Ulissidi" modern Italian explorers in Africa and the Near East, among them his journalist colleague Edoardo Scarfoglio.[81] In a series of articles Scarfoglio had praised Ferdinand de Lesseps, in his building of the Suez Canal, as a Homeric hero and gone on to advocate Italian colonialist intervention in Ethiopia. D'Annunzio takes up the Homeric motif by praising the revival of what he sees as the Homeric war ethos in the modern *Ulissidi*, "avid for conquest and for glory."[82] Although neither *Maia* nor *Beyond Love* should be read as vehicles for propaganda, central to both is the artistic imperialism advocated by Morasso and seen, in a different guise, in *Fedra*: the conviction that Italy will never renew itself without expanding beyond its borders paired with a "going beyond" in stylistic and aesthetic terms.

The question of whether *Beyond Love* should be read as an imperialist play has raised considerable controversy. Luigi Russo, in 1938, called it a tragedy that is "not poetry, but political action"[83] and a forerunner of Mussolini's colonialist policies. D'Annunzio himself corroborated this impression by writing in 1935 that in rereading *Più che l'amore* he thought, "What a stupendous work! It is the African tragedy of today!"[84] and by taking Corrado's

[81] See Becker, *Nationalism*, 77–87, for a discussion of Scarfoglio's influence on D'Annunzio and an interpretation of the imperialist agenda of *Maia*.

[82] Gabriele D'Annunzio, *Versi d'amore e di gloria*, ed. Niva Lorenzini (Milan: Mondadori, 1982), 2: 166, quoted in Becker, *Nationalism*, 84.

[83] Russo, "Il teatro dannunziano e la politica," 462.

[84] Letter to Gian Carlo Maroni, September 18, 1935, quoted by Andrea Bisicchia, *D'Annunzio e il teatro: Tra cronaca e letteratura drammatica* (Milan: Mursia, 1991), 124.

Latin line *teneo te, Africa* as the title of his book defending Mussolini's campaign in Abyssinia. For Paolo Alatri, the play presents a "manifesto of colonial intervention under the myth of Rome," an ideology that would become the foundation of fascist imperialism in Africa.[85] Antonucci, champion of the D'Annunzio revisionists, calls such commentators incapable of reading the text, claiming (along with the play's first spectators) that the so-called hero is simply a common criminal.[86] (One could, of course, raise the question of the political role of common criminality in the Italy of the 1930s.) Giovanna Tomasello makes the most interesting and convincing argument for the advocacy of imperialism in the tragedy. Drawing on D'Annunzio's poetry and rhetoric at Fiume as well as on *Più che l'amore*, she demonstrates how D'Annunzio clearly distanced himself from imperialist nations such as Great Britain, even going so far as to denounce British oppression in India, on the grounds that such colonization was the result of the base economic greed typical of an industrial bourgeois democracy. The Italian conquest of territories such as Libya, in contrast, represented for D'Annunzio not an invasion but rather a *recuperation* of a Latin Mediterranean unity broken by the medieval Islamic invasions. Thus "exotic" and "barbarian" Africa contains nonetheless a Roman or classical "beauty" that can be refound through an imperialistic archaeological and building project. Here we have an aesthetic ideal that would lend itself easily to the fascist propaganda regarding *mare nostrum*.[87]

If Corrado Brando were simply a common criminal, the play would be of no interest. Yet despite its defects, *Beyond Love* is a complex text that makes an important contribution to the search for modern tragedy. D'Annunzio criticism, here as elsewhere, tends to come down on the side of "politics" or the side of "poetry" viewed in strict binary terms. Like D'Annunzio's other modern tragedies, however, this play incorporates a fusion of aesthetics and politics. It is easy enough to find statements in the play linking Corrado's individualist adventures and exploits to a sense of Italy's mandate to revive the Roman empire and to a recuperation of classical beauty. In his own way, Virginio too participates in what we might call an aesthetization of action. Thus in the opening scene he tells Corrado that he feels in himself "a primitive sense of natural energies that made the soul of Greek statuary religious . . . That ancient sense becomes modern in me. . . . I feel my instinct tending toward the apparition of a new beauty . . . not for the ornamentation of the world but toward the conquest of the world" (94). Whereas Virginio's calling is to transform the city of Rome, Corrado's

---

[85] Alatri, *Gabriele D'Annunzio*, 257.

[86] Introduction to "Più che l'amore" in *Tutto il teatro*, 2: 73–74.

[87] Giovanna Tomasello, *La Letteratura coloniale italiana dalle avanguardie al fascismo* (Palermo: Sellario, 1984), chap. 2: "D'Annunzio: L'Africa fra bellezza e barbarie."

is to extend its boundaries. He tells his friend: "I have my thought, indeed I have my empire, a Roman word to make Italic: *Teneo te, Africa*. . . . Oh, if you had felt what I felt when beyond Imi we entered into an unknown region, when we stamped on the virgin soil the Latin footprint!" (96). That Corrado abandoned his profession as architect in Rome for African adventure is significant. If Rome could regain its power over the sea, he tells Virginio, "perhaps I could become a builder of cities on conquered land and rediscover that colonial architecture that the Romans constructed in the Africa of the Scipios" (99).[88] Thus the fulfillment of a modern Roman imperialism is for him at once archaeological and aesthetic. Recalling with Rudu their "conquest of the brutes and of destiny," at Olda, where they both fought and outwitted a tribe, Corrado shows his man the Roman coin found there which he always carries with him (131–32), a sign that their particular exploit has deeper roots in Rome's imperial destiny. We have here not "mere" poetry about imperialism divorced from political reality but a poetic binding of ancient and modern imperial destiny.

In this text shadowed by imperial Rome as *The Dead City* was by classical Greece, the culminating scene depicting the parting of Maria and Corrado suggests (through Racine) the pathos of Titus and Bérénice. The title, *Più che l'amore*, could be given to Racine's tragedy perhaps more fittingly than to D'Annunzio's. The same motif is central: woman, always consumed by love, no matter how strong and powerful she is, must cede to the superior destiny of man when he is called to go "beyond love." The destructive, sterile, Medusan "superwoman" attempts to castrate the hero; the ideal "superwoman" submits lovingly and heroically, in Maria's case also bearing his child. Maria expresses the gender roles succinctly: "For you, to live is to conquer; for me, to live is to wait" (125–26). Yet for D'Annunzio man's heroic destiny is also fueled and energized by his erotic attachment. The obvious difference between the classical and modern versions of the motif lies in the fact that no public interest is at stake: Corrado and Maria are isolated individuals, or perhaps a would-be emperor and a middle-class queen. Maria, however, rises sublimely out of her bourgeois context to become free and fearless, ready for sacrifice, more worthy of the coming heroic age than the hero himself.

Corrado's relationship with his Sardinian servant Rudu deserves some attention. As Giorgio Squarotti points out, D'Annunzio's use of dialect in their conversations is within *verista* (naturalist) conventions.[89] But Rudu is an aestheticized as well as a naturalist character. According to the stage di-

---

[88] Here the temptation to read D'Annunzio as a prophet of fascism becomes very strong. On the importance of architecture to the fascist colonial project, see Krystyna von Henneberg, "Imperial Uncertainties: Architectural Syncretism and Improvisation in Fascist Colonial Italy," *Journal of Contemporary History* 31 (April 1996): 373ff.

[89] Squarotti, *La Scrittura verso il nulla*, 257.

rections, he is dark-skinned "like a native of upper Egypt" and even resembles "Egyptian art of the Ancient Empire" (130). Like Sardinia itself, Rudu seems to stand between Rome and Africa, as if a primitive link to their intertwined destinies. Rudu, who calls Corrado "master" in an unnamed African language, also has affinities with the classical colonized helper and companion, the man Friday. A loyal and brave fighter in his master's African exploits, he incarnates as well the simple Italian peasants needed as soldiers in the armed forces of imperial Italy. The bonding of heroic visionaries and salt-of-the-earth people against decadent, bourgeois "plutocrats" figures importantly in D'Annunzio's political rhetoric as it will in Mussolini's.

The murder committed by Corrado is not only a means by which to finance his return to Africa but also a strike against the rule of "plutocracy" and the corruption of money. Corrado justifies himself to Virginio: "That man's life wasn't worth a wolf's life, because the wolf species is becoming rarer each day, whereas his brood is multiplying every day in ignominy, swarming and groveling, infecting everything it touches, sullying everything it devours" (138). This is strong language; even painfully evocative of later antisemitic propaganda.[90]

The would-be superman, in a state of delirium, exalts himself above the law and beyond good and evil. Yet he does so by vindicating the base and squalid crime for which, by his own negligence, he is caught. It is as if he cannot quite extricate himself from the structures of a society unprepared to receive or to nurture his visionary imperial aspirations. As in *Macbeth*, if much more crudely, potentially heroic qualities turn to destructive ones. D'Annunzio in his preface compares his hero to Sophocles' Ajax in his will to become something better than a man (531), to Antigone in his appeal to superior, unwritten laws (532), as well as to the murderer Orestes. Brando may be guilty of hubris, but his nemesis comes neither from the law of the gods nor the human moral order but from the limits of democratic "legalism." His last gesture—seizing "the arm which works best at a short distance" (147)—could be interpreted as a preparation for suicide to prevent being arrested. In the lyrical exode, however, he dies burned at the stake (147–48). D'Annunzio in his preface explains, "He will not kill himself, but will kill until he is killed" (534). If the details are not very specific, the intent is clear: the new Erinyes will seize their prey and the Dionysian hero will be immolated. The condemned man's last words, as quoted in the exode, are "Away, dogs, to your chain! My ashes are seed" (148). In the

---

[90] There is, to my knowledge, no evidence to suggest that D'Annunzio, whose close associates included Sarah Bernhardt and Ida Rubenstein, was antisemitic. Still, the fact that the murdered character portrayed so antipathetically was originally named Davide (see note 76) and that he was a moneylender may raise some doubts. But the character probably represents bourgeois money interests in general.

future, then, the new Erinyes (the police as representatives of bourgeois mediocrity?) are surpassed; the hero's sacrifice will make possible the perpetuation of his visionary projects by his physical and spiritual progeny. In suggesting that Brando is "burned at the stake," hardly likely in Italy of 1900, D'Annunzio deliberately flaunts realist conventions in his attempt to create a mythical tragic hero.

Più che l'amore can also be read metatheatrically. The stylistic tension between realist drama and classical-modern "sublime" tragic lyricism is recapitulated in the struggle between the striving and desire of the hero and his *adjuvant* and the power of money and mediocrity in their environment. In killing the usurer, the imperialist visionary would not only triumph over that power but, in a sense, "kill" realism and nineteenth-century drama to soar into a purified modern tragedy. Similarly, Maria would elevate herself "beyond love" in the sentimental, melodramatic tradition toward sacrifice and sublimity. But these modern avatars of Titus and Bérénice find themselves to be mere individuals, not representatives of social forces. The urge to fuse the classical-imperialist past with the technological-imperialist future, both politically and aesthetically, is in dramatic terms defeated by the reigning bourgeois order. It is, however, recuperated lyrically as D'Annunzio suggests in the end a future in which the ideal of artistic imperialism will be realized.

D'Annunzio's experiments with modern tragedy indicate the range of interests he incorporated into theater—from myth, to history, to contemporary life and politics. It is as if he were constantly searching for the ideal aesthetic form for the genre he felt certain was to replace nineteenth-century bourgeois drama. The poet's importance in adapting Nietzsche has not been sufficiently recognized. He was one of the first in Europe to attempt a practical application of the philosopher's radical theories. Not only did he derive a political significance from *Thus Spake Zarathustra* in his "La Bestia elettiva" as well as in his own political activity; he also understood *The Birth of Tragedy* in part as a call for the actual writing of modern tragedy. But politics and theater were never really separate activities for Il Vate, the poet-politician. The genius that interprets, forms, and expresses the collective desire of the masses through rhetoric in the piazza is another manifestation of that of the dramatic author who accomplishes ritual magic through poetry in the (preferably outdoor) theater. This genius, in D'Annunzio's theory and practice, may in turn inhabit the imperialist conqueror, the warrior, and the lover.

D'Annunzio's understanding of Nietzsche's Apollonian/Dionysian dialectic is crucial to this amalgam. Clearly the Dionysian is for him primarily female and the containment of Dionysian energy in Apollonian form takes place primarily through the transformation of the lover's domination of the Dionysian woman into poetry. On stage, the Dionysian actress transmits the poets' words to the masses. But the masses, too, are feminized, to be dominated by virile acts of poetry, political discourse, or conquest. The Dionysian-female can, however, take a dangerous as well as a benefi- cial form. As Medusa she threatens to wield her own phallic power, to cas- trate the leader and to reduce the poetic creator to stony silence. As Byzan- tium, she threatens to overturn the natural order of things, subduing Rome. The creation of tragedy, in D'Annunzio's metaphor, consists of the heroic act of slaying the Medusa and presenting her severed head to an au- dience brought to religious awe. Woman is sacrificed so that man can give form to her power; Apollo recuperates Dionysus.

D'Annunzio seems to want to write the heroic tragedy of "artistic impe- rialism" called for by Morasso, the optimistic tragedy of the modern hero who struggles with a form of ancient destiny but overcomes it, realizing "the victory of man." This, however, is not the tragedy he writes. His would- be tragic heroes are all problematic, somehow not adequate to the task that awaits them or to their encounter with destiny. Like Alessandro or Corrado, they may invoke the privileges of the superman but operate on the level of a common criminal. Even when, like Marco Gratico, they emerge victori- ous, they do not quite appear heroic. The women, far stronger figures, do not so much encounter destiny as incarnate it. As Medusas, superwomen, or both, they seem both not quite human and beyond human, more like forces of nature than tragic heroines. The tragedy that D'Annunzio actu- ally writes is not so much heroic modern tragedy as the tragedy of moder- nity. His heroes appear trapped between bourgeois, liberal "Italietta" and what he envisioned as an emerging virile, heroic, imperialist, neo-Roman Italy. Even though Ruggero Flamma and Marco Gratico may have discov- ered the secret of the new mass politics destined to replace the detested parliamentary squabbling, they have not quite mastered it, they are still products of their time, undone by Italy's own inadequacies. It is this ten- sion present in D'Annunzio's tragedies that must have prompted his ad- mirers during the *ventennio* to proclaim that his theater was "prophetic," that Mussolinian Italy was "spiritually prepared" to understand his plays as liberal Italy had not been. But Il Vate was not about to assume the role of John the Baptist. Wielder and creator of words himself, he would not allow even his own theatrical characters to upstage him. Why should he be domi- nated by a vulgar upstart politician who wasn't even a poet? If the role of poet/duce was not to be his, it was better to play that of the spiritual guide who had understood and poetically expressed before anyone else the na- ture of Italy's crisis and its destiny.

D'Annunzio's theater, it should be clear, has little in common with the propaganda plays encouraged by the fascist government, including the Forzano-Mussolini attempts at historic tragedy. His modern tragedies nonetheless anticipate fascist ideology and aesthetics thematically as well as stylistically. Promotion of imperialism, nationalism, "true" Italy, and the cult of *Romanità*; demotion of "plutocracy," democracy, the parliamentary system, and the bourgeoisie are some common themes. Another is the importance given to "religion": not to traditional Roman Catholicism but to a syncretic amalgam open to ancient and modern forms of paganism, Nietzschean ideas, and nationalism, with generous doses of Catholic liturgy and ritual. This is religion with very little theology but with an intense focus on the sacralization of the secular, religion in the etymological sense of binding the individual to a new and greater whole, intent on creating its own myths and incorporating them into ritual. In essence (with the important exception of the cult of the duce) it is already the "fascist religion" so called by Giovanni Gentile and analyzed by Emilio Gentile.[91]

D'Annunzio's primary contribution to the search for modern tragedy is not, however, ideological-political but aesthetic. Or rather, as I have argued, the two domains are in his work inseparable: the political is poetic and the poetic is political. Gramsci may have been right to say that D'Annunzio never had a political idea but only in the sense that for him politics is always merely a part of the whole. This is where his revisionist critics are, in my opinion, in error: to argue that he had nothing in common with fascism because he was, in his literary work, a poet and not an ideologue or a politician is to miss the point. The fusing of myth, history, and the present in an atemporal transcendence of "the error of time" is an aesthetic innovation with ideological overtones. To recuperate the classical past and the eternal folk within modernity is to deny the significance of the working out of time in history. The reshaping of the classical chorus into a *popolo* speaking in unanimous voice in dialogue with a hero, along with the concept of tragedy as the binding and fusing of the Latin crowd through the poetic word makes an aesthetic statement on the transformation of individuals and social classes into a consensual mass. Modern tragedy, in D'Annunzio's conception, has much to do with the revival of the sacred festival, the ritual and the rite that began to assume political importance during his days at Fiume and culminated in Mussolini's sacred festivals. The violent sacrifice central to Nietzsche's, and D'Annunzio's, sense of tragedy would continue as the Cult of the Fallen as Saviors of the Nation and the myth of the Great War crucial to the political rhetoric of both D'Annunzio and Mussolini. The cultivation of the tragic genre as a revolt against realistic drama would continue to be seen as consonant with the revolt against rationalistic, limited, inferior "bourgeois" systems in the search for a new politics of grandeur.

[91] For the importance of D'Annunzio's role in the construction of fascist "religion," see Emilio Gentile, *Sacralization of Politics in Fascist Italy*, 17, 22, 25.

CHAPTER THREE

Pirandellian Fascism, Metatragedy, and Myth

Pirandello and D'Annunzio, the two giants of early twentieth-century Italian theater, could in some ways hardly be less similar. D'Annunzio's flamboyant lifestyle and luxuriant, often esoteric literary style seem at the antipodes of Pirandello's puritanism and modernism. Pirandello was throughout his career a harsh critic of his rival. As early as 1898, in an essay on the author of *La Città morta*, he writes: "For him, renewing oneself means renewing imitable models. [To nourish the fame he has acquired] he needs to give a king to Rome today and to revive Greek tragedy tomorrow. [*The Dead City*] can be called Greek in so far as it takes place . . . near the ruins of Mycenae 'rich in gold.'" And the form can be called ancient, insofar as no one today, fortunately, speaks like the characters of this tragedy."[1] At the peak of Pirandello's fame, his opinions on D'Annunzio were heard by the entire literary world. In his essay on theater "Spoken Action," he criticizes the rival playwright's monological discourse in the theater—in D'Annunzio's plays one hears the author's voice, not the voices of the characters.[2] More controversially, in his December 3, 1931, speech to the Royal Academy of Italy on the occasion of the fiftieth anniversary of the publication of Giovanni Verga's *I Malavoglia*, Pirandello contrasts Verga's "style of things" with D'Annunzio's "style of words." Whereas Verga's style is devoid of literary affectation, D'Annunzio's represents a kind

---

[1] Quoted by Sarah Zappulla Muscarà in "Il Convegno Volta e la regia pirandelliana de 'La Figlia di Iorio,'" in *Pirandello e D'Annunzio*, ed. Enzo Lauretta (Palermo: Palumbo, 1989), 359.

[2] Luigi Pirandello, "L'Azione parlata," in *Opere di Luigi Pirandello*, ed. Manlio lo Vecchio-Musti (Milan: Mondadori, 1960), 6: 981–84.

of wallowing in the language of literature.[3] The speech was interpreted by some of the hierarchy as an antifascist statement on Pirandello's part, since he was directly insulting the writer adulated by the fascists.

The long rivalry seemed to end in reconciliation, indeed in a kind of apotheosis when, almost at the end of the lives of both celebrities, Pirandello directed *La Figlia di Jorio* for the Volta conference. The presence of Mussolini in a way consecrated the artistic fraternity. Of course, the deep differences were never really reconciled. But Pirandello may well have seen in his rival's tragedy of Abruzzo some real affinities with his own art, which exist despite the obvious differences. Both writers are products of the same cultural milieu: the irrationalist, antibourgeois, antidemocratic, antirealist culture that produced early fascism. D'Annunzio was more imbued with French culture and Pirandello with German, yet the influence of Nietzsche is more evident on D'Annunzio and that of Bergson more evident on Pirandello. Although he mentions Nietzsche infrequently, Pirandello was clearly acquainted with his thought. Like D'Annunzio, he may have drawn from Nietzsche an interest in the revival of myth and tragedy for modernity as antidotes to the despised realist "bourgeois" drama. As playwrights, D'Annunzio and Pirandello reject rational, linear discourse and structure as well as historical time for the creation of "totalizing," timeless mythological worlds.[4] And though neither was a practicing religious believer, both were intensely concerned with "spirituality" and religion in a broader, syncretic, "mythical" sense. Although Pirandello shows nothing of Il Vate's predilection for "possessing" crowds, he too, primarily in his later plays, was interested in moving beyond the confines of bourgeois theater toward communication, through myth, with "the people." Unlike D'Annunzio, Pirandello had no political ambitions, and indeed he claimed at times to be apolitical; unlike D'Annunzio too, he was a member of the Fascist Party.

The extent and nature of Pirandello's fascism have been a matter of much critical contention. Gaspare Giudice, in his 1963 biography, was the first to publish the facts on Pirandello's party allegiance (from 1924 until his death) along with many of his press statements on Mussolini and fascism. Giudice, however, argues that Pirandello grew disenchanted with the regime in the 1930s; that his fascism was "eccentric," and that there was no connection whatsoever between his literary work and his fascist "faith." Most Italian critics tend to argue that Pirandello was truly apolitical and that whatever fascism he espoused was simply opportunistic: he did all he

---

[3] Luigi Pirandello, "Discorso alla reale accademia d'Italia," Ibid., 6: 391–406.

[4] Both Robert Dombroski and Anna Meda conclude that Pirandello and D'Annunzio believe in the regenerative power of myth and use myth to refuse history and to create "totalities." Dombroski finds that such totalities are in fact totalitarian. See Anna Meda, *Bianche statue contro il nero abisso: Il teatro dei miti in D'Annunzio e Pirandello* (Ravenna: Longo, 1993), 332, and Robert Dombroski, "Aspetti di discorso mitico in Pirandello e D'Annunzio," in *Pirandello e D'Annunzio*, ed. Lauretta, 249–61.

could to get Mussolini to give state support to his theater. Robert Dombroski and Gianfranco Vené have both argued for a strong fascist presence in Pirandello's literary work, although most of their attention has focused on the novels. In a 1992 essay, I retraced Pirandello's affiliation with fascism, adding some press statements and other material not found in Giudice, and analyzed some of the affinities between his fascist beliefs and his theater.[5] I would now argue that Pirandello's approach to fascism was primarily aesthetic and that his apparent lack of involvement in contemporary politics cannot be used to argue that he was not "really" a fascist.[6] Indeed, the opposite may be the case: Pirandello may have taken the fascists seriously in their contention that theirs was a "spiritual" movement beyond "politics." We have no evidence as to how he reacted to *squadristi* violence and dictatorial policies. We do know that he chose to join the party just after the imputed assassination of the socialist deputy Giacomo Matteotti, when other intellectuals, revolted by fascist tactics, were leaving, and that he announced his support for the Ethiopian campaign in 1936. Certainly he had his differences with members of the hierarchy and certainly he was bitterly disappointed by the lack of support for his theater. His personal esteem for Mussolini seems to have diminished in his later years. Yet his "faith" in fascism appears to have been genuine and, on the whole, remained unshaken until his death. I will now attempt to trace the intersection of that "faith" with his aesthetics of modern tragedy.

Unlike D'Annunzio, Pirandello produced no substantive essays or sustained meditations on the theory of modern tragedy, nor did he write as many plays that he considered to be representative of the genre. His thinking on the subject must be found in sporadic comments in various writings. Yet he was just as concerned as his rival with the necessarily self-conscious attitude of the writer of modern tragedy, and many of his plays may also be read metatheatrically. The statement on modern tragedy most often cited as representing Pirandello's view has a somewhat suspect origin since it is spoken by the pretentious Anselmo Paleari, a character in the novel *The Late Mattia Pascal* (1904). In the course of telling the protagonist about an announcement of the tragedy of Orestes to be presented in a marionette theater, Paleari relates his "curious idea."

---

[5] See Gaspare Giudice in *Pirandello: A Biography*, trans. A. Hamilton (London: Oxford University Press, 1975), 143–65; Gianfranco Vené, *Pirandello fascista: La Coscienza borghese tra ribellione e rivoluzione* (Venice: Marsilio, 1981); Robert Dombroski, *La Totalità dell'artifizio: Ideologia e forma nel romanzo di Pirandello* (Padua: Liviana, 1978); and my "Fascist Discourse and Pirandellian Theater," *South Atlantic Quarterly* 91 (spring 1992): 303–31.

[6] This is not to say that Pirandello was uninterested in politics. His biography indicates strong concern with the problems of post-risorgimento Italy. See the papers in the collection *Pirandello e la politica*, ed. Enzo Lauretta (Milan: Mursia, 1992). The positions taken on Pirandello's fascism in this volume are quite diverse. See also Elio Providenti, *Pirandello impolitico: Dal radicalismo al Fascismo* (Rome: Salerno Editrice, 2000).

If at the climax of the play, just when the marionette who is playing Orestes is about to avenge his father's death and kill his mother and Aegisthus, suppose there were a little hole torn in the paper sky of the scenery. . . . Orestes would still feel his desire for vengeance, he would still want passionately to achieve it, but his eyes, at that point, would go straight to that hole, from which every kind of evil influence would then crowd the stage and Orestes would feel suddenly helpless. In other words, Orestes would become Hamlet. There's the whole difference between ancient tragedy and modern, Signor Meis—believe me—a hole torn in a paper sky.[7]

As Martin Esslin has pointed out, the Pirandellian dramatic protagonist prefigured by the puppet of Orestes goes a step further than Hamlet toward modernity. Not only has he become aware of the nonexistence of the gods and of an absolute moral law, he is also cognizant of himself as a *puppet*, that is, of the problematic nature of the self and its need to fashion various identities. But Esslin is wrong to conclude from this that Pirandello sensed the "death of tragedy" and the impossibility of writing it for the modern stage.[8] Rather, he envisions modern tragedy as writing the tragedy of the loss of the certainties presupposed by classical tragedy.

Less well known is another figure representing modern tragedy in an essay published eleven years before *Mattia Pascal.* Arguing that the discoveries of modern science and modern philosophy have left humanity without any illusion of certainty, stability, structure, or meaning, no longer the summit of God's creation at the center of the universe but whirling in infinite space, Pirandello sees the condition of modernity figured in King Lear.

What has become of this microcosm, this king of the universe? Ah, poor king! Don't you see leaping in front of you King Lear armed with a broom in all of his tragic comicality? With what madness? Once upon a time there was a superb castle, a marvelous castle built on a red cloud, a cloud that seemed to be made of flames. That castle was his kingdom, and the wind blew it away. The sun set, and the cloud changed: it became livid and then slowly black; finally it dissolved into water and its drops seemed to be tears.[9]

As Robert Dombroski has pointed out, this Lear is not Shakespeare's but Pirandello's: he will never be redeemed nor be made an authentic king through his suffering and insight ("to feel what wretches feel"); he will find

---

[7] Luigi Pirandello, *The Late Mattia Pascal,* trans. William Weaver (London: André Deutsch, 1993), 145.

[8] Martin Esslin, "Pirandello and Modern Drama," in J. L. DiGaetani, ed., *A Companion to Pirandello Studies* (Westport, Conn.: Greenwood Press, 1991), 261–65.

[9] In "Arte e coscienza d'oggi," first published in *La Nazione letteraria,* Florence, September 1893, reprinted in *Opere di Luigi Pirandello,* 6: 896.

no remedy for his dis-aster, his fall from the kingdom in the clouds, except in madness.[10] Pirandello carries his Lear figure through the centuries, having him meet Enlightenment philosophers, modern scientists, Darwin and Spencer, in his quest for truth (897–99). All he finds, in Pirandello's words, is "the concept of the relativity of all things" (900). Left naked, stripped of all his illusions and supports, Lear with his broom is *at once* tragic and comic, a figure of Pirandellian humorism. Nudity, however, is a condition that man cannot endure: he must clothe himself, construct an identity, if only in the garments of madness, to protect himself from such knowledge. The clothed Lear will reappear as part of the complex that makes up "Henry IV."

If Pirandello's Orestes puppet acts out the self-consciousness of modern tragedy, his Lear displays its potential comicality. Both of these attributes appear in Pirandello's concept of *umorismo*, a concept he seems to have derived from romantic irony and from Bergson's *Le Rire* and which he defines in his 1908 essay (translated as *On Humor*) as "the feeling of the opposite." The "humorist" writer, Pirandello argues, evokes in the reader responses that are at once comic and tragic, of distance and of pity. Although this "humor" is peculiar to modern literature, it does not lack ties with ancient Greece. Quoting an 1885 lecture by Giorgio Arcoleo, Pirandello maintains that Socrates taught that "the origin of happiness and sadness is one and the same . . . so that tragedy and comedy are made of the same stuff."[11] This perception, however, was not artistically realized in antiquity, with its clear generic taxonomy. Harmful to the development of the double "humoristic" vision in Italy was the strong rhetorical tradition that prescribed rules, thus inhibiting what Pirandello sees as an organic process of free artistic creation. To illustrate this notion, he creates a little allegorical comedy. The wardrobe master "Rhetoric" speaks to the "nude" thoughts that want to form themselves into a tragedy: "And you, you want to be a Tragedy? A real Tragedy? It will be difficult, I warn you. You have got to be solemn and light-footed at the same time, my dear. Twenty-four hours—that's all you have. And please stay put; choose your place and stay there. Unities, you must respect the unities. You know that? Fine. But tell me something: have you the blue blood of a prince in your veins? Have you studied Aeschylus, Sophocles, and Euripides? And what about the good Seneca?" (31). Whereas the rhetorical schoolmaster demands logical composition according to codified rules, the humorist advocates *decomposition*. Pirandello does not develop the implications of his ideas on humor for a theory of

---

[10] Robert Dombroski, "Nudità pirandelliane," in *Ars dramatica: Studi sulla poetica di Luigi Pirandello*, ed. Rena A. Syska-Lamparska (New York: Peter Lang, 1996), 55–68.

[11] Luigi Pirandello, *On Humor*, trans. Antonio Illiano and Daniel P. Testa (Chapel Hill: University of North Carolina Press, 1974), 10.

modern tragedy, but read with the passages on Orestes and King Lear, they suggest that a modern tragic hero, unlike his ancient counterpart, will be self-conscious, aware of all possible outcomes, including the comic ones, of his actions. If he might still manage to be "heroic," it will not be in the classical sense. Long before Ionesco, who claimed he could see no difference between tragedy and comedy, Pirandello realized the implications of the linkage of the two modes for modernity.

At the end of the essay, Pirandello does sketch out a possible modern tragic protagonist in an imaginary rewriting of one of the most heroic of tragic myths, that of Prometheus. The new Prometheus comes to realize that the spark of fire he has stolen for the presumed benefit of man brings only an awareness of the nothingness that surrounds him. The writing here resembles Franz Kafka's paradoxical parables. "Tomorrow a humorist could picture Prometheus on the Caucasus in the act of pondering sadly his lit torch and perceiving in it, at last, the fateful cause of his infinite torment. He has finally realized that Jupiter is no more than a vain phantasm, a pitiable deception, the shadow of his own body projecting itself as a giant in the sky, precisely because of the lighted torch he holds in his hand. Jupiter could disappear only on one condition, on the condition that Prometheus extinguish his candle, that is, his torch. But he does not know how, he does not want to, he cannot: and so the shadow remains, terrifying and tyrannical, for all men who fail to realize the fateful deception" (141). Prometheus's tragic consciousness, his awareness that an ethical absolute or the boundaries to hubris represented by Jupiter are a sham, a self-creation, but a necessary deception, evolves from the very decomposition of the foundations of ancient tragedy.

Read in conjunction with another passage from *The Late Mattia Pascal,* the Prometheus fable appears also to contain the germ of a political implication that Pirandello later developed. In a humoristic move similar to the recounting of the puppet Orestes story, it is from the mouth of a drunkard on the street that Mattia hears an opinion that was undoubtedly Pirandello's own. Our sufferings, the drunkard maintains, are caused by nothing more or less than democracy, the government of the majority. Why? "Because when power is in the hands of a single man, this man knows he is one and must make many happy; but when the many govern, they think only of making themselves happy, and the result is the most absurd and hateful of tyrannies. . . . I'm suffering because of a tyranny masked as freedom" (128). Here is a humorist who has decomposed an illusion to reveal that the worst tyranny is the masked tyranny, a tyranny that (in the same mode as an actor in a naturalist play) becomes the figure of the consummate hypocrite who encourages his public to believe that the mask he wears represents reality. This figure of tyranny deceives humanity in the manner of Prometheus's presenting his shadow as Jupiter but replaces the latter's tragic awareness with mere selfish greed. Prometheus, who cannot and will not extinguish the torch, seems to regard the "terrifying and tyrannical" shadow as a necessary illusion. "Mankind," in the words of Pirandello's contemporary T. S. Eliot, "cannot bear very much reality": if the masses realized that authority was only a shadow, anarchy would ensue. In the strangely Pirandellian (and Sorelian) words of another contemporary, the young socialist journalist Benito Mussolini writing in 1912, "Faith moves mountains because it gives us the illusion that mountains do move. This illusion is perhaps the only real thing in life."[12]

In contrast with "the worst of tyrannies," Prometheus's shadow is not disguised as liberty. The inverse is in fact the case. Prometheus uses his liberating flame to create the necessary illusion of authority, only himself humoristically and tragically aware of its deceptive nature. This Prometheus bears no resemblance to the actor-hypocrite of the naturalist stage who acts as if performance were reality but rather to the self-consciously theatrical actor as represented by Pirandello's "tragic emperor." The political implication emerges that since all social organization is by definition tyrannical, or in Pirandellian terms a "form" that can never encompass or adequately represent the multifarious quality of "life," the least harmful and the least deceptive form is that which presents itself as a tyranny, the rule of one man. The basis of authority for this type of ruler indeed resembles the "shadow" of the traditional European monarch whose rule was based on a now lost legitimacy. The new Promethean leader must base his authority on the necessary reality of illusion. His solitary, humoristic awareness of the deception makes him a tragic figure.

Pirandello's later, sporadic references to tragedy include more allusions to his famous distinction between "form" and "life." He first formulates this dichotomy—actually a never-ending dialogical movement—in the often-quoted passage from *On Humor*: "Life is a continual flux which we try to stop, to fix in stable and determined forms, both inside and outside ourselves. . . . The forms in which we seek to stop, to fix in ourselves this constant flux are the concepts, the ideals with which we would like consistently to comply, all the fictions we create for ourselves, the conditions, the state in which we tend to stabilize ourselves. But within ourselves, in what we call the soul and is the life in us, the flux continues" (137). Pirandello would later develop the notion of "constructions" or self-willed creations, including works of art, as examples of form, and the critic Adriano Tilgher would conceptualize the form/life antithesis as the very core of Pirandello's aesthetic, a concept taken to heart by the author.

---

[12] Benito Mussolini, "Da Guiccardini a Sorel," *Avanti!*, July 18, 1912, quoted in Emilio Gentile, *The Sacralization of Politics in Fascist Italy*, trans. Keith Botsford (Cambridge: Harvard University Press, 1996), 14.

An antifascist throughout his career, Tilgher was to my knowledge the first to link Pirandello's "philosophy" with the idealism of Gentile and with fascism. Writing in 1921, he explains Gentile's position that the ethical state is not an existing entity but continuously created by those who will it. Fascism is therefore an "absolute activism" stemming from relativism. He adds: "This point of view—a new proof of the absolute unity of every culture—finds its present expression in the art of Luigi Pirandello, the poet . . . of absolute relativism."[13] Along with Bergson, according to Tilgher, Pirandello demonstrates the uncertainty of our "constructions" of ourselves and of others, finding the only certainty, again like fascism, in *la vita vissuta*.

Tilgher's life/form formulation, as is well known, had a major impact on Pirandello's conception of his own work. It is thus not unreasonable to speculate that the critic's parallel between Pirandellian and fascist relativism may have strengthened Pirandello's sense of himself as the poet of the revolution—the Virgil, as he would imply later, to Mussolini's Caesar.[14] When Mussolini first received Pirandello at the Palazzo Chigi on October 22, 1923, the writer attempted to demonstrate a philosophical affinity between himself and Il Duce: "Mussolini knows, as few do, that reality is only in the power of man to create it and that it is created only by the activity of the spirit."[15] In the same article he is quoted as being pleased with Mussolini's praise of *Six Characters in Search of an Author* and *Henry IV.* In the October 28, 1923, issue of *L'Idea Nazionale*, devoted to the first anniversary of the March on Rome, Pirandello paid homage to Mussolini in terms that associate the life/form dialogue with his concept of tragedy.

> Mussolini can receive only blessings [Pirandello plays on his first name Benito, using the word *benedetto*] from somebody who has always felt the immanent *tragedy* of life which . . . requires a form, but senses death in every form it assumes. For, since life is subject to continual change and motion, it feels itself imprisoned by form: it rages and storms and finally escapes from it. Mussolini has shown that he is aware of this double and *tragic* law of movement and form, and hopes to conciliate the two. Form must not be a vain and empty idol. It must receive life, pulsating and quivering, so that it should be for ever recreated. . . . The revolutionary movement inaugurated by Mussolini with the march on Rome and all the methods of his new government seem to me to be, in politics, the necessary realization of just this conception of life.[16]

[13] Adriano Tilgher, *Relativisti contemporanei* (Rome: Libreria di scienze e lettere, 1922), 66.

[14] In an interview in *Le Journal de Paris* dated December 31, 1935, speaking of himself and Mussolini, Pirandello states that both activists and their interpreters are necessary to society. He adds, "Caesars and Octavians must exist in order for there to be Virgils."

[15] *Idea Nazionale*, October 23, 1923, 1.

[16] Cited in Giudice, *Pirandello*, 145–46; emphasis added.

Pirandello's biographer Giudice calls the statement "eccentric," as it undoubtedly was in comparison to the prosaic and political homages of the day. Yet it contains the germs both of Pirandello's aesthetic fascism and of his aesthetic of modern tragedy. In this potentially dramatic representation of Gentile's state as continuous creation, Mussolini appears as a Promethean figure, tragically aware of the relative nature of human constructions but nonetheless constantly creating them—casting shadows—for the benefit of humanity. The statement was made a few months before Pirandello formally joined the party, with the declaration that this was the time to affirm his fascist "faith," long nurtured in silence.[17]

In later statements on modern tragedy, Pirandello continues to refer to the life/form dichotomy. In one of a series of interviews in *Comoedia* titled "Pirandelliana" (March–April 1929), he is quoted as saying, "I see life as a tragedy. The tragedy consists in the conflict between stability and movement, life and form—not merely intellectual but deeply felt." He adds, significantly, that "humorism" does not exclude tragedy. In what was probably the last interview of his life, Pirandello explains that "necessity" in his theater means the double, contradictory exigencies of flowing life and stable form. In one of the few direct references he makes to Nietzsche, he states the difference between Greek tragedy and his modern tragedy. "Nietzsche said that the Greeks raised white statues against the black abyss, to hide it. Those times are over. I, on the other hand, shake them to reveal it."[18] The "white statue" metaphor seems to be Pirandello's own—at least I have not been able to locate it in Nietzsche. It indicates, if nothing else, his particular reading of *The Birth of Tragedy*: the white statues of Apollonian form curiously "hiding" rather than individuating the Dionysian, understood as chaos. The tragedy of modernity, Pirandello seems to be saying, lies in part in the revelation that the stable forms of antiquity are no longer sufficient to mask the chaos of existence. Modern tragedy is thus in part necessarily metatragic.

If Pirandello never wrote a formal poetic of modern tragedy or even developed his ideas on the subject at any length, his sketches of the modernized "humoristic" tragic figures of Orestes, Prometheus, and Lear, along with what we might call his construction of Mussolini as modern tragic hero, serve as prototypes for some of his own tragic figures. His notion of tragic conflict as the constant struggle between life and form figures importantly in his approaches to both fascism and drama. The later plays he called his "myths" become more self-conscious in their struggle to rewrite the ancient relationship between myth and tragedy for modernity and in their idiosyn-

---

[17] *Impero*, September 19, 1924, quoted ibid., 150.
[18] *Quadrivio*, November 15, 1936.

cratic approach to the regime's call for the creation of myths in the arts. Here I want to focus on the major types of Pirandello's approaches to modern tragedy: his great antihistorical drama *Henry IV*, his tragedy of motherhood, *The Life I Gave You*, and his "myths" of society, religion, and art in *Lazarus, The New Colony*, and *The Giants of the Mountain*. I shall also refer to other plays and to the evolution of his relations with fascism.

The international success of *Six Characters in Search of an Author* launched Pirandello's reputation as the modernist innovator of the European stage. Metatheatrical in conception, the drama can be read on one level as the definitive statement on the death of naturalist theater, or a play about the impossibility of writing a play that is mimetic, narrative, and linear. Peter Szondi rightly sees it, along with Bertolt Brecht's drama, as a major contributor to the demise of conventional European dialogical drama.[19] The *commedia da fare* (play to be made) has also been read as a statement not only on the crisis of authorship but also of authority: a portrait of the vacuum of leadership in postwar Italian society. Fragmented selves, living in their "eternal moment," the searching characters bring to the stage an agonizing portrayal of the dissolution of the bourgeois subject and its naive faith in temporal progression. The tragedy incipient in this metadrama portrays not only the crumbling of the foundations of naturalism but also the dissolution of the patriarchal family and the premise of authority that upheld it. If a bastard, prostituted stepdaughter can challenge and reveal the weaknesses of a legitimate father, what hope is there for reassembling the family, the traditional base of social order?[20] Clearly, as Pirandello will repeatedly state, an impasse has been reached, and the time is ripe for radical change and renovation in both art and society. It is not the premise of *Six Characters* to indicate the nature of the new order but rather to render, in humoristic terms, the tragic demise of the old.

The Antihistorical *Henry IV*

The creation of "humoristic" tragedy is more explicit and more fully realized in *Henry IV* (1922), with its major protagonist, the *faux* "great and tragic emperor." With a title that suggests a historical drama, Pirandello

[19] Peter Szondi, *Theory of Modern Drama*, trans. Michael Hays (Minneapolis: University of Minnesota Press, 1987), 77–81.

[20] In spite of her numerous tabulations on language and body language in *Six Characters* (it seems that women are touched more often than men and men speak more often than women), it is difficult to understand Maggie Gunsberg's conclusions that the play, along with Pirandello's other works, upholds the conventions of patriarchal society. See *Patriarchal Representations: Gender and Discourse in Pirandello's Theatre* (Providence, R.I.: Berg, 1994).

writes a self-conscious modern tragedy that is ahistorical and indeed anti-historical, that treats as constructions of costumed pageantry the two traditional bases of authority in European society: the monarchy and the papacy.[21] Even more radically than *Six Characters*, *Henry IV* reveals the dissolution of the individual subject: who, after all, is "Henry IV"? Although there is a plot of sorts—an "alienist," along with friends and relatives of a madman who believes himself to be the eleventh-century Holy Roman emperor, come to his fantasy castle in an attempt to bring him back to the "real world" and fail—only one genuine event, "Henry's" stabbing of his antagonist Belcredi actually takes place during the stage time. The real drama is more spatial than progressive in that it takes place on several temporal levels at once.

The setting is in a modern villa that has been turned into a stage-set medieval castle. Pirandello's elimination of the words "with meticulous historical reconstruction"[22] from an earlier version of the stage directions suggests an intention to accentuate the theatrical over the historical. The first scene, in which the "counselors" inform a new arrival that he must play his role in the eleventh-century court of Henry IV of Germany and not, as he had believed, in the sixteenth-century court of Henry IV of France, further emphasizes the playful nature of this pseudo-historical reconstruction. When the unnamed protagonist makes his appearance to the twentieth-century visitors dressed in appropriate costumes, he appears to be mad enough to believe that he really *is* Henry IV but at the same time seems to be playing. His hair, dyed blond in front but gray in back, allows him, as he points out, to live in two temporal periods at once: as a young man of twenty-six when he humbled himself before the pope at Canossa and as a mature man mourning the recent death of his mother. The death of his "historical" mother is also conflated with the recent death of his "real" sister, mourned by his nephew.

The superimposition of temporal periods is in fact the stuff of which the play is made. The forty-year-old Marquess Matilde Spina is confronted with a portrait of herself at twenty dressed as Mathilda of Tuscany at Canossa, a portrait of which her twenty-year-old daughter Frida will prove to be the living copy. Events from the eleventh century, from around 1920, and from around 1900 conflate with and separate from each other so that time seems

---

[21] Why did Pirandello specifically choose Henry IV as the subject of his one drama concerning a "historical" figure? I have not been able to find a satisfactory answer to this question. He may have known of the German dramas on the emperor in the eighteenth, nineteenth, and early twentieth centuries, mostly concerned with German nationalism. See the *Inaugural-Dissertation* by Reinhold Kolarczyk, *Kaiser Heinrich IV im deutschen Drama: Ein Beitrag zur Geschichte der politischen Tendenzliteratur* (Görlitz: NS-Druckerei, 1933). In this case he could have been writing directly "against" historical drama.

[22] *Un manoscritto inedito dell'Enrico IV di Luigi Pirandello*, ed. Livia Pasquzi Ferro (Rome: Bulzoni, 1983), xvii.

to stand still, or rather to become spatial. What we have is in fact the very opposite of historical drama: rather than development over and through time toward crisis and resolution, *Henry IV* postulates a refusal of temporality in a sealed, static world that by its very nature excludes change. What Henry calls "the pleasure of history . . . that is so great"[23] is in fact the negation of history as becoming. It is rather a pictorial, spatial view of history (the masqueraders, including Henry, derived their costumes from a magazine picture) resembling what the Father in *Six Characters* calls "the eternal moment." The play's last words, Henry's "per sempre" ("forever"), reject even the future possibility of progression.

The emperor Henry IV took refuge in affirming absolute imperial power at a time when it was threatened by the demands of the papacy; Pirandello's "Henry IV" takes refuge in a utopian medieval recreation as if refusing both historical change and the twentieth century itself. Ascanio Zapponi, fascist "lictor" for the theater, in an essay on Pirandello, puts forth a peculiar view of the Middle Ages to explain Henry's dilemma. Contrasting the "artificial construction" of democracy to the past, he expounds: "The Middle Ages: that was the time of force; legitimist to the point of being absurd, out of the fear it had of that mighty force that threatened at every instant to overthrow every law. . . . Man was bound to the law without hypocrisy."[24] In medieval society, according to Zapponi, laws emanated from the person of the ruler rather than from rational agreement, serving as a haven against anarchy. In the modern era, however, the basis of legitimacy has been destroyed and replaced by "artificial constructions."

Like Pirandello's figures of Lear, Prometheus, and Orestes, "Henry" seems to have understood the nature of modern society and to have derived his own tragic-comic consequences. As a young aristocrat, parading in a carnival as emperor, he might have been able to believe in some survival of legitimacy, but his fall from the horse had an effect similar to Lear's fall from the castle in the clouds, leaving him figuratively naked. Unlike Lear, however, he did not remain so but immediately clothed himself, not only in his costume but in the creation of his own "mad" universe—a totalitarian microcosm in which he forces all his visitors to play the game according to his rules. His self-conscious, totalizing theatricality paradoxically appears to the audience more "real" and less hypocritical than the normal social games played by the other characters and, by extension, in contemporary society. As he says to Belcredi, where would he go if he were to return to the "real world"? To the club, dressed up in white tie and tails? Twentieth-century people, according to him, merely engage in non-self-conscious masquerades. "Do you think you are living?"

---

[23] Luigi Pirandello, "Enrico IV," in *Opere di Luigi Pirandello*, ed. lo Vecchio-Musti, 4: 355.
[24] Ascanio Zapponi, "Pirandello rivoluzionario," *Scenario*, March 1936, 107.

he asks his "counselors." "You are merely rehashing the words of the dead" (350).

The major reversal occurs when the protagonist reveals that he is "not mad" or at least that he is aware of his play-acting. But it is because he lives self-consciously in a theatrical construction that he is able to expose the non-self-conscious "masks" (the marquess's makeup and hair coloring, the doctor's professional airs) of the aristocrats and the doctor who come to attempt to cure him. It is not only the life of the upper classes that seems to him stagnant and dead but also that of the common people, represented by the young men he has hired to be his "counselors." Your way of thinking and feeling, he says to them, is "that of the common herd—miserable, feeble, uncertain. . . . And those others take advantage of it and try to make you think and feel as they do . . . after all, what are they able to impose on you? Words, words, which can be interpreted in any manner. That's the way so-called public opinion is formed" (349).

The referent for "those others" is indefinite in this context, but the image of purveyors of words imposing their formulas on the credulous "common herd" parallels Mussolini's image of the socialists as "shepherds of the flock."[25] "Henry IV's" lucid-mad atemporal retreat figures his disgust with a society of talkers and pretenders along with his nostalgia for a world of legitimacy and organic wholeness. Like Pirandello's Prometheus, this modern tragic protagonist is fully aware that the legitimate authority that once gave coherence to the world no longer exists: all he can do is to mimic its illusion. He is in that sense comparable to Pirandello's characterization of Mussolini in his tragic awareness of the need constantly to construct new forms in an attempt to contain chaos. "Henry's" construction, however, remains in the theatrical-imaginary, with no effect outside the villa and with no indication that it might enter the theatrical-political.

In that it does not really propose a solution, the critique of modernity in *Henry IV* is a negative one, the portrayal of a vacuum without a suggestion of how the vacuum will be filled. The leader of the counselors, "Landolfo," explains that (in the manner of Pirandello's six characters) he and his colleagues are "like six puppets hanging on the wall, waiting for someone to take them and move them this way or that and to make them say a few words" (301). Similarly, the visitors to "Henry IV," wearing their medieval costumes, are unsure of how to play their parts, of what words to say. It is true that they are in a sense under Henry's direction, as they must take their cues from him, but his script is improvised and "mad," his fake castle an exposure of and a refuge from social collapse, not a solution to it. The vacuum is basically that in *Six Characters*, the absence of an author(ity) capable of bestowing meaning and unity on gestures and words—in a sense

---

[25] Benito Mussolini, "Pastori del gregge," in *Popolo d'Italia*, May 1, 1919, 3.

a reflection of prefascist Italy. Although Zapponi zealously reads Henry's final lunge toward Frida and his stabbing of Belcredi as the signs of a new, vital, "revolutionary" man,[26] they seem rather suicidal gestures, confirmations that the protagonist is unable to return to the twentieth century. His remaining "forever" in the domain of the atemporal and the fake-utopian is a kind of death in life but marked by the awaiting of an effective constructing "authority."

The Imbecile and Antipolitics

If *Henry IV* is a humoristic modern tragedy whose title announces it as historical drama but which refuses history, the one-act *The Imbecile* produced in the same year appears at the opening to be a political play but ends by affirming the "imbecility" of politics. The scene is in the office of Leopoldo Paroni, head of the republican party and director of a newspaper *Vedetta Repubblicana*. Paroni's sole desire is to have the socialist deputy Guido Mazzarini assassinated. When he learns that one of his colleagues, a certain Pulino, has committed suicide, he declares him to be an "imbecile" because he threw his life away instead of first assassinating Mazzarini. He, Paroni, would have paid for the trip to Rome! Luca Fazio, a twenty-six-year-old who appears to be extremely ill, closes himself in a room with Paroni and tells him that Mazzarini paid for his trip from Rome so that he would assassinate him, Paroni, before killing himself. Paroni at first takes this to be a joke, which in a sense it is, but at gunpoint from Fazio writes a declaration that *he* is the true imbecile. For Fazio, Paroni is a "buffoon" and "a little red man" whom he sees from "far away."[27] The spectator or reader surmises that Fazio is not in Mazzarini's service but rather disdains the political squabbling of all "little red men," be they socialists or republicans. That it is a young man (of the same age as "Henry IV" at the time of his fall) who is deathly ill and who has resolved to commit suicide suggests that a political system dominated by republicans and socialists allows neither hope nor future. Thus the play negates "politics" and again portrays a social and spiritual vacuum. "Politics," as in the rhetoric of D'Annunzio and the fascists, is associated with the meaningless squabbles and empty words of democrats and socialists, suggesting that the vacuum can be filled only by a movement that transcends politics as usual. Luca, like "Henry," is something of a lucid humorist whose life will end tragically, even if the play has nothing of the originality or the scope of *Henry IV*. The "political" tragedy like the "historical" one is overwhelmingly negative in its critique of modernity.

[26] Zapponi, "Pirandello rivoluzionario," 107.
[27] Luigi Pirandello, "L'Imbecile," in *Opere di Luigi Pirandello*, ed. lo Vecchio-Musti, 5: 663.

Telesio Interlandi, editor of the *Impero* and friend of Pirandello, claimed that while Pirandello was abroad he was persecuted because of his fascism. In a November 1, 1924, article on antifascism in general, he cites as an example a performance of *The Imbecile,* canceled at the last moment at a theater in Paris. The reason, according to Interlandi, was that Edouard Herriot, prime minister and "leader of the cartel of the left," was in the audience and people feared that he might be displeased by the bad treatment of the leftist protagonist and of the "sacred patrimony of Democracy." (This gives Interlandi the occasion to make ironic remarks on the practice of *liberté* in a so-called great democracy.) According to Renée Lelièvre, Charles Maurras also judged *The Imbecile* to be a fascist play critical of Herriot.[28]

Pirandello, very much in line with a certain vein of fascist rhetoric, always maintained it was not the province of the artist to make political propaganda but that the true artist, necessarily of his time, would do so instinctively, not on purpose. He expressed the idea most clearly in an interview published October 20, 1933, in *La Scena italiana,* quoted by D'Amico at the Volta conference: "A poet can sing the fascist Revolution. . . . But he must not do it on purpose. . . . If on the other hand he has the soul of a poet and he lives the Revolution lyrically and looks only at the necessity of his own inspiration, he can easily be the poet of the fascist Revolution." There were nonetheless certain fascist critics who complained that while Pirandello's writing did expose the "bewilderment" of prefascist society, it did not build on the positive contributions of fascism. To some extent Pirandello answered these criticisms in the creation of his "myth" plays; to the most literal-minded and propagandistically oriented of them he gave no satisfactory answer at all. Yet there was at least one positive value on which Pirandello's "lyrical inspiration" and fascist rhetoric coincided. This is the adulation of motherhood, or the mystique of the *madre/madonna.* In Pirandello's writing, as in early fascism, one witnesses a curious combination of a revolutionary, modernist critique of bourgeois institutions such as marriage and the family with an attachment to the most conservative values.[29] Pirandello's intense love of his mother along with his suspicion of his father are well known. Giudice suggests that one of the sources of his espousal of fascism may be his anarchic adolescent rebellion against his father in conjunction with his adoration of his mother, leading paradoxically to a final acceptance of the need for au-

---

[28] Renée Lelièvre, *Le Théâtre dramatique italien en France, 1855–1940* (Paris: A. Colin, 1959), 424.

[29] See Barbara Spackman's interesting analysis of this apparent dichotomy in Marinetti. *Fascist Virilities: Rhetoric, Ideology, and Social Fantasy in Italy* (Minneapolis: University of Minnesota Press, 1996), 7–10.

thority.[30] While the explanation smacks of pop psychology, it probably contains some truth. In any case it is clear that in Pirandello's theater, as in fascist ideology, there exists a "true" role for woman: that of mother.[31]

Mothers in *The Life I Gave You*

"La madre è una costruzione irreducibile" ("the mother is an irreducible construction") says Baldovino in *The Pleasure of Honesty* (2: 602), a phrase Zapponi glosses to argue that on this "instinctive" as opposed to "intellectual" basis, in conformity with fascist ideology, one can begin to construct ("Pirandello rivoluzionario," 107). Baldovino makes this remark just after delivering a most Pirandellian speech on the "construction" of one's personality in various situations. If our "constructions," as Baldovino maintains, are masks that hide our most intimate feelings—what we are for ourselves as opposed to what we are for others—then it appears that maternity is the one construction in which social role and intimate feelings coincide, a role so all-consuming that it eclipses all others. Paternity, as Baldovino himself will show by pretending to be the father of another man's child, can be intellectually constructed, whereas maternity need only be instinctively accepted. *The Pleasure of Honesty* ends "happily" with a triumph of maternity as Baldovino says to his wife, "With maternity, the lover (in you) had to die. Now you are nothing but a mother" (1: 644). The biological father, as often in Pirandello's theater, can be dispensed with.

Fathers are completely absent in Pirandello's female-dominated tragedy *The Life I Gave You* (1923). Only three men—the nephew of the protagonist donna Anna, a priest, and an old gardener—appear onstage, yet the action is dominated by donna Anna's dead son. Like "Henry IV," donna Anna lives in a solitary Tuscan villa in which she attempts, and fails, to create a fantasy world, ending in a kind of death in life. The difference between the two tragedies resides in the nature of the protagonists' "constructions": the man "plays" with history, constructing in fantasy until actual violence forces him to live in a self-conscious construction; the woman attempts to recreate the "irreducible construction," motherhood, taken from her by the death of her son.

Pirandello's religious syncretism is evident in the first act of the tragedy. A group of women singing Christian litanies for the dying in Latin and Italian acts as a tragic chorus, yet Pirandello's anticlericalism becomes evident

---

[30] Guidice, *Pirandello*, 33.

[31] I have discussed the various roles of women, particularly of the mother, in Pirandello's theater, in my "Woman or Mother? Feminine Conditions in Pirandello's Theater," in *A Companion to Pirandello Studies*, ed. John Louis DiGaetani (Westport, Conn.: Greenwood Press, 1991), 57–72.

in the figure of the priest don Giorgio when he attempts to comfort donna Anna with religious platitudes. In the exposition, we learn that donna Anna's son, who was away for seven years studying engineering and following a married woman with whom he was madly in love, returned to his mother two days previously only to die of an undisclosed illness. Donna Anna herself appears as a tragic figure apart from the others: "white," "hallucinated," and speaking in a "lucid delirium" (4: 457). Donna Anna, in fact, speaks in a language that the priest and her sister donna Fiorina cannot understand and which seems to them "mad." She is not mad in the sense that she believes her son will return to life, but she refuses his death by determining that "the life she gave him" will continue to exist. She will keep his room as it was, maintaining not that life is a dream but that the dream is life, and that since, in any case, we become "another" through age and change, we can make another live by giving him life in our imagination. This illusion sustained her during his seven-year absence; it must sustain her now.

Much of the second act of the play seems to exist only to illustrate the thesis that children, inevitably, "die" for the mother when they grow up and move away. The old nurse Elisabetta understands: "Children who leave die for their mother. They are no longer what they were" (478). Here we witness the return of donna Fiorina's son and daughter from the city, where they have matured and changed, become "other." In Pirandello's stage directions, their mother, realizing this, "will remain bewildered," suddenly becoming aware of "the tragic sense" of this fact (1: 474). The tragedy, in this play, has little to do with plot. It consists rather in the deepening of a theme, a continual anagnorisis, a lamentation as announced by the choral opening. Pirandello uses the realistic event of young relatives returning for a funeral for the completely nonrealistic purpose of suggesting that the change that children undergo in life prefigures their death for their mother.

Insofar as there is any action in this play, it begins at the end of the second act with the arrival of Lucia, the woman loved by donna Anna's son. By not telling her of the death, donna Anna finds another way of keeping "the life she gave" alive in the expectation of the young woman. A new development occurs when Lucia announces that she is pregnant with her lover's child (she has two other children by her detested husband). Donna Anna's illusion is now fulfilled: "Then he's really living in you!" (482) she exclaims. Her plan is now to keep Lucia with her so that the life she gave will be given back to her in the birth of the child. This hope, however, is temporarily frustrated when Lucia's mother, Francesca, arrives on the scene in the third act. Intent on taking her daughter back, she is horrified when she learns that the "mad woman" has not yet told her of her son's death. Once Lucia knows that donna Anna's son is dead, his mother sees him "really" dying. She now realizes that Lucia cannot give her back the life she gave. "When you give life . . . you will be the mother then, no longer I! No one will return to me here! It's over! You will have my son, little as he was . . . he'll be yours, no longer mine! You, you the mother, not me! And now, I'm dying, I'm really dying" (498).

Still, Lucia will remain with donna Anna, whom she now calls "mamma"—forever? Donna Anna foresees for her a repetition of the living out of the tragic destiny of motherhood. The mother's lot is to "break her body," giving life only to move into a status of death in life when her children—far away or dead—no longer belong to her. Donna Anna's last word—the last word of the play—is "death." Having lived entirely in the "irreducible construction" of motherhood, she "dies" when she no longer exists in that capacity. Or rather, she is transfigured into the death-in-life eternal figure foreshadowed by the chorus at the beginning: the *mater dolorosa*.

The modern version of the *mater dolorosa*, sometimes a "widow" of both husband and son, was a familiar one on the European scene following World War I. In the interest of glorifying sacrifice to the *patria* as well as in what seems to have been a fanatic fervor to increase the Italian birthrate, Mussolini attempted to raise the images of both the young mother and the sacrificing mother to a level of almost mystical veneration.[32] In 1923, the year *The Life I Gave You* was written, the first congress of fascist women was held. As recounted by Maria Macciocchi, both Mussolini's discourse and that of the fascist women themselves portray the Duce as not only the Super Male, Husband and Lover of all women, but also in some mystical sense as the father of their children. In the words of the marchesa di Casagrande's address to the Duce: "The mothers raised the children, but you inspired their birth; you placed in their soul not a torch but a living fire. . . . They are your soldiers, the purest flowers of the Italian spring. . . . Out of our love . . . under the auspices of Il Duce, we have convened here from all the lands that have heard the roar of the lion of Saint Mark, to sow the seed from which will sprout the flowers of the new spring."[33] Reproduction and maternal sacrifice—the tragic roles of women in *The Life I Gave You*—are here glorified through bombastic rhetoric and erotico-mystical devotion to Il Duce. Macciocchi theorizes that what fascist discourse really implies is the castration of all Italian males except for Mussolini—he alone will be Husband to the women and Father of the sons of the new Italy. Certainly the "giorno della fede," December 22, 1935, when Il Duce asked Italian

---

[32] See Maria Antonietta Macciocchi, *La donna "nera": Consenso femminile e fascismo* (Milan: Feltrinelli, 1977), and Victoria De Grazia, *How Fascism Ruled Women: Italy, 1922–1945* (Berkeley: University of California Press, 1992), 41–76.

[33] Macciocchi, *La donna "nera,"* 41–42.

women to give him their wedding bands to help support his Abyssinian campaign, must have had something of the aura of a mystical mass marriage. As throughout Pirandello's theater, mothers are cast in the role of "irreducible constructions," but biological fathers are disregarded or found wanting.

The Life I Gave You is particularly remarkable for its absence of fathers. Not a word is said about donna Anna's husband, who presumably fathered the son she has lost, or about the father of donna Fiorina's children, or about Lucia's father. The father of Lucia's two children is mentioned in passing as being odious, the father of her present child is of course dead, but his primary role in the play is in any case that of son. Even the chorus prays to the Virgin Mother, rather than to God the Father. The only "father" present, the priest, is completely ineffectual. Far from advocating patriarchy, as has been asserted, Pirandello in this play, at least, might be said to be representing matriarchy. Yet the nature of the mother's tragic condition does not indicate any basis of power. Rather, the past and expectant mothers here, choosing a timeless life in a solitary villa, seem, in the manner of "Henry IV," to be in stasis, waiting. As in *Jorio's Daughter*, the old order of patriarchy is dead; the new transformative one has not yet arrived, but the sacrifice of woman may prepare it. Did Pirandello come to believe that the self-created Father of Italy would displace the old bourgeois order of fathers, bringing glory both to the *mater dolorosa* and to the mother of the new sons?

Tragedy and "Myths"

The figure of the mother as the foundation on which a new order may be built appears more explicitly in the plays Pirandello called his "myths": *The New Colony* (1928), "the social myth"; *Lazarus* (1929), "the religious myth"; and *The Giants of the Mountain* (unfinished, posthumous, 1936), the "myth of art." The myth plays also represent a new approach on Pirandello's part to the attempt to create modern tragedy. His notions of myth need to be understood in the context of contemporary fascist discourse on the subject.

Pirandello began to speak of the idea of creating "myths" for the theater and to work on *The New Colony* as early as 1924, according to an interview.[34] Repeating that he continues to conceive of life as an incessant struggle between life and form, he states, "With *The New Colony*, I have proposed to show [*fare assistere a*] the birth of myth." In myth, he explains, the passions of a primitive humanity may provoke natural phenomena. In the same in-

---

[34] "L'Arte e il pensiero di Luigi Pirandello," *L'Impero*, November 11–12, 1924.

terview, he discusses his fascist "faith," maintaining that his art is close to "the renovating concepts of fascism." Politics too is an art, as well as a part of life, and therefore involved in the same conflict. Pirandello thus suggests not that his "myths" will provide resolutions to the conflict he has described as the basis of his tragic view of life but that they will represent it in new, perhaps "renovating" ways.

The notion that fascism represents a clean sweep, a new beginning in culture as well as politics, was common in the discourse of the time and evidently of interest to Pirandello. In a 1926 interview[35] the dramatist stresses the importance of creating *modern* myths rather than resurrecting ancient ones. Claiming that he is "ahistorical" and that history itself is a "construction," Pirandello affirms that the universal spirit of humanity is present in both ancient and modern myths. He thus comes close to D'Annunzio's concept of the "error of time," except that, unlike his rival, he does not believe that the myths of antiquity can be resurrected. Rather, the universal spirit must be given life in terms of modernity, set in modern times, not "clothed" in historical guise. In modern myth the transcendence of time and space will take place in a modern setting. Pirandello amplifies the notion that all myths deal with the relation of man to nature in that they show human passion provoking natural phenomena, giving as examples the sudden flowing of La Spera's milk in *The New Colony* and the "miracles" in *Lazarus.* At the end of *The New Colony*, "the myth of miracle and of faith is reborn." In another interview, Pirandello declares that he intends the audience for his "myth" plays to be more general, more popular than the "privileged" audience of his previous plays. This statement of course coincided with Mussolini's call for a "popular" theater. Pirandello here clearly declares his intention to create tragedy through myth, resurrecting an old form within a new one in order to involve the audience in a more spiritual participation. "Tragedy is always mythical. It has its beginning and end on the stage. The origins of myth are these: the elementary events of earthly cycles, dawns, sunsets, births, deaths."[36]

How, exactly, Pirandello intends to recreate myth and tragedy for the modern stage is not clear. Are myths "constructions" formed to give meaning to meaninglessness? Do they create heroes for our time? Is Pirandello proposing to fashion his own "white statues" against the "black abyss"? Was he influenced by Nietzsche's discussion of myth in the formation of tragedy? Certainly he sees myth in drama as another antidote to the mori-

[35] Romano Drioli, "*La nuova colonia* e *Lazzaro:* I nuovi lavori di Pirandello nel pensiero dell'autore," *Gazzetta del popolo,* June 12, 1926. Pirandello's statements on myth to the press have been collected and are discussed by Lucia Massi, "Pirandello's Theory of Modern Myths," *Yearbook of the British Pirandello Society* 6 (1986): 1–18. See also Meda, *Bianche statue,* 192–200.

[36] Alberto Cecchi, "*La Nuova colonia* di Pirandello, Intervista con l'autore," *Il Tevere,* March 16, 1928.

bund, bourgeois realist theater. The idea of creating "modern myths," for Pirandello a primarily artistic problem, was very much in the fabric of early twentieth-century intellectual discourse in diverse guises, the artistic and religious often conflated with the ideological and political. The word had a variety of connotations, all at least to some extent influenced by Nietzsche. For Sorel, myths had a crucial social function in that only they, drawing on irrational responses, could provoke the masses to action. Mussolini, who was interested in the idea from early in his career through Sorel, pronounced in 1922: "A myth is a faith, a passion. It is not necessary that it be real. It is real in the sense that it is a dagger, a hope, faith, courage."[37] Il Duce would also call for the creation of myths in the theater.

The theater director Anton Giulio Bragaglia, who worked closely with Pirandello, urged playwrights to create myths that would represent the fascist revolution.[38] The most enthusiastic and most developed call for the creation of "myths" by artists was made, however, by Pirandello's friend and fellow playwright Massimo Bontempelli, the creator of "magical realism" in Italy. Bontempelli, who became secretary of the fascist syndicate of writers and authors in 1928, published his ideas on myth in some of his articles in his journal *Novecento*, articles that were collected in the volume *L'avventura novecentista* in 1938. According to Bontempelli, the creation of new myths is imperative because of the contemporary historical and political situation: World War I created a tabula rasa from which a new epoch is beginning. There are three historical epochs: the classical, which ranges from pre-Homeric times to the time of Christ, the romantic, which goes from the beginnings of Christianity to World War I, and the present. The "misunderstood" Nietzsche is the precursor of the third epoch and of fascism. Since humanity is in fact beginning again, we must feel "elementary" and reconstruct from nothing, creating our own founding myths as did the other periods. The style of the present period will be "magical realism," which conceives of art not as an imitation of reality but as an exploration of mystery and of daily life as a miraculous adventure.[39]

Although he never really defines myth, Bontempelli very clearly links the concept to politics, seeing fascism (and to some extent communism) as the new system for the new era. Just as politics is rediscovering power, art is rediscovering magic. Moscow and Rome are the tombs of democracy; democracy's death necessitates new myths, new art forms. Bontempelli also apparently came to fascism through aesthetics. In November 1929 he writes: "My long-standing adherence to Fascism is due primarily to the fact

[37] Speech in Naples, October 24, 1922, quoted in Gentile, *Sacralization of Politics*, 82.

[38] Anton Giulio Bragaglia, "Propositi per il teatro sperimentale," *Quadrante* 6 (October 1934).

[39] Massimo Bontempelli, *L'Avventura novecentista* (Florence: Vallecchi, 1938), 500–502.

that I considered it to be a frank political primitivism, which joyously and with one clean sweep canceled the experiences of the outworn politics that had preceded it" (286).

Yet the new beginning, in both politics and art, Bontempelli warns, is not absolute: we cannot become Adam again; we have a past. The suggestion emerges that the creation of "new myths for new men" must of necessity be self-conscious, not "naive" like the myths of the pre-Homerics. Still, contemporary "new men" may be able to repeat the experience of the Greeks through the birth of a new theater. Responding enthusiastically to Mussolini's call for a "theater for the masses," Bontempelli argues that a new theater can be born from fascist mass political ceremonies and celebrations just as ancient Greek theater was born from the mysteries of Dionysus (385). To be truly popular, and not elitist, theater must rediscover the social and religious function of ancient tragedy through the creation of new myths (234).

Although Pirandello and Bontempelli did not have exactly the same concept of myth, their thinking on the subject was, as Gilbert Bosetti puts it, "dialectical," each influencing the other.[40] Certainly both share the notion that the "renovating" force of fascism requires the creation of new myths. Although Bontempelli develops the notion more than does Pirandello, they also agree on the necessity of myth in artistic creation as an antidote to a society overwhelmed with industrialism and materialism.

The New Colony

Intersections of the creation of new myths with social, spiritual, and aesthetic renovation and with the attempt to create new forms of modern tragedy appear in different guises in the three plays Pirandello called "myths." Like D'Annunzio's *Dead City*, Pirandello's *New Colony* made its first appearance outlined in a novel, *Her Husband*, published in 1911. The play composed by Pirandello's writer-character Silvia Roncella, differs, however, from the one written and directed by Pirandello twenty years later in that in Silvia's play, the mother-earth figure La Spera kills her baby son at the end of the play rather than surrender him to his father. Silvia is a "naive" and unlettered writer who had never heard of Euripides or Medea until critics pointed out the parallels. Pirandello, of course, was not so naive and

[40] Gilbert Bosetti, "De la poétique du mythe, de Bontempelli aux 'Géants de la montagne' de Pirandello," *Revue des études italiennes* 1–2, 40–71. Other discussions of the Bontempelli-Pirandello relationship include Corrado Donati, "Il rapporto Pirandello-Bontempelli dalla trasgressione grottesca al richiamo del mito," in *Luigi Pirandello: poetica e presenza*, ed. Walter Geerts, Franco Mussara, and Serge Vanvolsem (Rome: Bulzoni, 1987), 389–416, and Fulvia Airoldi Namer, "Pirandello e i miti di '900,'" in *Pirandello e la cultura del suo tempo*, ed. Stefano Milioto and Enzo Scrivano (Milan: Mursia, 1984), 339–49.

clearly seems here to have conceived of remaking the Medea story into what he would later call a "modern myth." In his own *New Colony*, however, he revises the classical myth considerably. There, La Spera does not imitate the act of Medea but rather is saved with her child on a rocky promontory as the rest of the island sinks into the sea.

A journalist writing in 1928 recounts that three years earlier Pirandello told him that he intended to write "a vast social drama of great poetry titled 'The New Colony.'"[41] Along with numerous reviewers, the commentator finds that the "myth" marks a significant change from Pirandello's previous "cerebral" drama. The new play is for him a "vast choral chant," a drama of "flesh and blood," an "almost classical tragedy." It is comparable to *La Figlia di Jorio* in that both are "tragedies of primordial creatures" that express "the soul of the race." Pointing out that the abject creatures in the play create their own law and morality by choosing a Leader (*Capo*) and an archetypal Woman ("vestal, nurse, consoler, queen, mother), he remarks that "no one could miss the social and ethical content of the tragedy." Disruption of the newly created order is brought about by the arrival of "sin and anarchy" on the island.[42]

Stylistic as well as dramatic changes from Pirandello's earlier work are indeed remarkable. In what could be construed as a response to the calls for "mass" and "popular" theater, Pirandello creates a popular chorus of sailors, smugglers, and criminals, including actual songs, using an earthy language. As Susan Bassnett-McGuire indicates, the play bears a superficial resemblance to Brechtian drama, complete with good-at-heart criminals and a capitalist villain (in Pirandello's play called Padron Nocio).[43] The differences between the Brechtian and the Pirandellian, however, are revealing, for it is not class conflict but rather the obliteration of class under a leader that is valorized in the foundation of the island community, although the capitalist, as in Brecht, will operate as a corrupter.

An old fisherman, Tobba, is the one to propose that the group sail off to create their "paradise" on the former prison and La Spera agrees that they will then either sink with the island or be reborn (*resuscitati*). Once the decision is made, at the end of the prologue, Pirandello introduces his first "miracle": milk begins to flow from La Spera's dry breasts; she can feed her child. Once on the island, La Spera is transformed from whore to angel of mercy, giving of herself to care for (but not to sexually satisfy) all of the men but belonging to the leader Currao alone. Currao's leadership is owing to his possession of her.

[41] Mario Corsi, "La Nuova colonia," *Comoedia* 10 (April 1928): 8.
[42] Ibid., 8–10.
[43] Susan Bassnett-McGuire, *Luigi Pirandello* (New York: Grove Press, 1983), 148.

Tobba acts as the keeper of the agrarian dream that promises happiness through cooperative communal work and the simple life, but the men begin to quarrel over questions of property and women. Here Pirandello's vision seems almost Rousseauistic—claims that a piece of land is "mine" come to disrupt the ideal of harmony. As often in Pirandello, sexuality seems to be associated with a fall, with sin. It is as if the men could enter their "new life" only if they could renounce the desire for actual women in order to venerate the Mother-Madonna-Saint. Without any legal system imposed on them from outside, the colonists must develop their own. In principle, the new institutions will be organic, communal, arising from collective need rather than abstractly conceived and imposed. This ideal is expressed by La Spera (speaking to Crocco): "None of us can be all if there are others. . . . I have understood that there is a way, yes, to be everything for everyone . . . that is to be nothing for ourselves. . . . If you open your hand to give and welcome everyone in yourself, you take everything, and the life of everyone becomes yours."[44] Currao (also to Crocco) explains it in more political terms: "Here there is no longer the law of others. There is yours . . . and ours, because we command ourselves, because we have recognized it to be just, as necessity has taught us. . . . No one imposes it on you" (1102). La Spera's version is closer to a Christian or at least a spiritually based ethic; Currao's is more practically reasoned. Both, however, are based on the notion of the possibility of a renovating, organic creation of law. Crocco, however, refuses to participate in the communal creation; furthermore, he wants La Spera for himself. At this point, the end of the first act, Pirandello introduces the second effect of his notion of myth as natural events caused by human emotions (the first being La Spera's milk at the end of the prologue): with Crocco's rebellion, the island begins to sink. Currao's stealing of their only boat leaves the colonists completely on their own: Tobba affirms that "the island will not sink, as long as we remain without sin" (1106).

Sin, however, is brought to the island by Crocco in the second act in the form of Padron Nocio with his boatload of women, wine, and other reminders of the corrupt city. Nocio comes, for one reason, to reclaim his son, to whom La Spera had acted as mother. But La Spera's position as mother-queen is threatened by the coming of the other women, and especially of Nocio's daughter Mita, for whom the *padrone* will arrange a marriage with Currao. Thus Crocco recalls La Spera to her former identity, naming her "disgusting whore" (1118), and proposes that Nocio, because he has "the means," become leader of the community with "a new government" (1121–22). Currao resists what he sees as the imposition of Nocio's laws on the community, along with the city vices, but the seeds of

[44] "La Nuova colonia," in *Opere di Luigi Pirandello*, ed. lo Vecchio-Musti, 5: 1099.

his own corruption are planted as he disputes with La Spera over their infant, whom he now calls "*my* son," thus thinking in terms of individual property. The end of the second act foreshadows that of the third as La Spera remains alone with the baby: "I'm not alone Nico, if they left me with you, with you, my love, with you, my joy, my Nico; my Nico" (1133). Although she too claims possession of her son, La Spera's discourse differs from that of Currao. Far from arguing by right of property, she regresses with the baby to a prelogical babble affirming the organic, unbreakable tie between mother and child, one that cannot be undone by the imposition of the father's law.

The third act works out the catastrophic consequences of Padron Nocio's invasion. One of the play's small realistic scenes serves as a *mise en abyme* of the return of property and greed to the community: three girls, attracted by a display of shawls and necklaces, argue over their possession with the refrain "questa è mia!" (1141). La Spera, having evolved from whore to mother-saint-queen to outcast, now envisions a new role for herself as sacrificial victim: "I am like the scabby sheep that no one must touch" (1138). To maintain his authority, Currao now needs the support not of the primordial woman but of the "boss," or capitalist money (1143). Thus the arrangement of marriage with Nocio's daughter: power is still attained through possession of woman but this time through an exchange between men. In the play, unlike the sketch, it is Currao, and not the *padrone,* who insists that he must have his son. And it is here that La Spera intervenes, pitting her notion of organically based law against the contractual one that Nocio has brought from the city. She argues: "If he really loved him, he would understand that my son must stay with his mother, because only I can give him *true* love. . . . These are not pacts that can be made. What? Make contracts on my blood? On my flesh?" (2: 1153). If Currao attempts to take the child by force, La Spera threatens, an earthquake will occur, and indeed it is this final "miracle" that brings the tragedy to its resolution. Against the background of the festival of carnivalesque "marriages" arranged by Padron Nocio, Currao reaches for the baby, La Spera grasps the child in a "mother's desperate embrace," and according to Pirandello's stage direction, "the earth, as if the trembling of the frantic, desperate embrace of the Mother [capital in original] spread [*propagarsi*] to it, truly begins to tremble" (1158). As the island and its inhabitants sink into the sea, La Spera remains with her child on a rock: "God, I am here, alone, with you, my son, on the waters!" (1158). It is as if La Spera has crossed the barrier that divides human life from the miraculous and the mythical, time from eternity. Through the magical effects of staging (which were not so easy to realize), she is to become one with Mother Earth. Pirandello's concept of myth— that the passions of primitive humanity provoke natural phenomena—receives its theatrical form.

Why Pirandello abandoned the Medea-like ending of the original version is not entirely clear. One possible motive is his determination to create "new myths," not to rehash the old. Also, the ideal of rebirth and regeneration seems to form one of the bases of his "social myth"—a notion better expressed through the figure of the Mother-nurturer than of the Mother-destroyer. The new, primal, organic society, founded on the renovated La Spera's maternal presence, has now tragically fallen and failed, but the mythical apotheosis, making of the sacrificial victim an Eternal Mother, promises its rebirth and regeneration; perhaps its eternal return. Like Pirandello's other mothers, La Spera is an "irreducible construction"—the one social role that cannot be acted or created but only instinctively accepted. For the "lictor" Zapponi, the mother, for Pirandello, as in fascist ideology, represents the instinctive, as opposed to intellectual, basis on which one can begin social reconstruction.[45] For Roberto Alonge, Pirandello's mythology of "Mother Earth" in *The New Colony* coincides with fascist discourse on the mother and with the fascist utopian vision of a return to a precapitalist, agrarian society.[46]

Certainly Pirandello's tragic vision in *The New Colony* is in conformity both with his definition of tragedy as the incessant and ever-renewed conflict between life and form and his understanding (via Gentile) of Mussolini's fascism as a continuous, ever-renewed, and nonstatic attempt to conciliate the exigencies of human vitality with the necessities of political structure. Thus the failure of one form (the first colony) does not mean the failure of the regenerative state. It is rather that the ideal form of a classless society unified by consensus under a leader must be wary of the menaces of bourgeois capitalism and legalism. All this does not mean that Pirandello was attempting in any sense to write "propaganda": it is rather that his aesthetic convictions coincide with his approach to fascism. The fact that this view had little to do with the brutal realities of the regime at the time poses other questions.

It is tempting to read in the "fall" of the pristine society through the introduction of money and greed a critique of the fascists' growing ties with capitalist institutions in contrast to their earlier "revolutionary" ideals. By marrying Padron Nocio's daughter and by dealing with him to share power on the island, it seems that Currao has in effect renounced the attempt to create a corporate society and has capitulated to the old order of power, wealth, and the contractual, abstract laws of "citizens." But there is no evidence that Pirandello was concerned with this development, and it would

---

[45] Ascanio Zapponi, "Pirandello rivoluzionario," 107.

[46] Roberto Alonge, "Subalternità e masochismo della donna nell'ultimo teatro pirandelliano," in Alonge, *Struttura e ideologia nel teatro italiano fra '500 e '900* (Turin: Stampatori Università, 1978), 200–233.

in any case be highly unusual of him to make such a specific reference in a play. Certainly his antidemocratic and anticapitalist sentiments remained unshaken: indeed, they were reinforced by his trip to America early in 1924.[47] What Pirandello has represented in his tragic "myth" is the losing struggle of an ideal organic, agrarian, and instinctively based social form against the degenerative forces of modernity. Yet the myth is potentially regenerative in that it postulates the possibility of a reconfiguration of the ideal social form constructed from the "blood" and "flesh" of the mother, perhaps by La Spera's son.

Paolo Puppa argues that *The New Colony*, although not propagandistic itself, contains thematic material that was prevalent in fascist discourse generally and specifically in the fascist theater of propaganda current at the time it was produced and thereafter. The fascists became engaged especially in the 1930s in what Puppa calls "a pathetic search for founding myths"[48] or for myths that would express the image of renovation and renewal they wished to propagate. Among these were the myth of the rural paradise as a solution to the corruptions of the city and the call to agriculture expressed in plays such as *Terra nostra* of 1933. The importance of representing the Italian mission to colonize, already emphasized by Mussolini in his call for writers to express "spiritual imperialism" in 1928, was of course renewed around the time of the Ethiopian campaign. Puppa also shows that during the years of consensus the Italian stage overflowed with plays extolling the value of maternity, while Mussolini was extolling the virtues of woman as generator for the Mother Nation.[49]

The fascist press was on the whole sympathetic to *The New Colony*. As the interviews quoted above indicate, the consensus seemed to be that Pirandello's theater was now turning from his former portrayal of the bewilderment and disintegration of the bourgeoisie toward a more "popular" theater and a more positive affirmation of "faith." Piero Fornaciari, in *Il solco fascista*, praised the presence of "humanity" in Pirandello's new play along with the "simplicity and clarity of its structure and language."[50] On the occasion of the revival of the play by an amateur (*filodrammatico*) company in 1938, the director Riccardo Marchi emphasizes its success as an example of "a choral spectacle conceived for the masses." With the use of Sicilian songs and ordinary people as actors, Pirandello has found the "wor-

---

[47] After he returned from this trip, Pirandello stated: "I am antidemocratic *par excellence.* The mass itself needs someone to form it, it has material needs and aspirations that don't go beyond practical necessities." He also reaffirmed his esteem for Mussolini, who "confers reality on things" (interview with Giuseppe Villaroel in *Il giornale d'Italia*, May 8, 1924).

[48] Paolo Puppa, "Motivi pirandelliani e condizionamenti di regime nel teatro italiano degli anni '30," in *Pirandello e la drammaturgia tra le due guerre*, ed. Enzo Scrivano (Agrigento: Centro nazionale di studi pirandelliani, 1985), 212.

[49] Ibid., 234–35.

[50] Piero Fornaciari, "*La Nuova colonia*," *Il solco fascista*, April 6, 1928.

thy interpreters of his popular myth."[51] Silvio D'Amico, in an essay translated into English and published in the United States, perhaps best expresses the critical consensus on Pirandello's evolution: "In recent years,
with the spread of the Fascist belief, especially since 1925, Pirandello has
insisted on a clear though tacit defense of his own position, repeating with
special emphasis the advice to look at his recent works." Whereas Pirandello's earlier theater succeeded in emancipating the Italian stage from
naturalism, *The New Colony* expresses a "glorification of maternity" and
Lazarus a "true faith" along with "new ardors of joy and earthly fertility."
Thus his theater, according to D'Amico, is turning toward an expression
of the "lasting values" of the fascist new order such as family, nation, religion, and the spirit of masses. Furthermore, it is becoming "religious" in
the original sense of creating a bond between the public and the stage.[52]

Lazarus and the Religion of Fascism

The question of Pirandello's "religion," not only in the theatrical sense,
elicited much debate with the 1929 production of *Lazarus*, which coincided
with Mussolini's Lateran accords with the Vatican. Was the new play anti-
or pro-Catholic? Should it be considered a tragedy or a religious parable?
Pirandello, who called it his "religious myth," seems to have composed it
between 1926 and 1928. That it was first staged in England, on July 29,
1929, and produced in Italy (by the Marta Abba company) only in December of that year is indicative of the material difficulties that Pirandello
was having in Italy as well as his disappointment that Mussolini's promises
to fund his state theater had not materialized. His letters to Marta Abba
during this period are full of bitterness on the situation of the theater in
Italy, and his problems with the regime at the time have been well documented by Giudice. Yet the difficulties seem to stem more from a disillusionment with the government's failure to live up to what he considered
to be fascism's goals (along with his personal ones) than from any loss of
his fascist "faith." His acceptance of an appointment to the royal academy
of Italy in 1929, his role in presiding over the Volta conference in 1934,
and his public support of the Ethiopian campaign in 1936 hardly indicate
a major falling-out. On April 27, 1929, he wrote to Marta Abba from
Berlin: "*Lazarus* has been written already for more than a year, and I myself did not want it to be performed in Italy without me . . . in this time of
conciliation with the Vatican I would like to make heard in Italy a courageous

---

[51] Riccardo Marchi, "Ripreso della *Nuova colonia*," *Scenario* 7 (June 1938): 320.
[52] Silvio D'Amico, "Italian Theater after the War," trans. Vivian Hopkins, in *The Theater in a Changing Europe*, ed. Thomas Dickinson (New York: Henry Holt, 1937), 221–84 (quote p. 239).

and salutory voice that would settle the modern conscience on the religious problem. . . . this would be the time to make heard a courageous voice on life and death, on the God of the living and the God of the dead (precisely Fascism and the Vatican)."[53]

Pirandello, whose anticlericalism was well known and explicit in his writing, is clearly aware of fascism's claims to be a "religion," though what, exactly, he means by fascism's "God of the living" is unclear. If fascist "religion" had a God, according to Emilio Gentile, it was either the state or Mussolini himself. It is highly unlikely that Pirandello had either of these in mind. More likely, he is simply referring to fascism's emphasis on vitalism and perhaps even to its incorporation of rural festivals celebrating the fertility of the earth into its cult.[54] Nor does the "God of the dead" seem to refer specifically to the Christian God but rather to what Pirandello sees as the austere and moribund religious doctrines and practices upheld by the Vatican. Pirandello apparently views the Lateran agreements as an opportunity for fascist "religion" to incorporate aspects of Catholic ritual, saving it from death, and thinks that *Lazarus*, although written earlier, speaks to the contemporary situation. An intertext of fascist religious syncretism is indeed evident in the "religious myth."

Pirandello attempts to explain the significance of religion in *Lazarus* in several interviews. In one he affirms that he is "ahistorical," that history is a "construction," and that he is not interested in reviving the biblical myth of Lazarus but rather in incorporating its "universal spirit" in a modern myth. He further comments that "the world beyond is created because men, who cannot succeed in discovering God in themselves, need to believe that He is present in the beyond [*al di la*]." He intends the play to move from a "transcendental" myth (the father Diego's strict Catholic faith) to a myth of an "immanent" God, God in our lives. (This is no doubt what he meant by the "God of the dead" and the "God of the living" in his letter to Abba.) The "miracles" in *Lazarus*, like those in *The New Colony*, derive from the nature of myth: human passion provokes natural phenomena.[55] Here Pirandello seems close to suggesting that religion, like myth, is another human "construction"—albeit a necessary one—but that the modern configuration of the myth must emphasize immanence, not transcendence. Pirandello's friend Lucio D'Ambra recalls the contiguity of Pirandello's literary and dramatic revolution with the fascist political revolution, claiming that both in their ways unmade and remade a world and that the two revolutions meet

---

[53] Luigi Pirandello, *Lettere a Marta Abba* (Milan: Mondadori, 1995), 154–55.

[54] In Gentile's view, the fascists never created a religion of nature like the Nazis but rather emphasized nature dominated by the work of man in their agrarian cults. See his *Sacralization of Politics*, 90ff.

[55] Romano Drioli, "*La Nuova colonia* e *Lazzaro*: I nuovi lavori di Pirandello nel pensiero dell'autore," *Gazzetta del popolo*, June 12, 1926.

in "the spiritual realm." The dramatist's present "melancholy" stems from the lack of governmental support for his work, yet his "new tragedy" reso-nates with the spiritual universality of myth. *Lazarus,* which Pirandello read aloud to D'Ambra and a group of friends, profoundly moved everyone.[56]

Both fascism's concept of itself as religion and the history of its rela-tionship with Roman Catholicism are important to elucidating the sub-text of *Lazarus.* We have seen how the fascists incorporated D'Annunzio's "spiritual," binding collectivity and their understanding of Nietzsche's Dionysian festival in their rituals and ideology. The "religious" element of fascism was stressed from the very beginning of the movement as an in-dicator of the chasm between this "revolution" and liberal democracy or Marxism. The cliché "fascist *faith*" was used throughout the duration of the movement to differentiate adherence to fascism from adherence to mere "political" parties. Giovanni Gentile contributed the most systemat-ically to the thinking about the spiritual side of fascism. In a series of speeches collected in the volume *Fascismo e cultura* in 1928 he insists on the importance of "faith" for fascism—defining this faith as moral, reli-gious, and patriotic but as something that is constantly changing and re-newing itself.[57] Fascism is a "religion," not just a political system, in the sense that it addresses itself to the whole of life, even the spiritual side.[58] The sacrifice to the nation and the "faith" required of Italians in the war have resulted in a vast spiritual movement or fascism as the "conscience of the new national soul."[59] An August 7, 1924, article in *L'Impero* titled "Il fascismo è una religione" lists the basic tenets of this "religion" for a public less sophisticated than Gentile's. They are, according to the author Elia Rossi Passavanti, faith in the *patria,* belief in "lived life," a love of Earth, and a veneration of "La Madre Italiana," creator of new generations for the country.

D'Annunzio had adopted elements of Christian liturgy in both his drama and his political rituals. Fascism, along with the D'Annunzian style, incorporated some of his Christian ritual and vocabulary. Along with D'Annunzio's influence, the Great War itself contributed to the develop-ment of a syncretic fascist-Christian mythology. Fallen soldiers become ven-erated as "martyrs" who sacrificed themselves so that the *patria* would be renewed. Thus death, in a fusion of Nietzschean and Christian thinking, is

[56] Lucio D'Ambra, "Malinconia autunnale di Pirandello (dopo una lettura del suo *Laz-zaro*)," *Comoedia* 10 (October 15–November 15, 1928): 9–11. Did Pirandello give the young hero of his play his friend's name?

[57] See, for example, his speech given to inaugurate a lecture series at the Istituto nazionale fascista di cultura on May 14, 1927, in Giovanni Gentile, *Fascismo e cultura* (Milan: Fratelli Treves, 1928), 90.

[58] Ibid., 57–58.

[59] Ibid., 169–70.

to be viewed not with despondency but with "tragic and vigorous optimism."[60] Immortality, it seems, could be attained not only by death in battle but also through service to Il Duce in his work of totalitarian renovation. Commitment to fascism involved a kind of rebirth. For Emilio Gentile, as discussed in the Introduction here, resurrection became "the founding myth of the Fascist symbolic universe."[61]

As the regime moved toward closer relations with the Vatican, it became necessary to define fascist "religion" in terms more conciliatory with Roman Catholicism. The rapprochement began as early as 1923, with the introduction of religious education in the public schools. By the 1930s, according to Alexander DeGrand, "Catholic culture did not so much challenge the regime as define fascism in a way that was compatible with religious faith."[62] Fascism, in its own interest, did nothing to discourage religious beliefs, and many fascists were also practicing Catholics.

Although Giovanni Gentile's writings, because of their advocacy of the totalitarian, ethical state as the source of morality, were placed on the index, Gentile also attempted to reconcile fascist ideology with traditional religion. In "Il problema religioso in Italia" he acknowledges man's need for God and the state's need for religion but also postulates a conflict between the ethical aims of the state and the transcendental aims of the church. There can be no "static" solution to this conflict, but since struggle itself is healthy, there can be a vitalistic one: "a mobile unity in eternal movement toward self-realization."[63] The suggestion emerges that whereas organized religion tends to fall into formalism, it can be vitally renewed through its contact with fascism.

A similar struggle informs the dramatic conflict of *Lazarus*, which pits a rigid, legalistic, and transcendental Catholicism represented by a father against a vital, natural, and immanent "faith" represented by a mother, with a young hero, the son, forced into the former, drawn toward the latter, but finally managing to incorporate both. The two "religions" are theatrically represented by two spaces: Diego's closed garden dominated by a crucifix, the setting of the first act, and the country house where his wife, Sara, lives, opening onto the lush green farm, "a paradise" (1188), setting of the second and third acts. The plot recalls the inner story of *Six Characters* in that the wife has left the husband to live with a simpler man and bear him illegitimate children. In this case the dispute that caused the rupture con-

---

[60] Camillo Pellizzi, *Problemi e realtà del fascismo* (Florence: Vallecchi, 1924), 165, quoted by Gentile in *Sacralization of Politics*, 26.

[61] Ibid., 39.

[62] Alexander De Grand, *Italian Fascism: Its Origins and Development* (Lincoln: University of Nebraska Press, 1982), 151.

[63] Gentile, *Fascismo e cultura*, 159.

cerned the upbringing of the children: Sara wanted them to live in the "country air" and according to her husband loved them with "too carnal" a love; Diego was determined to send his son to seminary. Thus Sara's desire for the country has caused her to live in sin but also in an earthly paradise with the man she loves, a peasant.

The dramatic action takes place through the invasion of one "world" into the other. Sara, radiating beauty and health and dressed in red, enters Diego's space of death to tell her estranged husband that their son Lucio has left the seminary, removed his cassock, and returned "to be born again of me, his mother."[64] The shock of this revelation causes Diego to run into the street, where he is hit by a car and killed, and the last word of act 1, pronounced by the doctor, is "dead." Thus the victory of the religion of life ironically brings about a death.

As in *The New Colony*, the "miracles" in *Lazarus* appear to be caused by an effect of human desire on natural phenomena. Here, however, they are at times uneasily at odds with the play's more realistic premises and attributed to acts of both science and God. When Diego's and Sara's crippled daughter, Lia, loses her pet rabbit, the family doctor is able to bring the animal back to life with a shot of adrenaline. In the second act, Lia proposes that the doctor attempt to resurrect her father in the same way. The modern Lazarus is indeed brought back to life by this "miracle" aided by science, but the result provokes a second disaster. As Dr. Gionni says: "He cannot admit this miracle, believing as he believes" (1191). Could he admit that, dead, he experienced nothing, saw nothing on the other side, and was brought back to life by man, not God? The resurrection into life, again ironically, entails a spiritual death. Diego appears onstage at the end of the second act in a moment of silence which is, in the language of the stage directions, "that of life appalled by death" (1209), so that the last word of this act is also "death." In the third act, Diego's "resurrection" provokes him to adopt a Nietzschean ethos: he tries to kill Sara's lover, Arcadipane, with the justification, "I can do anything!" (1220). God is dead; so is the law; everything is permitted.

All of the major characters have undergone, or undergo in the course of the play, a death and resurrection. Sara, telling Lucio of her rebirth in the country, stresses her hatred of the institutions of the city: "those churches, those houses, and the court" (1198). The court had judged her to be in the wrong, granting Diego custody of the children. As in *The New Colony*, the laws made by man that obtain in the city are shown to be inadequate before those of God and nature. Confronted by the illegitimacy of his union with Sara and his children, the "natural man" Arcadipane explains that "the law is that of God: there is no other" (1192). Sara's rebirth,

---

[64] "Lazzaro," in *Opere di Luigi Pirandello*, ed. lo Vecchio-Musti, 5: 1182.

like La Spera's, entails a liberation from the oppression of artificial law. In Sara's case, rebirth will be completed by the return of her legitimate children, Lucio and Lia, to be reborn in her, in a sense to become her "natural" children. Lia, at the end of the play, is the object of a miraculous resurrection, as she goes toward her mother, suddenly able to walk. The most important rebirth, however, is that of Lucio, because he is also the agent of the second, spiritual resurrection of his father. Lucio claims not to have lost his faith but rather to have gained it by taking off his priestly garb. His renewed faith, which he explains to Sara and the doctor, is somewhat questionable in its theological orthodoxy.

> Don't you see how it is? In order not to die, we annihilate life in the name of God, and we make God reign in some kingdom of death so that he can give us a prize or a punishment there. As if good and evil could belong to us, who are only a part of creation, whereas He alone, who is All, knows what He does and why He does it. . . . This should be for him [Diego], as it was for me, the true resurrection from death: to deny death in God, and to believe in one Immortality. It is not ours, it is not our hope of reward or punishment: it is to believe in this eternal present of life, which is God; that's all. (1195)

Belief in the hereafter appears here to be a "construction" created by men out of fear of both life and death. The "eternal moment," the ahistorical and circular time in which Pirandello's characters have always lived, now acquires a religious status: eternity is not beyond, at the end of time, but now. Lucio's faith annihilates any legalistic notion of heaven or hell to define God entirely in terms of immanence, as celebration of life, with Sara.

Described as "radiant" (1217) and at the end of the play "as if in a divine light" (1223), Lucio, as Anna Meda suggests, resonates with the mythological identities of Lucifer, Apollo, and Christ.[65] Like the "son of the morning," he has rebelled against (a certain concept of) God; like the Greek god of light, he shapes the Dionysian energies of the natural world into clarity of form; like Christ, he sacrifices himself so that others can be reborn. He accomplishes the latter by redonning his cassock so that, as Sara and the doctor say, "it will give him the strength . . . to accomplish the sacrifice . . . for the salvation of his father" (1217). Lucio will sacrifice himself by renouncing the joy of earthly life as lived and represented by Sara—a life he ardently desires. However—an example of the complex dramatic syncretism of this play—Lucio reconverts his father by preaching to him the new faith that he has discovered through rebirth in his mother. "Your soul is God, father; you say 'yours,' but it is God." "In God there is no death, and He is now again in you . . . here, eternal, in our moment." "You had closed your eyes to life, . . . and [God] now makes you

[65] Meda, *Bianche statue*, 260.

open them so that you will live it and let others live" (1222). When this statement prompts Diego to confess that he has done evil, Lucio tells him that he "assumes" the evil and "redeems" it. The play ends with Sara "transfigured, as by a reflection, from the divine exaltation of her son" (1223), receiving her miraculously healed daughter in her arms, and with the word, pronounced by the whole cast, "miracle." Lucio is thus transformed into a Christ figure, instrument of the salvation of Diego, the old Adam, and of Sara, the new Eve.

The physical resurrection of Lazarus by Jesus as recounted in the book of John, chapter 11, prefigures the resurrection of Christ and the spiritual resurrection of humanity. The same sequence occurs in *Lazarus*, but the name of Jesus, or of Christ, is never mentioned and a Christian connotation of the myth is questionable. Catholics were divided in their reaction to the play. The influential Catholic critic Silvio D'Amico skirted the issue of Pirandello's theological orthodoxy by pointing out the contrast between his new "faith" and his former skepticism.[66] A Jesuit close to the Vatican, Domenico Mondrone, described *Lazarus*, along with Pirandello's other plays, as "the most odious and absurd defamation of the fundamental truths of Catholic education and Christian faith."[67] Apparently oblivious to such criticism, Pirandello, in his last interview, called *Lazarus* a "modern mystery" and expressed contentment that it had been appreciated by Catholics and that none of his plays had been put on the index.[68] A Catholic critic argued in 1994 that Pirandello's vision of life in *Lazarus* is "evangelical."[69]

The pagan-Christian syncretism in Pirandello's "modern myth" recalls D'Annunzio's in *Jorio's Daughter*. Pirandello, however, is less interested in folklore than in a kind of Nietzschean-Dionysian worship associated with spring, women, and the promise of rebirth.[70] Certainly Sara could be seen as a Dionysian woman, although Pirandello's puritanism would hardly allow him to create one endowed with the excessive sexuality of D'Annunzio's. Yet a comparison of this radiant, beautiful, outspoken earth mother dressed in red with the silent, veiled mother in black of *Six Characters* shows how

[66] Silvio D'Amico, Review of *Lazzaro* in *Cronache del teatro* (Rome: Laterza, 1964), 2: 71: "A Pirandello who to the accusations made against him of spiritual Bolshevism, nauseating and nihilistic, answers (as previously in *The New Colony*) with an act of faith in fecund and immortal life."

[67] Quoted in Giudice, *Pirandello*, 198.

[68] Giovanni Cavicchioli, "Introduzione a Pirandello," in *Termini* (published in Fiume), October 1936, and in *Quadrivio*, November 15, 1936.

[69] Sergio Bullegas, *Pirandello e "Lazzaro": Il mito sulla scena* (Alessandria: Edizioni dell'Orso, 1994).

[70] Julie Dashwood, in "I momenti eccezionali di Pirandello: umorismo, novelle e 'paradiso terrestre,'" in Enzo Lauretta, ed., *Pirandello e l'oltre* (Milan: Mursia, 1991), 169–77, discusses parallels between *The Birth of Tragedy* and works by Pirandello, including *Lazzaro*.

far Pirandello had come in his celebration of Woman.[71] Although the power of Pirandello's Dionysian woman is through maternity rather than sexuality, it has a similar effect. As D'Annunzio's Dionysian women serve to energize male creators and leaders, so Sara effects the rebirth and "resurrecting" activity of the young hero.

Lucio then becomes a Dionysian-Apollonian hero, sacrificial but luminous. In Pirandellian terms, he gives "form" to Sara's "life." In the course of his last interview, Pirandello specifically evokes *Lazarus* in conjunction with both tragedy and contemporary philosophy.

> "In this nothingness, I hope to find everything," said Faust, adventuring into the infernal region of the Mothers. . . . The whole of my theater recognizes only one necessity, precisely in the Greek sense, a double and contradictory necessity of life: it must have consistence and at the same time it must flow. . . . This is the problem for life: not to remain a victim of form. And here is the whole tragic dissidence of the story of liberty. Nietzsche, Weininger, Michelstaedter wanted to make . . . form and substance coincide, and they were shattered. . . . In *Lazarus* I give the clearest answer to this fundamental dissidence.[72]

Did Pirandello actually believe that he had solved a major philosophical problem in *Lazarus?* The "answer" he gives is rather a dramatic and temporary one that corresponds to the development of his vision of modern tragedy. Whereas earlier tragedies such as *Six Characters, Henry IV*, and *The Life I Gave You* ended with a revelation of the "black abyss" and the inadequacy of "white statues," *Lazarus* not only posits the Dionysian as a positive, life-enhancing force but also envisions its possible containment in form. The form is a religion of some sort, but what? It is difficult to agree with Pirandello that his answer is "clear." In the drama, the form that resolves the conflict is Lucio's priestly habit. Putting it back on enables him to save his father from the extremes of rigid Catholicism and utter nihilism while sacrificing his own inclinations. But the cassock might also be seen as a theatrical costume which Lucio puts on in the same way that "Henry IV" wears his imperial garb. No longer believing in the substance—the authority of empire or church—one retains the form, creates the construction, plays the role. Like Henry, in this case, but with the major difference that he believes his role to be functional and beneficial rather than solipsistic and isolating, Lucio opts to play his part "forever." Such theatricality is not ab-

---

[71] The most thorough and convincing study of Pirandello's portrayal of women in the later plays, under the influence of Marta Abba, is Daniela Bini's *Pirandello and His Muse: The Plays for Marta Abba* (Gainesville: University Press of Florida, 1998).

[72] Ruggero Jacobi, "Pirandello parla di Pirandello," *Quadrivio*, November 15, 1936 (quotes from his interview in *Termini*).

sent elsewhere in *Lazarus*. In no other play do Pirandello's stage directions indicate so precisely the details of costume, particularly the costumes of Sara and Arcadipane. Sara, after all, was not born a peasant woman but had to put on a costume and play the part to become one. Acting like a peasant ("facendo la contadina," 1203), she tells her son, was the only thing that kept her from going mad. Like Lucio's in a sense, but as fulfillment rather than as sacrifice, her costume and role stave off chaos.

It would be possible to consider as a political parallel to Lucio's costuming the fascist government's rapprochement with the Vatican. Fascist "religion" cloaking itself in respectable, traditional garb accomplishes, as Gentile put it, a "mobile unity" of church and state. In the terms of Pirandello's letter to Marta Abba quoted above, such a costuming brings to the formal exterior of the Vatican's religion of the "dead" the vital interior of the Fascists' religion of the "living." While it is clear that Pirandello espoused the latter, he seems to have acknowledged the necessity of using the structures of the former.

Such an interpretation risks being reductive and does not deal with the aesthetic issues raised by *Lazarus*. Some of these are troubling. As a staging of "myth" the play is in many ways less successful than *The New Colony*. Realistic details get in the way of the "miracles": we are told, for example, exactly how Diego died and how he heard about his death certificate; we are made aware of Sara's economic situation. The shot of adrenaline is both overly precise and overly inaccurate—it seems to come from low-grade science fiction. It is more difficult to make the leap from the doctor's shot to the hand of God or from the mother's radiant love to the walking crippled child than it is to accept on a "mythical" level La Spera's causing the earth to move. But in spite of these and other flaws, *Lazarus* conveys at times an intense tragic suffering. Diego's spiritual anxiety and the consequences of his loss of faith, Sara's status as outcast, and Lucio's struggle and sacrifice all configure aspects of the modern individual's tragic encounter with a fate that is at once socially caused, provisory, and inexorable. The "miraculous" ending does not effect a resolution so much as a temporary stasis. While it is true that mother and child are reunited in a glorious rebeginning, we are not altogether sure that the syncretic fusion, or the costuming, achieved by Lucio can be maintained, or that Diego's reconversion will not give way to another spiritual crisis. Something of Pirandello's theatricality remains, fortunately, to keep the tragedy of modernity from giving way entirely to the modern equivalent of a mystery or morality play. Even in the "myths," Pirandello seems to be putting forward the metatheatrical problem of modern tragedy, writing, in a sense, the tragedy of the death of tragedy based on metaphysical certainties. His last myth will deal directly with the possibilities and limits of theater.

Art and Society in *The Giants of the Mountain*

The Giants of the Mountain is Pirandello's last play in the sense that it was never finished and that, according to his son Stefano, he was still working on it up until his death. According to Marta Abba, however, Pirandello had this "tragic myth" in his mind already in 1928; in May 1930 the maestro wrote to Marta that the work was almost finished.[73] There are many speculations but no evidence on the reasons why he was unable to complete the final "myth." The difficulties posed by an unfinished text have not prevented critical writing on it, especially in recent years. In spite of the problems it poses, *The Giants* is a much more original work than the other two myths, its metatheatricality in many ways harking back to some of the complex questions posed in *Six Characters* and *Henry IV*. I would like to call it a *tragedia da fare*.

Pirandello stated the theme he intended for the play on several occasions. In newspaper interviews in 1928 and 1929, he outlined the plot and explained that it centered on the conflict "between a spiritual world" and "the new materialistic world."[74] In a letter to Marta Abba dated May 30, 1930, he wrote that he considered the play to be "the tragedy of Poetry in the midst of this brutal modern world."[75] The letters also confirm the importance Pirandello gives to Marta's inspiration and his conception of her as Ilse and himself as the young poet ("the youngest of all"!) who writes the text inspired by her.[76]

Pirandello's somewhat reductionist formulations of the play's theme make it sound as if it might turn out to be simply another example in the long line of romantic and symbolist works pitting the fragile beauty of poetry and the poet against the insensitive, materialistic bourgeois world. The Pirandellian variations on the theme, however, transform it from simple conflict to complex maelstrom, perhaps leading the poet himself to confront problems that defied dramatic resolution. To attempt to write the myth of art was in a sense to confront the impossible task of writing the *Summum* of his entire career.

Of all the biographical, literary, and philosophical intertexts that can be found in *The Giants*, the most evident, and the most discussed, is the story of Pirandello's material difficulties with his own theatrical ventures. The fact that he uses the text of his own play, *La Favola del figlio cambiato* (*The Changeling*) as the text that the devoted actress Ilse tries unsuccessfully to present to an audience certainly indicates this as a real concern, although one that Pirandello must have added after his original conception of *The*

---

[73] Bini, *Pirandello and His Muse*, 125.
[74] Ibid., 124.
[75] Pirandello, *Lettere a Marta Abba*, 493.
[76] Ibid., 648. See also Bini, *Pirandello and His Muse*, 123–29.

Giants in 1929. *La Favola*, which was produced as an opera with music by Malipiero in 1934, was reportedly banned in Germany and received some hostile reception in Italy. This has led to speculation that it was perceived as anti-Nazi and antifascist. Reviews, however, were mixed and many quite favorable. While it is true that Pirandello did have enemies within the regime who no doubt expressed their displeasure, there seems to be no evidence of any charges of antifascism. Mussolini, who apparently liked the work otherwise, was said to be incensed by a scene in a brothel, contrary to "morality and family," and the Germans, too, objected to scantily clad women.[77] Pirandello defended himself in subsequent interviews. The Germans, he said, probably objected to the play because it is, in a sense, anti-Nordic; it represents a glorification of Mediterranean values. He agrees with the interviewer that it represents an "exaltation of maternal love and of the poetry of simple and natural life." The play's "meaning," as summed up by Pirandello, lies "in faith, in the strength of spirit against the fragility of matter." The nature of this faith corresponds to Pirandello's concept of fascism and of Mussolini—one which others in the hierarchy in 1934 might not have shared—"Everything may or may not be true; it's enough to believe it." He ends one of the interviews with a reaffirmation of his own "faith": "Today in Italy we have one great truth: the one that Il Duce has built with his most powerful and dynamic genius."[78] "Truths," for Pirandello here as elsewhere, are constructions, not absolutes; they can be "built" by geniuses and it is popular belief in them rather than external standards that makes them true. It is as if Pirandello himself wanted to keep on believing in the existence of the creative, dynamic, changing state that fascism purported to be as a movement, rather than the dictatorial regime that it had become in the 1930s.

Pirandello's problems with the reception of this particular play, however, were for him in a sense only a synecdoche for the greater problem of trying to get Mussolini to support his "Teatro d'Arte" as a state theater. Mussolini attended the opening of the theater in 1925, showing great enthusiasm over the production of Pirandello's folkloric and popular drama *The Festival of our Lord the Ship*, but his support waxed hot and cold with many words of encouragement and praise but no action. For Pirandello, failure to found the state theater was one of the major disappointments of his life's work. The ups and downs in his attitude toward Mussolini in the course of his negotiations are revealed in the letters to Marta Abba. A letter of February 1932 in which he distinguishes between Mussolini as man and as myth is particularly interesting. Sympathizing

---

[77] I have discussed the controversy surrounding this play more thoroughly in my "Fascist Discourse and Pirandellian Theater," 311–13.

[78] Interviews in *Quadrivio* and *Lavoro fascista*, March 1934.

with Marta, who was frustrated by her own attempts to get Il Duce's support for her company, he writes: "The man is . . . rough and coarse human material, made to command mediocre and vulgar people with contempt, capable of everything and incapable of scruples. . . . Whoever has the courage to tell the truth with head held high has 'a bad character.' [After Pirandello's pro-Verga, anti-D'Annunzio speech, Mussolini told Marta Abba that the maestro was a genius but had "a bad character."] And yet nonetheless, I recognize that at a time in contemporary political and social history as 'brutal' as this one, a man like him is necessary. It is necessary to maintain the myth that we have made of him and, in spite of everything, to believe and to keep faith in this myth as in a necessary hardship that it is sometimes useful to impose on ourselves. . . . [This is] the true proof of the disinterestedness with which we keep the faith in his myth."[79] The "vulgar" man is thus also the "necessary" dictator and the representative of the fascist myth whose "truth," although certainly not eternal, remained for Pirandello superior to any other political system for the present day. It was thus only fitting to put aside one's personal objections for a greater good.

If his faith in the myth remained constant, Pirandello's shifting attitudes toward the man are exemplified in a letter written only a month later. There he exudes an almost childlike enthusiasm. Il Duce, it seems, received him "with the greatest cordiality," "a beautiful intelligent smile on his lips," showing not only interest in but comprehension of Pirandello's latest plan for a state theater, which he promised to study carefully. Pirandello emerged from the interview "very happy with him and with me" and "full of faith and fervor."[80]

Of course, Il Duce's promises, this time as before and after, were never realized, and Pirandello's bitter disappointment was no doubt a factor in the making of *The Giants of the Mountain*, which postulates a conflict between "the fanatics of art" and the giants and their servants, bestial, materialistic "fanatics of life." Italian critics, with the notable exceptions of Roberto Alonge and Paolo Puppa, have almost universally identified the giants with the fascist regime, seeing in Pirandello's inability or unwillingness to finish the play a fear of censorship. The French critic Gilbert Bosetti, however, points out the reductive nature of this interpretation;[81] the Americans Jerome Mazzaro and Anne Paolucci argue that Pirandello's characterization of the giants could just as well represent American capitalism.[82]

---

[79] Pirandello, *Lettere a Marta Abba*, 930–31.

[80] Ibid., 952–53.

[81] Bosetti, "De la poétique du mythe," 70.

[82] Jerome Mazzaro, "Pirandello's *I Giganti della Montagna* and the Myth of Art," *Essays in Literature* 22 (fall 1995): 277. Mazzaro refers to Anne Paolucci, *Pirandello's Theater: The Recovery of the Modern Stage for Dramatic Art* (Carbondale: Southern Illinois University Press, 1974).

The fascists themselves, judging from a review of the 1937 production in the Boboli gardens in Florence, saw in the giants *both* "bolshevism" *and* "the gigantomachy of mechanical progress begun in America."[83] If Pirandello's difficulties with Mussolini and his theater no doubt figure into his creation, the myth grows to be much more complex.

A prime topos of both romanticism and symbolism, perhaps most memorably figured in Baudelaire, the theme of the incomprehension of art and the artist by a crass materialist society received a modernist formulation in the work of both Bontempelli and Pirandello. "Minnie la candida," the poetic woman lost in a mass, mechanized society, prefigures Pirandello's Ilse.[84] (One also thinks of Giraudoux's young girls and of the madwoman of Chaillot.) Both men see "myth" as a means of resisting both the stultifying rationalism of the bourgeois theater and the rampant materialism of contemporary society. But whereas Bontempelli embraced both mass spectacle in sport and technology in cinema, Pirandello (though he admired silent film) remained highly suspicious of technology, linking it to the triumph of the bourgeoisie, and continued to believe in the artistic superiority of theater. In August 1931 he wrote to Marta Abba from France that the current economic crisis demonstrates "the failure of the bourgeoisie in the entire world" and that it was in France, with the revolution, that the bourgeois order was born. Pirandello goes on to say that it was this bourgeois order that produced technology, which, applied to industry, is "a terrible form of madness." We have to simplify life, return to nature, and "destroy all the machines, all of them."[85] The outcry might be characterized as antifuturist, but the denunciation of bourgeois materialism and mechanism fits well within a certain vein of fascist ideology. Was Pirandello becoming more aware of the contradictions in fascism? While Mussolini continued to extol the virtues of rural natural life, he was embarking on a huge public works program designed to master and control nature.

Although the subtexts in Pirandello's life and thought may help us to approach his unfinished "myth," they do not give any answers to the problems it poses. The plot is fairly simple. Ilse, an actress, has devoted her life to playing the role of the mother in a poetic drama that turns out to be Pirandello's own *La Favola del figlio cambiato* (*The Changeling*). Her husband, a count, has spent his fortune on the endeavor. They have been unsuccessful, however, and only six members of Ilse's company, reduced to poverty, remain out of devotion to the countess. *La Favola* was written by a young poet who killed himself out of love for Ilse, and she has made it her

---

[83] *Lavoro fascista*, June 8, 1937, quoted in Paolo Puppa, *Fantasmi contro giganti* (Bologna: Patròn, 1987), 143–44.

[84] Suggested by Bosetti, "De la poétique du mythe," 46.

[85] Pirandello, *Lettere a Marta Abba*, 146–47.

Luigi Pirandello, *I giganti della montagna,* directed by R. Simoni, Florence, Boboli Gardens, June 5, 1937. From the Burcardo Library, Rome, Italy.

mission to communicate his theatrical poetry to the outside world. As the play opens, the troupe, pulling Ilse on a cart, arrives in a villa called La Scalogna, situated "in an unknown time and place, between fable and reality" (1307) and inhabited by the magician Cotrone and his band of quasi-human, quasi-fantastic creatures who seem to live as if in a theater with an endless supply of props, costumes, and even puppets. They are able to leave their bodies to exist as spirits and to see themselves dreaming. Cotrone invites Ilse and company to stay with them and, while reciting parts of *The Changeling,* tries to convince them to remain there, performing the poetic play in a world of pure art, rejecting the world that has grown incapable of understanding it. Ilse, however, continues to maintain that the play must be communicated to the world; where in the area can they perform it? The theater in the village is closing; perhaps it will become a stadium or a movie house. Cotrone suggests performing the play during a wedding feast about to take place among the giants who live on top of the mountain. At the end of the third act, the last one written, the onstage characters see the giants parading down the mountain on horseback, as the spectators hear the noise of the horses and an "almost savage" shrieking music. They are headed toward the village church for the wedding ceremony. The last written words, pronounced by one of Cotrone's group, are "I am afraid!"

The fourth "moment" or the "third act" (this contradiction is not explained) exists only as summarized by Pirandello's son Stefano according to his father's notes and conversation. The giants were never to appear onstage, but their servants, preparing the wedding feast, would receive the actors. The servants, however, having learned from their masters that the only important activity lies in "the possession of the strengths and riches of the Earth" (1373), know nothing of the theater but gross entertainment. When they jeer at the performance, Ilse shouts insults at them and they attack her, tearing apart her body until she dies. A butler comes to offer the apologies of the giants along with money, which the count accepts so he can construct a glorious tomb for his wife. The troupe exits, bearing the dead body of Ilse on a cart as they bore her live one in their first entrance.

Pirandello, or Stefano, explains the ending thus: "The poor fanatic servants of life, in whom the spirit does not speak today, but will be able to speak one day, have innocently broken, like rebellious puppets, the fanatic servants of Art, who don't know how to speak to men because they have excluded themselves from life" (1375). In this formulation, the conflict appears more as a variation of the endless life/form dialectic that Pirandello has always seen as the basis of the human tragic condition than as another variation of the romantic sensitive poet versus insensitive materialist society opposition. In the text as it stands, we know a great deal more about the fanatics of art than we do about the fanatics of life, although the latter give the title to the play. The only information we have about the giants comes from Cotrone, whose description is not entirely negative. They are not really giants but called so because they are big people who live on a mountain. They have shown courage and strength in accomplishing their various enterprises, which include the construction of aqueducts, factories, and roads, as well as agricultural development. Yet devotion to these works has left them "a little bestial" and swollen with pride in their victories (1360). The fact that they are about to celebrate a wedding in a church suggests that they have retained at least the forms of earlier civilization. They might be related to Padron Nocio in *The New Colony*, whose emphasis on material well-being and laws, represented by marriage, replaced the "natural" community. The problem here, however, lies not in the conflict between forms of social organization but in the question of the role and place of art in a society focused entirely on technical progress and material well-being. The giants' enterprises are not inherently evil but rather insufficient and dangerous in the sense that the material for them has eclipsed the spiritual.

From what little we know about them, the "giants" then seem to be mythological figures of a rampant materialism not unlike the forces that Pirandello, along with a strain in fascist ideology, saw as unleashed by the bourgeoisie in general and by American capitalism in particular. This does not of course exclude their possible relation to the growing importance of capitalism and technological enterprise in Italy or to other strains of fascism. Perhaps they cannot appear onstage because they have become dehumanized forces, representable only by the effects on their "servants." Cotrone's followers, in contrast, mythologically figure the opposite extreme, entirely devoted to the spiritual and oblivious of the material. In their villa, Cotrone explains, they may not have the necessary, but they have the superfluous in abundance (1136).

Cotrone's magic resembles philosophical idealism in that he claims to spend his life "inventing truths" (1342–43). He thus conforms to Pirandello's own essentially idealist position: there are no absolutes; truth is a perpetual invention of the spirit. One is reminded of Pirandello's tragic figures: the sketch of Prometheus casting shadows; "Henry IV" in a villa not unlike La Scaglona, desperately creating illusions in which he pretends to believe. Pirandello's "construction" of Mussolini also comes to mind, as, for example, in the statement he made back in 1923 at Palazzo Chigi: "Mussolini knows, as few do, that reality is only in the power of man to create and that it is created only by the activity of the spirit." (See note 15.) Cotrone's invention of "truths," however, does not constitute a creation of "reality"—it seems that unspecified activities of the latter sort resulted in his being expelled from the village (1344). His illusory inventions in the villa have no effect beyond the diversion of its fantastic inhabitants. He is not a tragic figure because he has divorced himself from all sources of conflict, choosing to live entirely in the imaginary and the marvelous, not, like "Henry IV," humoristically-tragically aware of an unbridgeable chasm.

If Cotrone is, as most critics have maintained, an artist, he is an incomplete one. The world of the villa is a Dionysian one peopled with music and dreams, in which dreams become playing "characters." As Cotrone says, "Dreams, without our knowing it, live outside of us, incoherent as we make them. You need poets to give coherence to dreams" (1359). The Apollonian ability to give light and form to the creatures of the night is lacking in the villa. The only poet in the universe of *The Giants* is a voice from behind the scenes: Ilse's young admirer, himself an unrealized character created by Luigi Pirandello, author not only of the poetic text preserved by Ilse but also of the text being spoken by the characters. Only a poet can communicate the truths of myth to the world, just as tragedy was born from the poetic incorporation of Dionysian ritual, but how is this communication to be achieved in modernity? This is the unanswered question of Ilse's mission.

The final scene might have represented a humoristic rendition of a Dionysian festival in which tragedy attempts to be reborn. The "Pantagruelian" banquet prepared for the giants was to be accompanied by "orgiastic screams and songs," dances, and fountains of wine (1372). Too busy to attend themselves, the giants have let it be known that it might be good for the actors to offer some means of "spiritual elevation" to the common people. But the gap has become too wide. If art is the only reality for the actors, the pursuit of material well-being constitutes the only reality for their audience: unlike their counterparts in ancient Greece, they have no common ground. The tearing apart of Ilse's body recalls the ritual dismemberment of Orpheus and Dionysus. With scenic effects difficult to imagine, however, her dismembered body was to appear "like that of a broken puppet." Ilse herself is prepared for supreme sacrifice, but the remains of her body, become as it were dead wood, will not as in the orphic mysteries accomplish rebirth. Sterile in body, Ilse seemed to be fertile in spirit, the "mother" of a work of art conceived through pure love. Now she recalls rather another tragic puppet, Orestes in *The Late Mattia Pascal.* The hole in the paper sky has become a chasm separating the material and the spiritual. If he had finished *The Giants of the Mountain,* Pirandello might have at last written the metatragedy of the problematic of modern tragedy. Instead, he has left the frames of a *tragedia da fare.*

Pirandello's incomplete tragic myth of the unresolvable conflict between the spiritual and the material is perhaps not so much a theatrical portrayal of the present as a visionary warning about the future. To reduce it to the biographical level, one could say that Mussolini's government, if it does not give Pirandello his state theater, will become like the world of giants. Pirandello's theater, in contrast, will become a hermetic, noncommunicating world of art. On a political level, if fascism does not remain true to its original "spiritual" mission, or its dialectical movement between the spiritual and the real, it will take on the worst traits of bourgeois capitalist democracy. Neither of these reductions, of course, contains the entire vision of the mythical metatragedy, the maestro's most complex statement of the dichotomy between the entities insufficiently formulated as "life" and "art."

Pirandello's tragic figures are all to some extent caught in the unsolved problematic of the writing of tragedy. Constructions themselves, their tragedy consists not in a confrontation with fate or the gods but in the awareness that these too are constructions without existence in any absolute sense. Like Pirandello's Prometheus, like his Mussolini, his tragic characters, aware of the death of the classical agon, cast shadows and create "realities." "Henry IV" recreates the trappings of the lost legitimate foundations of European society, only to expose the fact that the present is just as costumed and constructed. Lucio "resurrects" himself to appear in the costume of another hollow legitimate institution but attempts to renew it through a Dionysian vitalism. Only mothers, the "irreducible constructions," can experience something of the plenitude of tragedy without the self-conscious split. Donna Anna, learning that she cannot create life through the activity of the mind, becomes aware through suffering of the destiny of the mother's "broken body" in the loss of children. La Spera, bereft of everything else, remains on her rock with the certainty of motherhood. It is only through rebirth in the mother, and in nature, Pirandello suggests, that humanity can begin the necessary work of renovating and recreating both artistic and social forms. Like D'Annunzio, if with very different results, Pirandello equates bourgeois, linear, realist drama with parliamentary democracy: both are forms born of the rationalist mentality created by the French Revolution; both view human beings as abstract, definable entities rather than vital, changing beings; both construct time as historical rather than mythical. Radically new art forms as well as a radically new politics beyond conventional notions of "politics" are required for the new century. If Marxism is deemed to be as rationalistic as democracy, fascism seems to incorporate relativism, idealism, and an artistic, even theatrical approach to government. From the acceptance of Nietzsche's understanding that "nothing is true," it is possible—even while seeing the defects of the man—to arrive at an acceptance of the necessary myth of Mussolini.

D'Annunzio, although he never espoused this particular myth, helped to create it. Like Pirandello's, his aesthetic politics were to a large extent based on his conception of myth. D'Annunzio's drama seeks to abolish "the error of time" through conflating layers of ancient myth on the present; Pirandello's conflates historical periods or abolishes temporal and spatial referents altogether. Similarly, fascist discourse sought to recuperate antiquity within modernity, for example, the myth of Rome in contemporary imperialism, as it sought to obliterate class distinctions through the creation of mythical desire in the nation. We have seen how D'Annunzio's poetics of binding and fusing worked in similar ways.

Pirandello's poetics of "decomposition" seems to be in complete contradiction to D'Annunzio's poetics of fusion. Yet each begins by rejecting the "bourgeois" or naturalist notion of reality and arrives at an acceptance of the necessity of illusion. Both Pirandello and D'Annunzio retain one certainty: that of the authority of the poet and poetry. If Pirandello criticized D'Annunzio's excessively literary style, he never doubted the centrality of the author to the dramatic text. The poet decomposes, but then recomposes, bringing the audience into the necessary illusion.

For Pirandello, the poet and the dictator, both makers of words and realities, could be viewed as parallel and complementary; for D'Annunzio they were in competition. For both, however, the art of creating modern myth in the theater, like the art of governing, was ultimately a religious enterprise in the sense of binding together a crowd through the magic of words. Both D'Annunzio and Pirandello, in the spirit of fascist "sacralization," adopted syncretism through working pagan, Christian, folkloric, and modern stories and beliefs into a new identity. Both thus sought to recreate for modernity the most "religious" of Western dramatic forms, tragedy. Both, if they could, would adopt Nietzsche's theory to artistic creation, rebirthing tragedy from Dionysian festival. Yet whereas D'Annunzio ultimately writes the failure of modernity to produce a new tragic hero, Pirandello writes the hole in the paper sky widening into a chasm, the self-consciousness of modern tragedy ultimately and tragically withdrawing from life.

CHAPTER FOUR

French Aesthetic Fascism in the 1930s on Tragic Grandeur and Purity

Le fascisme. . . . C'est une conception subjective du monde et de la vie, une morale: c'est surtout une esthétique.

Jean Turlais, "Introduction à l'histoire de la littérature fasciste,"
Les Cahiers français 5 (May 1943): 25

Until fairly recently, and in some circles still today, French fascism was thought to be a foreign import, a primarily German ideology and politics briefly espoused by a few deluded Frenchmen but on the whole imposed on a nation whose traditions were profoundly antithetical to the movement. Studies by non-French scholars such as the historical ones by Zeev Sternhell and Robert Soucy and those oriented toward culture and literature by Alice Kaplan and David Carroll[1] have emphasized the indigenous French roots of and contributions to the movement, both in culture and ideology and in politics and economics. This is not to say that these scholars agree on all

---

[1] Zeev Sternhell, with Mario Sznajder and Maia Asheri, *The Birth of Fascist Ideology: From Cultural Rebellion to Political Revolution*, trans. David Maisel (Princeton, N.J.: Princeton University Press, 1994); Zeev Sternhell, *Neither Right nor Left: Fascist Ideology in France*, trans. David Maisel (Berkeley: University of California Press, 1986); Robert Soucy, *French Fascism: The First Wave, 1924–1933* (New Haven, Conn.: Yale University Press, 1986), and *French Fascism: The Second Wave, 1933–1939* (New Haven, Conn.: Yale University Press, 1995); David Carroll, *French Literary Fascism: Nationalism, Anti-Semitism, and the Ideology of Culture* (Princeton, N.J.: Princeton University Press, 1994), and Alice Kaplan, *Reproductions of Banality: Fascism, Literature, and French Intellectual Life* (Minneapolis: University of Minnesota Press, 1986). See also the essays edited by Richard Golsan in *Fascism, Aesthetics, and Culture* (Hanover, N.H.: University Press of New England, 1992), and (with Melanie Hawthorne) in *Gender and Fascism in Modern France* (Hanover, N.H.: University Press of New England, 1997).

important matters. Soucy has criticized Sternhell for neglecting the economic and social components of fascism in his focus on intellectual and cultural origins and for emphasizing the Marxist contributions to fascism over the conservative and right-wing ones Soucy deems more important.[2] Kaplan's approach, which embraces propaganda and popular culture, and Carroll's focus on intellectuals and "high" culture differ considerably from each other. Still, taken together, these studies and others make a strong case for the existence of a truly French face of fascism. Clearly, too, no other fascist movement attracted such a large number of intellectuals and writers, often drawn to fascism for primarily aesthetic reasons.

Implicit in these studies of French fascism is an element that has not yet been sufficiently foregrounded: the mutual impact of Italian and French fascism on each other was far greater than the influence of German Nazism on either of them. The Italian fascists' debt to Charles Maurras and Sorel, discussed in the Introduction, has been amply documented by Sternhell. Maurras in turn, and others in the Action française movement, whose distrust of German culture is well known, expressed admiration for the "Latin" dictatorship of Benito Mussolini, as well as for those of Francisco Franco and Antonio de Salazar. Coming to fascism through the influence of Maurras, Robert Brasillach, in attempting to conceptualize a French fascism, used Mussolini as his primary model.[3] Lucien Rebatet, in his *Memoirs of a Fascist,* making the somewhat exaggerated claim that no other movement attracted so many brilliant writers, states that "our patron was not Hitler but Mussolini."[4] Of course, there were elements in French fascism that were not specifically of Italian origin, most notably its antisemitism. This, however, does not signify a Nazi influence: the Dreyfus affair alone would suffice to show that antisemitism was hardly a German import. Edouard Drumont's *La France juive* (1886) had a deep effect on the French right as well as on fascist intellectuals. In oversimplified, but not false, terms, one could claim that French fascism, intellectually and culturally at least, was primarily a product of an Italian model partially derived from French sources combined with indigenous antisemitism. More important connections with German National Socialism came later, primarily under the Occupation when it seemed clear to fascist sympathizers (and others) that Germany, and not Italy, was destined to rule

---

[2] See Soucy, *French Fascism: The First Wave,* xiv, and *French Fascism: The Second Wave,* 8–12.

[3] See "Pour un fascisme français," in Robert Brasillach, *Oeuvres complètes,* ed. Maurice Bardèche (Paris: Au club de l'honnête homme, 1963) (hereafter *OC*) 12: 499–502.

[4] In the first volume of his memoirs, titled *Les Décombres,* Rebatet speaks of Mussolini's superiority to Hitler: "Hitler, with certain Wagnerian gifts, was nothing but a pupil of the great initiator of Rome whose genius created the politics of our century." In the second volume, he reacts to Mussolini's death thus: "But with the fall and the imprisonment of Il Duce, it was fascism that died. Well, we were fascists. Our patron was not Hitler but Mussolini, whatever faults he had committed. With him our *raison d'être* disappeared" (*Les Mémoires d'un fasciste* [Paris: Pauvert, 1976], 1: 28, 2: 115).

the "New Europe." Since French culture had Germanic as well as "Latin" roots, the association could be rethought. Even well into the 1940s, however, concern with defining a specifically *French* fascism continued to prevail.

One Germanic influence was, however, primary on French fascist intellectuals, and that was their discovery of the writings of Friedrich Nietzsche. Even here, however, we see an attempt, as on the part of Mussolini and Gabriele D'Annunzio, to "de-Germanify" Nietzsche, or to stress his affinities with Mediterranean, Latin culture, while (correctly) pointing out his severe criticisms of Germany. Although, as much recent work has stressed, Nietzsche had an important impact on "leftist" French ideology and theory, this should not obscure the fact that his work was *also* crucial to the right and to the neither right nor left fusions of developing French fascism. The turn-of-the-century French right associated with Charles Maurras would seem to have little in common with the "barbarian" Nietzsche, but the Maurassians made common cause with him to some extent for their own purposes. Certainly they agreed with Nietzsche's antidemocratic pronouncements in *The Genealogy of Morals*: the *ressentiment* of slave morality originating in the French Revolution results in a universal suffrage that obliterates the natural, hierarchical differences among individuals by transforming them into equal and abstract citizens. In *The Birth of Tragedy* they seem to have found congenial the praise of tragedy as European or "Aryan" culture's supreme form and the famous statement that the world can be justified only as an aesthetic phenomenon. They definitely took consolation in Nietzsche's later repudiation of Richard Wagner and of German culture generally along with his praise of France. Two articles in the *Mercure de France*, in 1895 and 1902, cite Nietzsche on the superiority of French culture, including the following phrase from *Ecce Homo*: "I believe only in French education [*Bildung*] and consider everything else which goes by the name of education in Europe a misunderstanding, let alone German education." Nietzsche is said to have seen victory in the Franco-Prussian War as a cultural disaster for Germany and to have contributed to the critique of the neo-Kantian ethics of the Third Republic.[5] For Maurras, Nietzsche, although unquestionably "barbarian," not only perceptively reinforces the case against democracy but also, ironically, may give his young French followers the desire to read Jean Racine again![6]

[5] The two articles are "Enquête sur les relations franco-allemandes," in *Mercure de France* 14, no. 64 (1895): 1–65, and "Enquête sur l'influence allemande en France," *Mercure de France* 44, no. 155 (1902): 289–383. This information and the quotation are to be found in Douglas Smith, *Transvaluations: Nietzsche in France, 1872–1972* (Oxford: Clarendon Press, 1996), 53. Smith also finds that later on, and through the 1920s, conservative commentators become less sympathetic to Nietzsche as he came to be identified with Prussian militarism (59).

[6] Charles Maurras, "Le Tien et le mien dans Nietzsche," in *Quand les français ne s'aimaient pas* (Paris: Nouvelle Librairie nationale, 1926), 117.

Thierry Maulnier

One of Maurras's disciples, Thierry Maulnier, publishing a book on Nietzsche followed by one on Racine, and reading the tragedian in the light of the philosopher, would seem to have taken his mentor's advice to heart. Maulnier, whom Sternhell calls the purest of the "spiritual fascists,"[7] and Carroll, similarly, identifies as a literary fascist "beyond Fascism"[8] does not deserve either label. Editor of the pro-fascist journal *Combat* in the 1930s, contributor to both *Action française* and *Je suis partout*, and generally espousing the goals of *La Révolution nationale*, Maulnier, unlike his friends and associates Robert Brasillach and Pierre Drieu La Rochelle, never joined a fascist party nor took any active role in politics. Highly critical of both Nazism and Italian fascism, as well as of the French parties, he seems to have envisaged his role as that of a theoretician, attempting to give an intellectual grounding to the antimaterialist, antidemocratic, "spiritual" rebellion prevalent among young Frenchmen opposed to the Third Republic and the "decadence" they believed prevalent in French society. Maulnier looked for the solution in what he called a nationalism beyond nationalism. The basic problem, as he envisioned it in *Au-delà du nationalisme* (1938), was "how to liberate nationalism from its 'bourgeois' character and the revolution from its 'proletarian' character, and how to interest totally and organically in the revolution the nation that alone can carry it out and to interest in the nation the revolution that alone can save it."[9] Obviously, none of the fascist movements in Europe, let alone any of the political parties in France, had achieved this ideal synthesis. One of his major criticisms of the existing fascist regimes was their tendency to compromise with capitalism. Carroll argues that Maulnier's contention that French culture has the potential to perform this salvific function is based on his conviction that the true culture of France is not national in any narrow sense of the word but rather the purveyor of the humanistic ideals of aesthetic and cultural wholeness dating back to classical Greece.[10] Maulnier's deep devotion to classical humanism, inherited from Maurras, plays itself out as an ideal and unrealized model for the "new man" envisioned by the revolutionary fascists and their associates. Although Maulnier was not a fascist in any conventional sense of the word, his literary and cultural writings clearly provided inspiration and grounding for those attracted to fascism through aesthetics such as his comrade at the Ecole normale and longtime associ-

[7] Sternhell, *Neither Right nor Left*, 213–65.
[8] Chapter 9 of Carroll's *French Literary Fascism* is titled "A Literary Fascism beyond Fascism: Thierry Maulnier and the Ideology of Culture."
[9] Thierry Maulnier, *Au-delà du nationalisme* (Paris: Gallimard, 1938), 249, quoted in Sternhell, *Birth of Fascist Ideology*, 236.
[10] Carroll, *French Literary Fascism*, 225–26.

ate Robert Brasillach. This theoretical or "pure" version of an aesthetic humanism coinciding with certain fascist aspirations can be seen in his two
principal works devoted to tragedy: *Nietzsche* and *Racine*.

Maulnier refers to "the tragic" in a political context in his preface to
Arthur Moeller van den Bruck's *Third Reich*, published in a French translation the same year as the first edition of *Nietzsche* (1933). Although he
takes care to distance himself from the young followers of the Führer
evoked in the book, stressing that the Germans are "our enemies,"
Maulnier does not fail to express his admiration for this "worthy" enemy.
"To die for a beautiful myth" (as did the author, who committed suicide)
"remains nonetheless one of the great privileges of man."[11] What moves us
in his book, according to Maulnier, is the author's "hard and proud passion, that will to grandeur, that tragic sense so striking in young Germany"
(8). With their critique of capitalism and Marxism, the Nazis have understood that the era of economics is being replaced by the era of will; that
Germany is entering into "a tragic epoch, in which the individual will have
to renounce all personal happiness" (8). What seems to appeal to him in
Moeller van den Bruck is the overcoming of Immanuel Kant by Nietzsche
and Bergson, although the latter two philosophers are not mentioned.
Whereas one aspect of National Socialism remains puritanical, Prussian,
and duty-oriented, van den Bruck displays its "spontaneous, generous, and
cruel" tendency, which causes him to speak of "purity" and of "a deep and
tragic virility, a natural bent for heroism, a disdain of happiness, a search
for sacrifice through the natural *élan* of being" (9).

The quarrel between France and Germany, Maulnier disingenuously argues, cannot be one of principles, for "if we contest the German principle
according to which a superior humanity has the right to subjugate an inferior humanity, why do we have colonies?" (13). The discord lies rather
in the inherent worth of the civilizations themselves, and for Maulnier there
can be no question about the supreme value of (a certain idea of) French
civilization. A young generation of Frenchmen, who resemble the Germans
in their disdain of happiness, their rejection of outworn values, and their
desire for sacrifice, is preparing to meet its worthy enemy. Maulnier states
categorically that "we feel closer to and more easily understood by a German national-socialist than a French pacifist" (16).

What Maulnier has clearly done in this preface is to disassociate the aesthetics of fascism from its politics. Thus he can express his contempt for
the "vulgar" political movements that cater to the masses in Italy and Germany (and in Russia) and for the specifically Germanic aspects of Nazism,
while admiring as it were the formal beauty and idealism of the young tragic

[11] Arthur Moeller van den Bruck, *Le Troisième Reich*, trans. Jean-Louis Lénault, introduction by Thierry Maulnier (Paris: Librairie de la revue française, 1933), 5.

heroes of Germany as described above. It is as if he were ready to welcome a tragic agon with the admirable enemy. The renunciation of an easy and decadent *bonheur* for tragic heroism, sacrifice, and *joie* would become a recurrent theme among the French fascists as it was for Mussolini's followers in their rejection of *la vita comoda*. One of Maulnier's objectives is to ally this new aesthetic with French classical humanism through a theory of tragedy.

Nietzsche (1933)

Apparently unperturbed by Nietzsche's violent attacks on humanism, Maulnier seems to want to reclaim the German's disruptive originality for a vitalistic development of Maurrasian classical humanism and the values of French civilization. In *Nietzsche*, he sees the idea of tragedy as *the* key to the philosopher's thought, *The Birth of Tragedy* as the basic work from which the others would spring, and Nietzsche himself as a tragic figure who throughout his life writes his own tragedy. Tragedy, unlike most philosophical speculation, is violent and combative. Maulnier goes so far as to argue that all true philosophy, instead of remaining abstract and *universitaire*, should represent "the extraordinary combat of man with the fundamental elements of the human condition: faith, despair, destiny, and liberty" and thus should be "pure, violent, and tragic."[12] Nietzsche is a "tragic thinker" in that his philosophy and his life become one and he invests them with heroism, sacrifice, self-transcendence and *grandeur*, opposing vitality to decadence.[13]

Tragedy and the tragic connote, in Maulnier's usage, a philosophical speculation, a way of life, and a literary genre, often conflated. The terms have political implications in that the "tragic man" is the superior man, most capable of and worthy of leading others. Tragedy is also a mode specific to Europe and even more to the Mediterranean, the area and the mentality, Maulnier implies, destined to dominate Europe and thus the world. By "Mediterranean," Maulnier clearly means only its European part, and through his understanding of tragedy Nietzsche seems to become an honorary Mediterranean. Whereas the "oriental" wants to sacrifice his personality to the world, the European "tragic man," exemplified by Nietzsche, wants to "virilize" his personality and oppose it to the world (269). The world, like man, is not a stable entity but a constantly evolving complex of "forces in struggle" (150), and the tragic mode reveals rather than obfus-

[12] Thierry Maulnier, *Nietzsche* (Paris: Gallimard), 21–22. The date printed on this *ninth* edition, 1925, is obviously a mistake—it is probably from 1945. The first edition, as far as I can tell, is by Librairie de la revue française, Paris, 1933.
[13] Ibid., 23–34.

cates this reality. Tragic European man is also "naked" in the sense that he does not hide his universal essence and his solitude behind national "clothes," for "the national idea is a non-tragic value" (70). Maulnier's notion of a European nationalism "beyond nationalism" is thus already incipient in this earlier work.

In many ways, Maulnier's book reads like Mussolini's (much shorter) 1908 essay on Nietzsche.[14] Mussolini also emphasizes Nietzsche's anti-German aspects: his Nietzsche is "French," "southern," and "Mediterranean" (99). For Mussolini, too, part of the greatness of Nietzsche's philosophy lies in the fact that it should not be read as an abstract system but rather "a myth, a tragedy, a poem" (99). The heroic Nietzsche, in "the tragic *grandezza* of his enterprise" (101), goes beyond the mediocrity of imposed morality to invent his own laws, overturning the Judeo-Christian slave morality. The Nietzschean superman, which Mussolini sees as the model for the coming generation, voluntarily, in living dangerously, encounters tragedy: "Every new conquest is a danger and a tragedy" (107–8). Like Maulnier too, Mussolini sees Nietzsche as writing the tragedy of his own life with that of his work. "Nietzsche was a poet and his work is the heroic poem of his life. Nor is its catastrophe lacking. . . . The superman is the symbol and the spokesman of this anguishing and tragic period of crises that the European consciousness is going through" (109).

Although Maulnier does not stress the superman as does Mussolini, he in a sense elaborates on Mussolini's notions of Nietzsche's life as a tragic poem and of Nietzsche as a Mediterranean figure. The philosopher's spiritual journey is first of all away from Germany, toward Greece—not Greece as a nation but Greece as the Mediterranean classical ideal. Nietzsche's singular contribution, however, is to discover that Dionysian forces and not Socratic rationality lie at the heart of Mediterranean culture. Nietzsche "opposes to the mournful and Christian pessimism of the Baltic the joyous and terrible cult of life" (68). His life then takes the form of a solitary tragic struggle. "For fifteen years, he plays on an empty stage a tragedy in the form of a monologue in which his voice is only heard by himself" (32). Nietzsche struggles to transcend the mediocre notion of morality that enslaves modern man. "Il s'agit de dépasser la morale, de vivre plus dangereusement que l'homme moral" (74)—one cannot help but think that Maulnier was hearing Mussolini's recuperation of Nietzsche in his slogan *vivere pericolosamente*. As the old values fall away, so do the false human support systems, the "reasons" we give ourselves for living. From this Nietzsche concludes not that life is not worth living but that the reasons themselves are

[14] Benito Mussolini, "La filosofia della forza (postille alla conferenza dell'on. Treves)," in "Il Pensiero romagnolo," nos. 48, 49, 50 (November 29 and December 6 and 13, 1908), reprinted in Enzo Santarelli, ed., *Scritti politici di Benito Mussolini* (Milan: Feltrinelli, 1979), 99–109.

without value (90). The Nietzschean critique thus destroys not only social, ethical, and metaphysical values but even the power of reason to reach objective truth. At this point, Maulnier makes a major leap in interpretation, attributing his own most un-Nietzschean term to Nietzsche.[15] What remains, according to him, is "purity": "the absolute purity of life, raised to the only value, accepted and cherished in its inevitable course" (93). Maulnier will elaborate on "purity," a term that, along with its associate "grandeur," will have an important fortune in fascist theories of both culture and tragedy in France.

Nietzsche thus appears as both tragedian and tragic hero, writing his own script but living his philosophical discoveries with the intensity of tragic suffering. The consciousness of the absurdity of the world entails a suffering that has no meaning but that brings the tragic hero to an encounter with "magnificent fatality," to sacrifice, and finally, through will, to victory (109). Tragedy for Nietzsche is not linear but "solar," an eternal cycle moving from catastrophe to renewal and back like Dionysus torn apart and reborn (174–75). As a tragic hero himself, Nietzsche struggles constantly with temptations to break his solitude, among them the temptation to accept happiness—*bonheur,* for Maulnier (as in fascist discourse generally) the refuge of the mediocre. This temptation comes in the form of "the little Jewish female intellectual" Lou Andreas Salomé (186), but it is rejected. Instead, he creates for himself tragic joy through the will to power—the extraordinary union of the cult of suffering and of the Dionysian embracing of life (chapter 9, "La Concupiscence de la douleur").

Nietzsche's life and work appear then as a constantly renewed trajectory toward "purity," or the rejection of ordinary life and its distractions for tragic perfection. Reaching the pinnacle, however, entails fall and catastrophe. For Maulnier, this means that Nietzsche's late work abandons the quest for Mediterranean classicism to "regress" to the cloudy myths of German romanticism. Since Nietzsche's late writings are vehemently anti-Germanic, antiromantic, and anti-Wagnerian, it is difficult to see what Maulnier means by this. He seems to have in mind primarily what he calls the "puerile" notion of the eternal return.[16] The return to "myth" obfuscates the clear vision of the fundamental duality of man's heroic combat with nature with a monistic fusion of man with nature. Thus Nietzsche falls from classicism into romanticism.

Nietzsche's life, in Maulnier's somewhat repetitious and digressive account, follows a tragic trajectory similar to the theory of tragedy he reconstructs. Tragedy is for Maulnier, as indeed it is for Nietzsche, clearly an

---

[15] I am grateful to John Burt Foster for pointing this out to me.

[16] According to Douglas Smith, the French Nietzscheans of the left could be distinguished from the Nietzscheans of the right by the former's emphasis on the eternal return and the latter's on the will to power. See chapter 3, "(De)Nazifying Nietzsche."

aristocratic literary genre as well as a mode of life in that it can be created, understood, or lived only by the superior. In an argument that reflects Nietzsche's own conflation of "race" with "class" (and that seems to prefigure some of Jean Anouilh's monologues) Maulnier states that "there are two races of men" (33). The first, those who belong to the "herd," are concerned only with living and with finding an easy happiness (*un bonheur facile*). They accept Christianity, the religion for the weak, with its mediocre virtues such as pity and its system of rewards and punishments. The second, the tragic men (it does seem that in life these are all men, though in literature Maulnier mentions Phaedra), eschew all moral systems and all rewards and punishments. The "purity" achieved by the tragic hero includes a single-minded (and Bergsonian) intensity of purpose, "the imperious *élan* that throws the human being into action" (241), vitality, the willingness to sacrifice, and the disdain for good and evil. These superior beings are accorded encounters with greatness and death ("des rendez-vous priviligiés avec la grandeur et la mort" [117]). Reading Nietzsche through the experience of the Great War, Maulnier, like Drieu La Rochelle, postulates a tragic man who values war above peace, quality above equality, free creation above servile conformity. Caesar and Napoleon, men who do not hesitate to live dangerously and confront destiny, serve as examples from the past. In modern democratic society, however, a "monstruous equality" threatens the strong and pure, imposing the values of mediocrity such as justice and the revenge of the weak on the strong. In the aftermath of the French Revolution, society reversed its authentic and traditional priorities: whereas it should be constructed to enable the great to flourish at the expense of the masses, it now functions the other way around (126–27), thus thwarting those capable of living tragically.

Although Maulnier gives several examples from Greek and from French neoclassical tragedy, it is clear that he is here more interested in tragedy as a concept applied to life and culture than to literature (he will turn to the latter in *Racine*). Politically, his sense of the tragic relates to the concept of a nationalism "beyond nationalism" and the superiority of European, particularly Mediterranean, culture. It is easy enough to see how he can move from his notions of the exceptional, spiritual tragic hero to the rejection of democracy and of socialist and capitalist materialism while embracing the idea of a strong leader or dictator. But one can also see why Maulnier, with his "pure" and elitist views, would not be likely to compromise himself with the day-to-day mass politics of fascism.

Maulnier does discuss solutions to the "decadence" of modern society in *Nietzsche*, but they are of a spiritual, aesthetic order, and precisely concerned with the possibilities of restoring the sense of the tragic to the privileged few through the recuperation of tragedy. It is of course just this endeavor that his tragic hero Nietzsche pursued from his rediscovery of

Dionysian energies at the heart of European civilization until his "catastrophe." Nietzsche at first found in Wagner's unification of drama and music the recreation of Greek tragedy for modernity but then—in Maulnier's view prefiguring his own fall—rejected him as too romantic and Germanic. In Maulnier's French interpretation—or distortion—of Nietzsche, the problem is formulated as one of how to restore *grandeur* and *pureté* to today's decadent Europe.

Maulnier elaborates on the problem and suggests a solution in chapter 7, "Your Dearest Enemy, Yourself." First, however, he feels called upon to contrast the art of the decadent present with the great achievements of seventeenth-century France. Tragedy, in a remark he attributes to Nietzsche but that sounds strikingly contemporary, is not an imitation of life but a "transmutation of life into discourse" (*transmutation de la vie en discours* [169]). This is the secret of classicism that he will elaborate on in *Racine*: the containment of the Dionysian by the Apollonian, of emotion by the Word; the union of interior richness and exterior simplicity, of lucidity and violence; what Maulnier calls in another striking formulation "un humanisme délirant" (178). Classical discipline does not mutilate or moderate passion but on the contrary makes it both more ardent and more intelligible (169). Modern men, however, the complex "men of decadence," have lost touch with their instincts and with simplicity, unity, and fervor of purpose (162). Their adversary, as the chapter title suggests, is in themselves. They cannot recapture innocent Dionysian fervor for they carry the baggage of their civilization with them; they must recreate it *self-consciously*. In what sounds like a Pirandellian formulation, Maulnier argues that modern tragedy thus requires a *mask*: it will have to be a "hypocrisie héroique" (167). The suggestion emerges that the possibility of a spiritual and cultural regeneration of modern Europe may lie in the creation of modern tragedy, even if necessarily self-conscious.

Maulnier does not develop his ideas on modern tragedy or on the restoration of the tragic in decadent modernity any farther than this. He does not even make clear when, in his view, the "modern" begins. "Classicism" sometimes refers to antiquity, sometimes to *le grand siècle*, and sometimes to an aesthetic that can, indeed must, be restored in modernity. At one point he says that all great men, again giving as examples Caesar and Napoleon, are "masked" (42). Does this mean that he sees Caesar and Napoleon as modern tragic heroes? Does modernity refer to everything that comes after the birth of tragedy in Greece? It would seem that Maulnier is really using the term in two ways: one referring fairly specifically to contemporary "decadent" France and another more loosely to European civilization after its loss of primal innocence. What is certain is that, through his reading of Nietzsche, he perceives that tragedy—in its Greek and French forms—represents the supreme creation of European civilization and that the restoration of an authentically tragic view of life is imperative to the future dominance of that civilization as well as to combating the internal "decadence" that threatens it. It is not surprising that the nation charged with a worldwide *mission civisilatrice* should have produced the tragedian most exemplary of the qualities of *grandeur* and *pureté*: Jean Racine.

Racine (1936)

For Maulnier, Racine in his very Frenchness became not only the summit and "purest" example of neoclassicism but also the universal, "beyond" national, transmitter of classical humanism. His tragedies exemplify the recuperation of primitive religious energies for the early modern age and the realization of the theoretical bases of Maulnier's "Mediterranean" Nietzsche: the containment of the violence of Dionysus within the formal purity of Apollo, the transmutation of life into discourse and cruelty into poetry and the transmission of the force of the superior (European-Mediterranean) civilization through its highest literary form. But Racine represents a summit of that civilization, which went into decline after him. Left implicit but unanswered is the question of how tragedy can be revived for the men of the decadent present.

Maulnier's Racine, as representative of one of the summits of civilization, is Bergsonian as well as Nietzschean. "In all of human history," Maulnier writes in the introduction, "the greatest *élan vital* and the supreme flowering of creative energies coincide with the triumph of formal perfection."[17] Racine is thus "civilized" not because he represses his violent instincts but because he gives form to them. The great summits of civilization, in which this ideal synthesis was realized, are Hellenic, Florentine, and French neoclassical. Maulnier does not even seem to conceive of civilization outside of western Europe, or indeed beyond nations touched by the Mediterranean. German and Shakespearean tragedy were no doubt too "impure."

Grandeur and *pureté*, the terms introduced in *Nietzsche*, surpass "Dionysian" and "Apollonian" in their importance to *Racine*. Maulnier uses them in part to contrast superior classical literary aesthetics with inferior romanticism and realism. Classical literature, Maulnier writes, is not a literature of "expression" because it gives primacy to what the poet creates rather than to what he feels or to what he imitates. As opposed to realism's "base submission to the object" and romanticism's emphasis on inspiration and interior images, classicism fosters the *grandeur* of creation, and "this

[17] Thierry Maulnier, *Racine* (Paris: Gallimard, 1936), 22.

grandeur is nowhere grander than in Racine" (52). Rather than submitting to the world, the classical creator would seem to exercise his will to power. Thus he *acts* by choosing among the "forces of the world," "those that he can bind in a bundle [*lier en faisceau*] to lead his audience to the denouement and his heroes to death" (53). One is reminded here of D'Annunzio's Nietzschean emphasis on the binding and fusing power of the dramatic poet over his characters and his audience.

"Purity," as an aesthetic criterion, also contrasts with the impure aesthetics of romanticism and realism. With Racine, it is realized in the perfection of composition and in a language that does not seek poetic effect for its own sake but puts poetry in the service of drama. Rejecting local color, realism, dramatic suspense and intrigue, and lyrical digressions, Racine depicts not the diversity of human beings but the pure confrontation of human *grandeur* with supernatural fatality. He is the poet not of life but of death, not of the *bonheur* that characterizes mediocre existences but of the great encounters with destiny (58). With such concentration, Racine's dramatic poetry succeeds in "creating in the crowd of spectators a unanimous and pure emotion" (108), of becoming "the means of that possession which tragedy affirms on the spectator, the instrument of the famous catharsis, which is . . . the transposition of the spirit into the mythical universe" (151). Again like D'Annunzio's ideal tragic poet, Maulnier's Racine *possesses* the modern (post-Hellenic) audience by reawakening yet controlling in them the violent world of ancient mythology.

While *grandeur* and *pureté*, in Maulnier's usage, are primarily aesthetic terms used to characterize Racinian tragedy, they also take on moral connotations when applied to Maulnier's Nietzschean concept of the Racinian tragic hero. Purity, for the civilized man represented by Racine, has nothing to do with the innocence of childhood but rather with the decision of the adult (although usually a young, passionate man or woman) not to compromise. Racine's heroes exhibit "the exaltation and intransigence which young men bring to sacrifice or love" (75–6); even his young girls are "hard, virile, and proud" (181). (It seems that this acquisition of "virility" is the only way for woman to enter into the tragic.) Racine's "pure" heroes are not in the class of heroic figures who deny death by perishing for a higher value but rather in that of tragic figures who affirm death by making a sacrifice with no "bargain." Their "purity" lies also in their lucidity: a consciousness of total catastrophe. Nietzschean heroes superior to the laws of morality, they know no limits; "everything is permitted" (192) to them. "The *grandeur* of defeats reserved to the tragic hero excludes . . . that offense to human purity which is morality" (191).

Having created his version of a Maurassian-Nietzschean Racine, how does Maulnier deal with his subject's Christianity? The key lies in his de-Christianizing of Jansensism. Thus "the cruelest and purest of poets could only find realization in the cruelest and purest religion" (242). Janenism is a "tragic" religion that emphasizes fate over innocence; *Phèdre* is not inspired by its sense of sin but rather by the resemblances between "the Dionysian cult of inevitable destiny and catastrophe and the religion of predestination and human misery" (243). If not really Christian, Racine's tragedy is nonetheless profoundly religious in that it concerns the struggle of man against supernatural forces rather than that of man against man and that it returns to the "purest sources of ancient tragedy" (243), reanimating the myths and religion of antiquity as in the time of Dionysian rites.

Maulnier's frequent use of the word "cruelty" in this work raises the question of a possible influence of or at least common ground with Antonin Artaud.[18] Certainly there are resemblances in the arguments of both that no true poetry is devoid of violence and in the critique of modern theater as timid and overly rationalistic. Racine's female characters, according to Maulnier, are even "crueler" than his male ones in that they are more entirely consumed by passion and will let nothing stand in their way. Maulnier's Racine is "cruel" in an Artaudian sense not only in that his tragedies are concerned with brutality, violence, and suffering but also in that they reawaken primitive passions within the spectator, liberating him or her from the rationalistic strictures of society and morality. In his *Introduction à la poésie française* (1939), Maulnier goes so far as to praise surrealism for its violent, liberating assault on rationality.[19] But he most decidedly parts company with the surrealists and with Artaud's theater of cruelty on formal grounds. The perfection of Racine lies in his ability to give *civilized* expression to primitive violence and religious fear, to transmute chaotic cruelty into clear language. Maulnier could never accept Artaud's valuation of the oriental theater's emphasis on gesture, sound, and visual effects over occidental theater's primacy of text. The humanistic tradition with which Maulnier allies himself postulates the essence of civilized humanity in the achievements of linguistic expression. Racinian tragedy represents the ultimate, for the modern world, of the Apollonian/Dionysian synthesis: "It is the confrontation, by a great civilisation, of its richest hu-

---

[18] For a comparison of Artaud with Nietzsche, see H. G. Kuttner, *Nietzsche-Rezeption in Frankreich* (Essen: Die Blaue Eule, 1984), 6off. Kuttner, however, makes a sharp distinction between the "Nietzsche of the Right" appropriated in Germany, especially by the Nazis, and a revolutionary "Nietzsche of the Left" received in France in a tradition from the surrealists through Deleuze. Like many other recent writers on Nietzsche in France, Kuttner does not even mention the importance of Nietzsche to rightist- or fascist-leaning writers in France such as Maulnier and Drieu La Rochelle. Naomi Greene, however, in "All the Great Myths Are Dark: Artaud and Fascism" in Gene Plunka, ed., *Antonin Artaud and the Modern Theater* (Toronto: Associated University Press, 1994), 102–16, brings out parallels between Artaud's work and aspects of fascist ideology.

[19] Thierry Maulnier, *Introduction à la poésie française* (Paris: Gallimard, 1939), 16–22. See the discussion by Carroll, *French Literary Fascism*, 233.

manism and its most perfect style of life with the primitive and pure sources of anguish, death, and pain" (109).

Any book on Racine by a French writer inevitably entails comparisons with his archrival Pierre Corneille. In contrast to his Racine, Maulnier sees Corneille as not so "purely" tragic. Corneille cedes to interests exterior to tragedy such as the heroic, the lyric, and the "romanesque." Whereas Corneille's subjects fight against circumstances and against each other, Racine's, pitted only against the gods, are certain of defeat and concentrate on accomplishing their destiny (157). They do not die for a higher cause but for themselves. It is because of its "purity" that Racinian tragedy fits naturally into the famous classical rules, whereas Cornelian tragedy does not.

Maulnier's aesthetics of tragedy, if they do not entirely justify labeling him a "spiritual" or "literary" or "pure" fascist, laid important groundwork for French aesthetic approaches to fascism. His concepts of *grandeur, pureté,* and the European tragic genius have some rather impure alliances. Edouard Drumont, in his influential antisemitic treatise *La France juive* (1886), had already complained about degeneration in the theater brought about by the influence of Jews. Making his own gloss on *The Birth of Tragedy,* he claims that the Jewish spirit destroys "the pure Greek creations of Aryan genius" and "the heroic soul of tragedy."[20] The idea of a "cure of purity" opposed to contemporary decadence, according to Robert Paxton, assumed importance in France in the fascists' appeal to youth in the 1930s and continued under Vichy. "Purity" had obvious racial connotations as well. According to Robert Brasillach, the desire of young French fascists was for "a pure nation, a pure history, a pure race."[21] The criteria of *grandeur* and *pureté,* the cornerstones of Maulnier's classical-Nietzschean aesthetics of tragedy, will become more politically charged aesthetic standards for judging modern tragedy.

Robert Brasillach

Robert Brasillach was Maulnier's classmate at the Ecole Normale Supérieure and like his comrade a rebellious disciple of Charles Maurras. From their teacher at the Lycée Louis-le-Grand, André Bellesort, they had received an induction to right-wing ideology through training in and admiration for the Mediterranean tradition of classical humanism as the central foundation of French culture. Although he was initially drawn toward Maurras's cultural-political movement, the Action française, Brasillach eventually rejected its conservative royalist-Catholic tenets to explore the

[20] Edouard Drumont, *La France juive* (Paris: Marpon and Flammarion, 1886), 2: 232, 249.
[21] "Pour un fascisme français," *OC,* 12: 501.

newer revolutionary movements, while retaining a fundamentally Maurassian humanism. Maurras's own admiration for the "Latin" dictatorships of Mussolini, Franco, and Salazar was influential in his transition to fascism. Like Maulnier, Brasillach approached fascism through aesthetics; unlike him, he came to support it in politics. Along with other French fascist intellectuals, Brasillach also came under the spell of the "barbarian" Nietzsche, whom he discovered, at least in part, through Maulnier. In his review of Maulnier's *Nietzsche*,[22] Brasillach expresses reservations about the German's romanticism and unreasonableness, repellent to the Latin temperament, while confessing that the book touched him deeply. After reading it, he felt "a bit drunk, possessed, and vanquished." In an article titled "Germanic Hellenism" written about a year later,[23] Brasillach appears to be wrestling with the thesis of *The Birth of Tragedy*. Marking his dissent from Maurras's traditionally classical concept of Greek beauty, he argues that while Germans such as Nietzsche may go too far in emphasizing the irrational and barbarian origins of classical Greek culture, it was important to recognize the existence of those origins.

Brasillach's struggle to reconcile the "Mediterranean" with the "Germanic" took place on both the aesthetic and the political fronts. Certainly throughout the 1930s the Mediterranean element, marked by his enthusiasm for Mussolini, dominated. In attempting to conceptualize a specifically French fascism, he also became interested in the leader of the Belgian Rex Party, Léon Degrelle, whom he visited in 1936.[24] Yet Mussolini remained his primary model for Mediterranean fascism. His novel *Les Sept couleurs* (*The Seven Colors*, 1939) praises the daring, heroism, and innovations of fascist Italy. In his prewar memoirs, he contends that the fascist "new man" had been born in Italy but deserved a Latin name applicable to the whole Mediterranean: *homo fascista*.[25] Even as late as 1942, he proposed as a model for French fascism Mussolini's (or Gentile's) theory expressed in the *Enciclopedia italiana* article that fascism is not a doctrine but rather a way of life forged in action.[26] A lover of the theater and a brilliant theater critic, Brasillach also viewed Mussolini in the light of that passion. In reviewing René Benjamin's *Mussolini et son peuple*[27] in April 1937, he notes with pleasure that Benjamin, student of Molière and dramatic author himself, has understood the importance of theatricality in fascism—a coupling that, he feels, most observers have viewed pejoratively or superficially. Recently

[22] In *OC*, 11: 328–31.

[23] "Hellenisme germanique," *La Revue universelle* 56 (January 1, 1934): 127, cited by William Tucker, *The Fascist Ego: A Political Biography of Robert Brasillach* (Berkeley: University of California Press, 1975), 73.

[24] See his essay "Léon Degrelle et l'avenir de 'Rex,'" November 1936, in *OC*, 5: 5–63.

[25] Robert Brasillach, *Notre avant-guerre* (Paris: Plon, 1941), 235.

[26] "Pour un fascisme français," 500.

[27] April 8, 1937, in *OC*, 12: 32–34.

returned from a trip to Italy himself, Brasillach sees in Benjamin's evocation of fascist Italy not only the resurrection of ancient Rome and the values of classical Latin literature but also a parallel to Corneille in mottoes such as "believe, obey, fight" or "Whoever is not ready to die for his faith is not worthy to profess it" (33). The beauty of Mussolini's rhetoric, with which he guides his people, makes the Italian dictator both "a great dramatic poet" and a director (*animateur*) who governs by poetry (33). Mussolini also appears as an actor as Brasillach recalls the beauty of his invocations to "the Latin sea" accompanied by "striking gestures" (33). His admirable sense of theatrical ceremony, coupled with his expression of a heroic conception of life, suggest to Brasillach not a superficial and facile showmanship but rather a recuperation for the modern age of *grandeur classique*. Brasillach himself seems to have "read" the February 6, 1934, riots after the Stavisky affair—the event that represented for French fascists the hope for an overthrow of the Third Republic and the establishment of fascism in France—through Drieu La Rochelle's novel *Gilles* as a recuperation of classical tragedy through political action. He did not, however, witness the events personally because he was at the time at the theater.

Brasillach's aesthetic-political attempts to create a "French fascism" were based not solely on the Italian model. In a series of lectures titled "Will Europe Be Fascist?" given to the fascist-leaning Rive Gauche Society in 1936,[28] he anticipated contemporary cultural historians by arguing that the origins of fascism were French, that Maurras had invented the term "National Socialism," and that French antisemitism preceded the German variety. Here too, he expresses an aesthetic admiration for Adolf Hitler as "a poet, a mythmaker, a Wagnerian orchestra conductor."[29] As antisemitism and the notion of the "purity" of nation and race grew more important in his thinking, he naturally became more interested in Hitler. Yet there is no reason to assume that he imported these ideas, which he correctly identifies as having French roots, from Germany. Although he eventually became fascinated by Hitler, as previously by Nietzsche, German culture, in contrast to Italian, always retained an "otherness" for Brasillach. He was disappointed by Mussolini's pact with Hitler in 1938.

Brasillach's tropes of Mussolini as dramatist and Hitler as musician are significant. Like D'Annunzio before him, he identified "Latin" culture with classical humanism and the preeminence of the word and Germanic culture with an emphasis on music and nonverbal effects. An important text in this regard is his "Cent heures chez Hitler" ("A Hundred Hours with Hitler"), consisting primarily of his observations of the Nuremberg cere-

[28] Alice Kaplan found these lectures in the French National Archives. She describes them in *The Collaborator: The Trial and Execution of Robert Brasillach* (Chicago: University of Chicago Press, 2000), 13.
[29] Ibid.

monies during a visit to Germany. Originally published in 1937, the essay was revised for inclusion in *Les Sept couleurs* in 1939 and again for *Notre avant-guerre* in 1941.[30] In Hitler's theatricality, as in that of Mussolini, Brasillach senses a totalitarian feeling of belonging to a community, the fusing of the crowd through the magic of the leader, the creation of an authentic political theater for the masses. Hitler's Germanic theatricality, no more superficial than its Italian counterpart, represents a "sacred rite" in which a sacrifice is accomplished (56, 61) and an aesthetic with *meaning* founded on doctrine (60). In the case of the Nuremberg pageantry, however, the aesthetic and its meaning are more difficult, more foreign than those of Mussolini's addresses to his flock. Germany, he muses, is "a surprising country, perhaps farther from us than the farthest Orient" (60). The German aesthetic is more archaic than classical: the stadium, which seats at least three hundred thousand people, is constructed with "an almost Mycenean architecture" (58). It is especially in the ceremony of the consecration of the flags that Brasillach perceives the "strangeness" of Third Reich ritual. Whereas in Italy he noticed posters everywhere, here there is a profusion of flags: the waving colors with their "crosses from the Orient" (72) produce a fluid and romantic effect in contrast to Italy's stable, framed verbal-visual icons. The flag consecration appears to Brasillach a religious act comparable to the Eucharist but more foreign since its underlying myths, like the flags themselves, seem to come from the "Orient." While he points out the irony in the fact that the nation that seems to reject everything out of the Orient (he is undoubtedly referring to the Jews) is in fact so "Oriental," he also recalls that important figures of German culture such as Goethe and Nietzsche were deeply drawn to the East (73). In his orientalizing of Germany, he was probably influenced by Maurras, for whom the Jewish, the Protestant, and the German all constituted "barbaric" and "oriental" threats to the French and therefore Western civilization.[31]

---

[30] The first version appears in *La Revue universelle*, October 1, 1937, 55–73; the second as part of the novel *Les Sept couleurs* (Paris: Plon, 1939 and 1985), 112–19 and 122–26; the third in *Notre avant-guerre* in the section titled "Ce Mal du siècle, le fascisme," 234–83. Brasillach's biographer William R. Tucker (*Fascist Ego*, 288) writes that since Brasillach was a POW when *Notre avant-guerre* was published, the proofs of "Cent heures" were given to Maurice Bardèche, who was asked to make changes to prevent a ban by German censors. See also Bardèche's comments in *Les Cahiers des amis de Robert Brasillach* 10 (December 1964): 50. It is true that there are passages in the 1937 version that express doubts on the future of Nazism and could even be construed as anti-German. Hitler, for example, is called "ce triste fonctionnaire végétarien" (this sad vegetarian functionary), 71. My references will be to the 1937 version except where otherwise indicated.

[31] Carroll points out this idea of Maurras and translates from his preface to *Romantisme et révolution* (Versailles: Bibliothèque des Oeuvres politiques, 1928), 4 as follows: "The fathers of the Revolution are in Geneva, in Wittenberg, and formerly in Jerusalem. They all derive from the Jewish spirit and from varieties of independent Christianity which rage in Oriental deserts or in Germanic forests, that is to say, at the different crossroads of barbarism" (*French Literary Fascism*, 75).

The cliché of Germany as a "musical" nation also dominates Brasillach's impressions. When he recalls listening to Hitler on the radio during the Nazi electoral campaign in 1933, his memories are neither of content nor of rhetorical effects but of "bells, drums, choruses, a musical magic." The Führer's voice "swelled, became rasping, completely filled the area, with something magic and terrible, and the word 'Deutschland' returned, passionately, every twenty seconds, like a sacred incantation" (70). (Tucker calls this "surely one of the most curious descriptions of the Nazi campaign ever penned.")[32] Whereas Hitler's voice at Nuremberg seems to Brasillach more "moderate" than his voice during the campaign, the ceremonies are filled with music from the orchestras and choral singing: "that musical enchantment without which Germany can conceive neither religion, nor nation, nor war, nor politics, nor sacrifice" (60). The mysterious spectacle overwhelmed by music and song seems to him to connote a ritual sacrifice, perhaps the sacrifice of German youth to their nation. The Germans express their patriotic devotion in a preverbal, preoedipal language: "that language of sounds and of the chorus which is the true maternal language of the German" (63).[33] We are surely here in the realm of the Dionysian, the orgiastic and ritual sacrifice rendered in choral music that came from the east and preceded the birth of tragedy. In Brasillach's reading, Germanic unlike Mediterranean culture seems incapable of containing Dionysus with Apollo and thus cedes to a romantic overwhelming of civilization by the primitive. He does not fail to point out that Germany's romanticism is part of its "strangeness."

If Brasillach's Hitler has to some extent succeeded in recreating a Dionysian rite and a pagan Eucharist, he also exhibits certain traits of a primitive tragic hero. "For this man . . . would sacrifice everything, human happiness, his own and even that of his people, if the mysterious duty he obeys ordered him to do so" (74). The sacrifice of *bonheur* to *devoir*: here is not only the Ur-plot of Cornelian tragedy but also a conflict central to Brasillach's own writing. Perhaps Hitler is not only orchestrating a sacrificial tragic ritual but is himself its symbolic victim.

Where is this all this heading? In the 1937 text (in contrast to the censored 1941 version), Brasillach manifests considerable skepticism about the durability of National Socialism and concludes that, if France may have something to learn from this form of totalitarianism, its ritual trappings are "certainly . . . not for us" (73). Also in the 1937 text, as well as in *Les Sept*

[32] Tucker, *Fascist Ego*, 68.

[33] Edouard Drumont, whose two-volume *La France juive* was the most influential piece of antisemitic propaganda in nineteenth-century France, also conflates to some extent Jews, Protestants, and other "foreigners." Interestingly, he sees the primarily musical Jewish culture as a threat to the book culture of the true French. "The very French book, the book that makes one think, the book that had such importance in the eighteenth century doesn't exist any more; it's music, art of feeling, of the soft and sickly, which holds the first rank. After the crocodile, the Jew is the most music-loving of all animals" (*La France juive*, 2: 264).

couleurs, Brasillach contrasts Nazism with Italian fascism. He can "understand" not only present-day Italian fascism but also its "immortal" quality, what will live on even after the fall of the Mussolini regime. "Hitlerism," however, raises doubts. "Tomorrow, will it be nothing but a gigantic historical curiosity? Isn't all of this too much?" (74). Brasillach seems to view the peculiar romanticism of Hitler with the distance and the fatalism with which Maulnier viewed Nietzsche's "fall" into romanticism. But the Führer, who neither contained the Dionysian with the Apollonian nor attempted to reconcile the Germanic and romantic with the Mediterranean and classical, remains more unknowable, more foreign than the philosopher. Yet because of its very strangeness, "oriental" Germany exudes a peculiar seductive power. If Brasillach was somewhat critical of but nonetheless "possessed" by Nietzsche, he became at once magnetically attracted to and repelled by Hitler.

In 1937, the year that he first published "Cent heures chez Hitler," Brasillach criticized the Germanophile and Hitler fanatic Alphonse de Chateaubriant for his "puerile" acquiescence to Hitler's attractions. While he concedes that Hitler's "poetry" undoubtedly has its "*charm* in the exact sense of the word . . . the distinctive feature of man is precisely to be able to resist charms."[34] Here Hitler takes on the traits of a woman: exotic, foreign, tempting, and "charming" but to be resisted by the man who would retain his national, masculine, or Mediterranean purity. Brasillach's feminizing, like his orientalizing, of the Germanic derives from Maurras, for whom Germans, along with Jews, appear as barbaric, "oriental," and feminine seductive threats to the integrity of classical (male) occidental culture represented by France and Italy. Yet Brasillach himself would eventually succumb to one representative of this "charm" while vilifying the other as the "foreigner" to be expelled from France.[35] In what became perhaps his most famous metaphor, he admits to "going to bed with" Germany.

After the defeat of France in 1940, Brasillach, in spite of his reservations, placed his hopes for the rise of a new fascist Europe in Germany. In a statement published February 19, 1944, and much quoted thereafter, he said the following:

> If one wants to know my whole opinion, I will say that I was not a Germanophile before the war, nor even at the beginning of the politics of collaboration; I was simply looking for the interests of reason. Now, things have changed. It seems to me that I have entered into a liaison with the German genius, and I will never forget it. Whether we like it or not, we have cohab-

[34] *L'Action française*, July 8, 1937, trans. and quoted in Carroll, *French Literary Fascism*, 116.
[35] See Carroll's summary of Brasillach's *Je suis partout* articles on the importance of expelling Jews from France (ibid., 112).

ited. Thoughtful Frenchmen [*les français de quelque réflexion*] during these years have more or less gone to bed with Germany [*ont plus ou moins couché avec l'Allemagne*], not without quarrels, and the memory will remain sweet to them.[36]

The prosecutor at Brasillach's trial, Marcel Reboul, used this quotation to great effect. After reading it aloud, he interpreted the accused man's "feeling" for Germany as the "feeling that dare not say its name, and which is *love!*"[37] The reference to Oscar Wilde's trial was not lost on the courtroom audience. Brasillach, who was reputed to have homosexual leanings, was being accused not only of collaboration but of deviant behavior with the enemy. Citing the fact that Brasillach received an early release from his prisoner of war camp, Reboul continued, "He sleeps with Germany, and the day after that fornication, they slip a return ticket in his palm" and "we understand . . . how your quasi-carnal love of brutal force could have pushed you to try and lead your country into the bed of such sweet memories."[38] In Brasillach's statement, however, it is not at all clear which country belongs to which metaphorical gender. *Les français* could easily be males seduced by a female *Allemagne*. This argument was brought out by Brasillach's defense attorney, Jacques Isorni, who claimed to have found the source for the metaphor in an often-quoted line by the nineteenth-century historian Ernest Renan: "Germany was my mistress."[39] (Kaplan shows that the trial was full of such trivializing, or obfuscating, debates.) What concerns us here is that Brasillach's words connote a seduction away from reason by *génie*; perhaps also from classicism to romanticism or from the Mediterranean to the Germanic; in any case from control to passion. Brasillach's *feelings* for the Germans, as opposed to his collaborationist activities based on pragmatic "reason," seem to have become active when the German army was close to defeat. Thus on September 4, 1943, he could write that after being a "collaborationist of reason" he had become a "collaborationist of the heart." Watching the Germans undergo their "tragic destiny" became for him a new aesthetic, theatrical experience, eliciting the emotion of pity and no doubt also terror in the spectator.[40]

That Brasillach took seriously the theatrical aesthetics of fascism and Nazism no doubt stems in part from his lifelong interest in the theater. In this domain too his interests seem to have been split, although not exactly along the lines indicated by his perceptions of Mussolini and Hitler. From

[36] "Journal d'un homme occupé," in *Une génération dans l'orage: Mémoires* (Paris: Plon, 1968), 487, entry dated January 1944. Also in "Lettre à quelques jeunes gens," in *OC*, 12: 612, dated February 19, 1944.

[37] Kaplan, *Collaborator*, 162.

[38] Ibid., 163, 164.

[39] Ibid., 178.

[40] "Naissance d'un sentiment" (*Révolution nationale*, September 4, 1943), cited in Carroll, *French Literary Fascism*, 121.

his classical education at the Ecole Normale, under the influence of the Maurassians, he inherited his veneration for the textual study of Greek, Roman, and French classical tragedy. As a theater critic, from 1931 to 1944, he developed a passion for modern dramatists such as Claudel, Pirandello, Giraudoux, Anouilh, and Henry de Montherlant as well as for productions by innovative contemporary *animateurs*, especially the Pitoëffs. The common thread binding his love of classical and modern drama was his strong belief that all great theater is first and foremost *literary*: against important voices in the contemporary theatrical world such as that of Artaud, and in spite of his great admiration for the Pitoëffs, he defended what Gaston Baty (sarcastically) called the reign of "Sire le mot." Like both D'Annunzio and Pirandello, in their different ways, like the critic Silvio D'Amico, and like Maulnier, he extolled the primacy of the word of the dramatic poet. Even in his modernist interests, he affirms his allegiance to classical, humanist, Mediterranean culture on guard against the too Dionysian or the too foreign.

In an essay titled "Le Théâtre littéraire,"[41] in which his primary interest is in tragedy, Brasillach follows Nietzsche in briefly tracing the development of Greek tragedy from its origins in the cult of Dionysus through its "purest" form in Aeschylus and Sophocles to its decadence beginning with Euripides. He departs from Nietzsche, however, in his emphasis on the importance of "the book" for the history of theater. When theatrical performance degenerated into spectacle for the entertainment of the masses, the essence of tragedy was preserved by obscure Alexandrians who wrote plays that were meant only to be read. During the Roman Empire, when popular spectacles abounded, the spirit of tragedy was kept alive by Seneca, whose poetic dramas were probably never performed on a stage, only read aloud. This does not mean that they are unrepresentable, even in modern times: Brasillach's earlier piece, "Sénèque le tragique" (1931), was dedicated "to Georges and Ludmilla Pitoëff who dare to play Seneca."[42] In that essay he stressed that since all tragedy demands a background of religion and that since Seneca was without religion, he replaced it with an awe before nature, death, and fate and with his poetic language. Here he emphasizes the dialectic in Seneca's characters between overwhelming passion and "that lucid consciousness that is without doubt the essence of classicism" (530). Seneca's tragedies are, even more than Greek tragedies, closed in a circle of fatality from which all hope is excluded and which leaves no resource but revenge (531). Seneca's genius lies in his ability to create a character like Medea, who is more than human, "a creation not conforming to the reality of the world, but conforming to that

---

[41] *OC*, 8: 525–53.

[42] *OC*, 8: 554–62. The essay includes Brasillach's translation of a dialogue from *Medea*, for him Seneca's greatest tragedy.

superior reality that one calls tragic reality" (530). Senecan tragic reality, created through poetry rather than through scenic effects, made possible the tragedy of Elizabethan England, French humanist tragedy, and eventually Corneille.

According to "Le Théâtre littéraire," the degeneration of French theater began with Denis Diderot and continued throughout the nineteenth century, although literary dramatists such as Alfred de Musset preserved poetic theater. It is the "horrible" realist aesthetic of the Third Republic, from Emile Augier to Henri Bernstein, that by imitating the language and manners of the man on the street rather than creating its own reality stands most in opposition to the spirit of tragedy.[43] (Interestingly, Brasillach does not even mention realism in comedy.) By the end of the century, however, "the fight to save poetry and intelligence on the stage" (541) was renewed in both France and abroad: Brasillach mentions D'Annunzio and Claudel, in whom he sees a continuation of the tradition of Seneca. Even modern tragedy must somehow impose a *sacred* language, taking seriously Mallarmé's "donner un sens plus pur aux mots de la tribu." Brasillach envisions his own curious version of a possible modern tragedy: "a drama whose heroes would be national heroes but in which, from time to time, the action would be commented on in Church Latin prose, vaguely modulated" (551–52).

Reading "Le Théâtre littéraire" along with Brasillach's theatrical impressions of Mussolini and Hitler helps to clarify the configuration of his aesthetic fascism. To be sure, both dictators emphasize ceremony and theatrics over "literature," but the Italian "dramatic poet" appears nonetheless to belong to the classical verbal tradition ranging from ancient Greece and Rome through Corneille. The "oriental" German spellbinder, in contrast, apparently untouched by Western classicism, relies not on the magic of words but on the seduction of sound and spectacle. Of course, one must not forget that Brasillach was *also* attracted to the wordless spectacle: he is after all coauthor of an important history of the cinema and a great admirer of silent film. Insofar as he conflated aesthetic fascism and theater, however, it is clear that—until quite late in his career—Brasillach attempted to guard the classical and Apollonian from being overwhelmed by the real seductions of the foreign and Dionysian. Like D'Annunzio, he clearly believed that the Latin theatrical genius lay in the manipulation of words. Yet certain romantic elements remain for him not only a temptation but also an important part of a theater that would otherwise become too academic and dry.

---

[43] Brasillach, unlike Drieu, does not here give an antisemitic twist to the "degeneration" of the theater, but one can again see a parallel with Drumont, who claims that the degeneration of theater in the nineteenth century is owing to the fact that it was taken over by Jews, who emphasized the spectacle more than the word (*La France juive*, 2: 232, 249).

Brasillach's book, *Pierre Corneille*, stemming from lectures that Brasillach gave at the Rive Gauche Society and published in 1938, represents a much more sustained although at times crude attempt to bring together theater, particularly tragedy, with Brasillach's ideas on fascism. Written just after Maulnier's *Racine*, and no doubt to some extent in rivalry with his school comrade and friend, it defends the heroic, nationalistic, and "romanesque" elements of tragedy that Maulnier had found "impure." It is in part a conventional *homme et oeuvre* study, in part Brasillach's own intellectual biography, in part an attempt to relate seventeenth-century absolutism to contemporary fascism, and in part an essay on the aesthetics of tragedy—ancient, neoclassical, and modern. Brasillach perceives three primary influences on Corneille's formation, influences which he no doubt sees in his own: Corneille's Jesuit education, his study of the classics, particularly Seneca, and his encounter with and attraction to what Brasillach calls the *romanesque*, by which he means in this instance the baroque, irregular, generically impure, and spectacular plays of Alexandre Hardy. From the Jesuits, in his school in Rouen, Corneille not only assumed the strong Christian belief that would remain with him the rest of his life but also learned the importance of developing a strong will. As part of their religious education, the Jesuits gave dramatic representations of the lives of saints and martyrs such as Joan of Arc—Brasillach even gives a list of such plays. "These tragedies," he claims, "already exalt the birth of French nationalism."[44] On the mind of a child, they would produce an "exaltation" fusing the hero with the saint and inducing a love of sacrifice (37).

From his reading of the "literary drama" of Seneca, Corneille must have appreciated the "violent taste for the absolute" (39) of the characters of the Roman tragedian. "They are of the race that goes to the very end" (40), under the influence of a "dictatorship of passion." Repeating his earlier essay on Seneca, Brasillach stresses what he sees as essential differences between tragedy and *drame*: tragic characters, unlike those of the *drame*, are intelligent; they analyze their passions; and tragedy demands a religious background which Seneca finds in nature and in man (41). Corneille, like Brasillach himself, would eventually translate Seneca's *Medea*. The violence and heroism of Roman tragedy along with the voluntarism, sacrifice, French nationalism, and Christian belief in the Jesuit plays would fuse in various ways in the development of Cornelian tragedy.

The third major influence on Corneille took place after he left the Jesuit school at age seventeen, as he became familiar with the baroque drama of his time by attending the theater. Alexandre Hardy's fantastic, tragicomic, more spectacular than literary plays induced in him a taste for the

---

[44] Robert Brasillach, *Pierre Corneille* (Paris: Librairie Arthème Fayard, 1938), 33. Subsequent references in the text.

romanesque, the fantastic, and the *invraisemblable,* as well as an aversion for what would become the neoclassical rules, a penchant for dreams and romantic love, and other "barbaric," "Shakespearean" elements which Brasillach finds present in modern cinema (161). Brasillach confesses that he has great sympathy for the "romanesque" element in Corneille and that he admires what he calls Corneille's "magical realism" (did he know Bontempelli?) in his early ballet-comedy *Clitandre.*

Although "literary theater," according to Brasillach, eventually wins out in the classical age and dominates Corneille's tragedy, the author of *Mélite* and *Clitandre* never entirely abandoned the *romanesque* of his youth. At the age of thirty, in Paris under Richelieu's protection, Corneille "marries Glory" by writing *Le Cid,* fusing his taste for adventure and romance with heroic tragedy. After the famous quarrel and the first of what Brasillach calls his "mysterious retreats," Corneille returns to the theater steeped in the Roman and Christian elements of his formation, temporarily stifling the romanesque. With *Horace* and its too exact adherence to the classical rules, what becomes known as the "Cornelian hero" is born. It is here that Brasillach suddenly, with no preparation, first applies his contemporary epithet to the writer of *le grand siècle.* "Thus it happens that the fascist writer simplifies, one must confess, that his ardor and his faith inspire in him works that are a little short, a little primary" (180). Brasillach himself devises a simplistic, updated interpretation of *Horace.* Noting that Leni Riefenstahl's title "The Triumph of the Will" (the title Brasillach gives to his part 2 on Corneille from 1637 to 1652) applies to Corneille and brings him close to the twentieth century, Brasillach remarks that the young Horatio would have "the vigorous ardor of a young Nazi" (182) if he weren't so stiff. Curiace, on the other hand, both "tender and virile," is in the situation of a soldier forced by a democratic regime into obligatory military service. The elder Horatio, too simple in his blind patriotism, fails to touch us.

Why does Brasillach suddenly call Corneille a "fascist" writer and what does he mean by it? Here, it seems to denote both a strict neoclassical formal structure and a fanatic devotion to patriotic duty that demolishes every other human sentiment through the "triumph of the will." Such rigidity and fanaticism, Brasillach seems to suggest, may be artistically harmful. His (relative) disappointment with *Horace* thus stems from the fact that the tragedy is *too* fascist! Perhaps he is warning his contemporaries that ardor, faith, and will do not suffice to create a great work of art. But Brasillach finds less rigid forms of fascism elsewhere in Corneille. One characteristic of fascism for him is the struggle of youth against age, and in *Le Cid* he sees the drama of a young fascist combating the ideals of an older generation (282).

Although Brasillach mentions Nazism in conjunction with *Horace,* his other references to fascism, if they are specified at all, are to its Italian face.

Taking up the Mussolini-Corneille connection mentioned in the Benjamin review, he observes that since Mussolini invited the Comédie française to perform Corneille in the Roman forum, he must have seen in the French tragedian "the brilliant, daring, antibourgeois, anticapitalist and antiparliamentarian precursor of modern fascism" (188). Here the "fascist writer" appears not as a slavish fanatic but as an adventurous revolutionary. Corneille's cult of Rome, which he develops from *Horace* on, prefigures Il Duce's. It is Rome's *power* that Brasillach's Corneille most admires. "Rome is the most striking example . . . of the domination of the world by power, and only by power" (292). Augustus, in *Cinna*, incarnates Roman grandeur because he pardons not out of pity and goodness but out of self-control and exercise of the will. Brasillach finds that the antidemocratic verses in *Cinna* still ring true: "When the people are master, they act in tumult: / The voice of reason is never heard." "The worst of States is the popular State" (290). Thus the Roman emperor, as for Mussolini, prefigures the fascist dictator. *Nicomède* creates a "daring, young, revolutionary" image of Rome. In that play, as in *Polyeucte*, Corneille's "romanesque" mixing of genres allows him to satirize the old bourgeoisie and "a whole gallery of *parliamentary* figures" (290, emphasis in original). *Seretorius*, on the other hand, portrays a tragic struggle between a "fascist" and an enemy worthy of him. If Seretorius resembles an antifascist brigade chief from a novel by André Malraux, his opponent Pompey, a "young Italian *avanguardista* who has become a general," remains "devoted to the dictatorship that saved his country from civil war." The subject of the tragedy is thus "the eternal struggle between fascism and antifascism" (384).

Positing an "eternal" quality of fascism, echoing the "immortal" nature of Italian fascism that he mentions in "Cent heures chez Hitler," allows Brasillach to find parallels between the twentieth-century movement and French royalist absolutism. The concept is implicit although not theoretically developed throughout *Corneille*. Brasillach seems to be suggesting that, in contrast to the historical narrative of the origins of the modern democratic republic, born from the French Revolution, fascism has always existed and will continue to recreate itself in new forms. If, however, one of Corneille's "fascist" characteristics is antiparliamentarianism, one has to assume that the adversary has also always existed in some form. The most important common characteristic of French absolutism and modern Italian fascism is their grounding in aesthetics, specifically theater and poetry. Italian fascism was born and is maintained "by the alliance of poetry and action, by the meeting of decorative passion and power, by the union of D'Annunzio and Mussolini. The same meeting, the same alliance, has already taken place once for French nationalism, through the spiritual friendship of Corneille and Louis XIV" (297). By accepting the contemporary Italian promotion of D'Annunzio as "the soul of fascism" and applying it to Corneille, Brasillach suggests not only that a national poet is essential to the fascist state; he also emphasizes the French contributions to "eternal fascism." The organic unity of the work of art—in Corneille's case, the binding of apparently conflicting influences into tragic form—mirrors the binding unity of the totalitarian state. Thus aesthetics and politics in *le grand siècle* attained an unprecedented unity as royal absolutism reigned in France and Corneille achieved absolutism in art (379). Yet ancient Rome was a model for the French monarchy, and an Italian, Cardinal Mazarin, who "put into his cardinal's coat of arms, like a revolutionary or a totalitarian dictator, the ax and the fasces" (378), was both instrumental in the creation of royal absolutism and patron of Corneille. Thus "eternal fascism" manifests itself as an intermingled Franco-Italian creation.

Yet Corneille, in his alliance with absolutism, also made specifically French contributions to the creation of "fascism." His cult of Rome was only part of his formation: his Christianity, allied through his Jesuit education with French nationalism, and his "romanesque" element, derived from French medieval and Renaissance literature, also contribute to his particular tragic and political vision. Both Christian and romanesque elements appear in *Polyeucte*, one of Brasillach's favorites, which he used for epigraphs for each chapter in *Les Sept couleurs*. Corneille may be "the most complete of our Christian writers before Claudel" (210); he is also a poet of chivalry; his martyr is a conqueror, like a knight of the Crusades, believing in the alliance of God and the superman and possessing a Jesuit will (225). At one point, Brasillach curiously calls this quality of Polyeucte "le nietzschéisme galant" (347). In the romance of Pauline and Sévère, Corneille brings out "romanesque dreams of dominance and sacrifice" (161). Through "triumphant grace" the city of Rome becomes the city of God; Corneille builds *Polyeucte* on *Horace* and *Cinna* like a cathedral. But *Polyeucte*, like *Nicomède* and *Attila*, takes place during the decline of the Roman Empire when the new forces of nationalism (Polyeucte is after all an Armenian) are beginning to arise. In *Attila*, dedicated to Louis XIV, Corneille puts these verses: "A great destiny is beginning, a great destiny is ending; / The Empire is ready to fall and France is rising" (294). Corneille admired in "the royal dictator" the incarnation of the nation (295). Heroic, chivalrous, nationalistic Christianity, represented by what Brasillach sees as the Joan of Arc of Corneille's childhood, contributes importantly to Corneille's aesthetic politics. Brasillach summarizes these as follows:

> Nationalism pushed to its most vivid particularism, incarnation of authority in a dominating and absolute figure, dictatorship, preferably royal dictatorship, opposition to liberal ideas, to parliamentarianism, to the old generations who never understood anything, hope in youth and the future, construction

of that future by faith, sacrifice, and everything that raises man above materialism, pride in the grandeur of flesh, but disdain for those who only have its appearance and form, these are, I think, the bases of what one could call Corneille's politics. Are they not strangely contemporary? (298)

Corneille, however, could not continue to identify completely with youth. Around the age of sixty, in Brasillach's biographical narrative, the tragedian comes under the influence of "le démon du midi," a late midlife crisis that makes him want to try something radically different. In his last works, the "temptation of the romanesque," always with him, transforms itself into the "temptation of tenderness." Citing Thierry Maulnier, Brasillach argues that this aspect of Corneille relates him more to the mixture of tones found in Shakespeare than to the "rigorous purity" of Racine. With Corneille as with Shakespeare, the dramatic machine can give way to a pause, to a dreamlike lyric interlude (436). In contrast to the rigorous *Horace*, love and politics, in the late plays, become inextricably mixed: "Politics takes on the face of love, and more and more a beautiful young woman, in the very center of the work, becomes the figure of dictatorship, liberty, fascism, and antifascism" (441). Brasillach does not give any examples of this, and it is difficult to see what he means. But his remarks on *Tite et Bérénice* (1670), one of Corneille's last plays, do show a new side to the "fascist" writer he has created. Brasillach would like to believe in the story of the contest created by the beautiful Henriette d'Angleterre, challenging Racine and Corneille to write a tragedy on the subject of the emperor Titus and queen Bérénice. Under her influence and that of the actress Marquise, the older Corneille becomes the "poet of virile tenderness" (442). Although critical opinion has traditionally found Racine's *Bérénice* superior, Brasillach argues that Corneille's version should not be neglected: he prefers Corneille's Titus, with his "desperate and fatalist heart," to Racine's, who talks constantly about killing himself but never does anything (445). Tempted by, but afraid of, happiness, Corneille's Titus revels in the poetry of despair. The mature Corneille transforms the confident line of Augustus in *Cinna*, "I am master of myself as of the universe," to "Master of the universe, but not of myself" (446). Thus the last incarnation of Corneille's conquering knight is in a sense defeated; he consents to lose everything except his honor. "Before the supreme temptation of tenderness, he still wants to believe in the help of will. But he touches us by his lack of conviction" (448).

Brasillach seems to be arguing here that Corneille's genius, his particular expression of "eternal fascism," is not limited to the creation of the better-known Cornelian hero of the period of the "triumph of the will" but encompasses both the romanesque and a more complex, mature, and more human side. Brasillach's own acute sense of the passage of time and nos-

talgia for a lost plenitude seem to find a corollary here. The conflict between *bonheur* and *devoir* or *bonheur* and *grandeur*, at the center of
Corneille's tragic universe, and often of Brasillach's literary one, may take
a variety of forms. Yet in Cornelian tragedy *devoir* and *grandeur* always
emerge triumphant, whether through the action of the single-minded soldier, the heroic and voluntaristic woman (Chimène), or the resignation of
the fatalistic emperor. Titus does not, after all, cede to the temptation of
tenderness. It is simply that *grandeur* acquires different tragic shadings.
Brasillach's final portrait of Corneille draws on his success in binding and
fusing a variety of styles into the creation of an original poetic world. The
true "classic" poet emerges not as a servile follower of rules or laws but as
an adventurous imperialist. "He is first of all an inventor, an explorer, an
Empire founder . . . [a] coloniser. He doesn't follow the laws, for he is the
one who makes them: genius is the only legislator. Classicism is the permanent Revolution" (486).

Here we are drawn back to D'Annunzio's poetry of imperialism, Gentile's
notion of the state as activist constant creation, and Mussolini's ideal of the
artist-dictator—strange company, from our present perspective, for
Corneille. Brasillach's images, more than his critical arguments, ground
his notion of fascism in aesthetics: the poet attached to the absolute
monarch or dictator does not merely follow the latter to create a reflective or propagandistic art; it is rather through the audacious creation of
his own world that he becomes the soulmate to the equally audacious creator of absolutism or totalitarianism. The parallel also emphasizes again
what Brasillach sees as the important French contribution to aesthetic fascism. Corneille's binding and fusing of the classical Senecan tragedy of the
Roman Empire with the French "Christian warrior" and romanesque traditions constitute his original creation of absolutism or "eternal fascism" in
tragedy. One of the implications of these arguments, which Brasillach and
his cohorts will develop later, is that if the poetic form of French absolutism
was neoclassical tragedy, the poetic form of French fascism (as presumably
of the D'Annunzian voice of its Italian counterpart) will be modern tragedy.

Because of his interests in the aesthetics and politics of theater, particularly tragedy, it is not surprising that Brasillach would try his hand at writing in the genre, though perhaps because of his critical interests in it, it
seems to have been a form that intimidated him more than the novel.
Brasillach's theatrical output is small but significant enough to merit a volume of his complete works with introductions by Maurice Bardèche and
Anouilh. It includes only two complete plays, *Domrémy* and *Bérénice*, a stage
adaptation of the trial of Joan of Arc, translations from Shakespeare and
Seneca, and two incomplete plays: *Les Captives* and *Septentrion*. Of these,
Bérénice is the only one that was ever produced. *Les Captives* (1934) is of in-

terest for its "romanesque" medieval subject (Roland and Charlemagne) and its attempt to apply the idea of a French text with a Latin chorus that Brasillach proposed in *Corneille*; *Septentrion* (1934), on the other hand, was to deal directly with the relations between the fascist leader and the poet and with the problem of conciliating fascism and monarchy in an imaginary modern setting. *Domrémy*, in which Joan of Arc never appears, treats the effect of the hero-saint on the ordinary folk of the village, in particular on her friend Hauviette, for whom knowing Jeanne necessitates renouncing *bonheur*. The trial adaptation presents Brasillach's concept of her as the virgin sacrificed for the nation and as a Cornelian heroine. The most representative text, however, for the intersection of fascism and modern tragedy, is *Bérénice*.

Brasillach clearly had in mind both (Maulnier's?) Racine and his own Corneille when he set out to write his "literary" modern tragedy on the rupture between the Roman emperor and the Oriental queen that had engaged both classical tragedians. But there were other reasons to attempt such a work for the contemporary world. Since his lycée years, Brasillach tells us in *Journal d'un homme occupé*, he had wanted to write such a play based on the "historical facts" that Bérénice was Jewish and that she was thirteen years older than Titus—facts that play no role in the existing versions of the story.[45] Those facts are indeed historical,[46] but Brasillach, in a letter written during the period of his vicious antisemitic journalism and a few months before he began writing the play, puts a particularly ugly spin on them.

> You ask me who is the real Bérénice . . . She is first of all the granddaughter of Herod who massacred the innocents, the niece of Herodiade, the cousin of Salome, which means that she is related to the most criminal family of Jewish (and historical) antiquity. Then she is a fat Jewess who was at the time of the break fifty-one years old (a 51 year-old Jewess!), *thirteen years* older than Titus. . . . All of that is *rigorously authentic*. You must admit that it is more Racinian than Racine, this carnal drama *à la Colette*, between a mature Chéri and a Léa from antiquity.[47] (emphasis in original)

Brasillach's poetic creation of Bérénice will be considerably more attractive than this so-called real portrait. He actually wrote his tragedy during the summer of 1940 while in captivity in a German Oflag—around the

[45] Cited by Maurice Bardèche, "Le Théâtre de Robert Brasillach," *OC* 4: 2.

[46] According to Ulrich Wilcken ("Berenike," in *Paulys Real-Encylopädie der klassischen Altertumswissenschaft*, ed. Georg Wissowa, vol. 3.1 [Stuttgart, 1897], 287–89), Bernice (b. A.D. 28) was the *great*-granddaughter of the Jewish king Herod and the daughter of Herod Agrippa I (d. A.D. 44). A Romanized Jew, she fell in love with Titus when he was twenty-eight and she forty-one. She lived with him in Rome for some time before popular opinion forced them to separate. On the death of Vespasian in A.D. 79, she returned to Rome to reclaim his affections, but Titus reluctantly sent her away. Wilcken's account is based on Josephus, Suetonius, Juvenal, and Tacitus.

[47] Brasillach's letter to Jacques Brousse, April 19, 1940, *OC*, 10: 549.

same time that another POW, Jean-Paul Sartre, was writing his "Christmas play" about a Jewish revolt against the Roman Empire, *Bariona*. It was given two public readings in two different Oflags where Brasillach was held but was never performed during his lifetime, though it was published in April and May 1944 in the journal directed by Brasillach, *La Chronique de Paris*. Bardèche speculates that the reason it was not produced during the Occupation was that since the play was "somewhat ambiguous on the Jewish problem" ("assez nuancée sur le problème juif") (!), it might not have passed the German censorship.[48] He also finds that Brasillach's fascism in the play was too "discreet" for the Germans. A more likely explanation is that Brasillach, perhaps seeing himself as a modern-day Seneca, consciously wrote in the genre of his beloved "literary theater" a piece to be read. There is no evidence that he ever tried to get it produced. The controversy surrounding the 1957 production of the play in a new edition with the most blatantly antisemitic lines cut and a new title, *La Reine de Césarée*, is a fascinating piece of French cultural history in itself.[49]

Like D'Annunzio's *Fedra*, Brasillach's drama from classical antiquity is heavy with intertextuality, but the tone is more Pirandellian than D'Annunzian in its ironic distance and its self-conscious theatricality. It is as if he applied Maulnier's idea that the only real modern tragedy must be *masked* and self-aware. Giraudoux and Anouilh are present too in the anachronisms, the characters' consciousness of playing a tragedy that has already been written, and the modern language, although Brasillach's veers toward a richer, more classical lyricism. The education of the *normalien* steeped in the humanities is evident: not only does Brasillach consciously adhere to the unities of classical tragedy; he names the five acts after the famous line of Suetonius that inspired Racine (*Titus Berenicen Invitus Invitam Dimisit*); he even quotes his predecessors. The variation on what is traditionally considered to be Racine's most perfect alexandrine at the beginning of act 2 would surely have the desired effect on a French audience:

Phenice: Dans l'Orient désert, quel devint votre ennui ...
Antiochus: Je vois que vous êtes sensible à la légende de la reine Bérénice.

On one level, *Bérénice* can be classified as a metatragedy.

The legend of Titus and Bernice contains a mythological and historical topos embedded in Western culture: the foreign, usually Oriental woman who threatens to subvert Western man or Western imperialism. Medea and Jason, Dido and Aeneas, Cleopatra and Caesar, Zenobia and

---

[48] Bardèche, "Le Théâtre de Robert Brasillach," 3.

[49] *La Reine de Césarée* was performed on July 26, 1957, in the Arènes d'Avenches in Switzerland and then in Paris, at the Théâtre des Arts, on November 15. The text was published the same year. Demonstrations against the performance were held in Paris (see Bardèche, "Le Théâtre de Robert Brasillach," 3).

Aurelian stand behind the queen of Caesarea and the Roman emperor as they do behind D'Annunzio's invented Basiola and Marco and Elena and Ruggiero. Bérénice also embodies, like D'Annunzio's Fedra, the Dionysian force that threatens to destroy Apollonian control, except that Brasillach distrusts the Dionysian a great deal more than D'Annunzio did. Like a good Hegelian, Brasillach endeavors to give his tragic antagonists equal weight, and following his interpretation of Corneille, he allows the "roman-esque"—the romantic and sensual aspect of the legend of the tragically separated lovers—to have its due. His Titus, like Corneille's, is subject to "virile tenderness."

Brasillach, it has to be said, has not written a piece of vulgar antisemitic propaganda or even a modernist Celinian one. The classical framework, the author's illusion that he has an aesthetic, intellectual, and "moderate" view of the "Jewish problem," along with his literary sophistication and po-etic language, keep the play from being a simpleminded struggle between "good" Romans and "bad" Jews. Perhaps this is what allowed Bardèche to say that *Bérénice* might not have passed the German censorship and the play's 1957 defenders to assert (naively?) that it was neither fascist nor anti-semitic. Yet fascism and antisemitism there are, and all the more insidious for being woven into (not merely cloaked by) the humanistic endeavor.

Those who argued that the tragedy is a purely literary piece with no po-litical agenda—or that it is even critical of fascism—have pointed out that Brasillach's sympathies are clearly with the mature and "tender" Titus, sen-sitive to the charms of the exotic, aging woman, rather than with the rigid young Roman Paulin, an invented character who spouts the pro-fascist and blatantly antisemitic lines that were cut in the later version. This is true: in fact, it may be argued that Paulin is for Brasillach a modern version of Corneille's "too fascist" young Horace,[50] whereas Titus reincarnates the character "tempted by tenderness" of his maturity. Yet what this apparent split allows Brasillach to do is to let his central characters play the individual drama of the Léa and Chéri of antiquity as well as the classical conflict be-tween *bonheur* and *grandeur* while displacing onto Paulin, through his dia-logues with each of the other characters, the collective *other* dramatic con-flict: primarily the struggle between the "criminal" race and the legitimate empire but also the struggle between West and East, youth and age, man and woman. Paulin, in spite of or rather because of his youthful rigidity, must safeguard the future by ensuring that the unthinkable does not occur: the Jews must not infiltrate Rome, the Orient must not threaten the Occi-dent, the colonized must not control the colonizer nor the female the male

---

[50] Henning Krauss, who argues that the fascism in *Bérénice* detracts from its aesthetic value, compares Paulin to Brasillach's portrait of Léon Degrelle in the *Oeuvres complètes*, 5: 6–63 ("Faschismus klassizistisch: Uberlegungen zum ästhetischen Wert von Robert Brasillachs *Bérénice*," *Romanistische Zeitschrift für Literaturgeschichte* 8, nos. 1–4 [1984]: 321).

nor age youth. It is Paulin, the representative of "the youth of Rome," as Bérénice calls him, who effectively manipulates the events of the drama.

From Paulin's point of view, Bérénice, the former but never forgotten mistress of Titus, has returned to Rome as queen of an inferior but nonetheless threatening enemy and it is imperative to drive her back. The threat is not only political but racial and sexual, and Paulin pulls out all the stereotypes. Bérénice is associated with perfumes, jewels, bazaars, odors, sweat, heat, disorder, wandering (144), dirt, magic, wiles, and what Paulin calls a "fantaisie coloniale" that seduced the youthful Titus (150). Bérénice accepts her status; she declares herself a loyal subject of the empire. It was after all the destroyer of the temple in Jerusalem who won her heart. She has even interiorized certain stereotypes of her people, calling the Jews "that bunch of merchants, philosophers, furriers, usurers, revolutionaries and bankers," incapable of fighting like men (156). All the same she has a political agenda: she wants a *place* in the empire, not only for herself but for the Jews. "You have to make a place for us, or we will make it ourselves" (156). The Jews may not be able to fight on the battlefield, but, as Paulin suspects Bérénice knows, they have the capacity to vanquish through subversion.

Since Bérénice's political intention as queen is inseparable from her erotic desire as woman, the collective drama, though usually hidden, will also play itself out in the emotional individual drama. "What I want and what I desire, are they not one?" she confides to her admirer Phenice, Paulin's fiancée. It is in fact Phenice who suggests to her the word she will use to overturn Titus's will: *rester*—she only wants to stay. Paulin has his own battle to fight on the sentimental front, and his quarrels with Phenice are to some extent a *mise en abyme* of the *grandeur/bonheur* conflict between the two protagonists.

The central scene of the play, act 3, the meeting of Titus and Bérénice, contains a mixture of moments of classical imitation, irony, self-conscious literary theatricality, and a gradually overwhelming lyrical eroticism. Here we are, say the protagonists of the metatragedy, as if in the theater, with the minor characters offstage, alone for the tragic encounter (158). The social drama, however, does surface in the individual one. When the queen makes her simple demand, *rester*, the emperor, like Paulin, seems to fear an attempt at Jewish subversion as a result. And after you, he says to Bérénice, come your brothers, "little bankers with good interest rates, furriers who tomorrow will have the richest cars and will lend money to *me*" (163). (There are several such self-conscious anachronisms in the play.) But Bérénice, silencing such objections with the evocation of memory and desire and the repetition of the word *bonheur*, recreates the image of herself as a combination mistress and mother: "We cannot separate ourselves from those days, Oh unarmed youth who slept in my arms like a child"

(164). And how does the queen complete her seduction of the emperor? By reciting the Song of Solomon—the rich, exotic, musical, Dionysian poetry of the Orient. (Bérénice's tempting of the emperor with *bonheur* recalls Maulnier's portrayal of the temptation of Nietzsche by Lou Andreas Salomé.) The older woman, the erotic mother, offering in her person the seductions of poetry, music, and perfumes, along with the illusion of the reversal of time and eternal youth, succeeds, in a classic perepeteia at the end of act 3, in enveloping in her orbit the will of the Master of the world. Titus may persist in calling her *étrangère* (foreigner), but he cries out, "You will stay!" (168).

In the fourth act, Paulin takes the action into his hands, intent on separating Titus and Bérénice, and also cognizant of being the instrument of a destiny predetermined by literary tradition. He puts to Bérénice directly the danger of her "whole tribe" invading Rome. Bérénice suggests a possible advantage: could not the Jews' talent for money and commerce help the great maritime empires of the future? To which Paulin replies, "What does it matter to me what the Empires of the future will do and the mistakes that they will make. . . . I speak for my nation, my eternal nation" (181). Having predicted, no doubt, the impure alliance of British imperialism and Jewish money dear to fascist and Nazi propaganda, Paulin upholds the purity of the Roman nation, race, and youth. He even presumes to lecture Bérénice on the true mission of the Jewish people: it is in cultivating their relation with the Eternal, not the temporal. But Paulin's real trump card is youth. "Tomorrow you will be old. Tomorrow, he will turn away from your cracked, loose, painted skin" (184). He is of course telling Bérénice what she, the Léa of antiquity, already knows. It is this personal self-consciousness that allows her to reverse her decision. She will leave— not because of warring races or the hostility of Rome—but because her age has passed the half-century, and she will not have her younger lover dismiss her.

Colette's sensual drama of the inevitable separation of the aging Léa and her young lover Chéri plays itself out in act 5. Titus's adieu to his mistress is full of tenderness and regret, but it also suggests a son's necessary, victorious rupture with his mother: "And I touch you with my hands, my beloved, my nurse, you who gave me pleasure as an immortal companion, consolation of the warrior going to sleep, o sweet maternal one" (196–97). Bérénice, on the level of the metatragedy, perceives another reason for their separation. "Glory has always been between us . . . the Occidental and the Oriental . . . We are victims of literature, Titus, and maybe of nothing else" (193). To which Paulin sententiously replies, "What you call literature, Madame, is the truth of the nation" (194). This is surely the voice of the Maurrasian humanist Brasillach, on several levels. On the one hand, characters in modern tragedy written from ancient material are "victims" of tradition through the self-consciousness of their authors. As Anouilh will tell his audience in 1944, "Antigone is going to die because her name is Antigone." What Paulin seems to suggest, however, is that a nation's (or perhaps the European) literary tradition carries a baggage of inevitable historical and political truths. The legendary couples mentioned above, like Titus and Bérénice, must also separate because Rome is destined to rule the world, the West is destined to subjugate the East, and, in contemporary terms, the Jews must be expelled from Europe. The historical conflation of "eternal fascism," with the addition of antisemitism, determines the denouement of tragedy and metatragedy.

The future, it seems, lies with the rigid twenty-year-old Paulins of this world rather than with the tender thirty-year-old Tituses. If Brasillach's literary and personal sympathies go to the latter, his political ideology is with the former, and the end of the tragedy, thanks to Paulin's manipulations and the fatality of literature, brings the two together. But Bérénice has also made what Paulin calls a "last calculation," an invention of Brasillach's. She is leaving, but she leaves behind her fourteen-year-old niece in Rome: "the age of Cleopatra," Paulin observes in the last words of the play, "when she met Caesar" (199). The seductive threat of the Jews and the Orient is not easily dismissed but requires constant vigil. Might not the emperor succumb again? The literary tradition in itself guarantees nothing: its lessons must be applied. The modern tragedian opens his resolution to a call for vigilance and action.

Bérénice, like D'Annunzio's *Fedra*, recuperates Racine and the tradition of classical tragedy for aesthetic fascism, but the differences between the two modern tragedies reveal not only the very different temperaments of the authors but also the evolution of the movement. Both plays foreground a trio: a Greek or Roman imperial ruler, a subversive foreign woman, and a young hero. In each case, Western imperialism is associated with possession of women, whether through amorous conquest or rape. *Fedra*, however, exalts the archaic, Dionysian, erotic force of its title character, just as early fascism portrayed itself as a vitalist force, transcending systems and legality. The demise of Hippolytus seems to show that the hero of the new Italy must possess such power so as not to be destroyed by it, as modern imperialism must incorporate its mythical foundations. *Bérénice*, in contrast, gives aesthetic form to the more virulent and antisemitic French fascism of the 1930s, while incorporating what Brasillach saw as the tradition of French classicism. The female foreigner has become a subversive danger— however enticing—which literary tradition, "the truth of the nation," shows must be rejected. And here the young hero—however personally unsympathetic—emerges victorious, fusing the future of the Roman Empire with the fascist ideal. Though it hardly deserves a place in the canon of modern drama, *Bérénice* represents to some extent a culmination of the reflections of a talented humanist and a perceptive drama critic on classical and modern tragedy. That literary humanism, unfortunately, cannot be separated from but is inextricably bound to an aesthetic commitment to fascism and a vicious antisemitism.

Pierre Drieu La Rochelle and the Search for Tragic Plenitude

Drieu La Rochelle, the most important French aesthetic fascist with Brasillach, differed considerably from his contemporary in approach and substance. Neither a disciple of Maurras's, nor a classical humanist, nor a devotee of Mediterranean culture, Drieu approached fascism with interests at once more pan-European and more modernist than Brasillach's. Rather than attempting to define a specifically French form of fascism, he hoped to integrate France into a totalitarian concept of the West. "My only connection to the Occident," he wrote in 1944, "but it is a strong one, is the connection of art. The Occident is artistic and political; it's the same thing."[51] Although Drieu wrote more on politics and political theory than did Brasillach, he could have said like D'Annunzio that art and politics were never separate in his thought. Even more strongly than Maulnier and Brasillach, Drieu looked to Nietzsche, whom he also read through the experience of World War I, for guidance in renewing the "decadent" present. A passionate theatergoer and critic, Drieu also saw the possibility of a rebirth of tragedy as integral to his concept of aesthetic fascism.

His account of his espousal of fascism in 1934, when he claimed that fascism entailed a restoration of the spiritual,[52] resembles that of a religious conversion. The discovery of fascism involved a discovery of the true self: like Pirandello, Drieu stated that he had been for a while "a fully fledged fascist without knowing it"[53]—in his case since the end of World War I. Since so much of his writing affirms the desire to recapture the plenitude of the war experience, and since fascism, in his view, comes closest to fulfilling that desire, this is in a sense true. Certain links among theater, tragedy, the war, and aesthetic fascism can be seen in Drieu's best-known fictional work, *Gilles* (1939).

Often called the Bildungsroman of fascism, *Gilles* contains a theatrical trajectory that parallels its hero's *Bildung*. In one of the novel's earliest scenes, Gilles and his friend Bénédict, both soldiers on leave in 1917, pick up two women who are on their way to the Comédie française to see Henri

---

[51] *Journal*, October 17, 1944, quoted in Carroll, *French Literary Fascism*, 125.

[52] Soucy, *French Fascism: The Second Wave*, 287.

[53] Pierre Drieu La Rochelle, *Socialisme fasciste* (Paris: Gallimard, 1934), 220, cited by Alistair Hamilton, introduction to Drieu La Rochelle, *Secret Journal and Other Writings*, trans. Hamilton (New York: Howard Fertig, 1973), xvi.

Bernstein's *Elévation*. While Bénédict proclaims that he would never go to see such a *saloperie* (piece of trash), the word that replaces the title as the characters' reference to the play, the two men decide to attend the play for the opportunity to fondle the women in their box seats. *Elévation* is described, by an omniscient narrator, as follows: "On the stage, the suffering body of the soldier was presented like a soiled host to the devouring pity of the public. Although half of the theater was filled with soldiers and their relatives, the audience was ecstatic."[54] Here are the elements of high ritual, the sacrifice of tragedy or mass, but grossly deformed. The potentially noble experience of war is parodied in its theatrical reduction; the sacrificial body of the soldier becomes, in simile, a *sullied* host; Aristotelian emotion among the Parisian public is transformed into a *devouring* pity and a cheap ecstasy. Following the technique of what Susan Suleiman calls the "amalgam" in *Gilles*,[55] Bernstein's theater acquires the associations of mediocrity and of *saloperie*: the enervating influence of women (a theme throughout the novel), easy sex, whoredom, disgust, moral turpitude, and especially the major theme of social decadence. (The fact that Bernstein is Jewish and the association of bourgeois theater with money, though not explicit in this scene, become clear after the reading of other "amalgams" in the novel.) An air raid in the midst of the play prompts Bénédict to long for a bomb explosion as the fitting interruption of "that trashy heroic play" ("cette saloperie de pièce héroïque") (35). Gilles, still naive and *ungebildet*, manifests his ignorance of both theater and heroism: "I don't know why you reject [*tu vomis*] that play. It is quite exact. Those are feelings that exist and that many people experience in that way" (39). It is of course the play's "exactitude," its imitation of and catering to the sentimental realism of a mediocre public, that make it unworthy in the eyes of Gilles's creator, although Bénédict skeptically doubts that anyone really believes in patriotism or sacrifice. The Comédie française itself, with its bourgeois public, appears in Drieu's writings on the theater as an outworn and decadent institution.

The scene that marks the culmination of Gilles's development, his epiphany at the end of the novel, stands in stark contrast to the above. As opposed to viewing a "trashy" play about the Great War while fondling "easy" women in a stuffy box in an outmoded theater, Gilles participates in an outdoor collective political action that undergoes an aesthetic metamorphosis into a modern experience of Greek tragedy. This is Gilles's experience of the February 6, 1934, riots in Paris over the Stavisky affair, the event that seemed to promise, for those who so hoped, the dawn of fascism in France and that was instrumental in Drieu's official "conversion" to fas-

[54] Pierre Drieu La Rochelle, *Gilles* (Paris: Gallimard [Folio], 1996), 34.
[55] Susan Suleiman, *Authoritarian Fictions: The Ideological Novel as a Literary Genre* (New York: Columbia University Press, 1983), 190–93.

cism. As mentioned in the Introduction here, Gilles experiences the Place de la Concorde transformed into an ancient outdoor theater and the event itself as a Greek tragedy. It even follows classical rules: Gilles tells a friend that it will not last more than twenty-four hours (435). Rather than imitating life in its tedious temporality, the riots-as-tragedy will condense it; the event will mark the end of history (433). Gilles is not just an interested spectator, he is "completely transfigured." If France was dying in its postwar torpor, it can now be, like Gilles himself, reborn. Here is the tragic "moment of truth" as in Sorel's myth of the general strike. Ordinary time and decadent existence cease: plenitude is recaptured in an aesthetic moment fusing myth, historical past, and future. In a brief essay written soon after the event, Drieu reflects on how the demonstrations reenacted and ritualized both the violent killing and sacrifice in the Great War and the Dionysian violence that, as Drieu learned from Nietzsche, lies at the heart of tragedy. Drieu "would have liked the moment to last forever":[56] the problem with the revolutionary epiphany and the tragic anagnorisis is that they may degenerate into the temporal worlds of day-to-day politics or realistic drama. Both Gilles and his creator approach fascism essentially as a quest for such aesthetic plenitude.

From the beginning to the end of the novel Gilles has moved from an indoor, artificial theater to an outdoor "real" one, from a public dominated by women to one dominated by men, from "devouring pity" to "fear and courage," from prose to poetry, from a dramatic travesty of tragedy to its realization in a transcendent "moment of truth." At the end of the epilogue, in which Gilles appears "reborn" as Walter in the Spanish Civil War, he prepares for actual death and rebirth through sacrifice in imitation of the Nietzschean tragic model. "Dionysus, Christ. Nothing is accomplished except in blood. We must constantly die to be constantly reborn" (501). Instead of a spectator gazing at the artificial enactment of a soldier's body presented as a sullied host, Gilles has become a sacrificial body prepared for eternal return.

Drieu undertakes a parallel search in his writing on theater. From his *Chronique des spectacles* in the *Nouvelle revue française* in the beginning of 1923 through his reviews of plays produced under the Occupation, he castigates theatrical decadence and searches for tragic plenitude. In the *Chronique*, which Rima Drell Reck calls "arguably his first real novel," he anticipates Artaud in calling for "more violent dramatic forms of ritual."[57] In the popular spectacles of the music hall, he had hoped to find the ritualistic mass communion, participation and violence absent from the written bourgeois

---

[56] Pierre Drieu La Rochelle, "Air de Février '34," *La Nouvelle revue française*, February 1934, 42, 568.

[57] Rima Drell Reck, *Drieu La Rochelle and the Picture Gallery Novel: French Modernism in the Interwar Years* (Baton Rouge: Louisiana State University Press, 1990), 13–14.

theater, but he soon became disenchanted. Far from being living popular theaters, the music halls display all too clearly the "splendor of money" that is the sign of their being financed by industrialists and of their decadence.[58]

The link made between bourgeois democracy, capitalist money, Jews, general "decadence," and the decline of the theater was not uncommon among fascist-leaning dramatists or drama critics. Henri Bernstein, in part because of the artificial realism of his plays and their success among the bourgeois and in part because he was Jewish, came to epitomize for them the "decadent" theater of the Third Republic they sometimes called *théâtre enjuivé*. In 1940, Drieu referred to Bernstein as "that old charlatan who has encumbered our stage for forty years with his low-level productions" and notes that he is "adulated . . . by all the pretty ladies of Parisian society."[59] Shortly before publishing that remark (accompanied by general antisemitic ones), it seems that Drieu actually provoked a physical fight with Bernstein in the Tuileries![60]

In Drieu's writings on theater, as in his journals and essays, one finds various outcries against French "decadence." Jews, moneyed industrialists, intellectuals, masons, parliamentary democrats, and women are responsible for the decline from a heroic and patriotic to a mediocre, pleasure-seeking, and individualistic mentality in France. A mediocre and decadent nation is incapable of either producing or appreciating great theater; the decline of theater in France is therefore symptomatic of the decline of the nation. Even the great theatrical classics cannot thrive in such an atmosphere. In a 1927 essay on the music hall in *Le Jeune européen*, Drieu refers to Parisian theaters as "those plague-ridden places" (*ces foyers pestilentiels*)[61] in which the classics die a slow death. (Drieu's metaphor has quite a different value from Artaud's plague!) In *Genève ou Moscou* (1928) he explores the theme of democracy as a destroyer of art. The modern petty-bourgeois spectator is incapable of the emotion demanded by a Corneille or a Shakespeare and goes to see the classics only out of habit.[62] The decadent state is incapable of realizing or producing a collective and poetic tragic theater. In 1935 Drieu writes that whereas *Horace* played at the Comédie française was "a joke," if it were played before Mussolini, Hitler, or Joseph Stalin, the play would reacquire its greatness because the faith and revolutionary fervor that unite spectators in totalitarian states would enable them to understand a "virile and inspired" theater.[63] But occasionally, even in France, he would encounter a

---

[58] *La Nouvelle revue française*, 39 (November 1932), 588.

[59] Pierre Drieu La Rochelle, *Journal, 1939–1945*, ed. Julien Hervier (Paris: Gallimard, 1992), June 9, 1940, 239.

[60] Ibid., May 22, 1940, 212.

[61] Pierre Drieu La Rochelle, *Le Jeune Européen* (Paris: Gallimard, 1927), 118.

[62] Pierre Drieu La Rochelle, *Genève ou Moscou* (Paris: Gallimard, 1928), 210–11.

[63] *Figaro*, May 23, 1935, 1–3, quoted by Jean Lansard, *Drieu La Rochelle ou la passion tragique de l'unité: Essai sur son theatre joué et inédit* (Paris: Aux amateurs de livres, 1985), 1: 57.

performance that moved him. The Pitoëffs' famous production of Pirandello's *Six Characters in Search of an Author* captured a "true tragic strength"[64]— because the author and directors came from totalitarian states? Louis Jouvet and Charles Dullin offer hope that new and intelligent theatrical production can emerge in France. Among French dramatists, he admires Claudel because he brings religion back to the theater and attempts to revive the collective festival that theater should be. In contrast to Brasillach, Drieu has no taste for Giraudoux, whose preciosity he considers a sign of decadence. Far from creating modern tragedy, Giraudoux simply "plays with the idea of disaster"; his tragedies are always resolved in comedy.[65] As we will see in the next chapter, Anouilh and especially Henry de Montherlant offer him hope for the creation of modern tragedy in France.

Along with other aesthetic fascists, Drieu believed Nietzsche to be the major precursor of fascism, though he also perceived that there could be a Nietzsche of the left as well as of the right.[66] Certainly Nietzsche was a major influence in his own approach to what he called "socialist fascism." He understands Nietzsche basically in the same way as Mussolini and Gentile: since the world has no general meaning but the one we give it at the moment, action and the will to power must precede thought.[67] Nietzsche is for Drieu, as for Brasillach, primarily a poet and an artist who inspired fascism with its "spiritual" quality, swept away the nineteenth-century belief in rationalistic progress, and brought Europe back to its origins with the myth of the eternal return and the understanding of tragedy. A blond Norman himself, Drieu did not share Brasillach's view of the Germanic as Oriental and strange, nor did he feel the need to create a Mediterranean Nietzsche. His fascist ideology being more European than nationalistic, he believed that France, with its mixture of Nordic and Mediterranean heritages, could serve as the model for the new, united Europe. This outlook would, of course, influence his eventual acceptance of Hitler and collaboration. Yet Drieu, like other intellectuals and aesthetic fascists, could never accept any regime entirely—in a sense he could not quite believe that the spiritual insights of Nietzsche could be realized in politics. Even his enthusiastic association with Jacques Doriot ended in disappointment. Already in 1933, he contrasted Nietzsche, who "wanted to keep humanity in a state of permanent revolution," with Hitler, whose regime was becoming conservative and institutionalized. Such seemed to be the fate of all revolutions.[68]

[64] Review in *La Nouvelle revue française*, June 1923.

[65] Pierre Drieu La Rochelle, "Mort de Giraudoux," *La Nouvelle revue française*, February 1944, in *Sur les écrivains*, ed. Frédéric Grover (Paris: Gallimard, 1982), 227–28.

[66] Pierre Drieu La Rochelle, "Nietzsche contre Marx," in *Socialisme fasciste*, 63–75. Drieu argues here that Nietzsche and Marx are not always as far apart as they seem to be.

[67] Ibid., 70.

[68] Ibid., 74–75.

In two brief essays on Nietzsche published in *Je suis partout* in 1939, Drieu stresses the central importance of *The Birth of Tragedy* for "the prophet of the twentieth century."[69] The book, he claims, was conceived during the war of 1870, and it was during the Great War that Drieu himself, and other Europeans, were first truly able to understand Nietzsche. The "call to violence" proclaimed by the prophet was not merely superficial but at the heart of European civilization. In showing that Greek tragedy and thus Greek culture were permeated with the Dionysian, Nietzsche overturned the myth of rationalism as Europe's guiding principle, bringing back the glory of the body as well as the sense of the sacred and the divine. Nietzsche is "the saint who announces the hero."[70] Like Brasillach, Drieu wants to reconcile Nietzschean atheism with what he sees as the medieval, virile, warlike, ascetic tradition of Christianity. Through a somewhat convoluted reasoning, Drieu attempts to show that since the Greek and Jewish traditions were intermingled from the beginning, Christianity marked the culmination of the blending of mysticism and rationalism. What Drieu seems to be interested in recuperating, however, is a kind of secular religion based on Nietzschean "poetry." To some extent the heroic prophecies of the saint have already come true. Though he might not recognize them as such, Mussolini, Stalin, and Hitler are Nietzsche's spiritual sons.

Drieu's war experience with its resultant cult of violence, killing, male bonding, sacrifice, and war itself as remedies for modern decadence find their justification in his reading of both *The Birth of Tragedy* and *The Will to Power*. If the sacrifice of the hero is at the heart of tragedy, violent sacrifice is at the basis of civilization and indeed of life itself. In *Etat civil* he writes, "Violent death is the foundation of civilization."[71] In *Straw Dogs* Drieu interprets in indirect discourse the thoughts of his hero, the collaborator Constant: "Life is a sacrifice. All the ancient religions that have known this human secret have taught it and practiced it. . . . The true religion is the Mexican religion: it splits a man down the middle and rips out his heart."[72] Here Drieu seems to bring Artaud's theater of cruelty along with Nietzschean tragedy to bear on a vision of violence as the alternative to decadence. It is a line of thought he later developed in arguing that Europe's salvation lies in its recuperation of a sense of the *tragic*.

The belief that France's decadence stemmed partly from its refusal to acknowledge its foundations in the violent and the tragic was instrumental in Drieu's welcoming of its defeat in 1940. In 1937 he wrote: "We have for-

[69] Pierre Drieu La Rochelle, "Encore et toujours Nietzsche" and "Nietzsche prophète du xxe siècle," in *Sur les écrivains*, ed. Grover, 91–96.

[70] Ibid., 95.

[71] Ibid., 219.

[72] Pierre Drieu La Rochelle, *Les Chiens de paille* (Paris: Gallimard, 1964), 73–74, trans. and quoted by Soucy, *French Fascism: The Second Wave*, 288.

gotten that life is tragic and that it is as impossible for a people [*un peuple*] as for an individual to hide from that terrible reality."[73] In the inaugural issue of *Idées* (November 1941), a journal advocating the *Révolution nationale*, Drieu published a short article titled "The Sense of the Tragic."[74] Here he claims that the defeat of France has at last brought back to the French the sense of the tragic that they had lost in their years of decadence and self-satisfied materialism. The existence of a nation is tragic because it is constantly threatened by destruction and even annihilation, a reality that is hidden by the false sense of security created by life in cities as well as by the ideology of progress and material well-being. Attempting to argue against a linear idea of history and for a sense of eternal return, Drieu cites historical examples to show that France's destiny, since the time of the Roman empire, has always been joined to that of Italy and Germany. Without a "tragic philosophy" there is only a sense of humiliation in defeat; with it there is a sense of destiny, of knowing joy through sorrow. If the tragic struggle for power has taken different forms throughout history, today it is shaped by "the present great convulsion of totalitarianism . . . the present conflict of communism and fascism on the debris of liberalism" (8). Seeming to slip into Hegelianism, Drieu argues that France must thus rise to the idea that seeks to impose itself on the world. Only by reintroducing the tragic into French thought will it be possible to face the challenges before the nation: "the adoption and adaptation of socialism by the ruling classes; the reconciliation of socialism and Christianity, and the reconciliation of the idea of the nation and the idea of empire or federation which is coming to us, blown by the East and the West winds" (8). Drieu's notion of "socialism" has to be read in the context of contemporary fascist parlance as a spiritual and aesthetic binding force, certainly not an economic system.[75] Yet Drieu was more interested than any of the other French fascists in the factors uniting left and right, communism and fascism, in opposition to democracy. It sometimes seems in the article that France should be prepared to join whichever side wins the tragic struggle. And yet it is clearly the defeat of France by Hitler that is addressed. After the battlefields of World War I and the abortive riots of 1936 comes another "return" of violence, suffering, and cessation of ordinary time offering the perception of a tragic moment of truth. It is as if the Dionysian had erupted once again, with the potential to cause the French to abandon their illusory faith in rationalism and to return to participation in the primordial nature of European man.

If Drieu believed in some sort of totalitarian European federation to which France should be joined, no doubt under Hitler since that was where the

---

[73] Pierre Drieu La Rochelle, *Avec Doriot* (1937), 104.

[74] Pierre Drieu La Rochelle, "Le Sens du tragique," *Idées* 1 (November 1941): 3–8, reprinted in *Chronique politique*, 324–29.

[75] See Sternhell, "Spiritualistic Fascism," in *Neither Left nor Right*, 213–65.

power lay, he was not really a political thinker and did not attempt to out-line such a system in any detail. Indeed, he was well aware that no system could ever realize the idea and that institutionalization of the permanent revolution was always bound to disappoint. The emphasis on process rather than realization is what made Nietzsche, especially the early Nietzsche, so appealing. Yet this did not stop Drieu from seeking both political and aes-thetic *forms* of the tragic struggle. Like Brasillach, if much less explicitly, he seems to sense an "eternal fascism" in Corneille and can thus hope for a res-urrection of stage tragedy in the French tradition if the French can reacquire their sense of the tragic. If his theater criticism in this vein in the 1920s and 1930s is primarily negative, stressing the lack of violence in popular theater and the skirting of tragedy in a Giraudoux, in the 1940s he will join the cho-rus of those fascist drama critics who envision a resurrection of tragedy. Again like Brasillach, he experiments with writing modern tragedy himself.

Drieu's total output of writing for the theater is slim: three published and produced plays, *L'Eau fraîche* (*Cool Water*, 1931), *Le Chef* (*The Leader*, 1934), and *Charlotte Corday* (1941); and four unpublished and unproduced plays and fragments, *Le dernier capitaliste* (*The Last Capitalist*, 1919), *Gille* (1931), *Nous sommes plusieurs* (*We are Several*, 1936), and *Judas* (1943).[76] The only two that had any success were the two he called his "tragedies," *Le Chef* and *Charlotte Corday*.

Drieu was quite clear about his intentions in writing *Le Chef*. Although he denied that the play was "political" in any narrow sense of the term, he stated that he wanted to "show the French that great eruption of collective mystique which, originating in Moscow, has overcome, in different forms— fascist, Hitlerian—a great part of Europe and is now pressing on our bor-ders."[77] The play was to be a "moral debate on dictatorship." In a piece titled "Mériter un chef," obviously related to the theme of the play, Drieu argued that a dictator comes from the creation of fascism, and not the other way around. A great man cannot be superior to his people or his time, and a true leader will be the "recompense" for "men of daring and will."[78] Drieu is again warning the French that unless they raise themselves out of deca-dence, they will not participate in the cataclysmic events of the present. Yet if they are prepared to accept a modern tragedy such as *Le Chef*, perhaps there is hope. The theatergoing public, he writes, is growing tired of little stories of adultery and may be ready for a play that confronts them with politics among men and the question of dictatorship.[79]

[76] For an exhaustive account of all of Drieu's writings for the theater, published and un-published, see Lansard's two-volume work *Drieu La Rochelle ou la passion tragique de l'unité*.

[77] Pierre Drieu La Rochelle, "Avant 'Le Chef': Ce que j'ai voulu faire. Ni pièce politique, ni pièce à thèse, ni pièce a idées," *Comoedia*, November 14, 1934, 1, 7,949.

[78] Pierre Drieu La Rochelle, "Mériter un chef," *Socialisme fasciste*, 126–31.

[79] Pierre Drieu La Rochelle, "Vers un théâtre politique," *Excelsior*, May 6, 1934.

Drieu began writing *Le Chef* in September 1933, thus shortly before his declaration of conversion to fascism. After having been refused by several directors, the play was finally produced by the Pitoëffs in November 1934. Although critical reception was generally favorable, it had only seven showings—Drieu himself, realizing it was a failure with the public, asked Pitoëff to withdraw it. He had believed that developments in Italy and Germany, as well as in France, had prepared the French public not for a propaganda play but for his authentic political tragedy; he now believed he was wrong. The text was not published until 1944, along with *Charlotte Corday*, and has not been reedited since. The Pitoëff production, with everyone in black shirts, was undoubtedly ingenious, but the text, as Drieu must have realized, is more literary than theatrical. As with other modern tragedies, it betrays a self-consciousness about the fact of writing tragedy, for example in its sometimes ironic discourse juxtaposing colloquial language with classical forms and references. Parallels are also made between politics and theater. While not metatheatrical at the level of *Bérénice*, it contains statements such as the one made by the hero Jean in act 4 that refers his interlocutor to "act 1 of this tragedy."[80]

Le Chef's defects lie primarily in the length and abstraction of its discourse and a too rigid stylization in its characters. Despite its shortcomings, however, it deserves to be recognized as standing in a continuum of political drama between D'Annunzio's *La Gloria* and French political drama of the 1940s such as Albert Camus's *Les Justes*, Anouilh's *Antigone*, and Sartre's *Les Mains sales*. Closer to *Antigone* in its ideological affinities, Drieu's play is a surprising precursor of Sartre's and Camus's in its subject matter and dramatic configuration. The three plays center around a political conflict involving questions of idealism/Realpolitik, friendship/ideology, political discipline/liberty which are played out between men with a woman relegated to a secondary, primarily sexual, role. Similarities between *Le Chef* and *Les Mains sales* are particularly striking.[81] Both use woman as a medium of exchange between men bonded by what can be read as an implicit homosexuality.

The setting of *Le Chef* is an imaginary Macedonia not unlike the Illyria of *Dirty Hands*. Drieu makes no attempt to follow the classical unities in his four-act tragedy as the place and the time as well as, to some extent, the action change in each act. The characters represent types drawn to politics: Jean the leader and compromiser (parallel to Sartre's Hoederer), Michel the idealistic intellectual (Hugo), Georges and Christophe, who operate mysteriously behind the scenes, Alexandre the youth, Léon the brute, and

[80] Pierre Drieu La Rochelle, *Charlotte Corday: Pièce en trois actes/Le Chef: Pièce en quatre actes* (Paris: Gallimard, 1944), 268.
[81] Frédéric Grover (*Drieu La Rochelle* [Paris: Gallimard, 1962], 78) notes that Michel's situation parallels Hugo's in *Les Mains sales*.

Pierre Drieu la Rochelle, *Le Chef,* at the Théâtre des Mathurins in Paris. The Pitoëff company, directed by Georges Pitoëff, November 1934. Permission granted by the Roger-Viollet photographic agency.

Cora the spy. Operating outside of the male group, Cora (like Sartre's Jessica) serves as an instrument of both discord and bonding, passing from Jean to Michel to Alexandre. The men wear costumes that are "half military, half athletic"; Cora is dressed "simply but provocatively," a code that signals immediately the male *Bund* and its female disrupter.

The first act takes place in a room used as a command post during an unidentified war. Three thousand men, represented by Léon, Alexandre, Christophe, and Michel, have accepted the title "La Brigade des Idiots," branding them as outcasts by the rest of the army. Why, then, do they fight? For the sake of fighting and because of the *chef* they have chosen, Jean. Jean, however, weary of the senseless war, makes a statement that seems prophetic of Drieu's vision of the destiny of France: "There are moments when one hopes for defeat in order to witness the fall of that old hierarchy allied with death against our youth." (164).

The action begins when Georges, a general who identifies himself as "a civilian dressed as a soldier" (169), proposes to Jean an alliance to stage a coup and rule at Pella, capital of Macedonia. Jean, disillusioned, prefers to desert, abandoning his men, an act that seems an incredible breach of faith to his loyal friend Michel. For Jean, however, such dependence amounts to a show of femininity: "You're reasoning like a broad [*gonzesse*] about to be dropped. I'm not married to you guys. Anyway, I'm divorcing" (180). The implicitly homosexual bonding of group with leader appears to be threatened by any display of "feminine" sentimentality. For the bonding to function, each man must, paradoxically, maintain his independence, his fundamental solitude. The idea recalls Mussolini's insistence on the strong individual within group fusion. Echoes of the fascist slogan "me ne frego" are numerous.[82] Léon to Michel: "Et puis, je me fous de toi, et de Jean par-dessus le marché" (156). Michel to Jean: "Tu nous l'as assez dit pourtant, qu'il fallait s'en foutre" (163). Jean's own *menefregismo* is affirmed by his decision to leave his men and desert to wander in solitude.

The second act takes place two years later in the back room of a café in the Macedonian capital, Pella. The war is over and Jean has returned to accept Georges's proposals and to attempt to form the "idiot" brigade into a political party, an action viewed by Michel as a compromise. Cora, who appears onstage for the first time, has become Michel's mistress. It is Cora who first identifies revolution with theater. A former actress, she has a new role: "I'm acting in a play that's beginning, the revolution" (190). Although she is not sure of what her role will be, it is clear for her that the lead will be played by Jean. "Jean is a magnificent actor. He loves his job" (202). Cora senses in her "woman's breast" "the obscure force" that is beginning to bring solitary individuals together, whether in the streets or the theaters (191). Act 2, which stages the moment of fascist bonding, is more lyrical and theatrical than it is dramatic. The plot barely develops, but the act culminates with Jean's harangue to his followers in a call-and-response format. The stage directions for Jean's speeches are in musical terms: "piano," "adagio," "plus fort," "moins fort," "allegro" (203–11). The actor-leader gradually acquires a D'Annunzian power to fuse and bind his subjects. He recalls the group's bonding in the trenches and their feeling that everything had to change. The moment to change has now come.

> Jean: Once we were different . . . during the war. Now again we are different. We don't know what it is, but it is enormous. . . . Are you going to stay as you are? You, the mature man, have you forgotten your youth? (Michel stirs.) Young man, have you known the hour of your youth? (Alexandre gets up and looks around with ardent eyes.) We don't know what we are going to do, but we are going to do something. We are going to do something.
> All: Yes!
> Jean: We will know who we are when we see what we have done. (205)

---

[82] According to Lansard, the text used in the Pitoëff production was even clearer in its references to Mussolini. Some of these were removed for the 1944 edition, when Il Duce's prestige had waned (*Drieu La Rochelle ou la passion tragique de l'unité*, 130, n. 63).

The directions describing Alexandre's "ardent eyes" may be difficult to realize onstage, but the crowd-leader dynamics here surely recall the *arditi* and the D'Annunzian style adopted by Mussolini. (Jean even proposes that they take up their old "cry" from the trenches [206]). So does the emphasis on youth and on unspecified action as opposed to coherent plan.[83] Yet Jean's last sentence quoted above sounds almost straight out of Sartrean existentialism.

Jean's rhetoric encompasses such contemporary fascist themes as the necessity to join left and right, the call for class fusion and revolutionary violence, the corrupting power of money, and above all the desire to create a society with *chefs* (208). The response to his speech at the end of act 2 reads like an opera libretto and could easily be sung. Like Brasillach, Drieu may also be thinking of Corneille's *stances* in *Polyeucte* and elsewhere: the lyrical pause in the dramatic action.

> Alexandre: We were lost in the big city.
> But we met a man.
> (All: A man.)
> We are bound.
> We are no longer alone.
> We have a friend.
> (All: A friend.)
> Look at us with envy.
> We have Jean.
> He is us, he is our blood.
> (All: Our blood.)
> Look at him.
> That is a man.

Drieu also adopts classical stichomythia.

> Léon and Alexandre (alternating)
> L.: We believe in nothing.
> A.: We believe in everything.
> L.: We only believe in the blood that flows in our veins.
> A.: In this blood that is fire from the sun.
> L.: No law except our own.
> A.: We have a law.
> (All: A law.)
> L.: We are alone.

[83] Lansard points out the parallels between the "dynamisme irrationnel" of Jean's words and those of contemporary, European fascist leaders. Léon Degrelle: "You must let yourself be carried forward. . . . You must act. The rest will come by itself." Oswald Mosley: "It would be foolish to describe precisely in advance the road by which we will attain our principles." Marcel Déat: "Fervor is sometimes better than light and clarity." In *Avec Doriot* Drieu himself contrasts fascist "struggle" and "action" with democratic "programs" (vol. I, chap. 1, "Le Théâtre," 58–59).

A.: We are all together.
(All: Together.)

The moment of ritual bonding fuses on an irrational, lyric, and musical level men of opposite temperaments such as Léon and Alexandre as well as logically polar entities such as nothing and everything, alone and together. The bonding can of course take place only through and by the leader, in whom the men invest their "blood." It is as if the group has become one mystical body. Leading them on to the next step, Jean envisions their role in the binding and fusing of the entire nation and continent. This time, however, he emphasizes action more than mystique and substitutes a metaphor of steel for that of blood.

Jean, *surrounded by all, toward Michel, allegro:*
Immediately,
Right away,
In this very second
We must build the tower of our despair and our pride.
In the blood and sweat of all classes,
We must build a nation that no one has ever seen,
A dense, tight nation, a block of steel, a magnet.
All of the filings of Europe will collect there, by
will or by force.
And then, before this block
Of our Europe
Asia, America, Africa will fall into dust. (211–12)

The group, metonymical with the nation and then with an ideal pan-European fusion of men and classes, culminates in the metaphorical steel block, a combined European military and political power. Subject to this final élan, Michel can do nothing but declare his adherence.

After the lyrical suspension of dramatic time in act 2, act 3 takes up the prosaic dealings and compromises of Realpolitik. It is a year later; the revolution is at hand, but Jean and Georges are dealing with the "President of the Bourgeois League" to get necessary funding. Michel revolts again, accusing Jean of treachery, and Jean in effect informs him that no one governs innocently. As in *Les Mains sales*, the ideological dispute between the leader and the idealist (Jean—Michel/Hoederer—Hugo) is confused by their rivalry over a woman, in this case Cora, who is sleeping with both of them. In the culminating scene, Michel reminds Jean that they both once had the same understanding of liberty: "the power that a man has from being linked to other men, outside of money" (246). For Jean, however, the cause is already tainted by money; they cannot do without it. No longer the D'Annunzian *chef* of act 2, Jean has become something of a bureaucrat, isolated with his telephone. Yet he convinces Michel to return to the fold once more by allowing him to go to fight in the revolution. Crucial to this scene is the nature of the new bond formed between the two men. Cora's sexual liaison with both of them has at once inflamed their rivalry and served to unite them. In their new union, whose basically homosexual nature surfaces again, Cora can be dispensed with. When Michel tells Jean he should get rid of Georges, Jean responds, "You're jealous! I need other men besides you" (245). Michel's desire for "liberty" seems now inextricably bound to his desire for Jean. What takes place is not his idealistic vision of mutual bonding of free men but rather, as Jean seems to realize, Michel's "female" subjugation to the fascination of the powerful "male."

The question raised in act 3 as to whether the present revolution, unlike its predecessors, can produce a true *chef* rather than another tyrant is addressed in act 4 which, like act 2, is more lyric than dramatic and takes place outdoors. It is a month later. The revolution has succeeded, but Michel, disillusioned with the number of bourgeois in the party, is plotting to assassinate his old comrade. Cora has taken on a new lover, the young Alexandre, who is conspiring with Michel. With the understanding that Alexandre will be spared, Cora, in her role as double agent, reveals the plot to Georges and Christophe. Offstage, Jean is conducting a popular festival in memory of Alexander of Macedon, with whose image he evidently hopes to identify himself. In contrast to the lyrical festivities in act 2, however, this celebration is treated with considerable ironic distance. Cora is the most cynical: "Alexander has been dead for two thousand years. . . . And making us slaughter sheep on a mountain top on the pretext that our ancestors, the Macedonians, were beautiful savages, doesn't make us any younger" (252–53). The ceremony is evidently put on to content the people, and Jean seems to be attempting a fusion of pagan and Christian ceremony with his rites. "Every year, my lieutenants will come to this mountain, the dwelling of the Macedonian gods who preceded Jesus" (263). It is Georges, this time, who takes up the theme of Macedonia and pan-Europeanism announced in act 2, but in a new register: "We will make Europe one. What Alexander once did for the Orient, Jean will do for the Occident" (264).

Is Jean the actor to play Jesus, sacrificial victim for love of humanity, or Alexander, powerful tyrant willing to sacrifice others to achieve his vision of empire? Neither, it turns out. Everyone becomes in some sense a traitor. The plot against Jean is thwarted, but Cora is also betrayed because Alexandre is killed. Michel and Jean, the antagonists/lovers, both miss out on the opportunity to emulate Brutus or Caesar, to kill the tyrant or to die the tragic death of an emperor. Metatheatrically, Drieu seems to be ascribing his inability to complete the play as tragedy to the fact that his own historical period is not yet a tragic one. Jean blames Michel for turning a potential tragedy into a "drame passionel" (268). Returning to the sexual theme, he tells his friend and antagonist that he merely "caresses" ideas whereas he, Jean, "marries" them. It is here that he makes the metatheatrical reference noted earlier: "I told you in the first act of this tragedy: you have always acted like a broad. You are all broads waiting for the male to be impregnated [*fecondées*]" (268). Michel's actions have stemmed not from his "ideas" but from his love of Jean, his desire to reestablish their "duo." It is then the female element, even in a world from which women are absent, that threatens to impede bonding and to turn tragedy into melodrama.

Is Drieu's critique here addressed to Mussolini, who perceived the crowd as female, responding to his super-male directives? Or to Hitler, who appeared to be closer to a tyrant than a *chef 182?* The play resolves itself as something less than tragedy with an ideological subtext implying that modern heroic tragedy will be attained only when men have made themselves worthy of a *chef.* In the meantime, compromise with dictatorship seems to be the only viable option. Michel realizes that he, and the others, have been too weak to establish a true bond with Jean. "Your heart is the only one beating in Macedonia; the other hearts are empty. You are not the strength, you are the weakness of men" (269). Instead of an exchange of brotherly blood, Jean's relationship with his followers is that of the "full" male filling the "empty" females.

Jean pronounces the line closest to a tragic anagnorisis in his acknowledgment of the truth of Michel's statement: "It is possible. I can't be nobler than my times" (269). Michel recapitulates his own recognition of this truth at the end of the play in what Jean theatrically calls his "last speech." "There is a terrible weakness in men who give themselves to another man. When there is a dictator, it's because there is no longer an elite; the elite is not doing its duty" (272). Both Michel and Jean are in the end right: Michel to see in Jean a dictator, no longer a leader, and Jean to recognize that a dictator is what his historical moment (and presumably that of Drieu's audience) calls for. The play ends with an affirmation of the notion that fascist "truth" is not eternal and stable but rather constantly shifting and improvised.

> Georges: When liberty is killed, it means it wasn't really living. There are seasons of liberty and seasons of authority.
> Christophe: Michel was right yesterday, and he will be right tomorrow.
> Jean: But I am right today. (273)

Before concluding on fascist tragic aesthetics in *Le Chef,* it is important to try to understand the curious subplot of the play that ostensibly has little to do with the major characters. This concerns Léon, the rough, tough, and drunken brute, whose "signature" is hanging women by their feet. He first explains this to Jean in act 1, where he confesses that he lost twenty of the men under his command by taking the time to rape and hang a village woman (165). Although Jean punishes him, he also laughs. In act 2, just before the lyrical "bonding" scene, Christophe says to Cora: "It's frightening how many women hanged by the feet there are since he [Léon] is the head of the attack sections!" (201). Léon, it seems, has been promoted, and the information on his behavior is given in an offhand, almost amused fashion—without reaction from Cora. In the second scene of act 3, Christophe informs Michel that Léon has hanged his latest victim (in a brothel) by her hair, not her feet, because he is "becoming a poet" (219). When asked what he will do on the day of the revolution, Léon replies: "I'll burn the brothels; that's where men's blood is wasted" (219). The stage directions that follow read: "*Christophe and Michel burst out laughing.*" In the fourth act, no more references are made to Léon's woman killing, but Léon acts as Jean's bodyguard, aiming at Michel but killing Alexandre (266).

The Léon motif thus runs throughout the play, functioning as a subtext that accompanies and underlies the drama of men, ideas, and revolutionary fervor. Léon's brutality is *funny* to the others—they laugh at him perhaps to establish their distance from him while at the same time apparently acquiescing in his actions. Léon is clearly *necessary* to the *Bund*: his credo of law-through-blood is a crucial element in the block of steel that will drive the revolution forward. His mission to eliminate all traces of the feminine from the masculine block seems clear enough. Jean needs Léon in part to do his dirty work, since he would hardly be capable of firing on his adoring Michel himself. If *Bérénice* achieves the necessary exorcism of female subversiveness through classical metatragedy supported by the manipulations of the "hard" fascist Paulin, *Le Chef* achieves it by a drama of "noble" male ideals supported by ignoble male brutality.

In the end the dictator, who has achieved his status in part through a theatrical "apotheosis" identifying him with the statue of Alexander the Great, is upheld by the "dirty hands" of the political Georges, the cynical intriguer Christophe, and the brutal Léon. A hollow actor-statue whose vacuum is filled by political-economic maneuvering, violation, and violence? It is tempting to see here a highly accurate parody of fascism. But Drieu has put before his audience in act 2 the possibility of an ideal bonding, a Dionysian ecstasy, a moment of truth. If the present historical moment necessitates a descent from the heights of tragedy to a compromise with drama, so be it: the point is to work toward a recreation of the ideal. Drieu himself (unlike Maulnier) felt that he had to take the plunge from aesthetic fascism into political fascism. In attempting to confront his audience with a "debate" on dictatorship, he has not created a simple piece of propaganda but is nonetheless clearly admonishing them to accept the present totalitarian states as historical necessities in the process of creating the New Europe.

One of the reviewers of *Le Chef*, using the terms in Maulnier's *Nietzsche* and *Racine* that become commonplace in fascist discourse, called it a "drama of *grandeur* and *purity* by which we are obsessed"[84] (emphasis mine). Grandeur and purity are also obvious concerns of Drieu in his other tragedy, *Charlotte Corday*, written during the winter of 1939–40 and performed in Lyon and Vichy in January and February 1942 by the "Les Quatre Saisons Provinciales" directed by Maurice Jacquemont. In these circumstances, Drieu seems to feel that it is possible to write a purer modern tragedy. Yet given the female role and the ideology of *Le Chef*, one might well wonder why his second heroic protagonist is not only a woman but a figure from the French Revolution.

Certain aspects and figures of the revolution of 1789 were admired by the French fascists and by the Vichy government, among them Charlotte Corday. She was one of the heroines idolized by Brasillach, the others being Antigone and Joan of Arc. All three had the "fascist" qualities of youth, insolence, and devout patriotism. Since they offered themselves as sacrifices to save their nation and died virgins, it seems that they could be forgiven for being female, or rather that they transcended the base and disrupting qualities of femininity. Charlotte, in the eyes of the fascists, embodied the aspects of the French Revolution that related it to their own revolution, while opposing its democratic excesses.

Drieu had another reason for liking Charlotte. Like himself, she was a Norman, and furthermore her great-grandfather, Pierre Corneille, was one of his Norman idols. Reinforcing his perception of Charlotte's heroic qualities was Drieu's belief—a prevalent one among fascists and Vichy supporters apparently derived from Drumont—that her victim Marat was Jewish.[85] *Je suis partout*, of which a special issue on the 1789 revolution dedicated "to the lofty and holy memory of Charlotte Corday" had appeared in 1939, corroborated Drieu's views in publishing the first tableau of *Charlotte Corday* in its July 9, 1943, issue. In the introduction we read: "Drieu's Charlotte is not an aristocrat, she's a 'fascist' *avant la lettre* who loved the social spirit of the Revolution . . . and who was horrified by revolutionary excess." A few days later, the Vichy journal *Combats* published the play's final scene, between Charlotte and Saint-Just. In the same issue, Jacques LaCroix wrote a piece arguing that the national holiday should be moved a day earlier to commemorate July 13, 1793, the day of Marat's assassination. "One hundred and fifty years ago, the sinister Jean-Paul Marat, whom there are good historical

[84] *Les Nouvelles littéraires*, November 24, 1934.

[85] In his *Journal*, 137, January 3, 1940, Drieu notes with pleasure that he is a Norman like Flaubert, Corneille, Poussin, and "Charlotte too!" He also writes, "Marat is Jewish." Drieu must have derived that idea from Drumont, who claims that the Jacobin's real family name was "Mara" and that once the family settled in Switzerland they became Protestant so as not to reveal their Jewish origins. Drumont, in his bizarre but highly influential book, even goes so far as to associate Marat's skin disease, his odor, and his ugliness with his being Jewish (*La France juive*, 1: 292).

reasons to believe Jewish, was executed by Charlotte Corday." Marat is said to be a "monster" in contrast to the "pure" figure of Charlotte, a Cornelian heroine, and Saint-Just appears as a precursor of fascism.[86] Clearly Corday and Saint-Just are being reinvented as the revolutionary figures who prefigured the *Révolution nationale*; Marat as the symbol of the revolutionary "errors" that became communism and democracy, in association with the Jews.

Drieu emphasizes his heroine's noble affiliations by calling her Charlotte *de* Corday and makes her Corneille's granddaughter instead of his great-granddaughter. She learned from her "grandfather" the meaning of "Roman and republican feelings" and to admire *Polyeucte* (22–23), whose *stances* she reads aloud in the fourth tableau. If the nobles would assume the leadership of the revolution, she argues, it might be saved (25). Charlotte, who has been in a convent but who seems to have retained of her religion only the need to devote herself to something (30), speaks on occasion like one of Brasillach's "insolent" fanatics and indeed like Anouilh's Antigone. "You have to stand there and cry out the truth until they kill you. You must never leave" (25). If she now devotes herself to the revolution, it is because the weak king is no longer a king and a new nation is in the process of being formed.

More simple in conception than *Le Chef*, the play consists of three acts and seven tableaux. In the first tableau, Drieu establishes Charlotte's Norman family background and the essentials of her character. The rest of act 1 and the first two tableaux of act 2 take place in Paris in the room of Simone Evrard where Marat is in hiding. Adored and seen as the martyr of the people by his faithful companion Simone, Drieu's Marat hardly appears "sinister" but describes himself as "ugly" and "dirty" (47) and comes across as primarily self-centered. All the other revolutionaries are persecuting him, he feels, but he could be the tyrant who could save France from tyranny! No direct mention is made of Marat's being Jewish, but a speech such as the following obviously suggested it to the audience: "Blood will flow and the people will come to me. Then they'll know who Marat is! They'll know that the inventor of modern science is also the inventor of modern politics. Yes, the persecuted one, the son of persecuted people. Persecuted in Spain, Italy, England, France. Finally triumphant" (51). Both Danton (act 2, 61) and Robespierre (act 3, 123) tell Marat that he cannot govern France because he is not French. He was a subject of the king of Prussia, then claimed to be English when he was living in England, and now claims to be French. According to Robespierre (126), his real name is Mara, without the *t*.[87] He thus fits the stereotype of the wandering, cosmopolitan Jew,

---

[86] Jacques LaCroix, "Il y a 150 ans, le geste héroique de Charlotte Corday," *Combats*, July 17, 1943.
[87] The notion obviously comes from Drumont. See note 85.

claiming roots that are not really his, the eternal foreigner. In addition, he is a journalist, an intellectual, and of course the apologist of radical popular democracy and regicide. Yet Marat seems to speak the "truth" for Drieu against Danton when he tells him that France will need a *chef*, a dictator, to replace the king (67–68).

Charlotte's "purity" consists in part of her single-minded devotion to the *grandeur* of the revolution, its "strength in moderation," and to overcoming its "ignoble" elements of useless violence and bourgeois mediocrity. But Charlotte is also "pure" because she succeeds in rising above politics into the domain of literature and myth. When her brother Alexis accuses her of "talking like a book," she hits her copy of *Polyeucte* and declaims, "There are books written by strong people and read by strong people. Those readers do not betray those authors" (77). This scene is shortly followed by her soliloquy at the center of act 2 and thus of the play (80–82). Here she tells us she has left the world of women to enter that of men but found them to be not as strong as she would have hoped. She is now alone with her soul but in communion with her grandfather Corneille and the Norman lineage of the Cordays. The nation is divided, suffering, being destroyed by the Jacobins. What can she do? She evokes her prototype, Joan of Arc, but there is no king for her to crown, no nobles to rally. There seems to be no solution but to find "a strong man to stop the evil" (82).

Charlotte, however, continues to find that strong men are in short supply. In Caen, the Girondin Bougon-Langrais declares his love for her and tells her he hopes to derive courage from her, but she scoffs at him. When the news arrives that his friend and leader Bayeux has been killed by the mob led by Marat, and she sees that he intends to do nothing, her own courage is inflamed. In act 3, still in Caen, she meets Barbaroux and informs him that the Girondins are cowardly and ineffective and that he should have killed Marat but that she will do it. Pointing to the statue of Brutus that has dominated several scenes, she says, "He was not a coward. I thought that we would produce a French Brutus" (110). Since this historical figure has not found its reincarnation, Barberoux proposes another: "But now, you will be our Joan of Arc" (111). At the end of the fifth tableau, Charlotte remains alone, exploring her identification with Joan. "When there are no more men in France, a woman rises up." A woman, in her role, has a certain advantage over men. "Since blood is necessary, it will stain my hands alone. After all, I am neither noble, nor plebian, nor royalist, nor republican. A woman, more than a man, carries the essence of the Nation in her heart, its unity, its purity, its eternity." Praying to God for the only time in the play, she presents herself as sacrifice: "I offer You my blood with that of Marat" (114). Leaving the men to squabble over ineffective "political" maneuvers, the virgin, almost transformed into an allegorical figure of *La Patrie*, purifies herself for the sacrificial act.

The third scene of the third act (tableau 6) finds Charlotte with Marat, who is in his famous tub, just after the departure of Robespierre and Saint-Just. But Drieu prefers the classical solution of offstage violence: the audience observes only her preparing the assassination before the scene changes to the final one, her prison cell. Here, Drieu has invented a platonic love scene, a meeting of sister souls, between Charlotte Corday and Saint-Just. He prepares this through the encounter of Robespierre and Saint-Just with Marat, where the two true French, and noble, revolutionaries establish their differences with the ignoble "materialist" Marat. Saint-Just says to Marat:

> What is gnawing at you [the word *ronger* suggests a parallel with his skin condition] is envy. I don't envy Robespierre, I admire him and devote myself to him, body and soul. And Robespierre will be a leader *[chef]* (he puts his hand on Robespierre's shoulder), but won't be a tyrant. In our Revolution, Marat, you only see the ugly side, the side of blood and tyranny. . . . There is another side that we see, it's the devotion of the greatest among us to the public good, to the law. (128)

Saint-Just thus embodies the ideals promoted but unrealized in *Le Chef*: devotion to a leader through virile fraternity, devotion to the purity of the nation. Apparently a precursor of the *Révolution nationale*, he has more in common with his noble enemy Charlotte Corday than with his associate Marat. In the course of their lyrical dialogue in her prison cell he gradually convinces Charlotte (whom he calls *petite Jeanne d'Arc manquée*) that they are of the same "race," of the "pure" revolutionaries, and that she would have found in him and Robespierre more worthy comrades than the Girondins. He invokes another historical precedent: "The Romans threw out a challenge to all the peoples of the earth in the centuries of centuries. Now, people will say, 'The Romans and the French'" (143). Like the Romans, the new French (and *sous-entendu*, fascist France in the wake of fascist Italy) are destined to unite Europe under the new idea. Both virgins, Saint-Just and Charlotte embody the pure youth, revolutionary fervor, and national devotion of fascist ideology. In the apotheosis of their idealized love, the gender hierarchy is rectified:

> Saint-Just: . . . I swear to you that I am as great as you.
> Charlotte: Greater. You are a man. (146)

If some of Charlotte's earlier statements might have given rise to fears of incipient feminism, that is set straight. Her glory is in her sacrifice. In her last words, "Death can only be heaven" (147), she seems to achieve the tragic plenitude sought by Drieu. "Heaven" of course is to be taken metaphorically. Charlotte may have strayed from the beliefs she was taught in the convent, but the fervor of her devotion to her cause is its own religion. Like all fascist heroes she dies young: such will be the fate of Saint-Just as well. Finding an ideal, spiritual love on the eve of their deaths, the two young heroes, like Antigone and Haemon, die tragically in part because they are spared the "dramatic" complications and "decadence" of sexuality. Dealing with a historical subject instead of with a myth created around contemporary events, as in *Le Chef*, and at the time when France's defeat seemed to have restored its sense of the tragic, Drieu has with some confidence written his modern tragedy.

Charlotte Corday is not metatheatrical and intertextual in the manner of *Bérénice* or even of *Le Chef*. Yet it is not lacking in self-consciousness. Drieu seems driven by a desire to conflate historical and literary predecessors: Corneille's Polyeucte, Brutus, and Joan of Arc stand behind Charlotte as Charlotte stands behind the National Revolution. The Christian martyr, the Roman republican, the royalist, and the "pure" revolutionary fuse in the creation of an ideal fascist. The discovery of historical eternal return along with literary tradition, myth, and Dionysian fervor merge in a search for eternal fascism. Yet Drieu's last play has none of the overt violence he advocated in his early writing on theater. In this primarily literary play, the violent is transmuted into the verbal, the Dionysian contained by the Apollonian.

What Drieu seems to seek in an ideal tragic plenitude is first of all the recuperation of the aesthetic experiences of brotherhood, sacrifice, violence, youth, purity, grandeur, and a sense of destiny that he felt in the war, in reading Nietzsche, on the "tragic night" of February 6, 1934, and finally in the defeat of France. Fascism, it seems, has the potential to give form to the fleeting but eternal moment as well as to provide the leader to achieve the binding of the group. The theoretical grounding in Nietzsche provides the eternal return as the basis for unifying myth and history with contemporary politics, the notion of philosophy and politics as action and improvisation, and the exaltation of tragedy as the aesthetic form corresponding to fascist plenitude. Self-consciously, in his two modern tragedies, Drieu attempts not a theater of propaganda but a recreation of the primordial European "totalitarian" literary form for his own time and the future. Yet it was perhaps only at the end of his life, in writing the scenario for his own suicide, that he came close to finding plenitude.

CHAPTER FIVE

Aesthetic Fascism and French Modern Tragedy under the German Occupation: Montherlant and Anouilh

The extraordinary flourishing of the French theater during the brief period of the German Occupation continues to pose unresolved questions. Was the Comédie française a haven for the dissemination of French culture and thus of nationalist spirit in defiance of the occupier or was it an institution subservient to the Nazis? Did Jean-Paul Sartre, in allowing Charles Dullin to produce *Les Mouches*, in fact collaborate with the enemy or did he, as he announced after the Liberation, send an encoded message of resistance past the censors? Was it possible for Jean Anouilh, one of the most frequently staged playwrights during the Occupation, to remain, as he claimed, a "bête de théâtre" completely unconcerned with politics? Is his *Antigone* a drama of resistance, a fascist-leaning "pièce noire," or an example of modern tragedy removed from political actuality? To what extent was the popularity of Henry de Montherlant's theater produced under the Occupation a result of its ideological subtext?

Perhaps one of the problems with the approach to relations between theater and ideology during the Occupation is that it has tended to remain colored by the passions of the time by forcing works into the classifications of "resistant" or "collaborationist," if not relegating them to the domain of the apolitical. Created in a climate saturated by propaganda, compromised by having to pass through the censorship of both the Vichy authorities and the Nazi Propagandastaffel, but received by a highly charged public eager to find political messages on one end of the spectrum or the other, the works created for the Paris stage from 1940–44 offer a unique relationship between text and reception.[1] Yet very few propagandistic or political plays were written or produced during the period, and the relationship between theater and ideology is more complex than has been realized.

Both the Vichy and the German authorities, as well as the drama critics of those persuasions in the press, seem to have had fairly clear ideas about what they expected from (and would not permit in) theater in the "new Order." There were of course important differences between the two. In general, the Vichy censors were more interested in matters of morality, notably in eliminating the theme of adultery from the Parisian stage, whereas the German censors were more attentive to references to Jews or to anything that could be construed as politically or ideologically unfavorable. Fascist-leaning Parisian theater critics, concerned with developing their own aesthetic of theater, tended to disdain incidents of Vichy puritanism such as the decision to ban *Tartuffe*.[2] It is perhaps in this context that one must place Anouilh's ironic comment on censorship in the Nazi-sponsored paper *La Gerbe* (April 12, 1941): "Well, I rejoice in this censorship. It will provoke the birth of a new *Lettres persanes* which we won't have to be ashamed of." The Parisian theater reviewers tended to look with disfavor on plays that were overtly propagandistic for the Vichy cause. The most influential of them, Alain Laubreaux, panned *Les Eaux basses* by André Roubaud for being a simplistic Vichy propaganda piece.[3] But critics and intellectuals writing in Vichy-sponsored journals such as *Les Cahiers français*, like their colleagues in the German-controlled journals and like Italian fascist intellectuals earlier, also purported to scorn crass propaganda in art in an attempt to develop a theatrical aesthetic befitting the National Revolution.

One of the clearest attempts to prescribe canons for the theater of the new era is the essay "Théâtre de demain," by Claude Vermorel in *La Gerbe*, January 2, 1941.[4] Vermorel argues that the theater of the "ancien régime" (the Vichy and fascist term for the Third Republic) reflected its period in its excessive concern with themes such as adultery and individual prob-

---

[1] For a good overview of theatrical production in occupied Paris, see Patrick Marsh, "Le Théâtre à Paris sous l'occupation allemande," in *Revue de la société d'histoire du théâtre* 3 (1981): 197–369. Serge Added, in *Le Théâtre dans les années Vichy, 1940–1944* (Paris: Editions Ramsay, 1992), gives a detailed historical, nonliterary account of the situation of the theater throughout France, based on archival material.

[2] See Marsh, "Le Théâtre à Paris," 213–14.

[3] This did not, however, stop Laubreaux from writing his own propaganda play, *Les Pirates de Paris* (on the Stavisky affair) under a pseudonym and then writing a favorable review of it. See ibid., 238–39.

[4] The case of Vermorel is perplexing. Drawing on the recollections of contemporary spectators including Simone de Beauvoir, reviews in the clandestine press, and his own reading, Patrick Marsh argues that Vermorel's play on the trial of Joan of Arc, *Jeanne avec nous*,

lems, as well as in the "surrealist" preoccupation with the inner life. "Mercantile liberalism, the self-critical reign of the individual, culminated in the economic crisis, poverty and capitalist disorder in the world . . . and in art . . . in the taste for rotten hothouse flowers." What is now called for is *not* propaganda for the moral order but a theatrical renaissance that will portray exaltation, joy, and a formation of "national myths." Among the young dramatists, Vermorel sees the most hope in Anouilh because of "his hatred of money . . . his striving for purity . . . his transition toward a healthy, strong, and noble theater." In the same vein, Jean Turlais, drama critic for *Les Cahiers français*, poet, and spokesman for aesthetic fascism,[5] writes that whereas Giraudoux belongs to "the age we want to vomit" (read the Third Republic), Anouilh, with his ferocious satire of the bourgeoisie, his portrayal of the purity of the young and the revolt of the oppressed, is the dramatist of the National Revolution. "For Anouilh on the other hand is with us, behind our barricade. I don't know if he has 'political opinions.' But it's enough for me to know that before a certain concept of society and of life, he has our same reactions, our disgust, our hatred. He is a revolutionary writer."[6] These writers, like many others in the collaborationist press, appear to be more concerned with the aesthetics and thematics than with the politics of theater. The two playwrights most consistently praised in the writings of fascist literati and journalists under the Occupation are Jean Anouilh and Henry de Montherlant. Parisian fascist intellectuals seem to have believed that a fascist literature was about to flourish in France and that theater might be its most important vehicle. Lucien Rebatet, while making the exaggerated claim that no other movement was supported by as many brilliant writers, lists Montherlant and Anouilh among those who

---

produced in January 1942, spoke more clearly to the Resistance than any other production under the Occupation and that Vermorel's intentions were clear (ibid., 292–94). Serge Added, however, points out the favorable reception of this play in the collaborationist press (including a review by Lucien Rebatet, who called Vermorel's *Jeanne* "la patronne d'un fascisme français") and concludes that it falls in line with Vichy-fascist Joan of Arc propaganda. The myth of *Jeanne* as a play of the Resistance, in Added's view, arose after the post-Liberation productions (*Le Théâtre dans les années Vichy*, 262–73). The play was first written in 1938 and contains no direct topical allusions. It is indeed difficult to reconcile the Vermorel author of "Théâtre de demain" in 1941 with the purported author and coproducer of a Resistance-oriented performance in 1942. Like Anouilh's *Antigone*, Vermorel's *Jeanne* offers an excellent example of the wide variations in reception of a highly charged public.

[5] Turlais, who eventually joined the French army and died on the front at the age of twenty-three, was part of the literary group at *Les Cahiers français*, along with Roland Laudenbach and François Sentein. Identified at one point as "a student of Nietzsche and member of the Milice" and called by Marcel Bucard "France's most committed fascist" (although he never engaged in politics), Turlais was also a poet. Montherlant called him "one of the best minds of the young generation." He was also a friend of Anouilh, Paul Serant [Paul Selleron], and Jean Genet. See Harry E. Stewart and Rob Roy McGregor, *Jean Genet: From Fascism to Nihilism* (New York: Peter Lang, 1993), 43, 114.

[6] Jean Turlais, "Le Théâtre de Jean Anouilh," *Les Cahiers français* 5, May 1943, 67.

were fascist sympathizers while emphasizing the importance of theater to fascist culture. Our "patron," he says, was not Adolf Hitler but Benito Mussolini, and theatricality is a necessary component in the tradition that includes Giacomo Puccini and Gabriele D'Annunzio. Rebatet also claimed that there were many sympathizers in the Comédie française.[7]

The search for a fascist modern tragedy, building on the ideas of Thierry Maulnier, Robert Brasillach, and Pierre Drieu La Rochelle discussed in the last chapter, continued under the Occupation. *Grandeur* and *pureté*, Maulnier's criteria in *Nietzsche* and *Racine*, took on additional connotations. "Purity," with its racial and political overtones, became a particularly loaded, polysemic term. In the mood of national self-recrimination created by the Vichy regime, a common notion was that "suffering purifies."[8] In 1942, a contributor to *Je suis partout* defined fascism as follows: "It isn't a party . . . it is above all a state of mind, a group of reflexes, an heroic way of conceiving life, . . . it is a constant willing of *grandeur* and *pureté.*"[9] In the theater, one "purification" project was the abolition of all the "bourgeois" values of the old regime in dramatic content and form.[10] Like the fascist intellectuals in the 1930s, the theater critics and literary journalists in the collaborationist press of the 1940s singled Henri Bernstein out as the bête noire of "théâtre enjuivé."[11] They call for a revival of the "Aryan" genre of tragedy as an antidote to the "decadence" inherent in the Jewish, capitalist, and democratic *drame.* This new, antibourgeois modern tragedy would be founded on both Nietzschean and classical French aesthetics. A fusion of *grandeur* and *pureté* with Dionysian violence and Apollonian form appears to be the primary characteristic of the ideal theater of the National Revolution. Readers and misreaders of Nietzsche argue that tragedy, with its "solar" ideology, its virile heroics, its emphasis on violence and sacrifice, and its aesthetic expression of the contradiction that lies at the heart of the

---

[7] Lucien Rebatet, *Mémoires d'un fasciste* (Paris: Pauvert, 1976), 41–47, 115, 120, 147.

[8] Robert Paxton, *Vichy France: Old Guard and New Order, 1940–1944* (New York: Knopf, 1972), 33–34.

[9] P. A. Cousteau, "Les Fascistes au pouvoir!" *Je suis partout,* September 12, 1943 (emphasis added).

[10] Regarding the theater, Henri-René Lenormand writes: "It is a question . . . of bringing the theater in line with the National Revolution, of sweeping away everything that still remains in it of partisan ideology, of conformity to the values of bourgeois democracy, of implicit or explicit eroticism. It's a question of making it healthy without making it bland, of purifying it without unmanning it" ("Pour un conseil de l'ordre," *La Gerbe,* November 13, 1941, 11). Lenormand later claimed that he had never collaborated and that he wrote articles for *Panorama,* "a paper of the infamous press," only to praise Giraudoux. He does not mention his numerous contributions to *La Gerbe.* See his *Confessions d'un auteur dramatique* (Paris: Michel, 1949–53), 2: 268.

[11] See for example André Fraigneau, "Couleur du nouveau théâtre français," *Les Cahiers français* 7 (July 1943): 31–37. The new public, he claims, comes to the theater not to escape but to "drink in common at the sources of grandeur."

world, was the Aryan form par excellence. They also applauded the numerous revivals of French classical tragedy, especially Pierre Corneille, and of Greek tragedy, which indeed met with popular enthusiasm.

An article in *Les Cahiers français* by Christian Michelfelder titled "Une époque tragique" gives perhaps the best summation of this attitude. (*Les Cahiers* specialized in cultural matters; for example, they published Jean Turlais's history of fascist literature.) Under the Occupation, Michelfelder opines, the French are fortunate to be living in a tragic period. Whereas materialism and "popular oriental philosophies" (read the Third Republic, the Jews, and what he calls "low" Christianity) are like weights that drag the human spirit down, the virile strength of the great agonistic civilizations of antiquity pulls it upward. Now that we are standing on the brink of an abyss, Michelfelder argues, we have the possibility of developing a new European elite. Yet at times his language seems straight out of contemporary Sartrean existentialism: "La vie ne peut donc être qu'un engagement total au bout duquel il y a la mort" ("life can only be a total commitment at the end of which there is death") and "Du sort de chacun dépend le sort de tous" ("The fate of all depends on the fate of each individual"). The tragic gesture of the tragic hero, Michelfelder concludes, will accomplish the sacrifice that will redeem the rest of us.[12] In articles in the Nazi-sponsored newspaper *La Gerbe* Michelfelder more specifically calls for a new poetic, literary tragedy to give aesthetic form to the spirit of the new age. Only a Nietzschean tragedy, bringing spectators together in Dionysian ecstasy while controlling them through Apollonian form, can elevate the French from materialistic concerns to grandeur, purity, and the cult of heroic violence.[13] The same Michelfelder interviewed Montherlant for *La Gerbe* on December 16, 1943, and published an essay on his theater in *Les Cahiers français* in May 1944. There he argues that only Montherlant has come close to creating the ideal tragedy for the National Revolution. Both *La Reine morte* and *Fils de personne*, the two plays by Montherlant produced under the Occupation, "burn with a flame that purifies."[14]

Other writers in the collaborationist press made more specific connections between political ideology and dramatic form. They reiterated the contention of Drieu La Rochelle and Brasillach that the Third Republic, and democracy in general, fostered a mediocre realism, or a tiresome and formulaic triangular comedy. The decline of the theater could be attributed to a Jewish influence epitomized by Henri Bernstein. Tragedy, how-

---

[12] Christian Michelfelder, "Une époque tragique," *Les Cahiers français* 3 (September 1942): 15–23.

[13] Christian Michelfelder, "Renaissance de la tragédie," *La Gerbe*, March 18, 1943; "Nietzsche et la tragédie," *La Gerbe*, June 22, 1943.

[14] Christian Michelfelder, "Le Théâtre de Montherlant," *Les Cahiers français* 11 (May 1944): 47–53.

ever, is not only Western (or Aryan) civilization's distinctive contribution to world culture but the proof of its superiority. The "virility" and "purity" of great tragedy are often opposed to the "feminine" softness and "decadence" of Third Republic theater. It is important to realize that arguments of this nature do not necessarily lead to an apology for German culture or its imitation. On the contrary, both the fascist and the Vichyite proponents of modern tragedy evoked the *grandeur* and *pureté* of Corneille and Jean Racine to demonstrate France's central role in the continuation of a Mediterranean form. Nor does their appeal to Nietzsche seem Germanophile or Nazi-influenced. It conforms rather to Thierry Maulnier's portrayal of a Mediterranean-oriented Nietzsche, particularly in his view of tragedy. What the French fascists sought in modern tragedy was a new but specifically French form.[15]

Enfin Montherlant vint

The collaborationist reviewers of Montherlant's modern tragedies *La Reine morte* and *Fils de personne* are almost uniformly of the opinion that these plays signal the long-desired cure for France's decadent theater. It is as if the critics are saying, "enfin Montherlant vint." If literary fascists sensed an affinity between Montherlant's aesthetics and their cause, they did not find in him a political activist. Ideologically close to Drieu in his disdain for the "decadence" and "mediocrity" of modern France, which he also associated with women, as well as in his nostalgia for the tragic plenitude of the battlefield, Montherlant unlike Drieu never made the leap into politics or joined a party. Indeed, Montherlant's own proclaimed ideological system of "sycretism and alternance" would seem to forbid traditional political allegiance. In this view, partially derived from Nietzsche, nothing is true and thus everyone is in some sense "right." Going back and forth between opposing ideologies or temporarily syncretizing them provides a means of giving a shape to life once the search for stable and rational truth has been abandoned.

And yet, early in his life, Montherlant had hoped to find some sort of fusion of aesthetics and politics in a political career, that is, if he could en-

---

[15] Here are some examples of writing by fascist critics. Alain Laubreaux, *Ecrit pendant la guerre* (Paris: Editions du centre d'études de l'agence Inter-France, 1944), 138: "Only defeat will rid us of Bernstein and the moral shit [*la merde morale*] that we're wallowing in, and vanquished France will become itself again." Claude Viriot, "La Tragédie, espoir national," *La Gerbe*, May 28, 1942: "Objective . . . amoral realism has had its day. . . . What is the form that can restore vitality to the theater? Tragedy." (He goes on to discuss the importance of reviving Corneille as an inspiration to modern tragedy.) Alphonse de Chateaubriant, "Literature and drama in the present time" (*La Gerbe*, April 1, 1943): "Tomorrow we must rid ourselves of yesterday's bad dream [the *drame* prevailing onstage] and return to the music of the world . . . from which . . . the new Apollonian dream will resurface."

gage in politics without losing his liberty. In this endeavor, his model—not surprisingly—was Gabriele D'Annunzio. According to Montherlant's biographer Pierre Sipriot, his admiration for D'Annunzio was first of all literary: reading D'Annunzio's novels, in particular *Il Piacere* and *Il Fuoco*, revealed to him what modern literature should be. In the early 1920s, Montherlant aspired to find a way of uniting politics and aesthetics in the manner of "the deputy of beauty," admiring also D'Annunzio's apparent role as the soul and poetry of fascism, unsullied by base politics. Yet Montherlant was unable, in the French context, to find a corresponding role and instead went into a period of "exile," traveling around the Mediterranean. Montherlant and D'Annunzio became personally close during the latter's residence in France and Montherlant acknowledged D'Annunzio's influence on him, particularly in *Les Olympiques*. After the publication of that elegy to sport and heroic pagan vitalism and probably on the advice of D'Annunzio, Mussolini expressed the desire to honor the French writer who had created "the literature we need."[16] Montherlant, for his part, apparently felt a certain admiration for Il Duce. Sipriot recounts that during a 1947 trip to Rome, he said that he bought a bust of Nero "because it is beautiful, because it resembles Mussolini."[17]

In addition to D'Annunzio, Maurice Barrès and Nietzsche were important influences on the young Montherlant. From Barrès, he seems to have derived, like Brasillach, an admiration for a certain heroic, chivalric, and nationalist concept of Christianity, though devoid of religion. With Barrès and D'Annunzio he also felt nostalgia for the passing of nobility along with a profound disdain for democracy. Reading Nietzsche, he was intrigued by the notion of the superman, the lesson of war and violence as the remedy for a weak people, as well as *The Birth of Tragedy*'s conception of the tragic hero and tragic form.[18]

The natural desire of man for war and its potential subversion through the influence of woman constitute the subject of Montherlant's first play, *L'Exil*, written on the eve of the Great War when the author was only eighteen, but not published until 1929. Based to some extent on Montherlant's own relationship with his mother at the time, this adolescent work, in Robert Brasillach's judgment, is not only one of his best plays but the one that gives "the key to everything that follows."[19] Brasillach may well have seen in it themes dear to him, such as the nostalgia for "collège" and the

---

[16] Pierre Sipriot, *Montherlant sans masque* (Paris: Robert Laffont, 1982), 1: 263. The information on Montherlant and D'Annunzio can be found in 1: 246–50.

[17] Ibid., 2: 269.

[18] Ibid., 1: 205–15.

[19] In *Le Petit parisien*, December 22, 1943, quoted by Montherlant in his 1954 notes to *L'Exil* in Henry de Montherlant, *Théâtre* (Paris: Gallimard, 1972), 11.

beauty of male bonding in both school and war. In the first act, the eighteen-year-old Philippe de Presles discusses with his dear friend Sénac his Nietzschean-aesthetic notions of the glories of fighting on the front: "Something magnificent and barbarous, Guérin, *The Centaur*, the afternoon of a faun. . . . But all that inferior humanity, born to be slaves, all those mediocre, ugly, stupid, badly dressed people, why can they participate in this glory? Do they have any right to it? What injustice!"[20] War, as Philippe sees it, will permit him not only to escape from contemporary mediocrity but to participate in the heroic model of classical antiquity: "We'll lead an admirable, free, ample, generous life, a life that can't be lived in our stupid era. . . . We'll be Achilles and Patrocles" (26). Yet Philippe succumbs to his mother's pleas that she needs him at home, and Sénac goes to war without him. Feeling that he is in exile from his true fatherland ("exilé de ma patrie profonde" [50]), Philippe sulks and complains to his mother, Geneviève, throughout the second act. Geneviève, who has been actively working in organizing ambulances and hospital care for the war wounded, is herself decorated as a war heroine, thus apparently making it necessary for her son to volunteer for service. Geneviève reluctantly consents, but it is, according to Philippe, "too late": Sénac has already returned from the battlefield. In talking with him Philippe becomes cruelly aware of the distance that separates the young aristocratic aesthete from the warrior: his friend has known real experiences of risk and death he does not share; they cannot be Achilles and Patrocles. Sénac's "intense life" has led him to admire the virtues of war more than those of patriotism: "Really, I like Germans who fight better than Frenchmen who stay at home" (64). Philippe now decides to volunteer for the front, but his goal, expressed in the final line of the play, has become that of rebonding with his friend through participation in the same experiences. "Farewell. I am leaving to make my soul like his, to find him again when I return" (65).

A distinct homosocial and homosexual desire, apparently unnoticed by critics of the play, is evident in *L'Exil*. Love of war is conflated with love of a man; both promise a mystical-erotic elevation and bonding in an arena uncontaminated by the mediocre concerns of daily life, represented in particular by women. Even though Geneviève is in many respects an admirable character (and Montherlant was devoted to his own mother), women, it seems, are by nature not only incapable of achieving this sort of transcendence but are also by nature inclined to try to prevent their men from finding it. They may exemplify lower forms of patriotism, as Geneviève does in her work with the wounded; they cannot achieve the warrior's glory that transcends patriotism. Brasillach was right to see in this youthful work germs that would come to fruition in the mature Montherlant. Here is not

[20] "L'Exil" in Montherlant, *Théâtre*, 24.

only the D'Annunzian glorification of the beauty of war in contrast with the mediocrity of ordinary life but also the "alternating" transcendence of patriotism in admiration for the enemy-warrior that Montherlant would develop in *Le Solstice de juin* (1941). Here, too, is an incipient distinction not so much between man and woman as between the principles of virility and femininity. The aesthetic approach to political reality is one with which Brasillach could surely identify. Even though Montherlant did not attempt to write a modern tragedy with *L'Exil,* the play exhibits Nietzschean overtones in the thwarted yearning of a modern young man to become a classical tragic hero.

Montherlant did not return to writing for the theater until 1928, when he chose to adapt the Cretan myth of Phaedra's mother, Pasiphae, into a modern tragedy. The year before, he described himself (in the third person) as a living tragic figure of modernity: "He gives the appearance of someone with a mad love of grandeur, who, in the impossibility of finding grandeur anywhere and nonetheless in the impossibility of denying it, ends up by dreaming of dying voluntarily for a cause in which he would not believe. This is the summit of the tragic." He goes on to say that a cause such as the nationalism of Barrès or the heroic adventurism of D'Annunzio or Byron could thus act as a "refuge" for him.[21] Here is the kernel of Montherlant's notion of "useless service," an ethos he developed not only in the 1935 essay of that title but also in several of his modern tragedies, most importantly in *La Reine morte.*

Pasiphae does not fit this particular tragic configuration. The "dramatic poem" is exceptional in Montherlant's dramatic corpus in its use of ancient myth and (with *Port-Royal*), its female protagonist. Inspired by fragments of a lost cycle by Euripides, Montherlant was interested in exploring the Cretan origins of the "solar myths" and their representation of the heroic vital principle in the bull, a mythical complex he had already used in his stories of bullfighting, *Les Bestiaires,* and to a certain extent in *Les Olympiques.*[22] Although I can find no mention of it, it seems likely that Montherlant knew his friend D'Annunzio's *Fedra* and D'Annunzio's intention of rendering the "monstrous" passion of the mother in the daughter. Like D'Annunzio's heroine, Montherlant's proclaims the necessity of a passion that goes beyond the limits of good and evil to reclaim the elemental and the Dionysian. "I am the daughter of the Sun, and I should restrain myself to loving only men? . . . And who ordered that limitation? . . . No, no limits! Like my father, to embrace, to penetrate everything that exists" (*Théâtre,* 85). Like Fedra too, this Pasiphae, in the throes of her passion, pierces the leaves of a tree with her hairpin (84).

---

[21] Unedited text, cited by Sipriot, *Montherlant sans masque,* 1: 431–32.
[22] See Montherlant's 1938 preface to *Pasiphae* in *Théâtre,* 75.

Although Montherlant's brief poem exhibits nothing like the elaborate literary and political intertextuality of D'Annunzio's drama, the tragic forces of the protagonists' opposition to social norms and morality parallel each other. Yet Pasiphae, as if in a nod of recognition to Montherlant's "useless service," recognizes that she expects neither happiness nor pleasure from her union with the majestic white bull. It is rather a question of doing what one wills, what others fear to do, thus joining the elect "nation of uncommon beings" (91). Since Montherlant does not choose to portray either the union of woman with bull or its dire consequences, the dramatic poem cannot really be called a tragedy in any usual sense. It is rather a poetic expression of the tragic conflict between elemental desire and the constructions of human morality. Just as Fedra had her poet, Pasiphae has a one-man chorus to give Apollonian form to her Dionysian expression of passion. As Pasiphae goes to her destiny, the chorus muses on whether "the absence of thought, the absence of morality, contributes much to the great dignity of beasts, plants, and waters" (92). The text thus ends with a suggestion of an amoral nature's superiority to humanity, a suggestion nonetheless expressed in poetic human language.

Although Pasiphae is undoubtedly the protagonist, she cannot really be said to be the hero. Her desire is not so much to act as to submit to the force of mythical virility incarnated in the bull. It is true that she consciously makes the decision to defy morality and taboo, but it is as if in doing so she accedes to what she recognizes as a greater strength, not only elemental virility but the "solar" principle Montherlant found in the bull in his writings of the 1920s and later recognized in the symbol of the swastika.[23] In his essay "Le Solstice de juin," published in the volume of that title in 1941, Montherlant interprets the victory of the "solar wheel" not only as a victory of paganism over Christianity but also as a vindication of his only credo, the principle of *alternance* derived from Nietzsche's eternal return. France must thus accept defeat as part of the eternal alternating order of things. To support his argument (or rather, his hymn to the German defeat of France), Montherlant invokes the mythical Cretan queen. "To be oneself and to become another! To become another self! (Pasiphae)."[24] By embracing the significance of the swastika, France can now leave behind its mediocre existence and partake in the vital revolution, just as Pasiphae seized the opportunity to realize her true self by transcending the merely human. It is tempting to speculate that Ionesco used *Pasiphae* as material for parody in

[23] In January 1938, introducing a lecture by the German "ambassador" in Paris Otto Abetz on "German Youth and Happiness," Montherlant said, "How could the author of *Les Béstiaires* consider the swastika with indifference?" (quoted in Pierre-Henri Simon, *Procès du héros: Montherlant, Drieu La Rochelle, Jean Prévost* [Paris: Seuil, 1950], 87).

[24] Henry de Montherlant, "Le Solstice de juin," in volume of essays titled *Le Solstice de juin* (Paris: Bernard Grasset, 1941), 309.

Rhinocéros, where his characters defend their metamorphoses by invoking the narrow limits of human morality and the superior appeal of bestial force.

Pasiphae was written in Tunis during the period of Montherlant's self-imposed wandering "exile" around the Mediterranean. It did not become known to the Parisian public until December 1938, when it was performed at the Théâtre Pigalle. Montherlant was at this time in Paris, frequenting the ultra-right group Rive Gauche, to which Brasillach presented his *Corneille.* The group was vehemently antirepublican but not at this time pro-Nazi: rather, it sought to oppose to both communism and "Hitlerism," "a certain idea of Europe, the fruit of its traditions and of its Latin sources."[25] Indeed, the group was horrified by the Munich agreements, which only exemplified French lack of resolution for war. It was to this association that Montherlant delivered his talk "La France et la morale de midinette" (France and the shopgirl morality) on November 29, 1938. Here he laments the "decadence" of France, the "feminine" and "Christian" conformity, weakness, and cowardice of the French people. France would be saved only by a new morality, transcending "shopgirl" limits and based on courage, strength, and "quality."

If Montherlant, like Brasillach, would eventually welcome the Nazi occupier, the cause does not seem to have been a wholehearted espousal of Nazi politics or philosophy. Like Brasillach, Montherlant approaches the defeat in primarily aesthetic and even theatrical terms: although he does not specifically invoke the tragic beauty of defeat, as does Brasillach, his praise of the "solar wheel," *alternance,* and the sacrifice of Adonis and his eventual resurrection suggests affinities with his reading of *The Birth of Tragedy.* In "Les Nuits de mai," Montherlant extols in terms that recall both Marinetti and D'Annunzio the beauty of the "spectacle" of war,[26] and in "La Paix dans la guerre" he suggests that the spiritual freedom people acquire in wartime has the capacity to elevate them to "tragic grandeur."[27] Montherlant's aesthetic approach to political events can be seen earlier in his essay "A Good Thing to Live in 1938," in which he evokes the "necessity of opposing forces, which was virtually a dogma with the Ancient Greeks," to justify his perception that no side or idea holds truth but that in the clash of opposites, all eventually fuse as one. "To enter the enemy's world and realize that you are in harmony with everything you find there, is a very significant experience. . . . Two antagonistic doctrines are merely different deviations of the same truth."[28] If any-

[25] Sipriot (*Montherlant sans masque,* 2: 122) attributes this quotation to Robert André, *Une passion ingénue,* but gives no further bibliographical information.

[26] Montherlant, *Le Solstice de juin,* 204.

[27] Ibid., 118.

[28] "A Good Thing to Live in 1938," in Henry de Montherlant, *Selected Essays,* ed. Peter Quennell, trans. John Weightman (London: Weidenfeld and Nicolson, 1960), 157, 161.

thing, this essay reads more like some of Gentile's and Mussolini's pronouncements on fascism than like Nazi propaganda. The squabbling of political parties for the fascists denoted bourgeois, rationalistic limitations: only the "spiritual" and "heroic" nature of fascism could accomplish the necessary transcendent fusion. Before Montherlant, the Italian fascists had adapted the Nietzschean idea that "nothing is true" to a doctrine of constant flux, vitalism, and action, surpassing rational argumentation. Montherlant's evocation of ancient Greek opposing forces in this context also underscores the link he perceives between the principle of *alternance* and his aesthetic of tragic agon. Both are centered in conflict and fusion.

Montherlant's welcoming of the Nazi Occupation stems then, in his perception, not from a desire to betray his country or an espousal of Nazi politics but rather from a heroic patriotism revulsed by France's current mediocrity and inspired by the idea of what France could be. As if in anticipation of this line of thought, he evokes his Italian model again in 1938. "Add to the list of patriots those who, at a certain moment, turned against their country.—When Giolitti has d'Annunzio bombed in Fiume, d'Annunzio cries out: 'O old Italy! Keep your old man, he is worthy of you. We are of another fatherland, and we believe in heroes.'"[29] The Giolitti government, the very incarnation, for the Italian fascists, of liberal democratic mediocrity, must have seemed to Montherlant an equivalent to Third Republic France. The superior race, the heroes, transcend the bourgeois notion of patriotism and, as Montherlant argues in *Le Solstice de juin* and elsewhere, may find common cause with the heroic aspirations and the virile force of their worthy enemies.

The publication of *Le Solstice de juin*, as well as Montherlant's public statements of praise of Vichy's new order, caused him to be accused of collaboration after the war. But it was generally believed that he saw the error of his ways after 1941 and that his collaboration was more or less harmless. His sentence was mild: he was forbidden to publish for a year. His supporters, including his biographer Pierre Sipriot, continue to maintain that Montherlant never collaborated during the war. Yet the evidence, not only for collaboration but for fascist sympathies, is considerable, both in his contributions to Nazi-sponsored publications such as *La Gerbe* throughout the Occupation and in his published letters to Roger Peyrefitte. Richard J. Golsan has reviewed the evidence and convincingly argued the case for Montherlant's collaboration in two important articles.[30]

[29] Henry de Montherlant, *Carnets, 1930–1944* (Paris: Gallimard, 1957), 302. For the D'Annunzio quote, Montherlant cites D'Annunzio's biographer Tommaso Antongini.

[30] Richard J. Golsan, "Montherlant and Collaboration: The Politics of Disengagement," *Romance Quarterly* 35 (May 1988): 139–49, and "Find a Victim: Montherlant and the de Man Affair," *French Review* 66 (February 1993): 393–400.

It remains for us to examine the two modern tragedies Montherlant produced under the Occupation, in the context of their reception. Critics in the collaborationist press welcomed both *La Reine morte* and *Fils de personne* as the fulfillment of the call for a modern tragedy befitting the National Revolution. Although Montherlant himself wrote very little on the theory of modern tragedy, he clearly wanted to create specimens of both "la tragédie en veston," or tragedy set in modernity, and tragedy for modernity but set in a mythological or historical context. Clearly, also, he always had in mind the lessons of Nietzsche. In a sense, *L'Exil* and *Pasiphae* can be seen as preparatory sketches for the more mature historical and contemporary dramas.

La Reine morte ou comment on tue les femmes (*The Dead Queen or How to Kill Women*) was published in 1942 and produced, with great success, at the Comédie française in December of that year. Although Montherlant dropped the second part of the title in subsequent editions, it remains revelatory of his tragic aesthetic. Originating as an adaptation of a sixteenth-century Spanish play, *Reinar después de morir* by Vélez de Guevara, *La Reine morte* appears to follow the classical convention of distance in time and place. Yet in the process of creating his own text, Montherlant erases the play's historical grounding by setting it not in medieval Portugal when the historical events took place but "Au Portugal—autrefois." In some respects, as critics have noted, the tragedy is more baroque than classical. Moving as it does between King Ferrante's dark, shadowy empty royal palace, Ines de Castro's contrasting sunny and life-filled dwelling and garden, and the prison where Ferrante confines his son, Ines's husband, Pedro, the tragedy disregards the unity of place, even as it exceeds twenty-four hours in duration. The action, too, contains unclassical subplots such as the Infanta of Navarre's inexplicable attraction for her rival Ines. And yet, a Corneilian conflict between love and duty appears to be at the center of the tragic action.

The plot is fairly simple. Old King Ferrante has sent for the Infanta of Navarre to come to Portugal to arrange her marriage to his son Pedro, thus solidifying Portugal's position against its rival Castille. Don Pedro, however, refuses, having long been in love with the noble but bastard Ines de Castro and having secretly married her and made her pregnant. Learning of their union, Ferrante complains that even though anything can be bought at the Vatican, the pope will never consent to an annulment because he is a political enemy. He puts Pedro in prison and the proud Infanta, offended at being cast off (though not by losing Pedro, since she claims to have no interest in men), prepares to set sail for Navarre. Ferrante's counselors advise him to have Ines put to death; the old king, charmed by the "aimable femme," refuses but then waivers. Learning of the situation from the betrayal of the king's page, the Infanta tries to convince Ines to accompany her to Navarre to avoid almost certain execution. Ines, of course, will not abandon the man she loves. Ferrante's counselors report that an attack by Africans on the coast indicates the weakness of the kingdom and that Ferrante must show strength. After a final interview with Ines, the king orders her execution and soon after dies himself. When Ines's body is brought into the room where the king's body lies in state, Pedro places a crown on her belly, and the courtiers, deserting the dead king, all move to attend the dead queen.

The central tragic conflict seems to resemble that outlined by G. W. F. Hegel as the model for *Antigone*: two irreconcilable but equally valid demands, one public and one private, lead to the working out of an inexorable and inevitable clash, resulting in tragic sacrifice. Montherlant's language and characters, however, subvert both the ancient and the classical French models of tragic agon. Sophocles' Antigone understands Creon's reasons of state but stands for a higher principle; Corneille's Chimène and Rodrigue undergo within themselves the conflict between the high demands of love and duty; Ines and Pedro, however, seem to be concerned with nothing but their private *bonheur*. Unable to convince his son to marry the Infanta, Ferrante decries Pedro's entirely personal preoccupations. "It's about you. And about your happiness. Are you a woman?" (115). Pedro does not dare to tell his father of his secret marriage; this task falls to Ines. When she explains that the reason for it was "to be happier," Ferrante exclaims, "Happiness, again! . . . It's an obsession!" (124). He then sentences his son to prison "for mediocrity." By contrast, the Infanta, with her "virile spirit," is "the son I should have had" (114). The Infanta herself later remarks to Ines that if she had married Pedro, she would have been the man (151).

Although the principal tragic struggle takes place in the dialogues between Ines and Ferrante, the conflict is thus defined not in terms of love against duty, nor even in those of man against woman, but rather as a principle of virility against one of femininity. It is clear, moreover, that these are not equal antagonists. They might also be called *grandeur* and mediocrity. It is true, of course, that the character of Ines is highly appealing to audiences—Montherlant himself remarked on how women love to applaud her. In fact, Ines's freshness, sincerity, and wholehearted devotion to love have caused some critics to remark that Montherlant here at last seemed sympathetic to women and thus could hardly be aligned with the reactionary or fascist camp. Without Ines's charm, however, there could be no conflict. It is her inadvertent seductive power that constitutes the greatest danger to Ferrante, weakening his resolve. Toward the end of the play, he understands that her strategy is to reduce him to the level of the merely human, that of mediocrity and *bonheur*. "What joy to be able to say to yourself, as women do: 'Even though he's a king, he's just a man like the others!' What a triumph for you! But I am not weak, doña Ines. That is a great error'" (172).

Classical tragic conflict is subverted by the character of Ferrante as well. The *raison d'état* he evokes in the first act while advocating Pedro's marriage to the Infanta slowly erodes, leaving him, approaching death, with a sense of emptiness and relativity. What is war? "Men who don't deserve to live. And ideas that aren't worth dying for" (163). In his most famous speech, Ferrante compares himself to a legendary suit of empty armor that sacrificed human lives randomly. At the heart of Montherlant's tragic vision, as Golsan has argued, is his notion of "useless service," a quest for nobility in action in the face of an awareness of the futility and meaninglessness of every cause.[31] Thus Ferrante's tragic anagnorisis leads him to the insight that he no longer has a reason to put Ines de Castro to death and yet must do so anyway. "Why am I killing her? There is doubtless a reason, but I can't distinguish it" (173). He is of course able to announce a public reason: to preserve the purity of the succession to the throne and to suppress the scandal she caused to the state (175). But more irrational motivations take precedence. Ines's announcement that she bears "a child of his blood" (168) does indeed precipitate Ferrante's decision but not for reasons of the purity of succession. He reacts: "A child! Yet another child! So it will never end!" (168). Ines's sense of plenitude, of utter contentment with her pregnancy, inspires in him a revulsion to what he calls her naïveté, which he claims to hate more than vice or crime (168). In the last, very moving dialogue between them, Ferrante opposes the disillusionment of age to Ines's young enthusiasm. He, too, loved his son Pedro when he was a child, but after the age of thirteen, the purity of childhood gives way to adult compromise, so that the man is "the caricature of what he was" (169). Ferrante, in his declining hours, is obsessed with the "pure," total worlds of childhood and death, his desires resembling what Jean-Pierre Faye describes in *Langages totalitaires* as fascism's reactionary impulses, its "grosses Zurück."[32] If an irrational drive toward totalizing purity becomes a preeminent goal, clearly the cluster of impulses represented by "woman"— happiness, compromise, mediocrity, weakness—must be sacrificed, whatever its appeal.

In the scene preceding this one (3.6), Ferrante announces to Ines his decision to have one of his officers killed, even though it is not clear that this officer is guilty of neglecting his duty to prevent the Africans from invading the Portuguese coast. To avoid being humiliated, the kingdom needs a "guilty" person, a sacrificial victim. But the political rationale may also have an irrational source related to the sacrifice of Ines. Femininity's threat to the "purity" of virility parallels the threat of foreigners menacing the "purity" of Europe. In each case a victim must be sacrificed to preserve a threatened integrity.

---

[31] Richard J. Golsan, *Service inutile: A Study of the Tragic in the Theatre of Henry de Montherlant*, Romance Monographs, no. 47 (University, Miss.: University Press of Mississippi, 1988).
[32] Jean-Pierre Faye, *Langages totalitaires* (Paris: Herman, 1972), 80.

Ferrante's tragic solitude manifests itself in the play's wordless final scene in which a crowd "of all conditions" from the palace kneel to pray beside the body of Ines as Pedro places the crown on her belly. Only one person, the young page Dino del Moro, remains beside the body of the king, but the final action consists of another act of betrayal by him as he walks over to join the crowd around Ines. In his "Notes de théâtre," Montherlant explains the ending thus: "Still beyond silence, there is terminal solitude, between abandonment and betrayal. And in the victory of the herd. The herd kneels around the body of Ines, and Dino del Moro joins the herd" (1377). Dino is thirteen years old, the age which Montherlant repeatedly designates as the threshold between the "purity" of childhood and the compromises of adolescence. Thus Dino's gesture could signify his moment of crossing over from purity to mediocrity. In a most untragic comparison in the same note, Montherlant compares Dino's "joining of the herd" to a boy joining his friends to go to a movie he's already seen, just because he doesn't want to be different from them. In this view, Dino prefigures the "mediocre" fourteen-year-old Gillou in Montherlant's next play.

In this final *tableau vivant*, Ferrante's tragic solitude then stands apart from the "herd" even in death. A 1942 entry in Montherlant's *Carnets* may help to shed some light on *La Reine morte*'s duality. Here Montherlant reflects on the French people's love of happiness, opposing it to a sense of the tragic. "From this taste for happiness comes the virtue or the vice, which the French of today have, of 'experiencing the greatest tragedies as bourgeois'" (329). This preoccupation with happiness, he goes on to say, explains the nation's lack of preparation for war. In addition, "it runs the risk of causing the revolution which will succeed the 'national revolution' to fail: [this revolution] will be endangered if, once peace is made, the return to prosperity overtakes it!" (330). What could this mean? Montherlant does not explain himself. Yet it is surely possible to read in this statement a suggestion that the National Revolution is preparing the Axis "New European Order" but that the French preoccupation with happiness will cause them to miss their opportunity to be part of it. In any case, Montherlant here, as well as in *La Reine morte*, restates a theme familiar to French fascist discourse at least since Drieu La Rochelle and probably originating with Mussolini's "Il Fascista è contra la vita comoda." A preoccupation with happiness is indicative of decadence and opposed to fascist (and tragic) *joy*. It is for the "herd" who have not perceived the meaningless void at the heart of things. In *La Reine morte*, Montherlant displays to his audience a tragic lesson on "how to kill women" or the necessity of sacrificing the principle of femininity and the mediocre happiness it incarnates while doubting that his portrayal of solitary virile *grandeur* will be understood. Although Simone de Beauvoir exaggerates when she writes, "It is easy to imagine Ines de Castro in Buchenwald" and Ferrante as Himmler, she is on target in her opinion

Henry de Montherlant, *La Reine morte,* directed by Jean-Louis Vaudoyer, Comédie française, Paris, December 1942, with Jean Yonnel in the role of Ferrante and Madeleine Renaud as Ines. Permission granted by the Roger-Viollet photographic agency.

that the king sacrifices Ines because "the solar principle must triumph over terrestrial banality."[33]

La Reine morte was well received by fascist intellectuals. Lucien Rebatet praised the play, singling out Ferrante's sentencing his son to prison "for mediocrity."[34] Drieu La Rochelle saw in *La Reine morte* an expression of his own preoccupations in *Le Chef.* "There is no leader [*chef*] except where there is a people who deserves him." Although fifteenth-century Portugal had a great king, a "dictator of genius," he remained in solitude because his people wanted only to be left in peace to make love. He then had to kill in order to rule. Drieu finds that Ines, though necessarily and tragically sacrificed, is a "true woman" in that she understands the great man and is in fact secretly in love with her father-in-law. Drieu also praises Montherlant's poetic diction, extolling, like Brasillach, the virtues of "literary" theater.[35] Writing in *Le Petit Parisien* (December 12, 1942) Alain Laubreaux claimed

[33] Simone de Beauvoir, "Montherlant or the Bread of Disgust," in *The Second Sex,* trans. H. M. Parshley (New York: Random House, 1974), 240, 243.

[34] Rebatet, *Mémoires d'un fasciste,* 2, 148.

[35] Pierre Drieu La Rochelle, "La Reine morte," *La Nouvelle revue française,* February 1943, in *Sur les écrivains,* ed. Frédéric Grover (Paris: Gallimard, 1982), 237–44.

that he heard in the performance a language not heard in the French theater for years. The conflict of love with *la raison d'état* is in the great French tradition and has profound political significance (though he doesn't say what it is). The reviewer in *Aujourd'hui* (December 19, 1942) restates the fascist line that Third Republic theater suffered from banality, as well as from the lack of heroism and virility. Montherlant, however, has restored the French tradition to the Comédie française with "his male energy and his taste for *grandeur*." André Castelot, writing in *La Gerbe* on December 17, 1942, quotes its editor, Alphonse de Chateaubriant, in calling *La Reine morte* a "French victory." Nor was he alone. In line with Brasillach's call for a French fascism, it was not mere subservience to the Nazi occupiers that the Parisian collaborationists sought but rather a specifically French aesthetic expression of what they considered a supranational ideal. Several critics in the collaborationist press formulated Montherlant's achievement in terms of the victory of virility over femininity, the latter associated with decadence, the Third Republic, or theater à la Bernstein. Henri-René Lenormand, writing in *Panorama*, finds a moral lesson for France in Montherlant's "Nietzschean" portrayal of tragic conflict: "We must become virile." The moral of *La Reine morte* is more crudely formulated by one Lucien Louvel, writing in the Vichy-sponsored journal *Combats*, September 11, 1943. Taking his inspiration from the 1942 subtitle, Louvel praises Montherlant's "virile morality" and concludes, "We must kill women, that is to say cowards, the weak, the sentimental, everything opposed to the rectitude of duty. . . . Yes, prison for the mediocre! Alas, when will we get to that point? Alas, if we had only gotten there, in France."

Montherlant himself, it must be said, never descended to this level. And yet his own articles and interviews published in collaborationist journals surely contributed to the encouragement of such interpretations. *Aujourd'hui* published on its July 4–5, 1942, front page a discussion by Montherlant of "the hero." This piece contains, in conjunction with some of his ideas on tragedy, one of the writer's most unambiguously profascist statements. In defining the problem of "quality" posed by the hero in Europe, Montherlant writes of a present "struggle of the heroic elite of the new European civilization against low Europeans." Although Montherlant does not define what he means by *"les bas-Européens,"* the use of the term in a Nazi-sponsored paper was no doubt clear enough to the readers. In conformity with his arguments elsewhere, he goes on to state that "Europe was going to die of mediocrity, without the shock it had in 1939." In attempting to define the "elite" European hero, Montherlant makes use of Nietzsche in the same manner as Christian Michelfelder in his *La Gerbe* article on tragedy. Striving after *grandeur*, the hero has the ability to blend will with necessity. Sometimes dominating events, sometimes dominated by them, he is "at ease in the tragic." "Dionysian when he is overcome, Apol-

Ionian when he overcomes, he endlessly participates with joy in [*il jouit sans cesse de*] nature and himself." Writing in *Panorama*, December 16, 1943, Montherlant seems to support the reviewers who find a social or political "moral" in his modern tragedies. Both of his tragic heroes—Ferrante in *La Reine morte* and Georges in *Fils de personne*—are, he says, heroic in their rejection of mediocrity and their sacrifice "to what France should be."

With *Fils de personne ou Plus que le sang* (*Nobody's Son or More Than Blood*), first performed at the Théâtre Saint-Georges on December 18, 1943, Montherlant seems to have decided to attack directly the problem of French "mediocrity" with a tragedy set in modernity. In his preface, however, Montherlant makes it clear that his modern tragedy should also resonate with mythological and historical intertexts. He defines the play's subject thus: "A child is sacrificed by his father to 'a certain idea that the latter has of man' (one could just as well say: to a certain idea that he has of what France should be)." In "sacrificing" his son, the main character, Georges, acts in the tradition of the Japanese samurai so admired by Montherlant: "he immolates what he holds dearest to his demanding personal morality." Georges also finds a mythical avatar in Agamemnon, tragically sacrificing his child for his country, and parallels the Jacobins and the Spanish inquisitors in their rigorous ideal that cruelty is necessary to salvation.[36]

Living in 1940, Georges can hardly accomplish a sacrifice on the order of those of the Trojan War or the Inquisition. A combatant in the "phony war," an escaped prisoner, and one who claims to have suffered in *la débâcle*—the defeat and the exodus of the French—Georges feels that he is living in "exile" in the free zone, where he practices law in Marseille. He has installed his former mistress, Marie Sandoval, and their son, Gilles (called Gillou) in a villa near Cannes. Although Georges had abandoned Marie when she was pregnant, after a chance encounter with her and Gillou in a metro station in Paris, he decides to become a true father to the boy. This plan is interrupted by the war, when he is able to see Gillou only during his leaves. The play, which is set in the villa from October 1940 through January 1941, thus concentrates on Georges's attempt to be a father, his gradual realization of Gilles's fundamental "mediocrity" or "lack of quality" and his final decision to abandon him again, "immolating" him, as he intends, "to something high and pure" (260). Georges's judgment of Gillou is constantly intermingled with his ideas about France. When Marie points out that the boy is affectionate, Georges responds, "One can't make a nation with affectionate men" (248), and when she objects that her son doesn't have to be exceptional, he answers that "the nation needs its sons to be so . . . only individuals can save honor in France today" (250).

[36] Henry de Montherlant, Preface to *Fils de personne*, in *Théâtre*, 211–14. See also the epigraph from *Agamemnon*, 205, and Montherlant's note, 265, comparing Georges's silence in the fourth act to Agamemnon's veiling his face when he immolates Iphigenia.

A father's condemning a boy he did not help to raise for being "of bad quality" certainly seems unjustified in any realistic, domestic dramatic framework, and many spectators of *Fils de personne* reacted against what they considered to be a display of unnecessary cruelty. Yet Montherlant was clearly attempting to heighten the play's realistic fable to a level of more general social significance. In the essays "La Qualité" and "Avenir de la qualité humaine" published in *Le Solstice de juin*, he explains what he means by "quality." The individual is a microcosm of the nation, and one must be demanding with both. Quality is an "undefinable" notion, independent of intelligence, morality, and character. It is possible to conceive of an education for quality, but the French educational system, encouraging conformity and suppressing originality, does just the opposite.[37] Montherlant's diatribes against the popular culture of his day equal those of our contemporaries. Magazines, popular music, radio programs, and especially the cinema produced for the masses, along with attempts at "edification," all contribute to the mediocre mentality of present-day French youth. Montherlant seems unsure of whether "quality" is something innate, perhaps aristocratic, or whether it can be environmentally induced. Perhaps those who have quality can flourish only if the environment permits. Montherlant ends his essay on the future of human quality with an appeal for censorship, for a government that would act as a sort of "inquisition," permitting only works of value to circulate.[38]

In his literary works, Montherlant seems to believe that "quality" is something generally lost at adolescence, when a boy passes from thirteen to fourteen years of age. (He is generally unconcerned with quality in women, although the figure of the virile Infanta is exemplary.) Ferrante claims to have loved Pedro as a child but to have perceived his fundamental mediocrity from the age of fourteen on. Gilles is fourteen years old. At some point (his fourteenth birthday?), as his father tells him, Gilles passed over from the "marvelous domain of those whom I trust completely into the banal domain of those whom I distrust somewhat" (254). Gilles and his mother are also surrounded by the examples of popular culture so decried by Montherlant: Marie reads illustrated magazines, Gilles buys lottery tickets, loves "idiotic" films, sings "stupid" songs, gets good grades in school, and, in the crucial scene in which his father lectures him on the morality of the superior, lets himself be distracted by reading magazines (255). Georges finds numerous examples of his son's mediocrity throughout the play. Gilles has no interest in sports, no passions, no sense of rebellion, no ambitions, and the manners of a little Parisian; it is evident that he has been raised, and spoiled, by women. He would try to evade military service if he were called.

[37] Henry de Montherlant, "La Qualité," in *Le Solstice de juin*, 153–56.
[38] Henry de Montherlant, "Avenir de la qualité humaine chez le Français moyen," in *Le Solstice de juin*, 249–72.

Money seems more important to him than principles. When Georges tells him that he takes the cases only of people who seem to him to be in the right, Gilles asks him if he didn't become a lawyer to make money (234).

In all this, Gilles is no doubt, for Montherlant, a representative of the banal, mediocre, and decadent youth of the French nation. Yet Montherlant's dramatic sense keeps the play from being a mere diatribe of a father with aspirations for "quality" against a boy without it. Gilles and Marie are in a sense right and often sympathetic, whereas Georges is for the most part insufferable. Marie clearly loves her son and correctly reproaches Georges for his years of neglect; Gillou is tender, sweet, and engaging and wishes that his parents would get back together. Marie also wants to be happy: it turns out that the reason she wants to take Gilles to Le Havre, where her parents live and where the danger of being bombed is great, is that she has a lover there. For Georges, this is proof of her inferiority to him, a comparison he states succinctly: "I sacrificed him to the idea that I have of man. She sacrificed him to the need she has of a man. . . . Son of woman? No, nobody's son, like the others" (260–61).

Montherlant also intends to portray a tragic conflict within Georges himself. "Ah, Marie," he sighs in the third act. "I am suffering on account of him. I love him, and I would like to esteem him as much as I love him, and I can't" (252). Yet it is difficult to see how this 1940 version of the Corneilian struggle between love and duty could have been convincingly rendered on stage since Georges' (and the author's) preoccupation with "quality" so clearly outweighs any sentimental attachments he professes to have. The real tragedy, for Montherlant at least, seems to lie in the fact that a whole generation of French youth, "abandoned" by their fathers, is being raised to be of "bad quality." "Nobody's sons" lack not only the rigor, discipline, and high aspirations of paternal guidance but even, perhaps, true maternal devotion. The *tragédie en veston* contains a plea for a "new order" in France.

For contemporary reviewers, *Fils de personne* exemplified the possibility of both Corneilian and Nietzschean modern tragedy. The collaborationist press again found Montherlant worthy of their expectations. Jean Turlais praises him for daring to write, against modern trends, a play in the seventeenth-century "moralist" tradition. Montherlant's affinity with Corneille is apparent here in Georges's will to *hauteur* and his choice of the "inhuman" in the manner of Rodrigue and Polyeucte. Cruelty, as Montherlant shows, is essential to the conception of human nobility. The "dramatic violence" of the father's sacrifice of his son speaks to contemporary France in its plea for grandeur in the face of mediocrity and severity against indulgence.[39] Alain Laubreaux praised the play's "dramatic rigor"

---

[39] "Morale et tragédie" was published—as far as I know for the first time—posthumously on the occasion of the revival of *Fils de personne* in *La Table ronde*, December 1948, 2080–84.

and its severe judgment of contemporary mediocrity.[40] Armory, writing in *Les Nouveaux temps*, December 28, 1943, calls Montherlant "the most Nietzschean of the Latin spirits" in creating an expiatory victim for the sake of social grandeur. Although Georges is antipathetic as a person, he is heroic in his aspirations for "a magnificent remaking of the country." Lenormand, in *Panorama*, January 6, 1944, praises the play's "Nietzschean tragic form" along with Georges's samurai morality and his "proud disdain of mediocrity." The moral lesson seems to be that France must create "superadolescents" in order to elevate itself from decadence. Michel Mohrt finds that Georges shows courage in choosing, against the *morale de midinette* incarnated by Marie Sandoval, a vision "stronger than blood" for the France of tomorrow.[41] Several critics see in *Fils de personne* a conflict of virility against femininity like that in *La Reine morte*. Thierry Maulnier judges that Georges, like Ferrante, struggles against the corrupting "demon of feminine mediocrity" within himself. For Louis Chéronnet, in *Beaux-Arts*, *Fils* is a new version of "how to kill women" in that through Gillou, Georges seeks to "kill" Marie. Antoine Fléchier compares Georges's sacrifice of Gillou to the tragic sacrifice of the being one loves in *Bérénice*. "Titus immolates Bérénice to the idea that Rome has of Titus, Georges Carrion immolates his son to the idea that he has of his son."[42]

The last comparison could be more aptly made with Brasillach's *Bérénice* than with Racine's. Although Brasillach's play is much more evidently literary and metatragical than Montherlant's, both self-consciously strive to rewrite for modernity the classical conflict between love and duty. Love, although it retains its emotional pull in theatrical as well as in human terms, has become something to be surpassed, a lower, "feminine" aspiration, like happiness, that must be overcome by a "virile" will to preserve national integrity in a tragedy worthy of the new order. Montherlant's aesthetic of modern tragedy can indeed in this sense be encapsulated in his title "how to kill women."

Jean Anouilh and the Collaborationist Press

If fascist and collaborationist writers waxed most ecstatic over Montherlant's achievements in the genre of modern tragedy during the Occupation years, they also placed high hopes on Jean Anouilh. Anouilh's thirteen journalistic contributions to the collaborationist press reveal even less political in-

---

[40] Alain Laubreaux, "Emile 43 ou de l'induction," *Je suis partout*, December 24, 1943.
[41] Michel Mohrt, "L'Education des garçons selon Montherlant," *Idées*, July 1944.
[42] The last three studies are cited by Montherlant himself in his "Notes" to *Fils de personne* in *Théâtre*, 275, 269, 270.

terest than do those of Montherlant, but they certainly indicate that he did not object to being associated with those who regarded him as congenial. One of the issues frequently discussed in the press was the need for a state-supported theater, a demand usually accompanied by an attack on control of the theater by capitalist money or Jewish interests. Articles in *La Gerbe* in 1940 and 1941 call for a "corporative" state theater.[43] Three of Anouilh's articles deal with the topic of the adverse effect of money on theater.[44] In "Propos déplaisants" (*La Gerbe*, November 14, 1940, 9) Anouilh warns of the danger of a theater controlled by money and calls for a talented public, as opposed to a merely paying public. "Soliloque au fond de la salle obscure" (*La Gerbe*, January 23, 1941, 11) consists of an imaginary, satirical confrontation with a fat bourgeois couple who demand to see a realistic play about their lives with no "playing" in it. The theater manager informs "Anouilh" that he will have to "grow up" and conform to these demands because the theater needs money. In "Propos confus" (*La Gerbe*, December 11, 1941) Anouilh again laments the control of money over the theater by arguing that *générales* (dress rehearsals) are superior to ordinary shows because the nonpaying public understands the theater better.

André Barsacq, Anouilh's director, also pronounced himself in favor of "corporative" state support for theater by the National Revolution. *Les Nouveaux temps*, a pro-Nazi journal, reports that Barsacq held a joint press conference with Lieutenant Baumann (responsible for theater at the Propagandastaffel) on January 9, 1941. The question of Jews in the theater was also raised in the course of the conference. Baumann "alluded to the numerous eliminations of corrupt persons in the theater . . . which will finally permit French theater to find its way again."[45] Like Dullin and every other theater director in occupied Paris, Barsacq of course had to agree to eliminate all Jewish personnel if he wanted to keep his theater open. Other changes had to be made as well. Pirandello's plays were on the whole absent from the Parisian stage during the Occupation because the translator of most of them, Benjamin Cremieux, was a Jew.[46] Barsacq, however, staged *Vêtir ceux*

---

[43] See, for example, Georges de Wissant, "Le Théâtre et l'état," *La Gerbe*, December 5, 1940 and Alphonse Sèche, "Sur une corporation du théâtre," *La Gerbe*, March 20, 1941. Charles Dullin also published a series of articles lamenting the influence of "big money" in the theater and calling for a "corporation" (*La Gerbe*, July 25, August 15, 22, 1940, and *Comoedia*, June 21, 1941).

[44] The references for these articles, along with those for virtually all of the reviews and criticism written on *Antigone* in French (and many in English and German) are to be found in Manfred Flügge's exhaustive and heavily documented thesis, *Verweigerung oder Neue Ordnung: Jean Anouilhs 'Antigone' im politischen und ideologischen Kontext der Besatzungszeit, 1940–1944*, 2 vols. (Rheinfelden: Schauble Verlag, 1982). Flugge's research efforts have greatly facilitated my work.

[45] Quoted in Marsh, "Le Théâtre à Paris," 206.

[46] According to Marsh, ibid., 212.

qui sont nus, originally translated by Cremieux, with the credit "Adaptation d'André Barsacq" in the fall of 1941.[47] Barsacq's company, "La Compagnie de quatre saisons," also mounted plays in the Pétainist "camps de jeunesse."

The theme of corruption by money, including attacks on capitalists, Americans, and Jews, a constant in Vichy propaganda generally, was also considered acceptable subject matter for "revolutionary" drama. In two articles published in *Aujourd'hui*, like *La Gerbe* a German-sponsored paper, Anouilh develops his own variations on this theme, one of long-standing importance to him, along with another "revolutionary" theme, the exultation of youth as agents for change. In "The Wound of Money" (September 22, 1940), Anouilh argues that if the present generation is "wounded" by money it is ultimately the fault of the French Revolution. The ideology of 1789 replaced a hierarchy based on tradition with one based on money. The youth of the present must reconstruct a world in which money no longer controls social relations. The young people Anouilh imagines as filling this role have the characteristics of his young, intransigent characters such as Thérèse in *La Sauvage*. He even uses a stage metaphor to describe them. For the middle-aged and compromised it is difficult to confront "those who have the effrontery to appear on the stage of the world as pure and demanding as we would have liked to remain." "A film that you will never see" (October 5, 1940) describes a film Anouilh had planned before the war about two young lovers whose love is ruined when each discovers that the other is rich ("the Rockefeller and J. P. Morgan type"). Commenting on the social significance of the proposed film, Anouilh speculates that everyone in France, even "the poorest among us," seems to have lived through "that idyllic time compromised by money." The producer, Anouilh says, told him he was afraid of the story because when young writers turn to such subjects, the revolution is near. Anouilh concludes with what can only be construed as an apology for the National Revolution as the solution to the problems caused by money. "At that time, he could not imagine the form and the detour that the revolution would take. . . . One must push open doors for a long time so that revolutions can pass through them."

Anouilh's Theater in the 1930s and 1940s

The notion of money as the corrupting force in bourgeois society and of the revolt against bourgeois values by an uncompromising "pure" youth—a theme current in fascist literature of the 1930s—is one that in-

---

[47] Program in "Fonds Rondel," Bibliothèque de l'Arsenal.

formed Anouilh's drama long before he wrote about it for the press. Having grown up poor, he was indeed obsessed by the effects of money, or the lack of it, on all social classes. In *L'Hermine* (1931, performed 1932), *La Sauvage*, (1934, performed 1938), *Le Rendez-Vous de Senlis* (1937, performed 1941) *Léocadia* (1939, performed 1940), and *Eurydice* (1941, performed 1942), money serves as an important element of the signifying system and the dramatic conflict. The young protagonists of each of these plays seek an ideal happiness only to be blocked and generally defeated by a powerful, money-controlled social order. Only in *Léocadia*, with its fairy-tale decor and structure of fantasy, does the love between the prince and the Cinderella figure Amanda end the play on a note of triumph. In that play (serialized in *Je suis partout* in 1940) we are dealing, however, not with the bourgeoisie, for whom money serves as an instrument of social control, but with an isolated, archaic aristocracy that has used its money to create its own protective, timeless, imaginary world, much as in Pirandello's *Henry IV*. The substitution of the truthful, independent, and poor Amanda for the glittering, successful, foreign diva Léocadia in the prince's world signifies not only a replacement of inauthenticity by authenticity but also a collusion between the social strata Anouilh admired—the aristocracy and the "lower" classes—leading to the exclusion of the bourgeoisie, along with the foreigners. Because of the fairy-tale atmosphere and because the world created by the money of an eccentric duchess is hermetic and theatrical, Amanda's incorporation into it is not fraught with the dangers present in the other plays.

In *L'Hermine*, Frantz's determination to obtain money in order to obtain happiness, along with what he calls his "great thirst for purity,"[48] results in his murdering the rich aunt of Monime, the young woman he loves, and the loss of Monime's love, recuperated when he confesses and is arrested. The bourgeois order, maintained materially if defied spiritually, is defended by an American banking couple. Thérèse, *la sauvage*, also seeks happiness through leaving the sordid, poverty-ridden world of itinerant musicians in which she has grown up for the comfortable, money-protected one of her lover, the wealthy and "happy" Florent. Unlike the aristocratic fantasy world of *Léocadia*, however, the world of Florent's upper-middle-class family is gradually understood (from Thérèse's point of view) as exploitative, having created its narrow sense of *bonheur* as a result of greed and at the expense of those who continue to struggle to make a living. Thérèse's "savage" revolt against the bourgeoisie— "All of you disgust me with your happiness" (194)—echoes the antihappiness rhetoric in Montherlant and Drieu, grounded in Mussolini's call to oppose "the easy life." In *Le Rendez-vous de Senlis*, the protagonist Georges, who lives at the expense of his rich

---

[48] *L'Hermine*, in Jean Anouilh, *Pièces noires* (Paris: Calmann-Levy, 1942), 78.

(offstage) wife, attempts to flee the money-controlled world by creating a theatrical one for the pleasure of the young girl he loves, Isabelle. Here too, the power of money overcomes the opposing dramatic force of love as Georges's parents, friend, and mistress, who also live from his wife's wealth and are afraid of losing their means of support, expose the sham "family" that Georges had attempted to create with actors in a rented house in Senlis. Yet in this case Isabelle accepts Georges in spite of his theatrics, and at the end of the play we are led to believe that Georges will have the courage to leave his wife for Isabelle. Thus the possibility of escaping from a milieu conditioned by money and characterized by corruption and hypocrisy is envisioned. As in *Léocadia*, the escape route seems to be via the theatrical and the imaginary, with the help of a young woman outside the social order.

In *Eurydice*, Anouilh attempts a metatragic tragedy in rewriting a myth for modernity. The "darkest" of these plays, *Eurydice* offers only death as a possibility of escape for the young and "pure." In this modern tragedy, the milieu of both protagonists, Orphée and Eurydice, is that of Thérèse in *La Sauvage*—what one might call the artistic underclass—with the difference that no aristocratic or bourgeois world promises happiness as an alternative. The influence of money here manifests itself entirely among the have-nots or by its lack. The desire for money and the promises it seems to hold (food, sex, comfort) is what sustains Orphée's father in his indomitable pursuit of "life." This in turn leads to Orphée's perception that an acceptance of life would mean stepping into the role of his father. That recognition and the choice it entails culminate after the father's virtuoso tirade toward the end of the play, after Orphée has lost his Eurydice.

> Ah! money, money! But that's all of life, my dear boy. You're sad, but you're young. Imagine, you can become rich. Luxury, elegance, good food, women. Think about women, son, think about love! . . . But all of life isn't there. There is respectability, social life. You become strong, powerful, a captain of industry. You give up music . . . Administrative meetings, among sly foxes, where the fate of European economy is worked out. (But you fool them all).[49]

Orphée's father, the failed "artist," imagines a successful future for his son in terms of a bourgeois *drame* ending happily with sexual, monetary, and social satisfaction. Commenting to Orphée on his father's speech, Monsieur Henri, the figure of destiny, observes that "life," for the father and his ilk (and presumably for a middle-aged Orphée), resembles nothing so much as bad theater. "That clowning, that absurd melodrama, that's life.

---

[49] *Eurydice*, in Jean Anouilh, *Eurydice suivi de Roméo et Juliette* (Paris: Editions Folio, 1991), 158–59. Subsequent references will appear in the text.

That heaviness, those theatrical effects, that is indeed life" (167). At this point, M. Henri can make his offer of "an intact Eurydice, the true face of Eurydice which life would never have given you" (167) and a world that is "pure, luminous, limpid" (168). Anouilh's Eurydice in fact resembles Pirandello's Ersilia or his "unknown woman": she is, for herself, nothing, but according to the perception men create of her, pure and luminous, or pathetic and ordinary. Orphée's acceptance of M. Henri's creation of Eurydice and his offer—the choice of death over life, purity over compromise, tragedy over *drame*—was already made in the third act. When in conformity with the mythical figure whose name he bears he turned to look at Eurydice, he told her, "I love you too much to live!" (130). Already in the second act, although Orphée still believes in the possibility of ordinary happiness, M. Henri has singled him out as belonging to the "race" of human beings for whom the compromised life is impossible. In this speech, Henri is certainly the mouthpiece of his author.

"My dear boy, there are two races of beings. A numerous, fertile, happy race, a big lump of dough to be kneaded, those who eat their sausage, make their children, count their pennies . . . people for living, everyday people. . . . And then there are the others, the nobles, the heroes. Those whom one can very well imagine stretched out, pale, with a red hole in their heads, one moment triumphant with an honor guard or, in other circumstances, between two policemen: the upper crust" (97–98). The first type belongs theatrically to the *drame*, the second to tragedy. It is an opposition Anouilh will develop further in *Antigone*.

Anouilh's young heroines, as David Grossvogel has pointed out,[50] all show (like Drieu's Charlotte Corday) a tendency toward masculinity. Modeled perhaps on a combination of Frantz and Monime in *L'Hermine*, Thérèse, Isabelle, Amanda, and Eurydice are all "thin" and "hard," without softness and sensuality. In addition, Florent describes Thérèse as having "a kind of virility" (143) and calls her "my little man" (199). Orphée remarks to Eurydice that they are like two "little brothers" (62, 72) and calls her "my little soldier" (88). Their heroic "purity" seems somehow to derive from their transsexuality. We will return to this phenomenon with Antigone, who is no exception.

The affinity between the aesthetics and thematics of these plays and the expectations of aesthetic fascists and collaborationist critics did not go unperceived. Jean Turlais, in his "Introduction à la littérature fasciste," enumerates a tragic sense of life, a morality based on "vivere pericolosamente," a portrayal of "the disgusting baseness of capitalist and bourgeois

---

[50] David Grossvogel, *The Self-Conscious Stage in Modern French Drama* (New York: Columbia University Press, 1958), 158–59.

society," and a vindication of the oppressed and the outsiders in that society as characteristics of fascist literature. He adds: "It is significant that young fascists are beginning to reclaim outcasts and their threatening solitude. In our heart, we want to link them to the early plays of Anouilh."[51] In a review of the *Pièces noires* and *Pièces roses*, the same author praises *L'Hermine* for its opposition of the purity of youth to the greedy stupidity of the rich, claiming that the play portrays "all the horror of a society in which nothing pure can exist without killing."[52] *Léocadia*, which was serialized in *Je suis partout*, was judged by the collaborationist press to be "exquisite";[53] Armory in *Les Nouveaux temps* (December 9, 40) praised it for its antirealism and poetry. Reviewing *Le Rendez-vous de Senlis* in *Le Petit Parisien*, Alain Laubreaux remarks that although the play is not as "perfect" as *Léocadia*, it is further proof that Anouilh is the "first" dramatic author of the present. André Castelot in *La Gerbe* (February 6, 1941), calls *Le Rendez-vous* a "great play" based on the dreams and poetry of youth. Robert Purnal, in the *Nouvelle revue française* (April 1, 1941), finds that this play exposes "the other side of bourgeois morality" while "R de B" in *L'Illustration* (February 19, 1941) remarks that, as in his previous plays, Anouilh displays a ferocious and "revolutionary" irony toward hypocritical bourgeois morality.

Although the Vichy press on the whole judged *Eurydice* to be "depressing" and even "harmful" for French morale during the Occupation, Parisian critics such as Laubreaux and Brasillach considered it to be a great modern tragedy.[54] Brasillach, in a 1943 essay titled "Jean Anouilh or the Myth of Baptism," finds "baptism," in the sense of a desire to abandon a sullied past for a figurative rebirth into a new and pure life, the unifying motive in Anouilh's plays through *Eurydice*. He admires the attack against the bourgeoisie in all of his theater, particularly that of Thérèse in *La Sauvage*. "Her words, pronounced with a biting humor that seems to make Jean Anouilh the Henry Monnier of the P.S.F., legitimate all revolts and all assassinations" (412). Brasillach does not, however, develop this political parallel between revolt in Anouilh's characters and the legitimacy of violence. While he criticizes Anouilh for sometimes being too romantic (too many "madonnas of the gutter") and using a language often too common and vulgar (as opposed to the literary theatrical language to which Brasillach aspired), he praises the use of myth in the modern world of *Eurydice* for allowing the audience to see the aspirations of the pure in heart in the midst

---

[51] *Les Cahiers français* 5 (May 1943), 32.
[52] Ibid., 68.
[53] *Paris-Soir*, November 30, 1940; *Aujourd'hui*, December 3, 1940.
[54] Flügge, *Verweigerung oder Neue Ordnung*, 1: 216–17.

of the corruption caused by bourgeois society. In a footnote he mentions the admirable scenes portraying the heroine's desire for purity in Anouilh's "chef d'oeuvre," *Antigone*, upon which he will comment more at length.[55]

La Bataille d'Antigone

While *Le Rendez-vous de Senlis*, *Léocadia*, and *Eurydice*, all produced under the Occupation, were applauded by a much wider audience than fascist sympathizers, they nevertheless reinforced a certain view of Anouilh. Yet in a period when public and critics were hyperattentive to political overtones or allusions to contemporary events,[56] no one, to my knowledge, saw such in any of these plays. The same cannot be said of *Antigone*, which despite the author's and producer's disclaimers seems to have been "read" at least to some extent politically by almost everyone who saw it performed during the last months of the Occupation or the first after the Liberation, as well as by numerous critics since then. Claims that the play is resistant, collaborationist, or apolitical have been put forward with equal fervor. A journalist in Geneva compared the *bataille d'Antigone* to the *bataille d'Hernani*.[57] Debate has tended to center on the question of who "wins" in the struggle between the two antagonists. Even later critics take opposing positions along these lines. George Steiner in his *Antigones* (1986) affirms that there can be "no real doubt" that Anouilh's Créon wins; Leo Weinstein in 1989 states that Antigone's call to resistance is a "message" that "seems unmistakably clear."[58] It is perhaps just this either/or approach with the often concomitant identification of Créon with the Pétain government and Antigone with the Resistance that has confused the issue. If it is possible to attempt a political reading of *Antigone* today, it must be done by first rehistoricizing the text in the context of both Anouilh's cultural environment and contemporary reception.

Sophocles' heroine was hardly a newcomer to the twentieth-century French stage when Anouilh's play (written in 1942 but first performed on February 4, 1944) appeared at the Théâtre de l'Atelier. Jean Cocteau did a "free adaptation" (in a colloquial idiom although without anachronisms)

---

[55] Robert Brasillach, *Oeuvres complètes*, ed. Maurice Bardèche (Paris: Au club de l'honnête homme, 1963) (hereafter *OC*), 8: 409–14, quote on 412.

[56] According to Patrick Marsh (*Le Théâtre français sous l'occupation allemande*, 273–88), prompt books censured by the Germans show that they tended to cut out anything that could be construed as a reference to the contemporary situation. The public, however, notably applauded lines such as "En prison se trouve la fleur du royaume" ("The flower of the kingdom is in prison") from *La Reine morte*, and "Liberty to captive souls," from *Le Soulier de satin*.

[57] Flügge, *Verweigerung oder Neue Ordnung* 1: 324.

[58] George Steiner, *Antigones* (Oxford: Clarendon Press, 1986), 193. Leo Weinstein, *The Subversive Tradition in French Literature* (Boston: Twayne, 1989) 2, 126.

of the Sophoclean tragedy in 1922 which Arthur Honegger used for his 1927 opera.[59] The Occupation years, in the words of André Fraigneau, saw "une crise d'antigonnite."[60] The Sophoclean tragedy (in their own French translation) was put on by the Groupe de théâtre antique from the Sorbonne at the Odéon National Theater in 1942; a version by Léon Chancerel, written for the Scouts de France in 1934, was staged by Vichy for the "Chantiers de la jeunesse" in 1941; the Cocteau-Honegger opera was revived in 1941, 1943, and 1944; also in May 1944 Thierry Maulnier's adaptation of Robert Garnier's *Antigone* of 1580 was mounted at the Théâtre Charles de Rochefort and in August the troupe from the Odeon National Théâtre staged Sophocles at the Sorbonne.[61] Clearly, the German and Vichy censorship did nothing to discourage and indeed seemed to have encouraged the presence of Antigone, and clearly too the theme was one that spoke to the audience of the day.

What appealed to the French so much about Antigone? Simone Fraisse notes the tendency in the French right, beginning with *Action française*, to compare Antigone with Joan of Arc in "purity" and their vocation for sacrifice.[62] For Charles Maurras, Antigone like Joan was a guardian of the legitimate order (and the real anarchist was Créon!).[63] Brasillach, who did a translation of Sophocles' *Antigone* and a poem on Antigone along with his two texts on Joan of Arc, was fascinated by the myth of the "sacrificed virgin."[64] In terms that echo his definition of fascism, he writes that he admires the two heroines for their "insolence," their refusal to compromise, their fidelity to a higher truth beyond civil laws, and their quest for *grandeur*. Antigone is a pagan prefiguration of Jeanne in that each invokes "eternal laws stronger than temporal and written laws."[65] Jean Turlais also

---

[59] Arthur Honegger and Jean Cocteau, *Antigone: Tragédie musicale* (Paris: Editions Salabert, 1928).

[60] *Comoedia*, March 13, 1944, quoted in Flügge, *Verweigerung oder Neue Ordnung* 1:255.

[61] This information, with more detail, can be found in Flugge, *Verweigerung oder Neue Ordnung*, 255–59, in a section titled "Der Antigone-Stoff in der Okkupationszeit." See also Steiner, *Antigones*.

[62] Simone Fraisse, "Antigone," in *Dictionnaire des mythes littéraires*, ed. J. P. Bertrand (Paris: Editions du Rocher, 1988), 90–92.

[63] Maurras wrote an essay for the Lyon-edited *Action française* (May 25, 1944) titled "Et si l'anarchiste était Créon?" In Maurras's reading of Sophocles' tragedy, it is Antigone, daughter of the royal family, who incarnates "the very concordant laws of man, the gods and the city. And who violates and defies all of them? Creon. He is the anarchist. No one but him." See also Maurras's poem "Antigone vièrge mère de l'ordre" (1946) in *Oeuvres capitales* (Paris: Flammarion, 1954), 4: 358–60. In the same vein, Maurras wrote that Joan of Arc's revolt against the laws of the English was *legitimist*. "The characteristic of her political work was to *recognize, affirm, announce, and consecrate* the legitimate king" ("Le Bienfait politique de Jeanne d'Arc," *Oeuvres capitales*, 2: 309).

[64] Anne Brassié, *Robert Brasillach ou encore un instant de bonheur* (Paris: Editions Robert Laffort, 1987), 290.

[65] "La Jeune fille Médée," *OC*, 11: 41. In "Pour un fascisme français," *OC*, 12: 502, Brasillach defines fascism as "an anticonformist, antibourgeois spirit in which disrespect plays a part."

admired the "insolence" and the "superior truth" of the two "fraternal heroines."[66] Because she could be identified with anti-English French nationalism, Joan of Arc was one of the figures that the Propaganda-Abteilung wished to promote in occupied France.[67] Conflated with Joan, and sometimes with Charlotte Corday, Antigone fits into Vichy (and fascist) propaganda themes such as the refusal of bourgeois modernity, the nostalgia for a preindustrial society along with the notion that France "fell" with the revolution, the defense of an elitist social hierarchy and/or the natural wisdom of the "people" against the power of money and the rule of abstract law, the cult of youth (living dangerously and dying young), the rejection of mediocrity, and the espousal of sacrifice for grandeur. As with Anouilh's young women protagonists, there is a curious tendency to masculinize these "fraternal heroines." Maurras, who no doubt influenced Brasillach's opinion, called Joan of Arc "a great states*man*."[68]

If the National Revolution made every effort to recuperate them, veneration of Antigone and Joan of Arc was not limited to the right. The Resistance, in something like a war of symbols, had its own agenda for the maid of Orleans, in particular. One has only to imagine the English of the fifteenth century as Germans of the twentieth to make Joan of Arc into a Resistance heroine.[69] Claude Vermorel's *Jeanne avec nous* (performed January to March 1942) was applauded by Resistance supporters and viewed in both the clandestine and post-Liberation press as a Resistance play while the Vichy and fascist press praised the play and "their" heroine (see note 4). As for Antigone, Simone Fraisse remarks how the

---

[66] Jean Turlais, 'Le Théâtre, les sources de la grandeur," *Les Cahiers français* 5 (May 1943): 65.

[67] Flügge (*Verweigerung oder Neue Ordnung*, 1: 112) cites a June 6, 1940, paper by the "French specialist" Professor Grimm urging that both Joan of Arc and Napoleon should be promoted as anti-English propaganda motifs. Marsh ("Le Théâtre à Paris," 287–94) describes how the Joan of Arc theme was exploited by the collaborationist press and promoted by Vichy. Both Alphonse de Chateabriant and Pétain gave speeches emphasizing that their heroine demonstrated the necessity of binding a group through a leader. In May 1942, a group of musicians and poets, including Claude Vermorel, did a broadcast on Jeanne at Radio France. According to Jean Plumyène and Raymond Lasierra, the Jeanne d'Arc symbol was used to "bind" the right and left aspects of fascism, and Jeanne was conflated with Doriot (*Les Fascismes français: 1923–1963* [Paris: Seuil, 1963], 127). See also Gerd Krumeich, "The Cult of Joan of Arc under the Vichy Régime," in *Collaboration in France*, ed. Patrick Marsh and Gerhard Hirschfeld (Oxford: Berg, 1989), 92–102, and Gabriel Jacobs, "The Role of Joan of Arc on the Stage of Occupied Paris," in *Vichy France and the Resistance: Culture and Ideology*, ed. Roderick Kedward and Roger Austin (Totowa, N.J.: Barnes and Noble, 1985), 106–22.

[68] "It is as if Joan of Arc had been a general and a great statesman [un grand homme d'état]" (Charles Maurras, "Jeanne d'Arc et la monarchie," in *Dictionnaire politique et critique* [Paris: Cahiers Charles Maurras, 1975], 55, originally published in *Action française*). See also Peter D. Tame, *Le Mystique du fascisme dans l'oeuvre de Robert Brasillach* (Paris: Nouvelles éditions latines, 1986), 182.

[69] She was in fact so portrayed by Resistance writers. See, for example, Jacques Dastreé in *Résistance*, January 13, 1943, and R. P. Brückberger's "La Marseillaise de Clairvaux," in *La Patrie se fait tous les jours*, ed. Jean Paulhan and Dominique Aury (Paris: Editions de minuit, 1947), 387–92.

mythical "no" sayer denoted resistance to those so inclined under the Occupation to the extent that, against the intentions of the authors and directors, the public read a Resistance message into the Antigones of Léon Chancerel (staged at the Vichy chantiers de la jeunesse) and Anouilh.[70] Béatrix Dussane, Henri Amouroux, and Hervé Le Boterf also corroborate from firsthand observation the tendency of Resistance sympathizers in the audience to "adopt" Antigone while collaborationists applauded along with them.[71]

Before looking into the press reception of *Antigone* in more detail, let us examine the text. Anouilh's play is both "darker," as he says, and lighter than Sophocles' tragedy. Lighter because of its self-conscious theatricality and its playing with modernity (the anachronisms, the colloquial language); darker because the characters by assuming their roles are aware from the beginning of their inevitable doom. Like Brasillach's Bérénice and Titus, Anouilh's antagonists are "victims of literature." Antigone must die and Créon must put her to death because their names are Créon and Antigone; their only freedom lies in playing their roles well; the tragedy, in a sense, is already over. Thus Anouilh's play opens after Antigone has already attempted to bury her brother rather than, like Sophocles', before the deed. The characters in *Antigone* resemble those of Anouilh's mentor Pirandello in *Henry IV*, who instead of enacting a historical drama, play at a history that has already occurred. The chorus, functioning critically and metatragically at a crucial moment, reinforces this particularly fatalistic view of tragedy while arguing, in simple, colloquial terms, for tragedy's superiority over *drame*.

[70] Fraisse, "Antigone," 92, and *Le Mythe d'Antigone* (Paris: Colin, 1974), 121. In Fraisse's view, Anouilh's rehabilitation of Creon meant that he intended to write a pro-Vichy play.

[71] In a section titled "*Antigone: Une apologie de la Resistance ou un plaidoyer pour la collaboration?*" Hervé Le Boterf, while pointing out that Anouilh would have had none of this in mind when he wrote the play in 1942, observes that at the performances, "The resisters claim Antigone, symbol of revolt against a government deprived of dignity . . . just as certain partisans of collaboration assimilate the king of Thebes to Pierre Laval, forced to believe in German victory rather than see his country swallowed up under the tide of Bolshevism" (*La Vie parisienne sous l'occupation* [Paris: Eds. France-Empire, 1974], 1: 251). Henri Amouroux also finds that the spectators identified Creon with the "realist" Laval and Antigone, prisoner of guards dressed in leather, with Resistance victims (*La Vie des Français sous l'occupation* [Paris: Livre de Poche, 1971], 2: 250). Béatrix Dussane, in her *Notes du théâtre, 1940–1950* (Paris: Lardanchet, 1951), recalls that nothing, during the Occupation, could keep people from the theater and in particular from *Antigone*. "Antigone's refusal became the symbol and the sublimation of the personal refusals of all and every one. Her stubbornness, her 'I am not here to understand, I am here to say no,' may seem inexplicable to audiences in happier times, but they struck to the heart people watched by the Gestapo, and familiar with every misery. . . . This is by no means imagination: I felt like that myself when I saw the play, and others have confessed to the same experience" (trans. and quoted by Harold Hobson in *The French Theatre of Today: An English View* [London: Harrap, 1953], 45).

It's clean, tragedy. It's restful, it's sure. . . . In drama, with its villains . . . its persecuted innocence . . . those gleams of hope, it becomes horrible to die, like an accident . . . the nice young man could have perhaps arrived on time with the police. . . . In tragedy . . . everyone is innocent. . . . It's a question of distributing the roles. And then tragedy is restful because there's no more hope, vile hope; one is at last caught like a rat . . . there's nothing to do but cry out what one had to say. . . . And for nothing: to say it to oneself, to learn what it is. In drama, one struggles because one hopes to get out. It's base, it's utilitarian. In tragedy, it's gratuitous. It's for kings. And there's nothing more left to try, at last![72]

The tragedy/drama opposition here recalls the two "races" of humans described by Monsieur Henri in *Eurydice* and makes it clear that Antigone belongs to the "race" of the royal, heroic, and tragic. While partially recapitulating Nietzsche-inspired right-wing anti–Third Republic rhetoric, Anouilh also gives a reductive view of tragedy. He carries Brasillach's literary and metatragical approach to modern tragedy a step further. It seems that since all tragedies have already been written, the modern tragedian can only replay them, in a low key. The weight of the tragic tradition no longer permits a sacrificial victim/hero for the community but only an affirmation of the individual. Anagnorisis leads not to reversal and change but to nostalgia and to Antigone's ultimate statement of purpose, which is *pour moi.*

Antigone is punctuated by signs designating childhood and death, the womb and the tomb, and the twenty-year-old title character is defined dramatically by two intersecting desires: a refusal to abandon the innocence, purity, and totality of childhood, and a determination to "say no and die" to the adult, corrupt world. After the prologue, on a stage lit by a "gray and livid" dawn, perhaps suggesting prebirth or death, Antigone and her nurse engage in a dialogue resembling that between an overprotective mother and a recalcitrant but still dependent child. Antigone has just emerged, as it were, from the world of the dead; we later learn that she had gone to accomplish her funeral rite. Following the scene between Antigone and Ismene, we see an Antigone regressing even further, seeking the maternal protection of "nursey stronger than nightmare . . . nursey stronger than death" (32). In the scene with Hemon, her nostalgia for childhood takes the form of imagining (in the past conditional, since it can never be) her own child, her own protective maternity. "I would have squeezed him so strongly that he never would have been afraid. . . . He would have had a little, badly groomed mommy—but surer than all the real mothers in the world with their real breasts"(40). But this ostensible dream of maternity is eclipsed

---

[72] Jean Anouilh, *Antigone* (Paris: La Table ronde, 1982), 58. Subsequent references are given in the text.

in the desire to be a child: what Antigone is imagining here is herself as a child (a "little mother") playing at being a "real mother." Similarly, her act of loyalty to her brother is an act that mimics child's play. She tells Créon that she dug the dirt to cover Polynices' body with his little shovel that they used for making sand castles. In the tomb, Antigone finds the only possible fulfillment of her desire for the secure totality of childhood. The messenger, describing her death, tells us that she hanged herself with the strings of her belt, "which look like a child's collar" (118).

Créon, it is well known, strips Antigone of every conceivable rational motivation for her act and her decision to die, but by mentioning the simple word *bonheur* provides her with insight into the overwhelmingly *irrational* motivation that has been hers all along. The climactic moment of the drama comes when Antigone screams out the words defining the nature of her desire for which Créon has no answer and which confirm the identity of the totalizing worlds of childhood and death. "I want everything, right now—and that it be whole—or I refuse! I want to be sure that everything today should be as beautiful as when I was little—or die" (95). *Bonheur* clearly has two different significations for Créon and Antigone. For the former, it means maturity, acceptance, simple pleasure ("a book one likes, . . . a child who plays at your feet, a tool to hold well in your hand" [92]); for the latter it resembles, as for *la sauvage*, *la vita comoda*. Antigone in fact "quotes" her predecessor: "All of you disgust me with your happiness" (94). The pleasure that Antigone seeks is far more intense than that of calm and compromised adult *bonheur*; it resembles rather a mother-bound, totalizing *jouissance*.[73]

In the process of formulating her utopian desire, or, as the chorus says, of "becoming herself," the orphan Antigone seeks not only maternal protection but also paternal authority. "Like your father," Créon remarks after the tirade above. Antigone echoes, "like my father, yes!" and begins to speak in the first person plural. "We are among those who pose questions up to the end. . . . We are among those who . . . jump on . . . your vile hope." Créon also calls her "little Oedipus" with "the pride of Oedipus" and remarks that she considers herself invulnerable because she is "of royal race." Antigone now reaches back beyond her corrupt, modern, "hoodlum" brothers (as Créon describes them) to identify herself with the true, the legitimate king. An identification with the father's authority has replaced, or rather superimposed itself on, the desire for the protective body of the

---

[73] Developing Julia Kristeva's cryptic statement, "Le fascisme est le retour du refoulé dans le monologisme religieux ou politique" ("Fascism is the return of the repressed in religious or political monologism") (*Polylogue* [Paris: Editions du Seuil, 1977], 17), Alice Kaplan stresses the neglected role of mother-bound or "oceanic" pleasure in fascist texts (*Reproductions of Banality: Fascism, Literature, and French Intellectual Life* [Minneapolis: University of Minnesota Press, 1986], 10–25).

mother. Speaking in the royal we, Antigone incorporates herself into the mythical, royal, utopian past while echoing the chorus's commentary contrasting royal tragedy and vile hope. Antigone seems to relegate Créon's attempts to save her to the base domain of *drame*. Although he is also of the house of Thebes, Uncle Créon is clearly to be considered of another stripe.

Antigone fits better into the imaginary role of "little Oedipus" than into that of "little mother." (It is perhaps significant that Jocasta is mentioned only once, by the nurse. If Antigone seeks maternal protection, she certainly never identifies with her mother.) Her gender, like that of Anouilh's other young women protagonists, is questionable throughout the play. The prologue, introducing the characters, emphasizes the difference between the pretty, feminine Ismene and the thin, plain Antigone. When she went to visit Hemon, hoping that he would love her "like a woman," she dressed herself in Ismene's clothes, makeup, and perfume, as if, to appear to be a woman, she must disguise herself as Ismene. For her, unfitness for the conventional feminine role means unease with her gender: "Haven't I cried enough because I'm a girl!" (29) she confides to Ismene. During their agon, Créon tells her: "I have often imagined it, this dialogue with a pale little young man" (84) and finally sees in her himself at twenty, "a little skinny pale Créon like you" (91). Créon's solution to the Antigone problem is to reinstate her definitively in the feminine role, to see her happily married to his son. It is the masculinized virgin, like Joan of Arc and Charlotte Corday a rare combination of *pureté* and *dureté*, who poses a threat to the very foundations of the social fabric.[74]

One way of describing the conflict between this mid-twentieth-century Antigone and her antagonist is in terms of the opposition between *mystique* and *politique*, as rendered poetically by Péguy and taken up by fascist literati. Fascist ideology, as we have seen, presents itself as "above" mere politics, in the domain of art and religion. Jean-Pierre Faye's description of fascism's reactionary desire for the night, the earth, the past, and death, paradoxically combined with its "revolutionary" drive,[75] applies even better to Antigone than to Ferrante. Even in a fascist state, however, someone must handle the day-to-day political work of governing. And if one accepts the role of a Pétain or a Laval in a collaborationist government, political considerations may well outweigh the mystical. It is this type of role to which Créon has said his "yes."

---

[74] Antigone's gender, or at least her gender role, has of course been problematic in various ways throughout the Antigone tradition (see Steiner, *Antigones*, 144–51). For Josette Feral, "Antigone is not a woman, or at least she does not conform to society's image of a woman. She is actually representative of the woman who refuses her condition as woman and pays for her transgression of the laws with her death" ("Antigone or the Irony of the Tribe," review essay on Luce Irigaray and Kristeva, *Diacritics*, 8 [fall 1978]: 2).

[75] Jean-Pierre Faye, *Langages totalitaires* (Paris: Herman, 1972), 80.

Jean Anouilh, *Antigone,* directed by André Barsacq, Théâtre de l'Atelier, Paris, February 1944. Jean Davy in the role of Créon and Monelle Valentin in the role of Antigone. Permission granted by the Roger-Viollet photographic agency.

In conformity with his role, Créon immediately suspects a political (and economic) plot when first informed of the attempted burial of Polynices. "The friends of Polynices with their gold blocked in Thebes, the plebeian leaders stinking of garlic, suddenly allied with princes, and the priests trying to fish out something" (50–51). Motley factions of the Resistance? Bourgeois bankers, communists, Charles de Gaulle, and leftist priests? Brasillach did not fail to point out the parallel.[76] Créon also questions Antigone over possible political motives. "Why are you making this gesture then? For the others, for those who believe in it? To organize them against me?" To which Antigone gives her much quoted response: "For nobody. For myself" (73). Once Créon understands that Antigone's motives are anything but political, that they belong to the order of irrationality or *mystique,* he is able to understand, even to identify with his niece, to see his former

[76] "Polynices was a traitor, around his name were grouped all the hopes of the dissidents: the bourgeois whose money was blocked, the disturbed and unhappy proletariat, the priests. . . . What a magnificent summary of so many contemporary tragedies!" He concludes that Antigone is not fighting for Polynices but for herself, against mediocrity, for "the disincarnate ideal against realism" ("Chronique de Paris," *OC* 12, 698).

idealistic self in her. "I would have done the same thing as you at twenty" (91). Créon now argues that Antigone should not allow herself to be mixed up in "mere" politics. He paints Eteocles and Polynices as *both* trying to assassinate their father (their heritage and tradition), motivated by money, willing to sell Thebes to the highest bidder (89). Fundamentally, then, Créon and Antigone agree on their rejection of modernity as well as their disgust with the power of money. As Créon explains the "backstage" or the "kitchen" of the political stage to Antigone he also reveals his utter cynicism about the governing process. Government for Créon has nothing to do with the rational rule of law and everything to do with the theatrical symbolism of a rotting body imposing obedience on the "brutes" that he governs. If Créon and Antigone (like Ferrante) have looked as one into the heart of chaos and emptiness, the differences between them emerge in their resultant actions. Créon's compromise is to attempt to make the world appear to be "a little less absurd" by imposing social order while seeking a private "happiness"; Antigone's intransigence results in a quest for purity and for a totalitarian utopia attainable only in death.

"I've got the bad role," Creon tells Antigone, "and you have the good one" (75). Even if this Creon "wins" the debate, as he surely does, anyone who plays Creon, as Anouilh later observed, can only play a losing game. Anouilh's Creon may be the best of all possible Creons, but the parameters of the myth prevent the complete rehabilitation of the man of state. Maturity condemning youth immortalizes youth. Yet Créon is sympathetic to the contemporary reader in that his avuncular concern for "little Antigone" differentiates him from Sophocles' austere tyrant (although unlike the latter he never changes his mind). He was sympathetic or antipathetic to the viewer of 1944, through his resemblance to a head of state attempting to govern in difficult times.

What I have attempted here is a reading of the play based on neither political allegory nor atemporal philosophy. Rather, I suggest that the text of *Antigone,* although *not* a *pièce à thèse,* is, even more strongly than Anouilh's earlier work, permeated by an ideological subtext informed by aspects of aesthetic fascism. With her cult of youth and refusal to grow old, her resounding "no" to everything resembling bourgeois mediocrity and "happiness," her ideal of "purity," her notions of the superiority of her "race," her courting of danger and death, her rejection of "politics" and law, and her guiding principle of irrationality, the character of Antigone reverberates with themes dear to French fascism since the 1930s. Créon's plea for understanding the "necessities" of politics, his role as "*chef,*" his view of government as theater, his acceptance of absurdity, and his clinging to "happiness" bring his outlook closer to that of Vichy, although his point of departure is the same as Antigone's. Except for its colloquial language, *Antigone,* with its embodiment of *pureté* and *grandeur* and its adherence to the superiority of tragedy over *drame*, also fits the reigning fascist aesthetics of theater. The impact of the tragedy stems from the conflicting yet fundamentally accordant desires of the antagonists. If Créon continues politics as usual at the end by going off to a council meeting, it is nonetheless the oceanic, totalitarian desire of Antigone to return to a pure and perfect childhood that prevails. Créon's last words of advice to his young page are, "It would be best never to grow up" (122).

Critical reception of *Antigone* in the collaborationist press was overwhelmingly enthusiastic, although not always in agreement.[77] After the *Pariser Zeitung*, the first and most influential critic to review the play was Alain Laubreaux, who wrote in both *Je suis partout* and *Le Petit Parisien*. For Laubreaux, the play transcends mere "politics" to represent "the revolt of purity against the lies of men." Although this revolt is admirable, it must be condemned in the social order for it would lead to chaos. Thus Laubreaux, while claiming to be nonpolitical in his judgment, clearly praises the fascist qualities of Antigone's *grandeur* and *pureté* while ultimately condoning Créon's strong-fisted order.[78]

Although a few collaborationist writers take the part of what they see as Créon's order against Antigone's anarchy, most seem to agree with Laubreaux that both antagonists are in a fundamental sense right. Roland Laudenbach, while making the inevitable comparison between Antigone and Joan of Arc, argues that Antigone represents virtue and heroism and Créon the legitimate authority of the state. Both, in contrast to the stupid mediocrity of the guards, are right. Anouilh's modern tragedy thus succeeds in illustrating Nietzsche's contention that tragedy stems from the Aryan perception of contradiction at the heart of the world.[79] A populist version of the same argument is made by Pierre Clémenti in an article titled "Antigone or the Great Fear of the Bourgeoisie." "Jean, you got them all," he writes in *Le Pays libre* (March 5, 1944). The bourgeois, with their idiotic love of "liberty," are both "crushed by Créon, the statesman" and "humiliated by Antigone, too sublime for their cowardice." The dialogue between Créon and Antigone will someday belong to the "true France."

In his review, Brasillach is surprised that so few commentators have noted "the deep political import of this play." Créon, the *chef*, effectively represents an intelligent defense of order, yet Antigone's "savage" protest "against

---

[77] For a thorough list of virtually all of the contemporary reviews of *Antigone* along with detailed summaries of many of them, see Flügge, *Verweigerung oder Neue Ordnung* 2: 47–72. My conclusions are based on these as well as on my own readings of reviews in the Bibliothèque de l'Arsenal and the Bibliothèque nationale, including some (notably in *Les Cahiers français*) not mentioned by Flügge.

[78] Alain Laubreaux, "Du théâtre!" *Je suis partout*, February 18, 1944, and review in *Le Petit parisien*, February 19, 1944.

[79] Roland Laudenbach, "Sainte Antigone," *Les Cahiers français* 11 (March 1944): 70–75.

all the duping enterprises" is equally convincing.[80] For some commentators, Antigone is an "anarchist" and Créon a "fascist," yet both are compelling. In the classical tradition, Antigone elevates herself above realism, both aesthetic and political. One critic writes, "In the brutal materialism of our epoch, Antigone is the swan song of idealism. . . . Her revolt is magnificent from the human point of view, but . . . harmful from a social point of view." [Antigone is] "drunk with sacrifice, determined and obstinate like Joan of Arc" (Jean Laurent, *Vedettes*, April 1944). The fanatic, antisemitic *Au Pilori*, in an article titled "Notre Antigone," also claims that the "no" of Antigone ("the worthy daughter of proud Oedipus") is dangerous but as necessary to the world as Créon's laws. The play is "ours" because it is in the true French (presumably not Jewish or foreign) classical, tragic tradition.

The single review in the clandestine Resistance press, Claude Roy's in *Les Lettres françaises* (no. 14, March 1944), comments ironically on *Au Pilori*'s title. "Notre Antigone et la leur" opposes Sophocles' Antigone, symbol of resistance to tyranny, to "theirs," that is, Anouilh's, who in "fundamental connivance with Créon" disdains humanity for "purity." Whereas Antigone's motivation for her "no" is reduced to "for myself," true resisters are saying "for us, for men." Roy goes so far as to accuse Anouilh of being a naive admirer of the Führer. Such nihilism leads to fascism. "By accepting despair and the feeling of the vanity of everything, one ends up by acclaiming the first strong arm that comes along." After the Liberation, Roy's line of argument was taken up by writers in *Action* (October 6, 1944), *Les Lettres françaises* (October 7, 1944), and *La Pensée* (December 1944). In the latter, Pol Gaillard reaffirms the idea that Créon and Antigone share a "common nihilistic religion" and comments further: "Antigone's 'resistance,' in which some people wanted to see the image of ours, has no human value." The social class that Antigone represents is the one that received Hitler with open arms.

Other post-liberation reviewers, in *Libération*, *Le Peuple*, and *Le Réveil des jeunes*, attempt to avoid political controversy by concentrating on the play's dramatic qualities. But the interpretation of Anouilh's Antigone as a representative of the Resistance and of Créon as the Vichy government, the reception espoused by Resistance-sympathetic spectators under the Occupation, also begins to take shape in the press at this time. The reviewer in *L'Homme libre* (September 29, 1944) sees in Antigone the sister of all those who dared to say "no" until death; the one in *Le Front National* finds an "antifascist accent" in Antigone's resistance to "the tyrant Créon" (September 30, 1944). The first American accounts of *Antigone* (like much American criticism since) tout it as a play of the Resistance.[81]

---

[80] *La Chronique de Paris* (March 1944), in *OC*, 12: 699.

[81] See Leo O. Forkey, "The Theatres of Paris during the Occupation," *French Review* 22 (February 1949): 299–305, and Edmund G. Berry, "Antigone and the French Resistance," *Classical Journal* 41 (October 1946): 17–18.

What of Anouilh's position in all this? He and Barsacq seem always to have maintained that the play and the production had no political or ideological content. In his memoirs, Anouilh recalls awaiting the revival of *Antigone* after the Liberation with some trepidation since the *Lettres françaises* had called it a "Waffen SS" play. He defends himself, as usual, by claiming political ignorance— "My conscience was clear . . . I knew almost nothing about the Resistance at that time"—and was gratified to see that the play was well received.[82] It is surely time to dispel once and for all the notion that Antigone represents the Resistance and Créon the collaborationist government, or rather that particular response should be seen as a reading of spectators conditioned by highly charged circumstances of reception. Yet this does not mean that Anouilh should be relegated to the domain of "pure" theater. His articles for the German-sponsored papers, as well as his plays produced under the Occupation and in particular *Antigone*, all place him in the context of French fascist aesthetic ideology of the period.

Anouilh and his critics who insist that his theater is not political are in a sense right. Certainly there are no overt political references in his plays of the 1930s and 1940s, and Anouilh apparently had even less interest in politics in the usual sense than did Montherlant. The only political circumstance that stirred him to act and speak out was the brutality of the postwar "purge" in France. Two of his postwar plays, *The Lark* (on Joan of Arc, 1953) and *Poor Bitos* (set during the French Revolution, 1956), allude to and in no uncertain terms condemn the *épuration*. But the event in the purge that "overwhelmed" Anouilh, as he said in a 1972 interview, was the execution of Brasillach. Having led the attempt to collect signatures for the petition to prevent the execution, Anouilh claims to have been disgusted by what he saw as the hypocrisy of those who refused. All of them, he says (without mentioning names), frequented Otto Abetz's parties, Maxim's, and "the other places where one went at the time." Because of his anger against de Gaulle after the execution, Anouilh would not allow his plays to be performed in state theaters.[83]

The trial of Brasillach must have seemed to Anouilh, as it did to many who witnessed it, the enacting of a drama with enormous social and emotional resonance, or the staging of a real-life modern tragedy.[84] Writing about it in essays published some twenty years later, "Février 1945" and "Salut fraternal à une ombre," Anouilh finds the best way of describing the

---

[82] Jean Anouilh, *La Vicomtesse d'Eristal n'a pas reçu son balai mécanique (Souvenirs d'un jeune homme)* (Paris: La Table ronde, 1987), 166.

[83] Interview with Anouilh by Nicolas de Rabaudy, *Paris Match*, October 21, 1972, 88.

[84] See the analysis of Brasillach's trial as a three-act drama by Alice Kaplan, *The Collaborator: The Trial and Execution of Robert Brasillach* (Chicago: University of Chicago Press, 2000), 150–88.

trial in parallels from his own theater. In "February 1945," speaking of Brasillach's accusers, he quotes (without citation and with modifications) the passage from *Eurydice* equating life with bad theater. "Those gross theatrical effects, that absurd melodrama, that sinister clowning, those half-ridiculous villains stinking of convention, with their uniforms, their Legion of Honor decorations, their glory, their big words—that was it, that was indeed life."[85] The condemned Brasillach, in contrast, in Anouilh's "fraternal salute," appears as youth eternalized, indeed as reentering childhood, something like Orphée accepting M. Henri's offer of purity over "life" or tragedy over *drame*. But the courtroom agon fuses finally with Anouilh's supreme achievement in modern tragedy.

"The little boy who looked death in the face remains standing and intact—eternally. . . . The man with the sentence, thinking that he was suppressing him, has preserved him. Whatever words he uses to intoxicate himself with, Creon always plays a losing game."[86] Anouilh does not specify whom he has cast in the role of Creon, but it is clear that "the little boy" is playing Antigone. His life-art comparison does have some validity. Brasillach's exit line, in response to his sentence— "It's an honor!"—helped to solidify the condemned man's image as a tragic hero.[87] Creon may have been the judge, Maurice Vidal, who sentenced him, or perhaps de Gaulle, who refused to pardon him. In any case, the opinion de Gaulle expressed on Brasillach's execution, as reported by Pierre de Boisdeffre, does sound curiously like what Anouilh's Créon might have said. "Perhaps justice did not demand his death, but the health of the state demanded it."[88] Thus the man of state who seemed to play Pétain or Laval in 1944 can become the hero of the Resistance in 1945: "whatever words" he uses, he is Creon. De Gaulle, of course, was no "uncle Creon," and it was in any case too late to try to send the little boy back to his room. But Brasillach, transgendered like Antigone herself, becomes in Anouilh's vision a sacrificial victim incarnating purity, *grandeur*, and the uncompromising choice of death over mediocre life—the last tragic hero of French aesthetic fascism.

[85] Jean Anouilh, "Février 1945," in Pol Vandromme, *Un auteur et ses personnages* (Paris: La Table ronde, 1965), 180.

[86] "Salut fraternel à une ombre" appeared as the preface to Brasillach's collected works for the theater (*OC*, 4: xii).

[87] Kaplan, *Collaborator*, 187–88.

[88] "La justice n'exigeait peut-être pas sa mort, mais le salut de l'Etat l'exigeait" (Pierre de Boisdeffre, "Apologie pour un condamné," *Le Monde*, February 18, 1975, referred to by Herbert Lottman in *The Purge* [New York: William Morrow, 1986], 139).

Conclusion

Anouilh's rethinking the trial of Brasillach as a new *Antigone* reminds us that the conflict between the aspiration to "purity" and the realities of "politics" lies at the heart of the tragic vision of the aesthetic fascists. Whether Creon appears as a defender of the republic or a compromised dictator, he plays, in this theater at least, a losing game. Ordinary life, as Anouilh's recapitulation of *Eurydice* for the trial states, resembles bad theater. The desire for tragic catharsis, as conveyed by Montherlant's Ferrante and Georges, entails a desire for purification from mediocrity. Brasillach's "intact" purity was, to be sure, sullied by writing that mingled aesthetics with the most sordid politics, yet his appearance, onstage as it were, allows Anouilh to reconfigure him as the scapegoat of "literature" sacrificed to "politics." The tragic hero, for the aesthetic fascists, may be violent and transgressive; he or she must not be compromising or "political." Pirandello, who, when he joined the fascist party, saw Mussolini as a modern tragic hero, eventually learned to distinguish between the flawed Mussolini the man and the ideal Mussolini the myth. D'Annunzio both kept his distance from and gave his support to Il Duce, confident in the superiority of his own role as "the soul of fascism" to the operations of its body.

The aesthetic approach to fascism, if it attempts to distance itself from "politics," inevitably espouses aspects of fascist political ideology just as fascist politicians embraced aesthetics. The pronouncement by D'Annunzio—"art and politics were never separate in my thought"—encapsulates important strands of the early twentieth-century culture from which aesthetic fascism grew as well as the attempts by Mussolini and Hitler to represent themselves as ruling by poetry or creating of their states totalitarian works of art. Fascism appealed to artists to the extent that it presented itself as a primarily aesthetic phenomenon—vitalist, relativist, but totalizing in the manner of *l'art pour l'art*. The fact that those who were drawn to fascism through aesthetics can be accused of political naïveté should not obscure the complexity or the importance of their commitment.

The search for modern tragedy was—as I hope to have demonstrated here—a crucial component of aesthetic fascism in Italy and France. The ideal modern tragedy was of course never found: this in itself is indicative of the perpetuation of the activist component of fascism for which no form could ever adequately capture the continuously changing and creative "spirit" of the movement. In both theory and practice, however, from turn-of-the-century French and Italian aesthetic-political discourse through writing on and for the theater in Paris under the German Occupation, a rebirth of tragedy appears essential to the dawning of a heroic new age. The inclusion of the discussion of aesthetic form with more general cultural phenomena was made possible by the great German theorists of the nineteenth century—Schelling, Hegel, and Schopenhauer—who defined the notion of the "tragic" as an ontological reality beyond the theatrical genre. The most important influence on the rethinking of the significance of tragedy for fascist modernity was of course Nietzsche's *Birth of Tragedy*. This fact should not be interpreted as an argument for a return to the now discredited view of Nietzsche as one of the prime fathers of fascism. It is a particular way of reading Nietzsche that is in question. Walter Benjamin pinpointed an opening in the text of *The Birth of Tragedy* conducive to some of the links we have seen when he argued that with Nietzsche's statement that it is art that gives significance to life, that existence can be justified only as an *aesthetic* phenomenon, "the abyss of aestheticism opens up, and this brilliant intuition was finally to see all its concepts disappear into it." Aestheticism, according to Benjamin, led to a rejection of art grounded in history. In the case of the modern understanding of Greek tragedy, it led from a view of the chorus—along with the audience—as exercising a reflective role to a view of chorus and audience joined together in ecstasy.[1] Certainly, as D'Annunzio understood well, the ecstatic binding and fusing of the dramatic poet, through actors, with his audience, represented the same phenomenon as the binding and fusing of the crowd with the political orator—the form of new mass politics to be realized by D'Annunzio himself at Fiume and his successor in Piazza Venezia.

Although the concept of aesthetic fascism, along with certain generic definitions of fascist ideology, can be extended to all European fascisms, including German National Socialism, the bond between the Italian and

---

[1] Walter Benjamin, "Trauerspiel and Tragedy," trans. John Osborne, in *Tragedy*, ed. John Drakakis and Naomi Conn Liebler (London: Longman, 1998), 107.

French varieties nonetheless has certain distinguishing features. From the early 1900s, French and Italian thinkers, in contact with each other, mingled aesthetic with political discourse in antidemocratic, nationalist, and revolutionary rhetoric. Although the writers from each country had specific goals, each saw in the other a "sister" Latin nation, heir to a superior culture. All were interested in abolishing the heritage of 1789 and the Enlightenment to retrieve a sense of the true nation. Ironically, the influence of the German Nietzsche only reinforced the sense of the importance of a common Mediterranean heritage in this Franco-Italian culture. The young Mussolini, in 1912, wrote on the anti-German, "French" aspect of his idol Nietzsche. With *The Birth of Tragedy*, Nietzsche seemed to have revealed that not only was Greek tragedy the primordial form of European art but the Enlightenment view of classical antiquity was discredited. Tragedy, grounded in the ecstatic and the spiritual, appeared as the opponent of rationalism, democracy, and Socratic "decadence." Dionysian excess, transgression, and purification through suffering seemed immediately applicable to present "revolutionary" thinking. For Mario Morasso, only a modern tragedy could give adequate aesthetic form to the dawning age of imperialism. For Edouard Berth, the revolutionary Dionysian Sorel together with the Apollonian classical and conservative Maurras would bring about the fusion of left and right preparing the birth of a new *grand siècle.*

If Italian and French aesthetic fascists welcomed the discovery of Dionysian ritual, they believed their understanding of it to be different from that of the Germans. A consistent theme in all of the writings discussed here is the prime importance of the word in both aesthetics and politics. D'Annunzio distinguished his ideal theater from Wagner's in that Wagner placed music and spectacle above poetry. Although other theatrical effects were not negligible for D'Annunzio, it was primarily through verbal enchantment that the orator in the piazza like the "tragic poet" through actors in the theater would achieve the desired binding and fusing of the wielder of words with the crowd. Similarly, Brasillach, comparing Mussolini's theatricality to that of Hitler, contrasts the congenial, understandable, powerful discourse of the first to the "foreign," "uncanny," if strangely seductive, musical and spectacular effects of the second. Brasillach also argued strongly for the superiority of *literary* theater to a theater based on spectacle. For the Latin sisters, it seems, Dionysus, though never to be denied, had to be always contained by Apollo. Rereading Racine through Nietzsche, Thierry Maulnier indeed saw this balance as the distinguishing feature of French classicism.

Although they continued to think of themselves as French fascists rather than followers of the Nazis, the French writers who had looked primarily to Mussolini in the 1930s began under the Occupation in the 1940s to envisage their nation as part of a New Europe under Germany. The defeat itself became in their vision a manifestation of France's tragic destiny, a catastrophe that would lead from mediocre existence under the Third Republic to purification and renewal. Writing from Belgium on April 28, 1942, Paul de Man observed that now that Europe was entering an era of "suffering, exaltation, and intoxication," France would at last have to change its cult of reason.[2] The sentiment he expressed was basically the same that had led Brasillach, Drieu, and Montherlant to welcome the German invasion. Participation in the Dionysian wave that was in the process of destroying Europe's outworn institutions and ideologies seemed to them not only the most exhilarating but also the only possible course for the future. At the same time, however, the French aesthetic fascists had no desire to assume a German cultural identity and were on the contrary eager to redefine a French one. This meant preserving the legacy of the classical Mediterranean, along with French, classicism and the link with the Latin "sister." In occupied France as earlier in fascist Italy, journalistic writing on tragedy as the ideal form for the culture of the National Revolution abounded. The terms that Maulnier had applied to French classicism, particularly Racine—*grandeur* and *pureté*—became both key words in fascist ideology and canonical standards in the search for a modern French tragedy worthy of the new age. Racist connotations, however, particularly of the latter term, became more explicit. Aesthetic "purity" conflated with the notion of a Europe "purified" of Jews.

Although they differ widely in many respects, the critical and theoretical writing on modern tragedy and exemplary modern tragedies by aesthetic fascists in the early days of Italian fascism and in the later flowering of the French variety show important common aspirations. Tragedy, seen as an outgrowth of the violence, sacrifice, and rebirth at the origins of European civilization, seemed destined to return to renew Europe after the experience of the Great War. The mythologizing of World War I as a great tragic moment took place on both the propagandistic and the literary levels. For Drieu La Rochelle and Brasillach, in the wake of Sorel, the riots in Paris on February 4, 1934, recaptured the war's tragic exhilaration while prefiguring the possibility of the dawn of fascism in France. Theatrical portrayals of the struggle of the hero against destiny and the sacrifice of a martyr-victim for the renewal of the nation both predate and postdate these events. They configure the tragic form in plays as divergent as *Jorio's Daughter*, *The Ship*, *Lazarus*, *Charlotte Corday*, and *The Dead Queen*.

A formal concern that permeates the boundaries between aesthetics and politics is the association of bourgeois, nineteenth-century realist drama with the inadequacies of parliamentary democracy. Both the realist aesthetic and the parliamentary system embody linear, historical, rationalis-

---

[2] *Le Soir*, quoted in Jeffrey Mehlman, "Perspectives: On Paul de Man and *Le Soir*," in Mehlman, *Genealogies of the Text* (New York: Cambridge University Press, 1995), 120.

tic, or dialectical modes of thought which the new political-aesthetic discourse wants to replace with transcendent, spatialized, and totalized "art." In Italian writing about the necessity for going beyond bourgeois theater, the bêtes noires are the French practitioners of the well-made play such as Scribe and Dumas or Zola's naturalism. For the French aesthetic fascists, the prime bête noire becomes Henri Bernstein, representative not only of the theatrical realism supported by the plutocratic bourgeoisie but also of the presumably insidious phenomenon of *théâtre enjuivé*. The return to tragedy thus incorporates a cure of "purity" through the recuperation of what Drumont and his followers, expounding on Nietzsche, called the pristine "Aryan" form. This politicized revolt against nineteenth-century realism helps to explain why so many of the plays considered here are in part metatheatrical. In *The Dead City*, D'Annunzio stages the importance of the rediscovery of tragedy for modernity; in *Beyond Love*, he demonstrates formally and thematically the conjunction of going beyond realist drama with going beyond liberal politics, plutocratic economics, and bourgeois morality. *Six Characters in Search of an Author* suggests the crisis of authority in liberal Italy while demonstrating the present impossibility of writing a naturalist play; *Henry IV* "plays" with historical drama, finding the tragedy of modernity in a crisis of legitimacy. Brasillach's *Bérénice* portrays nostalgia for the recovery of French classical tragedy as an incarnation of "the truth of the nation"; the chorus in Anouilh's *Antigone* explains the aristocratic superiority of tragedy over *drame*.

Related to the rejection of historical, realist, and linear drama is the search for refuge in timeless worlds of the imaginary past, childhood, or death; a kind of preoedipal *jouissance* that Pirandello's travestied "Henry IV" calls "the great pleasure of history." Anouilh's Orphée chooses death and Eurydice over mediocre "life" (or bad theater); his Antigone, like Montherlant's Ferrante, accepts death over compromised "happiness." Pirandello and D'Annunzio attempt to create modern tragedies that reconfigure timeless "myths"; Drieu creates an imaginary Illyria for the setting of an ostensibly political drama that resolves itself in lyricism. Even plays that appear to be historical, such as *The Ship*, *Bérénice*, *Charlotte Corday*, and *The Dead Queen*, conflate the present with the past, imposing myth on history and subordinating plot to poetic "truth."

Female roles in these plays diverge widely but show some important correspondences. For D'Annunzio, woman is primarily the vehicle of Dionysian erotic forces, or, in a more threatening mode, of Medusan castrating ones. She must in any case be mastered and subdued by the Apollonian male or decapitated by Perseus. The Dionysian-Medusan woman, as in the figures of Basiliola in *The Ship* and Elena Comemna in *Glory*, may also incarnate the foreign, "oriental," or Byzantine power that threatens the virile destiny of Rome. Here D'Annunzio connects with an old historical-mythological tradition, one that is recuperated by Brasillach in *Bérénice*. For Brasillach, however, "oriental" has become primarily "Jewish" and the destiny of the Roman Empire fused with the destiny of modern fascism. The seductive oriental woman remains a fascinating and powerful antagonist: the tragedy lies in the necessity of her sacrifice.

While D'Annunzio enacts more sacrifices of women than any of the other authors, Montherlant's tragic aesthetic is founded on "how to kill women." Montherlant creates a Dionysian woman similar to D'Annunzio's Phaedra in his Pasiphae. In most of his theater, however, women embody not so much the threat of erotic seduction or oriental power as the temptation to settle for mediocre happiness. Ines de Castro's youth, beauty, and maternity represent for Ferrante an impediment, and then a sacrificial victim, to his pursuit of "useless" *grandeur*. Georges Carrion sacrifices a son too much under the influence of his "mediocre" mother "for the sake of what France should be." In Montherlant's early *L'Exil* as in Drieu's *Le Chef*, women threaten to impede transcendent male bonding.

As mothers, and as virgins, however, women can themselves become tragic figures. Whereas in Pirandello's theater, the sexually active childless woman tends to appear as a "construction" or an empty shell given identity by whatever man she is with, the mother, in his words, is "an irreducible construction," the foundation on which society can be built anew. Pirandello's veneration of motherhood in *The Life I Gave You* and *The New Colony* theatricalizes Mussolini's promotion of the cult of the *madre-madonna*. The tragic catastrophe occurs with the separation of mother from child and heroic renewal in their reunion in death or myth. The virgin heroines Antigone, Joan of Arc, and Charlotte Corday were particularly favored by the French aesthetic fascists. For Charles Maurras and his followers, Antigone and Joan represented a continuity from classical antiquity to the French Middle Ages: each was the vessel of royal legitimacy, incarnation of the "eternal truth" of her nation. Charlotte Corday in a sense completes the fascist amalgam by adding the revolutionary component to the reactionary one. In Drieu La Rochelle's tragedy, she confirms her "purity" by assassinating the presumed Jew and leftist Marat. But these strong women serve their nation primarily by their sacrificial death. The values of the nation may be incarnated in a quasi-mythological female figure, but the implementation of power has to lie in the hands of men. The killing of women—pure or impure—assures the grandeur of tragedy.

As Nietzsche revealed to them the origins of tragedy in primitive religious ritual, his followers found themselves confronted with the question of religion's role in the creation of tragedy for a modernity with no unifying myth. D'Annunzio and Pirandello partially solved this problem by adapting to the needs of their theater syncretic religions along the lines of the religious syncretism advocated by Gentile and other fascist theorists.

Thus in *Jorio's Daughter* and in *The Ship* we see enactments of rituals concocted from primitive Italic traditions, paganism, Eastern and Western Christianity, all fused in the Bard's poetry and culminating in the purifying sacrifice of a woman. Pirandello, in *Lazarus*, attempted to blend what he specifically identified as fascism's "God of the living" with aspects of Christianity, while discrediting the legalism of the Vatican, which in his view upheld a "God of the dead." His tragic hero, sacrificing himself for the renewal of his community of loved ones, was to be at once Christ and Dionysus. Fascist drama critics spoke much about *religio* in its etymological sense of binding of the audience with stage in great drama in the same manner as Il Duce bonded with his public in the piazza. These critics found such a "religious" ecstasy realized in the outdoor productions of D'Annunzio's tragedies during the *ventennio*. In France, too, there was much talk of the revival of "religious" drama in outdoor theaters. The French writers whose plays are discussed here, however, seem to have abandoned any hope of recreating a religion for modern tragedy.

At the heart of aesthetic fascism there is a void, or as Benjamin puts it, an abyss. The attempts to recreate syncretic religions, like Mussolini's and Bontempelli's call for the constant creation of new, changing "myths," only points more clearly to its presence. Pirandello's metaphor captures the aesthetic of the poet of relativity: his creations, instead of creating white statues to hide the black abyss, shake them to reveal it. Into the abyss, as it were, jumps the "artist," molding and forming what was once a collection of abstract individual "citizens" into a carefully shaped consensual mass, a *popolo* or a *Volk*. Fascism in a sense mourns Europe's lost legitimacy of king and church, having nothing with which to replace them but art. This sense is already present in D'Annunzio with his nostalgia for the passing of the aristocracy, his disdain of democracy, and his pursuit of a politics of beauty along with the creation of a Medusan modern tragedy. It stands behind "Henry IV"'s fake castle and the vacancy of authority in the search of the six characters. D'Annunzio will propose a renovating myth of artistic imperialism; Pirandello will create his own religious, social, and artistic myths. But whereas D'Annunzio in a sense masks the void with ecstatic poetry and the fusing and binding techniques of his tragedies of possession, Pirandello's self-conscious "constructions" emphasize its presence. The tragic hero is the one who recognizes the necessity of creating new truths in order to mask for the common folk the demise of truth: in one avatar Prometheus, in another Mussolini. Aware of the necessarily self-consciously theatrical nature of both modern politics and modern art, Pirandello in a sense writes the tragedy of the end of tragedy.

A primary concern of the French aesthetic fascists is the rejection of both Third Republic positivism and the rationalism of the spirit of 1789. Like the Italians, the French saw the devastation of World War I as a tragic and heroic purification of their nation's ills, but they deplored the "decadence" that reinstated itself after the war. With the passing of both royalist legitimacy and revolutionary rationalism, however, what can fill the void? Once again the answer is, aesthetics. One "myth" that Drieu La Rochelle, Brasillach, and Montherlant propose is the model of a "virile," militant, medieval French Christianity but an aesthetic Christianity devoid of religious faith. Drieu creates the image of a lyrical binding around the personage of the *chef*, but expresses doubt that his own country is prepared for such a leader. Montherlant's heroes come face to face with the void as they adopt an ethic of "useless service" figured by the suit of empty armor performing executions. If the substance is missing, the beautiful, masked forms of the chivalric and royal past, as in *La Reine morte*, can be recreated for the stage. Anouilh's Antigone and his Créon, stripped of their religious and political beliefs, face the void clearly: Créon with his admission that the rotting body of Antigone's brother is only a product of his political "kitchen;" Antigone with her answer to Créon's question on her motives, "Pour rien. Pour moi."

The void revealed in the tragedies of aesthetic fascism is fundamentally the same as that theorized by existentialism and represented in the arts and thought of the "absurd." The existentialist generation also turned to modern tragedy: Camus's *Caligula*, along with his *Letters to a German Friend*, perhaps best portray the similarities between the absurdist and the fascist encounter with the void. It is the reaction or the solution to the encounter that, at least ostensibly, diverge. Sartre attempts in *The Flies* to write "the tragedy of liberty," based on the agony of individual choice. Postwar theater, however, perhaps in part in reaction to the adulation of tragedy under fascism, seems on the whole to renounce the attempt to write modern tragedy. With the influence of Brecht, the idea of the theatrical audience becomes critical rather than consensual. Ionesco, whose experience of fascism was considerable, claimed that he could see no difference between tragedy and comedy. In *Rhinocéros*, it is the comedy of fascism that reveals its tragedy. Beckett, who most powerfully put on the stage the apprehension of the void, does so through the convergence of comedy and tragedy.

Modern tragedy, of course, is not necessarily "fascist" as a genre. Yet under the combined influences of aestheticism, the reading of Nietzsche, and the desire to recover the ancient and classical past for modernity, it was one of the aesthetic forms most adaptable to the illusory and theatrical ideology of fascism.

Index